Love and Marriage

Love and Marriage

Literature and its Social Context

Laurence Lerner

Edward Arnold

© Laurence Lerner 1979

First published 1979 by
Edward Arnold (Publishers) Ltd
41 Bedford Square, London WC1B 3DQ

British Library Cataloguing in Publication Data

Lerner, Lawrence
  Love and marriage.
  1. Love in literature   2. Marriage in
  literature   3. English literature – History
  and criticism   4. Literature and society
  I. Title
  820′.9′354   PR149.L/

  ISBN 0-7131-6227-9

Printed in Great Britain by
Butler & Tanner Ltd, Frome and London

By the same author:

Criticism
The Truest Poetry: an Essay on the Question, What is Literature?
The Truthtellers: Jane Austen, George Eliot, D. H. Lawrence
The Uses of Nostalgia: Studies in Pastoral
An Introduction to English Poetry

Poetry
Domestic Interior
The Directions of Memory
Selves
A.R. T.H.U.R.

Fiction
The Englishmen
A Free Man

To Natalie
'Yes, yours, my love, is the right human face.'

Contents

The Contest of Love and Marriage
Tristan   1
Romeo and Juliet   5
Wives and Daughters   8
Tristan in context   11
Romeo and Juliet in context   14
Wives and Daughters in context   24
Excursus on Realism   32

The Paradoxes of Love
Love's Unreason   36
Religion and Love   41
Who is Beatrice?   46
Sarah's Lover   50
Love and Death   53

Choosing a Mate
What is the Extended Family?   61
The Arranged Match   65
Propaganda for Romance   76
Alternatives to Realism   80
The Newcomes   88
Esther's Suitors   94
Botho's Dilemma   97
Romance and Real Life   101

Married Love
Protestant Marriage   111
Adam and Eve   114
Marrying Laura   120
Spenser or Shakespeare?   125
The Angel in the House   130
The Angel in Literature   143

The Brangwens   153
Phallic Marriage   160

Feminism and Love
An Anti-Marriage League?   167
Marriage and Liberation   170
Love and Liberation   175
Sisterly Imaginations   182
Protofeminism: Charlotte Brontë   187
Protofeminism: Samuel Richardson   201

Sex
Forms of Reticence   213
Forms of Outspokenness   220
Sublimation   226
Poetry and Eroticism   234
Conclusion   244

Index   259

Preface

What is love? And what can we know about it? 'In a yet unpublished monograph,' writes a sociologist, 'the writer has developed a theory of intersexual attraction and love which holds that love is an affectionate response to one who is instrumental in the gratification of an individual's needs.' That is one way of looking at it, which we shan't be able to avoid, and one kind of vocabulary, which I shall do my utmost to avoid. Another way of looking at it is that of the poets. 'Tis not hereafter, sing the drunken old men in *Twelfth Night*: present mirth hath present laughter. It is a prick, it is a sting, suggests George Peele: it is a pretty pretty thing; it is a fire, it is a coal. And how many other things too, pretty or stinging: a red red rose, an ever-fixed mark, a sickness full of woes; it is of God and passes human wit, but it has pitched its mansion in the place of excrement. It is begotten by despair upon impossibility. And so on and so on: the poets never tire of this senior–junior giant dwarf Dan Cupid.

It? Is it one thing? Can we clear up the babel of voices telling us what love is by saying that they are talking not of one but many things? If we ask what relationships are described by the word, the answer will be a list of perhaps four or five—sexual love, parental (and filial) love, friendship, spiritual (and divine) love. Damon loves Chloe and Robert Browning loved Elizabeth Barrett; a mother loves her child, a man loves his mother; the love of David and Jonathan surpassed the love of women; the mystic loves God, and God so loved the world that he gave his only begotten son. The distinctions are important, but they will not sort out the babel for us, for it is almost entirely concerned with the first: there are poems about the love of God, but on the whole when the poets say 'love' without qualification they mean Cupid—that is, sexual love. That is what the arguments are about, and that is what this book is about.

And what is marriage? An honourable estate, ordained for the procreation of children, for a remedy against fornication, for mutual society, help and comfort. A sexual union with economic cooperation, involving residential cohabitation, and forming the basis of the nuclear family. The purposes of marriage in the Christian service, and the functions of marriage according to the anthropologists: are they polar opposites, or saying the same thing? To say of marriage that it is commended of Saint Paul, and to be taken in hand reverently, discreetly, advisedly, soberly, may be solemn obfuscation; to speak of social functions without reference to holiness or mystical union may be reductivism; or it may be in the nature of the institution that it can be defined in two kinds of language, even though it took us centuries to devise the second.

The history of love and marriage can study three things. First, there is what people actually do. At what age do they marry, and does that vary with sex, social class and sibling order? How many children do they have, at what intervals, and how many grow up? What forms of sexual activity take place before marriage, and what after (frequency of intercourse, positions used, accompanying rituals)? What do husband and wife do together, and what apart (work, eat, pray, sleep)? The list is very long, and of every item we can ask if it has changed over time. Second, there is sentiment. What do lovers feel about each other, and how does it differ from what married couples feel? How does married love change in the lifetime of the couple, how has it changed over the centuries? And third there is ideology. The members of any society have a picture of what its institutions are, ideally, like. The purpose and functions of marriage, the duties and responsibilities of the partners, the dangers and wickedness of neglecting these, are discussed in sermons and marriage manuals, improving tracts and radical pamphlets. The threefold division corresponds to William J. Goode's distinction between real behaviour, real ideals and ideal ideals. Only for the third of these is there clear and abundant evidence: it is always easy to find out what people thought ought to be done, by themselves and (especially) others, and if there is a difficulty in writing the history of the ideology of marriage, it is because there is too much material, not too little. For the first, real behaviour, there is in principle no problem of evidence, but as we go back in time (before the social survey, before the census) it becomes more difficult in practice. But what is evidence for the history of sentiment? The work of those social historians who believe that *la vie intime* has a history which can be studied (Aries, Flandrin, Shorter, Stone and many others) has been invaluable to me in writing this book, but it has left me profoundly sceptical about the problems of evidence. We cannot go back and ask Mrs William Temple or Mrs James Boswell if they loved their husbands very much ☐ mildly ☐ sometimes ☐ not at all ☐ , and we would not trade their letters for the answer if we could.

To illustrate the problem, let us look at the main thesis of Lawrence Stone's monumental *Family Sex and Marriage in England 1500–1800*. This concerns the supposed rise of affective individualism. In the course of the eighteenth century, Stone believes, English men and women developed stronger affective bonds, in the family and perhaps in all their relationships. In earlier times, social relations were cool, even unfriendly: most people 'found it very difficult to establish close emotional ties to any other person'.

How could one show this? Stone is shrewd at using linguistic or material evidence, but these are incidental: what really matters is what people have said about their feelings. The comments of observers, always unreliable, are by definition useless in this case: how could they know that in future ages affective life would grow richer? And even if we find cool statements at one time and, in a later age, warm statements in the same situation, how can we know what has changed, the emotion or its expression? Stone quotes the correspondence of John Dickinson and his wife Mary, at the end of the eighteenth century: 'I love you as much as it is possible for one human creature to love another.... I have only time to say that I love you dearly...', and claims that it 'exudes a warmth and an emotional commitment that is very hard to find in the sixteenth and early seventeenth centuries'. This is doubtless true, but the Dickinsons were writing in the age of sentimentality: because Yorick and the Man of Feeling shed tears of sensibility, and were admired for doing so, can we conclude that mankind's heart had grown softer? If *Sense and Sensibility* were read in Stone's spirit, Marianne would represent the new, and Elinor the old; and Marianne, who expresses her feelings with passion, would be an example of affect, while Elinor, who bottles hers up, would belong to the cool world without emotional involvement. This is certainly not Jane Austen's intention: she wrote the book to tell us not to judge on appearances. True, there is a rhetorical problem here: the fact that all our evidence for Elinor's inner sufferings is accompanied by an insistence on how well she controlled it has the effect on the reader of giving him a very theoretical or cursory picture of her feelings compared to Marianne's passionate drama. It is meaningful in a literary context to say that Elinor does not suffer, because her suffering is not expressed. But that is because her reality is created solely by the author's words: there is no pre-existing Elinor that Jane Austen is telling us about, because fiction is fictitious. But if *Sense and Sensibility* were a historical document we would have to entertain seriously the view that the grief that does not speak whispers the o'er fraught heart and makes it break.

There is of course one other source I have not yet mentioned, the most familiar of all, and that is literature. This book is mostly about literature, for two reasons. The first is purely personal: I am a student of literature, and that is what I know and want to write about. The second is that most of what we know about love comes from the poets. It is therefore very tempting to regard literature as the answer to the social historian's problems, the true quarry for evidence about the history of sentiment. This is especially plausible if we adopt those theories that regard literature as directly inspired by social reality, without the intervention of ideology. Nonetheless, I have felt I must resist the temptation, for a simple and inescapable reason. If one is going to compare two things, it is necessary to establish each of them independently first. The social historians who distrust novels may be missing all the fun, but they do enable us to compare literature and society without arguing in a circle.

The purpose of this book, then, is to describe the way our literary tradition has perceived love and marriage, beginning from the relationship between the two, which it has seen as one of contest; then to explain the concept of love that has made such a conflict seem inevitable. Then, having established the literary vision of the subject, I turn in the third chapter to the social reality of marriage, both the ideology and what we can know about the actual practice, and ask how literature has responded to this, concentrating on the favourite topic of choice of mate. As society developed a view of married love very different from that discussed in the first two chapters, there were some attempts to find literary expression for this; their very limited success offers a counter-tradition to that of romantic love, and the fourth chapter, which discusses this, can thus be seen as a kind of riposte to the first. I then turn to the most influential of recent criticisms of love and marriage, those that have emerged from feminism, and ask how they are reflected in the fiction of women writing today, and how far they are implied in the fiction of earlier, protofeminist novelists: doing this forces us to ask what it means to claim that a novel implies ideological positions that no one has yet formulated. Finally, I lie down where all the ladders start, and discuss the sense in which sex is the basis of love, and what this means for literary expression.

A work of literature has three main determinants: the society, the literary tradition and the individual author. This book will not be greatly concerned with the last: although every book is, in the end, the work of an individual, a study of general patterns will not deal with what makes one writer distinctive, and my examples are chosen because they illustrate (or seem to refute) a general trend or theory. But the other two contexts—that of literature and that of social reality—are important to my argument, and a few preliminary remarks on method seem necessary.

Can we even speak of a literary tradition? Is it not a verbal fiction, distracting attention from the fact that literature consists of nothing except particular poems and stories? Such scepticism can be dealt with in the way nominalism always can, by distinguishing what the individual work has in common with others from what makes it unique. If the common elements are consciously formulated, we call them conventions: if not, recurring patterns—of imagery, of action, of motivation, and so on. If we attribute to tradition an immanent rather than a transcendent existence, these conventions and patterns *are* the tradition. Verbal fictions are, after all, necessary for making general statements.

But it is also possible to resist too much concern with tradition not because it is fictitious but because it is reductive. Modern readers often feel that what one work has in common with others is precisely what makes it undistinguished; and that the best way to illustrate a tradition is from the minor writers, who lack the uniqueness of the great. Since I have no wish to write about Googe's sonnets or Mrs Craik's novels, does this not present me with a problem: will not any discussion of *Othello* or *Middlemarch* which is concerned with what they are truly like be incompatible with an interest in tradition?

I believe, on the contrary, that a masterpiece may exemplify the tradition as well as, even better than, a minor work. In turning Arthur Brooke's *Tragicall History of Romeus and Juliet* into a taut, fast, moving play, Shakespeare removed irrelevancies, emphasized the tragic nature of the love, and showed how intimate, and how destructive, is its involvement with family life. The contest of love and marriage which emerges so hesitantly from Brooke's long and often tedious poem is enacted with great skill and concentration in Shakespeare's more single-minded construction. There are, in the end, two very different ways of conceiving the relation of minor work and masterpiece. The more usual one sees lesser works as tame and commonplace, the masterpiece as complex and unique; this has its truth, but so has the alternative view, which sees the lesser works as awkward and superficial, the masterpieces as profoundly in touch with the archetypes that move and convince us. By this view conventions can represent not the obvious patterns that the masterpiece transcends, but the significant patterning that only the masterpiece attains.

As for the relation between literature and social reality, it is not easy to summarize the view that informs my discussion, and, since this is not a work of literary theory, not possible to defend it at length. Briefly, then: it must be clear to anyone with a touch of scepticism that ideology is not always in close touch with real behaviour: that is one reason why reliable evidence for the latter is so hard to come by. There is a view, held in a different ways by different schools of criticism, that literature is a direct, even inarticulate, response to social behaviour: Lucien Goldmann's theory of homologies is an influential recent version of this, claiming that literature bypasses ideology by responding directly to patterns of thought and conduct that have not yet been formulated theoretically. I believe, in contrast to this, that the literature of love and marriage is drenched in ideology. It engages in constant dialogue with the ideals and criticisms of marriage, and with doctrines of the true nature of love. But on the other hand its relation to ideology is not the subservient one that moral critics like to attribute to it, of illustrating orthodoxy or making virtue delightful: the literary imagination tests our ideals and our moral beliefs, by measuring them against the feel of real experience. This is why literature is, in the end, the profoundest record we have of our real ideals.

I owe the usual thanks to friends, colleagues, students and family who have listened patiently to the contents of this book in lectures, argued with it in seminars, and (most valuable of all) read and criticized earlier drafts of it. For this I am grateful to Peter Burke, Patrick Grant, Peter Hennock, Stephen Medcalf, and above all Tony Nuttall and Tony Thorlby, whose criticisms have led to endless and fascinating arguments and (often) to illuminating my own position to me. For all faults, eccentricities and complications of presentation I must admit sole responsibility.

1

The Contest of Love and Marriage

If we are to believe the poets, love and marriage exist in a state of conflict: love exists outside marriage, or ceases when marriage begins, or enters marriage only to destroy it. The aim of this first chapter is to tell the story of how European literature has presented this conflict: it is the one purely literary chapter in this book, questions of how that literary tradition relates to social reality being saved for later discussion.

But how can one discuss anything so vast as a literary tradition? I propose to survey the forest by beginning with three large and interesting trees; then, after I have looked at each as a thing in itself, by comparing it with some of its immediate neighbours, to show that it was not chosen at random.

Tristan

Tristan and Isolde is the greatest of medieval love stories. It made no memorable impact on English literature, and has come down in four main versions, two French and two German, of which the most important is that of Gottfried von Strasbourg, composed at the beginning of the thirteenth century, which I shall take as the text for this discussion.[1] Tristan was the posthumous son of Rivalin, prince 'of Brittany', and Blancheflor, sister of King Mark of Cornwall, brought up by Rual, Rivalin's faithful steward. He grew up skilled in music and languages, and found his way to the kingdom of his uncle, Mark. After a conventional series of adventures (giant-slaying, poisoned wound, cure by Queen Isolde of Ireland, wooing for Mark, dragon-slaying) he is bringing Isolde, daughter of the Irish Queen, across the sea to be his uncle's bride: her handmaid Brangane has been given a love potion by Isolde's mother, intended for her and Mark, but Tristan and Isolde drink it by mistake.

> In an instant that arch-disturber of tranquillity was there, Love, waylayer of all hearts, and she had stolen in! Before they were aware of it, she had planted her victorious standard in their two hearts and bowed them beneath her yoke. They who were two and divided now became one and united.[2]

Isolde declares her love by means of a verbal trick; asked what was distressing her, she replies 'lameir' (the sea; bitterness; love), and this precipitates a mutual declaration. Once in Cornwall, they enter on a long series of deceptions, sometimes duping Mark and sometimes not, sometimes protecting their honour by equivocal oaths and tricks, sometimes banished, sometimes recalled. In his wanderings Tristan fights for the King of Arundel (? in Brittany) and is fascinated by his daughter, also called Isolde (Isolde of the White Hands); he marries her, but the marriage is not consummated. Wounded by a poisoned spear Tristan realizes he is dying, and sends for his Isolde, the only one who can save him. Told that the approaching ship has black sails he believes that his Isolde is not on board, and dies heartbroken. Isolde arrives too late and dies of grief in his dead arms.

Gottfried's doctrine of love is expounded for us in a digression inserted just after the lovers' declaration. It begins with a lament on the shabby way we love nowadays, cultivating love with guile and deceit, sowing failure and disaster, selling it in the open market: we have trampled under foot its true basis, which is Fidelity. Fidelity there clearly does not refer to marriage, since Tristan and Isolde, patterns of fidelity, deceive King Mark, often very elaborately. The guile and deceit which have crept in nowadays to destroy love must refer to lovers deceiving each other; and the discourse is followed by an account of how happy these two lovers were for the rest of the voyage, because they dropped shyness and gloried in their intimacy. This was right: 'for lovers who hide their feelings, having once revealed them ... are robbers of themselves'.

This discourse is not the only moment when the poet tells us his view of love. We have already been told that love is the arch-disturber of tranquillity, and have been given many of the famous paradoxes: 'the pleasing malady that works such miracles as changing honey to gall, turning sweetness sour ... robbing hearts of their natures, and standing the world on its head'. Early in the poem, in the account of Rivalin and Blancheflor, we are told how love's clinging sweetness ensnares the lover so that he cannot get free; how it turns him into a different man, granting him a new life, in which all he does is chequered with strangeness and blindness. And when Tristan and Isolde have declared and consummated their passion, the perfection of their union is rendered by simple symmetry in the verse:

> Thus he was she and she was he. He was hers and she was his. There Blancheflor, there Rivalin: There Rivalin, there Blancheflor! There both, and there true love![3]

Love is bitter-sweet, is the pleasing malady; we are told this not only through verbal antithesis, but in the whole conception of the story. The perfection of the union brings an intensity of happiness, not only on the voyage, but in all the hours the lovers are able to steal together; but at the same time it is ineluctably tragic. This is clear from the beginning, for instance in Brangane's horrified response when she learns they have drunk the love potion: 'that flask and the draught it contained will be the death of you both.' A love so blissful cannot have a happy outcome.

To set against these two pairs of perfect but tragic lovers, we have three marriages. First, there is that of Tristan's guardian Rual, who pretends that Tristan is his son in order to protect him from Morgan, who has conquered his father's kingdom. We do not see much of his good wife, worthy, constant, chaste Floraete, who readily agrees to pass Tristan off as her own son—though we may notice that, to make no mistake about family relationships, Rual commands her to do this most strictly on pain of death. But though Rual is a minor character, whose feelings are not our concern, we do learn about one very powerful feeling, his love for Tristan. He has three sons of his own, but he leaves them and his wife to go and look for Tristan when he has been abducted by pirates, resolving never to return till he has heard news of his whereabouts. He wanders in search of him for more than three years till his clothes are in rags and he has lost all traces of nobility, bearing his load of shame like a vagabond born and bred. Great devotion is necessarily irresponsible: it is as if fatherly love, like sexual love, only attains true intensity outside marriage.

Then there is the marriage of Isolde to Mark. Cuckolds are never dignified, and the range of attitudes suggested towards Mark never includes true tragic grandeur. He is, to begin with, a victim of the bedtrick: to conceal her loss of virginity, Isolde arranges for her maid Brangane to replace her on the wedding night. The trick succeeds, as the bedtrick traditionally does, and to make matters worse for Mark, Gottfried tells us, when Isolde has slipped into Brangane's place and he clasps her close and resumes his pleasure, 'to him one woman was as another'. It is difficult to know how far to invoke realistic notions of plausibility for this: if we are allowed to, we have a Mark who cannot tell who the woman is but can tell—in the dark—whether she is a virgin: not only contemptible but rather unpleasant.

It is difficult for the modern reader to be sure what the attitude to Mark was meant to be. He is torn by inner conflicts in a way that might almost be tragic, except that contempt is always too near. Gottfried gives him dignity and deprives him of it as Tolstoi does with Karenin, that supremely complex study of a cuckold. And so after Mark's blind agony has led him to banish the lovers ('it was death to his reason that his darling Isolde should love any man but himself'), he is reduced to a wittol by the trick of the sword. The lovers, sleeping together in the *Minnegrotte* or cave of love, have laid a naked sword between them to deceive spies, and sure enough Mark sees them, and sure enough he is deceived because he wants to be. His gullibility is due to the blindness of love, 'that foolish insensate blindness of which a proverb says "Love's blindness blinds outside and in"'. Gottfried has already taken the trouble to explain that despite the false versions of the story that are found, Mark did not drink any of the love-potion, and Mark's love, we see, has many of the symptoms but none of the dignity of Tristan's. It does not seem excessive to call him a parody of Tristan.

We can go further: for when the lovers' assignation in the orchard is betrayed to Mark, the episode is narrated in terms of an analogy with the Fall: 'Now Tristan did just as Adam did; he took the fruit which his Eve offered him, and with her ate his death.' Mark's role in this parallel is that of God, but the poet's comments once again deprive him of all dignity: he is a parody of God.

If Isolde's marriage is a parody of her love affair, Tristan's is a parody of both love and marriage. Since Gottfried's poem breaks off just where he is about to marry the second Isolde, most of this episode has to be supplied from the old French version of Thomas, which was almost certainly Gottfried's original, and of which (by one of the strangest coincidences of literary history) we possess the last part, beginning just about where Gottfried leaves off.

Tristan marries Isolde of the White Hands because of her beauty and because of her name: Thomas explains, at rather tedious length, that neither of these would have been sufficient reason without the other. The marriage is never consummated, though the bride loves and longs for Tristan, because his will to do the deed is conquered by his love. In this obvious sense the marriage is a travesty, and it turns Isolde of the White Hands into Tristan's enemy. Her bitterness is brilliantly rendered in the taut irony of the incident when her horse slips and the water splashes up her thigh—where Tristan's hand has never sought her. From this it is a natural step to the bitterness that makes her lie to the dying Tristan, and cause his death.

Not only is this a grotesque parody of marriage, but the account of Tristan's hesitations reduces him to something more like King Mark. In this form of storytelling (as Wagner clearly perceived) the most powerful effects occur when total commitment clashes with the facts of the situation, not when the characters are in inner conflict. Descriptions of that are patronizing, even mechanical, so that Tristan's uncertainty whether he should sleep with his bride sounds as pathetic as Mark's uncertainty whether he should believe the lovers innocent.

It is love then and not marriage which has all the dignity in this story. The same is true of our next example.

Romeo and Juliet

'Oh she doth teach the torches to burn bright': Romeo's first glimpse of Juliet transforms his world, and the line tells us, instantly, that it is a play about the transfiguring power of love.

If there ever was a play which had to be in poetry, it is this: for only through heightened language can the heightened quality of the love-experience be conveyed. Falling in love can be seen both as extraordinary and as completely natural, as an experience that takes us out of the every-day onto a higher plane, and as one that takes us from sophistication and artificiality into true simple feeling. It is therefore necessary for the poetry of the lovers to be tugged in two directions: towards formality, which provides conventions that take us away from the ordinary, and towards simplicity, to express the need to drop conventions for genuineness. The dialectic between these gives the language its force: to surrender to either extreme would destroy it.

The extreme of formality is represented by the opening exchange of the lovers: their near-stycomythia composes a sonnet, full of word-play upon the love–religion parallel. The passage asks to be spoken in two different ways, and good actors will convey both: on the one hand it should move slowly, with a solemnity appropriate to the dance taking place and (even more) to the fact that this is the tremendous experience of their lives, for which only religious imagery is adequate; but on the other hand there is (certainly from Juliet, possibly from Romeo too) a playful handling of the religious analogy, almost a feeling that a girl must know how to look after herself by keeping the implications of the words at bay:

> For saints have hands that pilgrims' hands do touch,
> And palm to palm is holy palmer's kiss. (I.v.99)

If the last line is spoken with the emphasis on 'palm to palm' (come now, not lips!) it is fencing; if on the last three words, then the fencing can dissolve in the bliss of what is happening to her.

The extreme of directness, on the other hand, is found at the end of the balcony scene, when Juliet calls Romeo back, asks him something trivial, and confesses 'I have forgot why I did call thee back'. There are no metaphors, no heightened diction, simply the language of being tongue-tied: it could be *Love Story* or *West Side Story*, it could belong with our modern celebration of inarticulateness—and yet it couldn't, simply because of the interplay between this and the rich metaphoric language we have had. Such immediacy derives its literary power from the way it breaks free of a previous formality.

Between these two extremes we can see the dialectic of style actually taking place, for instance in the following:

R: Lady, by yonder blessed moon I vow,
    That tips with silver all these fruit-tree tops—
J: O, swear not by the moon, th'inconstant moon,
    That monthly changes in her circled orb,
    Lest that thy love prove likewise variable.
R: What shall I swear by?
J: Do not swear at all.
    Or if thou wilt, swear by thy gracious self,
    Which is the god of my idolatry,
    And I'll believe thee.
R: If my heart's dear love—
J: Well, do not swear.   (II.ii.107)

They are trying to break free of the convention that they desperately need. Romeo's two lines are lovely and totally predictable; Juliet interrupts to plead, Let us not have these conventions, but she can only do so by describing the moon in equally conventional language. This leaves Romeo inarticulate. For a moment Juliet accepts this, then tries to make up her own convention; as soon as she hears what Romeo makes of it she realizes that he has dropped once more into a protestation that is removed from experience, and she reaffirms her rejection, even if it means silence. She has discovered that what she originally meant was not 'swear not by the *moon*' but a wider prohibition, telling him in general terms not to speak like that. Yet for lovers, striving to escape from ordinariness, there is no other way to speak.

I have tried to suggest by looking, however briefly, at the self-consciousness of the writing, how the special nature of the love experience is conveyed; but I could have set about it in a much more obvious way, by saying that Romeo and Juliet fall in love at first sight, that they compare love to religion, that they feel premonitions of disaster from the beginning. That would have told us nothing about the particularity of this play, but would have stressed what it has in common with others. Both of these matter: for masterpieces are both highly individual, and the most perfect examples of tradition.

And marriage? The main married couple is Juliet's parents; and thinking of Romeo, we ask with astonishment, was Capulet ever in love with his lady? Did he tell himself that she taught the torches to burn bright, did he climb orchard walls, and swear by the moon to her, and could we conceivably imagine him killing himself for love? We see Capulet in two moods, fussy and authoritarian. He fusses over the ball, making an old man's jokes ('She that makes dainty, She, I'll swear, hath corns'), ordering the servants about ('more light, you knaves! and turn the tables up'), a well-meaning, slightly tedious host. We see the same Capulet when he arranges the match with Paris, a little smug in his confidence that his daughter 'will be ruled In all respects by me'—but why not, for she has never crossed him yet?—and more than a little fussy as he hesitates between Wednesday and Thursday for the wedding. Well-meaning, yes, but there are ominous touches even here: 'mark you me', 'and there an end'. He is used to getting his way, and perhaps the later scene when he plays the heavy father is not wholly unexpected. It is a marvellous piece of comic writing, adjusting the blank verse to the speech rhythms as only Shakespeare can do.

> How, how, how, how, chopped logic? What is this?
> 'Proud'—and 'I thank you'—and 'I thank you not'—
> And yet 'not proud'? Mistress minion you,
> Thank me no thankings, nor proud me no prouds,
> But fettle your fine joints 'gainst Thursday next
> To go with Paris to Saint Peter's Church,
> Or I will drag thee on a hurdle thither.   (III.v.149)

How utterly different this movement from 'Earth hath swallowed all my hopes but she' and yet (this is what we mean when we speak of Shakespeare's characterization) it is clearly the same man. Capulet is a wonderful creation, but he lives in a different world from the lovers. The feelings he displays are the pleasure of authority, the wry jokes of old age, and affection for his daughter. There is no sign of affection for his wife: the nearest is when he calls on her to share his grief—'O heavens! O wife, look how our daughter bleeds'—and even there he is simply including her in a feeling that is paternal and familial, and he calls her, as he always does, simply 'wife'. She has no identity and receives no feelings as an individual, and marriage has nothing to do with romance.

In proposing *Romeo and Juliet* as a play about the contrast between love and marriage I have ignored what some may feel is a fatal objection, the fact that Romeo and Juliet do actually marry. Now I do not believe this is an objection at all, for what does that marriage consist of? Not of domestic arrangements, children or even cohabitation, but of one marvellously beautiful *alba*. The song of the lover compelled by dawn to leave his mistress was a popular medieval genre, and examples range from the simple and fragmentary to the rich complexities of the *Minne-singer*—from, say, the simple assertion that the nightingale has ceased to sing and the watchman on the tower is calling the lovers to awaken, to Heinrich von Morungen's 'Owe, sol aber mir iemer me'.

> Oh will there never be a morning,
> When he will simply stay?
> When as night passes we'll no longer

Need to sigh and say
'Alas, look, it is day:'
As he, when last he lay
With me would often say.
Then the day came.[5]

We can never say much about the situation depicted in an *alba*, for
lyric poetry after all is not about situations; but we can say with some
certainty that the lovers are not married. The intensity comes from the
certainty that they must part, and often there is just enough narrative
to make it clear that their assignation was a furtive one. The parting
of Romeo and Juliet in III.v is a marvellous example of the transposition
of lyric into dramatic. Almost every detail belongs to the tradition of
the *alba*: the song of the nightingale and of the lark, the fading of the
moon, the image of the envious streaks. Sometimes it is the man who
longs to stay, sometimes the woman who longs to retain him: Shakespeare takes advantage of these alternatives to depict the wavering situation of pleading, danger, longing, resignation, decision; and the songs
of the two birds, losing none of their lyrical beauty, acquire a dramatic
function.

The 59 lines of this scene are the only lines that Romeo and Juliet
exchange after they are married: an *alba*, followed by brief arrangements
('I will omit no opportunity That may convey my greetings ...') and
then by dark foreboding ('O God, I have an ill-divining soul!'). With
a marriage like that, who needs adultery?

Wives and Daughters

Elizabeth Gaskell's novel *Wives and Daughters* (1864) tells the love
story of Molly Gibson, and the story of her father's second marriage,
to Hyacinth Clare, widowed governess of the local great family. Since
the author wishes to show the misery of unrequited love, Roger Hamley,
the hero, is given the lengthy error of falling in love with the wrong
girl, Molly's stepsister Cynthia, pretty, vivacious, superficial and (as he
eventually discovers) unworthy of him. The story ends happily, but we
have not got the picture of Molly's happy love, since Mrs Gaskell did
not live to write the final chapter. It can hardly have shown greater
emotional intensity than the picture of her wretchedness, when Roger
proposed to Cynthia:

For a few minutes her brain seemed in too great a whirl to comprehend
anything but that she was being carried on in earth's diurnal course, with
rocks, and stones, and trees, with as little volition on her part as if she were
dead.

At this high moment, the author leans on Wordsworth: a sure sign both that she knows her limitations, and that she means to make this a moment of great emotional power.

But Molly too had earlier made a mistake, and her first impression of Roger had not been at all favourable. This is worth looking at closely, for in seeing how Mrs Gaskell here departs from a convention of the love story we can see how, in an oblique fashion, it is still at work in the book. The convention is that of love at first sight. When Molly first comes to stay with the Hamleys she has not met either of the sons. The elder, Osborne, writes poetry and is the apple of his mother's eye; the younger, Roger, is to turn out a great scientist, but his sharp practical mind has so far struck his family as pedestrian and insensitive. The first one to meet her is Roger, and she is not impressed.

> He was a tall powerfully-made young man, giving the impression of strength more than elegance.... He had a trick of wrinkling up his eyelids when he wanted particularly to observe anything, which made his eyes look even smaller still at times.

It is meant to be an attractive portrait, but too real to please Molly at first, since it fits none of her stereotypes of the fine young man. To her he seems 'heavy-looking, clumsy, and a person she was sure she should never get on with'; worse still, as a departure from romantic expectations, 'he certainly did not seem to care much what impression he made on his mother's visitor'. Mrs Gaskell has deliberately botched the first meeting of the lovers: they are distracted and inattentive, and neither feels that the other doth teach the torches to burn bright. Molly however (or her author, or an alliance of the two) is saving the magic of a first meeting for Osborne, who, she has settled, is the really attractive brother. When Osborne turns up she is 'talking poetry and romance' with his mother, and the garden is 'brilliant with autumnal flowers and glittering dew-drops'. Osborne is 'beautiful and languid-looking ... dressed to perfection but with easy carelessness'—not quite what Molly was expecting, and her first response is to try to reconcile the ideal with the real.

> The ideal was agile, yet powerful, with Greek features and an eagle eye, capable of enduring long fasting, and indifferent as to what he ate. The real was almost effeminate in movement, though not in figure; he had the Greek features, but his blue eyes had a cold, weary expression in them.

Neither of these meetings fits the convention of will being overruled by fate, but they depart from it in different ways. The meeting with Osborne is a partial fit: the setting is right, the young man is partly right, but so conscious, even rational a response is not the stuff that fate is made of, and we can see that romance is soon going to fade into the light of common day. The meeting with Roger does not even look like the convention, but it does contain an irritation that can lead to heightened emotional tension—just as Molly's later feeling that she would rather never be married at all than marry an ugly man, '—and dear good Mr Roger is really ugly; I don't think one could even call him plain', is not perhaps just the simple moralizing (Roger is dear and good rather than handsome) that it might seem, but also an awareness of his physical presence—the kind of aversion that can turn into an attraction deeper than liking. Of the two meetings, the one that contains less trace of the convention of fate is psychologically closer to it: Mrs Gaskell thus showing herself a true realist, rejecting convention for what she sees as psychological truth.

That then is love, rendered without any powerful originality of language, but with a keen sense that the experience is special. Mr Gibson's marriage is not special but a real and complex human situation that the author understands very well. He marries Hyacinth, not because her eyes through the airy region stream so bright, but because he wants companionship and a domestic manager, and he thinks Molly needs a mother. She is not perfectly suited to these roles, for she is vain, stupid, snobbish and self-centred, and gradually he finds this out. But it is not a matter of disillusionment—it is not (for instance) like Troilus finding out this is and is not Cressid, for he is a shrewd and realistic man who knows he has to come to terms with her imperfections, and we are shown how he adapts to disappointment: when he decides to speak and use his authority, and when he finds it best to say nothing, how he chooses his words and when he—occasionally—loses his temper; set against his wife's not very subtle schemings, her use of tears as a weapon, her acceptance of his authority on one level and readiness to ignore it quietly on another. It is all matter-of-fact, detailed, perceptive, and needs no poetry.

Three works: poem, play and novel, from the thirteenth, the sixteenth and the nineteenth centuries, and (inevitably) with increasing authorial independence. In the case of *Tristan*, the story now seems to us like a communal possession of its age: it does not matter greatly that we have to move from Gottfried to Thomas when the text gives out, and we can never be sure, when we admire, if the credit belongs to one or the other, or a common original, or the tradition. In the case of *Romeo and Juliet* we have the immediate source, we can see what Shakespeare himself contributed, and we also know that the story itself was already popular. Gottfried offers an example of a traditional tale well told, Shakespeare is the transmuter of genius, turning a traditional tale to his own incomparable gold. In the case of *Wives and Daughters*, the author made up the story. Though representative it is original, a narrative made direct from raw material.

Though their relation to it develops, each work has a tradition behind it, and our next task must be to relate it to that. I have chosen the three works because I believe they are representative, and to show this they must be put in their literary context—other medieval romances, other Renaissance plays, other Victorian novels.

Tristan in context

That the Tristan story was widespread in the Middle Ages is obvious; and it is equally obvious that it must in some measure have been disapproved of. What for example is the significance of the complaint of Fénice in Chrétien's *Cligés*,[6] that she would rather be torn limb from limb than be regarded as another Isolde (or, as she is in old French, Iseut)? On the basis of this, the romance has been described as an anti-Tristan; but if we look at what Fénice says,[7] we see that she cannot bear the thought of sleeping with one man when she loves another (hence the magic potion that deceives her husband and keeps her virgin for Cligés). What distresses her about Iseut is not that she slept with Tristan, but that she slept with Mark. In another passage,[8] refusing to go off with Cligés by saying 'Everyone would speak of us as they do of Iseut the Blond and of Tristan', it is clear that what she objects to is being talked about. So far from being an anti-Tristan, *Cligés* is very close to it in narrative detail, and based on the same conception of love, as an overwhelming experience that takes complete possession of one. Love is illness, is fire, is bitter-sweet; when Cligés goes off to win honour in Britain without confessing his love, simply saying he is altogether hers, her reflections leave us in no doubt that sexual love is unique and extreme; for in her anxiety that she may have overinterpreted his remark, she says,[9] 'I must not assume I was the cause of it, for one is always loth to leave people whom one loves and knows.' The use of the same word for the love she longs for (*amor*) and for the more ordinary feeling she contrasts it with (*qu'on aint*, whom one loves) cannot hide the enormous difference. Such after all is the nature of the word 'love': to name this incomparable experience we still, today, use the same word that describes our affection for parents, friends and chocolates.

To some medievalists, the differences between Gottfried and Chrétien are of great significance: the former is seen as part of a dark wild northern tradition, the latter as part of the sunny sophistication of courtly love as derived from the troubadours.[10] But what they have in common is much more important. Both speak of love through paradox and conceit; for both it is adulterous, and contrasted with marriage; for both it is so powerful as to be irresistible; above all, for both it is unique.

I have glanced at *Cligés* in order to rescue it from the charge of being, in any important sense, an anti-Tristan; but if we are looking for a medieval love story to place next to that of Tristan and Isolde we have a far more famous example, that of Lancelot.

There are two main versions of the Lancelot story and this time they really are very different. That of Chrétien is called *Le Conte de la Charette*,[11] because the knight who sets out to rescue Guinevere (we only learn later that he is Lancelot) is told by a dwarf that the only way to find the Queen is to mount the cart he is driving. Every reasonable argument is against doing this: Chrétien explains at length how degrading such a cart is (it carried criminals, and to mount it was to lose your legal rights), and Lancelot is not only publicly humiliated when he mounts it, but it does him no apparent good, since Gawain, who refuses to mount, comes to the same destination. Worst of all, the Queen, when he does find her, is angry with him because (and it takes a long time and near suicide to worm it out of her) he had hesitated for two steps before mounting. It is clear that love is deeply at odds with the norms of the society and with good sense.

In the other version[12] the adulterous love is closely connected with the downfall of the Round Table, for, though there is no direct causal link, it is suggested that by going off to France to fight Lancelot, Arthur left his kingdom vulnerable; and after the death of Arthur, Lancelot returns to England to slay Mordred's sons. He then becomes a hermit, and dies the holy death of the converted sinner.

The parallel with the Mark–Isolde–Tristan triangle is obvious, though the emphasis has shifted. In the Tristan story the lovers ruin their own lives, in this one they are part of the fall of a civilization: perhaps that makes Tristan and Isolde, in the end, the supreme example of love's doom. There is also a difference between the two heroes: Lancelot's talent is for fighting, Tristan's for singing. Lancelot's way of showing his love for Guinevere is to win tournaments or slay enemies against overwhelming odds, and since the eternal jousting and lance-splintering of the (usually disguised) knightly hero is, in all medieval literature, one of the elements that least speaks to us today, this is another reason why Lancelot now lives less vividly in our imagination.

The most moving statement of Lancelot's passion was added by Malory to the French original. After the Queen has entered a nunnery, Lancelot declares that he will do the same, as he almost did when the quest of the Holy Grail led him to forsake the vanities of the world:

> And therefore, lady, sythen ye have taken you to perfection, I must needs take me to perfection, of right. For I take record of God, in you I have had mine earthly joy, and if I had founden you now so disposed, I had cast me to have had you into mine own royaume.[13]

There is a pall of doom over this of a different kind from the lament of Isolde over the dead Tristan: in this case, both lovers are alive, and their greater sense of the public reverberations of their affair involves a recantation amid disaster.

Tristan and Isolde: Lancelot and Guinevere: and (especially for English readers) Troilus and Criseyde. All are representatives of courtly love; a sentiment that goes back to the troubadours, in which love is illegitimate and furtive, addressed to a woman who is disdainful, often unjust, and worshipped by a lover willing to perform any service imposed on him. Such love is an art, with rules like chivalry, set forth in such treatises as the *De Arte Honesti Amandi* of Andreas Capellanus, in which seduction techniques are classified according to the social status of the parties, and which contains the famous judgement of the Countess of Champagne, that love is not possible between a married couple.[14]

The term 'courtly love' was coined in 1883 by Gaston Paris:[15] its most famous exponent in English is C. S. Lewis; and the idea has now fallen a victim to the inevitable swing of scholarly opinion.[16] In both this chapter and the next I shall continue to use it, and ought therefore, however briefly, to defend the concept against the recent attacks. As representative of these, I choose A. Kelly, who claims that there was no serious incompatibility between love and marriage; and that a great deal that looks extramarital may have involved clandestine marriage. In particular, he claims that Troilus and Cressida, in Chaucer's poem, are secretly married, so that their love is not adulterous.[17] Kelly's case is made with great learning and skill; but I believe it misconceives the nature both of marriage and of literature. Marriage, unlike love, is necessarily public: it is the institution by which society regulates the sexual and reproductive life of a couple, and no society is without a system of marriage laws. 'In every human society,' says Malinowski,[18] 'a man and a woman who attempt to behave as if they were married without obtaining the appropriate social sanction are made to suffer more or less severe penalties.' The medieval church was right in its opposition to secret marriage[19] because it was an attempt to conform to the letter while defying the spirit of the institution. Clandestine marriage is not in practice very different from adultery.

Kelly's misconception of literature, shared by many distinguished medievalists, is of great importance in this discussion, since it represents a pressing danger for books that attempt (like the present one) to place literature in its social and intellectual context. It is a misconception shared by other distinguished medievalists—E. T. Donaldson, for instance, who protests: 'If the student has been told that adultery is a basic ingredient in courtly love, he will be discomfited, to say the least, to have to accept in place of adultery, such substitutes as fornication, frustration, idealization, madness, matrimony or death.'[20] Both these scholars are treating poems like legal documents: instead of deriving the essence of a literary work from its symbols and its action, they argue with it, paying great attention to its explicit statements, treating plot as something given and therefore unimportant. Donaldson's list is deliberately and rhetorically miscellaneous; if we sort it out, we can see that many of these 'substitutes' lead to the same artistic effects, and the same imaginative vision, as adultery. The resemblance is not discomfiting but revealing. In contrast to this, I shall attempt constantly to treat a poem as a work of imagination, whose soul is plot and whose meaning resides in its symbols.

Romeo and Juliet in context

To the enraptured lover, his mistress seems larger than life, his experience is of a bliss surpassing all other pleasures. Only great poetry can rise to the expressing of such feeling, and the greatest of poets is Shakespeare.

> Tempests themselves, high seas, and howling winds.
> The gutter'd rocks, and congregated sands,
> Traitors ensteep'd to clog the guiltless keel,
> As having sense of beauty, do omit
> Their common natures, letting go safely by
> The divine Desdemona.... (II.i.68

> O my soul's joy,
> If after every tempest come such calms,
> May the winds blow till they have wakened death,
> And let the labouring bark climb hills of seas,
> Olympus—high, and duck again as low
> As hell's from heaven! If it were now to die,
> 'Twere now to be most happy, for I fear
> My soul hath her content so absolute,
> That not another comfort like to this
> Succeeds in unknown fate. (II.i.84)

Both these speeches come from the scene of the arrival in Cyprus, which is the high moment of the action of *Othello*, and from which everything descends in rapid but complex development to the tragic end. The first, by Cassio, loyal lieutenant and devoted admirer, celebrates Desdemona by the traditional device of the pathetic fallacy: the elements have spared Desdemona because, 'having sense of beauty', they have not dared to destroy her. It is not the only conventional device that Cassio uses: Desdemona is 'our great captain's captain', in the military imagery so common in love poetry, she is 'the riches of the ship', and he prays both for her safety and Othello's. The lines have some individual and Shake-spearean life ('gutter'd rocks'), but within a general framework of the traditional. A lesser dramatist would have given that speech to Othello himself; it is only when we hear Othello's lines that we realize the ordinariness of Cassio's. It is not only that Othello's are more splendid poetically (there is nothing of Cassio's as marvellously mimetic as 'And let the labouring bark climb hills of seas', with its one labouring adjective among the monosyllables), or that they contain proleptic elements appropriate to the hero rather than the lieutenant, but above all that they contain an intensity of emotion to make us realize that Cassio's poetry was, after all, simply that of compliment.

Here then is the pinnacle of love, placed at much the same point of the action as the stycomythia-sonnet of Romeo and Juliet; four acts later, both pairs of lovers are dead. But although in both plays love's bliss ends in death there is an obvious and important difference, the difference expressed in a great deal of traditional, especially Bradleian, criticism by calling *Romeo and Juliet* a tragedy of fate, *Othello*, a tragedy of charac-ter. External circumstances determine Romeo's fate, Othello is respon-sible for his own. I do not want to reject this familiar view, but to point out a corollary of it, that Bradley himself gives no hint of. What does the 'tragic flaw' of Lear or Hamlet or Othello, tell us about them, and about fatherly affection, revenge or love? The answer, surely, will be alarming: love, we see from this play, is *dangerous*. If it is something within the hero that causes the tragedy (and causes the death of Desde-mona), we must ask ourselves if even within the high idealization of that poety ('O my soul's joy ...') there is the stuff of tragedy, even of murder.

If such love is dangerous, what does it threaten? It threatens, surely, stable social relationships. There is no more place for Othello's excesses, his idealization, his exotic charm, his ultimate foreignness, his striking of his wife, in the institutions of civilized Venice (and on one level, if not the deepest, Venice is the hero of this play) than there is place for the love of Lancelot and Guinevere in the institution of the Round Table—the difference being that in the one case the institutions survive the self-destruction of the individual, in the other case the civilization is destroyed. Such intensity of idealization, teetering if things go wrong to such intensity of retributiveness, seems quite incompatible with the complexities of interaction by which two people learn to know one another, each adjusting to the other's individuality. In short, it threatens marriage.

Shakespeare's other great love tragedy, *Antony and Cleopatra*, is the very opposite of *Othello* in both plot and poetry: its vast untidy structure, with its innumerable rapid changes of scene, its huge number of characters, its action stretching from Egypt to Rome in one direction and Parthia in another, and lasting for an indeterminate number of years, invites us out into the infinite reverberations of its wildly inventive poetry; whereas *Othello* is the most tightly constructed of all Shakespeare's tragedies, the one which almost observes the unities, uses virtually no prose, builds each scene carefully to interact with the others, echoes with the most complex Shakespearean irony, and whose poetry is intricate and inward looking. So it is appropriate that in *Antony and Cleopatra* love is the rival to political and marital responsibility in a gigantic clash of loyalties, whereas in *Othello* marriage is destroyed from within.

It is necessary for Othello's marriage to be on the one hand something settled and solid, so that we may see the full extent of the destruction, and on the other hand something that never got going, so that we may see the appalling—and rapid—inevitability of the disaster. To achieve this paradox Shakespeare used the celebrated double time scheme.[21] We no longer believe that the sustaining of two incompatible time schemes in the play is a sign of Shakespeare's clumsiness, or even of the fact that he knew what he could get away with: it enhances the play, for both versions contribute something positive. By the short time scheme (which is the more prominent) the action takes 48 hours, and the couple sleep together only once: a couple who sleep together only once is a common feature in stories of extra-marital love, and the repeated sharing of the bed is the most obvious, and one of the commonest ways of representing marriage—as we see from the longer time-scheme:

> What sense had I of her stol'n hours of lust?
> I saw't not, thought it not, it harm'd not me:
> I slept the next night well, was free and merry;
> I found not Cassio's kisses on her lips.   (III.iii.344)

In Cinthio, Desdemona and the Moor are married for years. Shakespeare used that version in speeches like this one in order to convey the full horror of jealousy, contrasting it with this domestic familiarity; and in doing so he has, after all, made it a marriage. Here at least for a moment he is showing us intensity of passion in a marital setting.

One brilliant detail removes the double time-scheme when it is no longer needed, in Act V. This is Desdemona's instruction to Emilia to lay on her bed her wedding sheets. No doubt this assumes the longer time-scheme (the phrasing is odd if she means the sheets she'd had last night, even if these had already been changed and were ready again), but at the same time it abolishes it. Once again, it is to be the bed of lovers, of the virgin bride, not the familiar domestic couch. The fact that we can see the bed as both familiar and terrifyingly strange expresses the ambivalence of love, the content so absolute that it can commit murder, so that the perfect marriage is the most deeply threatened.

There is no Elizabethan tragic dramatist to compare with Shakespeare. Middleton and Webster have great power, and the former deals with love and marriage, but for a sustained body of tragedy that explores the nature of love it will be more rewarding to turn to Racine. Virtually all his plays are love tragedies, and the enormous care with which he devised his plots shows that he had worked out all the possibilities of construction offered by love intrigue. Basically, he uses two plot devices, which we may call the dilemma and the chain. The dilemma occurs when a character is torn between love and principle, as when Titus loves Bérénice but knows that a Roman emperor cannot marry a queen. The chain occurs when A loves B who loves C, and so on. The longest chain occurs in *Andromaque*, where Oreste loves Hermione who loves Pyrrhus who loves Andromaque—who loves her dead husband. The two devices are not mutually exclusive: *Phèdre* can be seen as a chain (Thésée–Phèdre–Hippolite–Aricie, except that Aricie returns Hippolite's love) or as a dilemma if we realize that Phèdre's love is in any case unlawful since she loves her stepson.

A Racinian tragedy involves an unstoppable force meeting an immovable obstacle. The plot devices provide the obstacles; the forces are the passions. In Corneille the passions might be reasonable and yield to the situation, but in Racine they are incapable of compromise. He is not really very far from his master Euripides, in whom the passions are gods. In *Phèdre* love is actually called Venus, and though the name is a metaphor, the nature of the belief involved may be very similar in the two dramatists.

> Je reconnus Vénus et ses feux redoutables,
> D'un sang qu'elle poursuit tourments inévitables. (*PH.* 277)

She does not 'recognize' Venus in the way one might recognize a goddess who appeared on stage; but such appearances in Euripides derive their power from what we have already seen of the torments of those they pursue. The use of 'Venus' is not mere ornament in *Phèdre*: the power of her passion is such that she is driven to attribute it to an external force, and it is from this feeling of helplessness that Racine's most celebrated line draws much of its power: 'c'est Vénus tout entière à sa proie attachée'.

The nature of Racine's poetry derives directly from his conception of the passions: to the helplessness of the character we must add the convention of articulateness. The relation between reason and the passions in these tragedies is paradoxical. When it comes to action, reason can do nothing; but when it comes to expression it is supreme. The character who is quite unable to control his passions is able to express them with total lucidity:

—De victimes moi-même a toute heure entourée,
Je cherchais dans leurs flancs ma raison egarée.
D'un incurable amour remèdes impuissants!
En vain sur les autels ma main brulait d'encens. (*Ph.* 281)

—Je le vis; son aspect n'avait rien de farouche;
Je sentis le reproche expirer dans ma bouche;
Je sentis contre moi mon cœur se déclarer;
J'oubliai ma colère, et ne sus que pleurer. (*Iph.* 497)

The first of these is by Phèdre, central character of her play; the second by Eriphile, who hovers on the fringe of the action of *Iphigénie*. Both are hopelessly in love, with a man who does not care, and both express their despair in verse of perfect symmetry. Such poetry is limited: stating one's plight in ringing tones, balancing verbs against one another in that perfectly adjusted instrument, the French hexameter, perhaps, comes too close to being a splendid opportunity for the actress, but at the same time it is a triumph of classical art.

The perfectly controlled statement of uncontrolled feeling is also found in Shakespeare's sonnets:

Past cure I am, now reason is past care,
And frantic mad with evermore unrest;
My thoughts and my discourse as madmen's are,
At random from the truth vainly expressed. (no. 147)

Yet for all their perfect rhetoric, these lines are a long way from Racine: the word-play, the piling up of epithets, yield an altogether more complicated poetry than Racine's perfect poise. Shakespeare's quatrain ends with a rising hysteria that sounds less controlled than the voice of the *Comédie française* actress.

Dramatic poetry like this belongs most appropriately to the protagonist. Eriphile has a peripheral role in *Iphigénie*: she is there because needed for the plot, but having landed himself with a cypher Racine added to her part the more interesting element of hopeless love. When she expresses this, we feel she needs, like Phèdre, a play of her own: such poignant lucidity suggests the tragic heroine.

Poetry like this is essentially unironic. It contrasts with the speeches of (say) Achille in this play, or all the characters in *Andromaque*, whose perception of the situation is limited and constantly corrected, for us, by the limited perception of others. *Andromaque* is a developing structure of clashing attitudes, in which the ironic possibilities are endless, and in which each speaker can shift his attitude and play on our varying sympathies. But Phèdre knows her plight with all too tragic clarity; as does Titus, and, when she has attained her final understanding, Bérénice.

Bérénice was described by Sainte-Beuve as 'tout à fait dans le gout secret et selon la pente naturelle de Racine: ... du Racine pur, un peu faible si l'on veut'.[22] It is a play virtually without plot or incident. Based on a single sentence from Suetonius, telling how Titus, having offered to marry Bérénice, was compelled to send her away once he became emperor, against both their wishes, it simply shows us Bérénice realizing that the marriage is off, and learning to accept this. It could have been constructed as a chain, but Antiochus, who loves Bérénice, is reduced to a looker-on at what is essentially a long interrupted dialogue between the two lovers. This gives Racine the opportunity to deploy his splendid baroque gestures involving kingdoms as toys and wedding presents, or to show us the theme of the human being inside the monarch. (Bérénice like Cleopatra, both less and more convincingly, is no less but e'en a woman).

The two extremes of Racinian tragedy are represented by *Andromaque* and *Bérénice*. In the one, love hurtles violently against obstacles it has refused to recognize, and the play ends in death and disaster, the women dead, Oreste mad; in the other, love admits the impasse, and expresses itself in the *tristesse majestueuse* of resigned acceptance, and the play ends like an aria. In both, love is essentially unhappy love. It cannot be tamed, it cannot overcome the obstacles, and it does not issue in marriage.

So far I have treated *Romeo and Juliet* as a tragedy, and the parallels drawn have been with other tragedies. But it was written between 1594 and 1596, and the vocabulary and versification give it the feel of the comedies Shakespeare was writing in the mid-1590s. For a full sense of the context of the play, we need to look at the comedy of love as well as its tragedy.

It is obvious how the comedy of love will begin and end. Boy and girl meet and fall in love in Act I; they marry in Act V; something has to fill up the intervening space. On one level, everything that happens in between must function as an obstacle, delaying their union.

> Ay me: for aught that I could ever read,
> Could ever hear by tale or history,
> The course of true love never did run smooth,
> But either it was different in blood ...
> Or else misgraffed in respect of years ...
> Or else it stood upon the choice of friends ...
> Or if there were a sympathy in choice,
> War, death or sickness did lay siege to it.

This is clearly a literary passage, meant to sound like a recital of the narrative forms of love. Hermia hasn't yet any experience, she is simply classifying (more graciously than the clumsy prose of this book) the ways a love story can unfold. Most of the obstacles she lists are external: war, death or sickness, and above all family: and the play built on these will be a story of adventures—how to overcome the obstacles, how to outwit the parents. *A Midsummer Night's Dream* itself reminds us of a simple and famous example of this, the story of Pyramus and Thisbe, separated by a wall, destroyed by a lion. It hardly seems fair to these lovers to take their story from Shakespeare's parody, but the mechanicals did at any rate get the facts right. The Pyramus and Thisbe story is relevant to that of *A Midsummer Night's Dream*, in which the lovers also escape into the woods, but relevant only as a point of departure: if they had met lions in the woods, if after many adventures they had reached the wealthy aunt, the play would have been a comedy of love's adventures. Instead, what they find in the wood are the obstacles that result from love itself, confusions of identity, rivalry and quarrels, resulting from the fact that choice of the beloved object is after all as arbitrary as being in the way when the juice of a flower is squeezed. When these complications are cleared up, the original obstacle is not overcome but simply removed, as Theseus now decides it's time for a happy ending and, for no reason whatever, overbears the will of Egeus so that the couples can all be knit in the Temple.

What Shakespeare has done to the plot is playfully to turn the adventures into a rehearsal of love's inherent difficulties. For adventures are not in the end very interesting in a love story, their relation to the love being merely accidental. What can Pyramus say, when he finds Thisbe dead?

> I am cause of this felonie,
> So it is reason that I die
> As she is dead because of me.[23]

That is what Pyramus says in Gower's version. But he is not the cause; or if he were (say for turning up late) it would be for a reason accidental to the love. It is when the obstacles are internalized that the details of the action, and the language of the lovers, constitute an exploration of the nature of love.

A blending of internal and external is provided by the familiar theme of the heroine in disguise. The cause for Shakespeare's heroines dressing up as pages is usually an adventure impinging on them from without (Viola's shipwreck, Rosalind's banishment) though it is also, on occasion, the fact that the man has gone off (Julia, Helena); but when the disguised girl meets her lover we have an opportunity for something far more interesting than adventure. In the case of Rosalind and Orlando, for instance, the disguise gives Rosalind two personae, and enables her to express two contrasting attitudes to love. The first essential for any actress playing Rosalind is to realize that two selves can only be mingled if they are, in the first place, separated; and to divide the whole of her part, in the scenes with Orlando, into those remarks she makes as Ganymede, and those in which Rosalind breaks out. Thus after teasing Orlando about horns, and after his reply, which ends 'and my Rosalind is virtuous', 'Ganymede' replies, 'And I am your Rosalind.' Celia's intervention—'it pleases him to call you so'—is surely a hasty re-erecting of the barrier that Rosalind's impetuosity has knocked down, and makes it clear that 'I am your Rosalind' came of an impulsive need to tell the truth. The clear distinction between the two sets of remarks is much easier to sustain because of the Elizabethan convention of the impenetrability of disguise: simply because the audience is willing to omit questions of whether Orlando is likely to spot who she is, she can play her dangerous game of brinkmanship with superb theatrical effect, unhindered by naturalistic probability. There is scope for different interpretations, of course, of which remarks are to be spoken in which persona.

> *Orlando:* Then love me, Rosalind
> *Rosalind:* Yes, faith will I, Fridays and Saturdays and all
> *Orlando:* And wilt thou have me?
> *Rosalind:* Ay, and twenty such (IV.i.104)

The last remark is obviously by Ganymede, but what about the previous one? I have seen a Rosalind say 'Fridays and Saturdays and all' in the teasing voice of Ganymede, and another say it in uncontrolled surrender, on the brink of betrayal, and each was superb: there is even scope for variety if it is taken as a Ganymede remark, on whether the whole sentence is playful or whether she pulls herself up after saying 'Yes faith will I' as Rosalind. But although the details of application are variable, there can be no doubt that a clear cut alternation is essential.

This alternation of personae corresponds to two contrasting attitudes to love, the lover's and the cynic's. Rosalind believes men are trustworthy and love will last, Ganymede doesn't. Ganymede's cynicism is explicit, Rosalind's trust bursts out through her loss of control. And so the retelling of those beloved stories of faithful lovers takes on a unique flavour:

> Troilus had his brains dash'd out with a Grecian club, yet he did what he could to die before, and he is one of the patterns of love. Leander, he would have liv'd many a fair year though Hero had turn'd nun; if it had not been for a hot midsummer night, for (good youth) he went but forth to wash him in the Hellespont, and being taken with cramp, was drown'd, and the

foolish chroniclers of that age, found it was Hero of Sestos. But these are all lies, men have died from time to time, and worms have eaten them, but not for love. (IV.i.88)

Why is that last sentence among the most moving in all the literature of love? Because everything in the situation has shown us that Rosalind doesn't 'really' believe it. She is hopelessly in love herself, and her scepticism and commonsense are a kind of antibody, engendered by the passion in her veins. She is all Ganymede now, in the sense that she's not betraying herself, but I would like to see an actress say it smiling, as if that was her happiest moment.

Disguise was a standard device of Elizabethan love comedy, but no one else used it with the consummate skill of Shakespeare. Beaumont and Fletcher's *Philaster*, for instance, shows at least as good a theatrical sense as *As You Like It* (to which it is indebted), but with none of the same psychological exploration. In *Philaster*, two sympathetic women both love the same man; and we are not told that the hero's page is really the heroine in disguise until she is unmasked. This is a better recipe for suspense and excitement, but we have only to think of what would be lost from the scenes between Julia and Proteus, Rosalind and Orlando, Viola and Orsino, if we did not know who the pretty youth was, to realize the difference between true drama and theatrical competence.

Adventure is not essential to the comedy of love. Why should not the intricacies and obstacles of courtship make their own pattern? There is after all a good analogy for this, that of dancing. The couple perform elaborate movements as an expression of their ambivalent relationship, involving attraction and repulsion, delay and consummation: the most beautiful movements are often those involving most opposition, yet all their driving force comes from the impulse towards union.

We owe the love comedy based on the courtship dance to John Lyly. Almost all his plays show several pairs of lovers involved with one another through rivalry; they end happily, through magic or impossible magnanimity; and they have little action, consisting largely of the recital in patterned prose of the dilemmas of love:

> Unfortunate Apelles, and therefore unfortunate because Apelles! Hast thou by drawing her beauty, brought to pass that thou canst scarce draw thine own breath? And by so much the more has thou increased thy care, by how much the more thou hast shewed thy cunning:... O Campaspe, Campaspe, art must yield to nature, reason to appetite, wisdom to affection?[24]

The speech is three pages long, and never for one moment does art yield to nature, or the careful antitheses to the impulses of appetite. Lyly was a schoolmaster, and wrote his plays for children: to hear a trained boy picking his way through these rhetorical figures would make it clear what an elegant game they are, a delighting in verbal skill, not a rendering of experience. Few famous writers can be less congenial to the twentieth century than Lyly. Our love poetry tends rather to the coital grunt and the gasp than to these polished recitations. Are *Campaspe* (1584) and *Endimion* (1591), then, mere historical cuiorisites or is there some way of bringing their intricate patterns to life? For Shakespeare there was: the method of parody. Shakespeare's early comedies, and especially *Love's Labour's Lost* (1595) are closely related to Lyly; and so is *Romeo and Juliet*. In both these plays there is actual dancing, as well as the dance of words; in both there is euphuistic verbal intricacy:

> 'Is love a tender thing? It is too rough,
> Too rude, too boisterous and it pricks like thorn.'
> 'If love be rough with you, be rough with love,
> Prick love for pricking, and you beat love down.' (*R. & J*, I.iv.25)

The relation of such a 'set of wit well-played' to Lyly is twofold: the verbal skill of the original is both bettered and rejected. To say that Shakespeare is parodying Lyly is true, if we remember that the good parodist needs the same skill as his victim—and in this case has more. The way to bring artificial verse to life is to insert reminders of the actualities of experience which it ignores: as Mercutio's bawdy wit mentions aspects of love that would hardly have been in place in the mouths of those clever schoolboys—or perhaps it would be truer to say that it incorporates the jokes that the schoolboys made offstage. The verbal dance of *Love's Labour's Lost* is superb, and makes Lyly look an amateur; yet it is full of suggestions that we should not take it too seriously and at the end, in the moment of marvellous simplicity when Marcade brings the news of the Princess's father's death, all dancing ends, and any wooing that takes place now needs to be direct: 'Honest plain words best pierce the ear of grief.' Yet Berowne has said this before, and not found it easy to carry out ('Sans sans, I pray you'), and his honest plain words now include 'Behold the window of my heart, mine eye', and even a request that takes us back to courtly love, 'Impose some service on me for my love.'

The rejection of eloquence under the power of true emotion is a recurrent theme in Shakespearean comedy: yet the artistry that is rejected is also retained, sometimes with marvellous subtlety. Romeo's calf-love for Rosaline is completely euphuistic, full of references to Cupid the marksman, and not unsuitable for Lyly's boys (perhaps the references to chastity are a little explicit, but by the time Mercutio has made fun of them they are made to seem innocence itself.) Only after meeting Juliet is he capable of the directness of:

> I shall forget, to have thee still stand there,
> Remembering how I love thy company.   (II.ii.172)

Yet though Romeo learns simplicity when he falls in love, he does not lose his eloquence, and his highest poetry (like that of Viola) comes from the interplay of simplicity and wit, immediacy and formality.

Here then are some of the possible variants of the comedy of wooing. What they all have in common is the overcoming of obstacles, and what all the interesting ones have in common is the acting out of a pattern of coming together and staying apart, of emotional surrender and sceptical detachment, that corresponds to the emotional experience of preparing for sexual union.

In medieval romance, love exists outside marriage and is adulterous, with tragic consequences for the lovers, and perhaps for the society. In Shakespearean tragedy we may have the same pattern, or love may enter marriage, but only to destroy it. In Racine, unlawful love is doomed, and may destroy the lawful in the process. These are tragic patterns, and with love comedy we are in another world, but we are still never shown the successful incorporation of love into marriage. The comedy ends in a wedding: the dance concludes, and the couple live happily ever after. We do not look beyond the ritual ending to see how time will keep the promises. One of the fathers, Prospero, actually points this out:

> So glad of this as they I cannot be,
> Who are surprised with all.

The tired sympathy of middle age has its place at the wedding too—or, in the case of *The Tempest*, is so prominent that even the wedding is pushed beyond the edge of the play.

Wives and Daughters in context

From *Wives and Daughters* we can move out first to another work by Elizabeth Gaskell herself, then to the novels of other English women of the nineteenth century. In *Cousin Phillis* (1863) Mrs Gaskell tells, in a hundred pages, a charming and shrewd story about family life and attitudes to work, and places at the centre a tale of unrequited love. The story of Ebenezer Holman, farmer, minister and inventor, is told through leisurely description, vivid dialogue, and mild irony: it shows a keen awareness of social change, and a keen eye for matter of fact details. The story of how his daughter Phillis was disappointed in love needs a different kind of writing—this, for instance:

Phillis said nothing. She kept her head bent down over her work; but I don't think she put a stitch in, while I was reading the letter. I wondered if she understood what nosegay was meant; but I could not tell. When next she lifted up her face, there were spots of brilliant colour on the cheeks that had been so pale before.... Once my eyes fell upon her hands, concealed under the table, and I could see the passionate, convulsive manner in which she laced and interlaced her fingers perpetually, wringing them together from time to time, wringing till the compressed flesh became perfectly white.[25]

There are many passages like this. They differ from the technique of the rest of the story in two ways. First, they show us Phillis entirely from the outside. Usually, we are told a good deal about what is going on mentally, both because the characters speak their thoughts and because the narrator speculates, interprets, adds earlier or later details. But here, suddenly, a gate has come down: we simply watch. Paul does not even say, for some time, what is obvious to him and us, that what we are seeing is her love and this reticence adds to the feeling of our being helpless spectators. We are in the presence of something it would almost be an impertinence to interpret.

Second, there is a new concentration here on the physiological. The effect of this is striking, but also limited, for the bodily details observed are a little too predictable. In both these passages there is a touch of power: in the 'two spots of brilliant colour', the adjective mocks the meaning of the spots in a fine verbal gesture, and 'laced and interlaced' is a cool verbal rendering of the action of the fingers. But in both cases too there is too much that is easy and ordinary: 'that had been so pale before' uses its plangent vowels and elegiac rhythms in a way that is ultimately glib, and even 'brilliant' is a conventional enough term for spots of colour in the cheek; and there is too much of adjectival protest in the 'passionate convulsive manner'. Elizabeth Gaskell's fine distinction as a social novelist is not quite matched by her handling of young love's tragedy.

Both absence and modesty prevent Phillis from uttering a word of rebuke to or about her lover; so the traditional isolation of the lovers— the physical isolation of Tristan and Isolde banished to the forest, the emotional isolation of Romeo and Juliet from the bawdy quarrelsome world of Verona, their stylistic isolation as they take refuge in dark word play (lamier) or passionate metaphor ('here is thy sheath')—now becomes the isolation of Phillis alone, loved by all her family and all who know her, but silent in her suffering, surrounded by a pool of silence.

If marriage is made of prose, then Jane Austen is just the writer for it: her marriages are famous—and so of course, are her love stories, but how much of the passion of love do they express? The best place to look for it is in her last and sunniest novel, *Persuasion*. When Anne and Wentworth have at last come together and declared their love,

> they slowly paced the gradual ascent, heedless of every group around them, seeing neither sauntering politicians, bustling housekeepers, flirting girls, nor nursery-maids and children....

This is the total indifference of lovers to the outside world—a prose translation of, say:

> Take you a course, get you a place,
> Or the King's real or his stamped face,
> Contemplate, what you will, approve,
> So you will let me love.[26]

Now there is in *Persuasion* one wholly delightful description of a happy middle-aged marriage, that of the Crofts. Mrs Croft has 'bright dark eyes, good teeth, and altogether an agreeable face'. She looks older than her years because of her weather-beaten complexion, 'the consequence of her having been almost as much at sea as her husband', a practice she stoutly defends: 'I can safely say, that the happiest part of my life has been spent on board a ship.' When on land, her pleasure is to go driving with her husband; and his habit of overturning the gig and tossing her out adds an extra zest to the outings. Now Wentworth, like Admiral Crofts, is a sailor, and full of vitality: is this not a glimpse of what Anne's married life will be like?

No doubt it is; and yet, as we read, the thought is impossible. To move from one literary mode to another is to move between incompatible worlds: there is a jollity about the Crofts that puts them in the world of the comic, and that would be fatal to the intensity of Anne's experience. In a world in which time moves steadily forward, in which Anne Elliott becomes Anne Wentworth, one could picture her still having good teeth, and being tossed out of her gig; but fiction does not use time in that way. The mode of experience of the lovers could not change so radically and still belong to the book.

Persuasion is the only novel in which Jane Austen seriously tried to express the experience of love; her careful skirting of it in all the others can be seen in the detatched language of the proposal scenes. Darcy, for instance, 'expressed himself on the occasion as sensibly and as warmly as a man violently in love can be supposed to do'. It is a commonplace of Jane Austen criticism that she never writes a scene which could not come from her own experience—there are, for instance, no scenes in which only men are present. When she wrote *Pride and Prejudice* she had never heard a proposal, and there is surely an uneasy consciousness of this in 'supposed': ardent lovers belong not to personal experience but to literary convention, and what they say is what they are expected to say. In *Emma*, she simply surrendered to this awkwardness and deliberately laughed it off. 'What did she say? Just what she ought, of course. A lady always does.' Who can say whether the unembarrassed warmth of *Persuasion* has anything to do with Jane Austen's now richer emotional experience? Her disastrous one-day engagement to Harris Bigg-Wither is hardly likely to have taught her much about love's happiness, though it does tell us she had by then heard a proposal; the mysterious love affair, perhaps in Devon, perhaps with a clergyman, is too ill-documented to be counted as real knowledge.[27]

Of marriage, on the other hand, Jane Austen knew all she needed. She knew it as an observer, but that was the appropriate knowledge for this shrewd, edgy observer's art. The taste of her marriages is often sour: who would care to be married to Mrs Bennet, or Mr Grant, or either of the Middletons? The Bennets, her most famous married couple, have a good deal in common with the Gibsons: a husband far more intelligent than his flamboyant, self-pitying wife, and realistic enough to know that he must accept the situation and make the best of it. Jane Austen's comedy is broader than Mrs Gaskell's and Mrs Bennet is coarse to a degree that would deeply offend the easily offendable Hyacinth Gibson; but that is simply a question of degree. There is a more important difference:

> 'My dear Mr Bennet,' said his lady to him one day, 'have you heard that Netherfield Park is let at last?' Mr Bennet replied that he had not. 'But it is,' returned she; 'for Mrs Long has just been here, and she told me all about it.' Mr Bennet made no answer. 'Do you not want to know who has taken it?' cried his wife impatiently. 'You want to tell me, and I have no objection to hearing it.'   (Ch. 1)

This snatch of dialogue ends with Mr Bennet making explicit the satiric point it has built up to. Similarly, when the first letter arrives from Mr Collins (in chapter 13), and Mrs Bennet delivers herself of a diatribe against 'that odious man' (the estate is entailed onto him), it is Mr Bennet's comment—'nothing can clear Mr Collins from the guilt of inheriting Longbourn'—that expresses the illogic of her position. In both cases, we can say that his function is very close to the author's; he it is who makes the point she has set up. When Jane appears to have been jilted by Bingley, he remarks:

> So, Lizzy, your sister is crossed in love, I find. I congratulate her. Next to being married, a girl likes to be crossed in love a little now and then. It is something to think of, and gives her a sort of distinction among her companions.

It could be a recipe for a plot: being married and being crossed in love are the interesting situations. Is it callous? Well, if it is, is not Jane Austen's fiction—is not all fiction—callous? Wanting people to be happy would mean wanting them not to be worth writing about.

Now Mr Bennet is not a good father: his ironic detachment has meant neglecting his children. We are meant to be aware of this throughout, and he grows aware of it at the climax, after Lydia's elopement: 'It has been my own doing, and I ought to feel it.' It does not last long: in the very act of reproaching himself, he retains his irony. Elizabeth tells him not to be too severe upon himself:

> You may warn me against such an evil. Human nature is so prone to fall into it! No, Lizzy; let me once in my life feel how much I have been to blame. I am not afraid of being overpowered by the impression. It will pass away soon enough.

Mr and Mrs Bennet are not treated alike. The wife is allowed to expose herself by her garrulousness, and is put down by occasional savage analyses ('She was a woman of mean understanding, little information and uncertain temper'). The husband has a much better understanding, and is enlisted by the author as an ally in the putting down. But this leads to a probing into the nature (and motives) of satire. Mr Bennet's hope of finding Mr Collins as foolish as his letter suggests, and his insistence that Wickham is his favourite son-in-law, are the remarks of an eager ironist; and make it clear that the ironic and the moral attitudes are, in real life, incompatible. Most notable of all is the remark, perhaps a little clumsily explicit, which he makes on almost the last occasion we hear him: 'For what do we live to make sport of our neighbours, and laugh at them in our turn?' Is not the spiritual emptiness of that remark all too accurate an indication of the basis of much that is most brilliant in Jane Austen's fiction?

That there is a tension in Jane Austen's universe between the ironic and the moral is often dismissed as the oversophisticated interpretation of modern critics.[28] So far is this from being the case, that I believe she was aware of the tension herself. Her novels encourage in us a clear and merciless awareness of the spite, vanity and selfishness of others; but her moral code insists that we tolerate those we have to live with. For the family is like the ship in Conrad: an enclosed world from which there is no escape, in which the passions must be controlled or someone will be hurt. Satire does not encourage tolerance, yet Jane Austen would have found the world intolerable if it were not for satire.

This problem rises to the surface through her treatment of marriage, as it could not in her love passages. Anne Elliott lays aside her irony when Wentworth enters the room: she has no duties towards him, only the unquestioning longing for his love. They will have to learn the balancing act between satire and tolerance when they deal with Anne's family, but they will learn it together, for love all love of other sights controls: they will enjoy their one world together. I say 'will': but novels, as we have seen, do not really have a future tense. Their love exists outside time: it is in time that we laugh at our nearest, and put up with them. It is in time that marriages take place.

For my next example, I turn to our greatest woman novelist. There are no profounder studies of marriage in English than the stories of the Casaubons and the Lydgates in *Middlemarch*. George Eliot is at her finest in these sad, clear-eyed accounts written with ruthless probing and profound compassion. To choose one example from so rich a book seems hopeless: almost at random, I will take the quarrel between Causaubon and Dorothea in chapter 29.

This chapter begins with the famous shift in point of view (One morning.... Dorothea—but why always Dorothea?) that reminds that there are two to a marriage. It then gives us a careful account of Mr Casaubon's anxieties: the difficulty of making his 'Key to all Mythologies' unimpeachable, the annoying reception of his preliminary pamphlets, his suspicion that his old acquaintance Carp of Brasenose is among his hostile critics, and the tensions (digestive as well as mental) brought on by the new pamphlet he is working on. It is a brilliant account of the difficulties of the scholarly life, as led by a man of no great mental powers but as much sensitivity as the rest of us. Imperceptibly to himself, Mr Casaubon's inner struggles have shifted from the agonies of real creation to the equally distressing agonies of the trappings—worry about the reception of his work, brooding on the Latin dedication 'about which everything was uncertain except that it was not to be addressed to Carp'.

Perhaps no contribution that George Eliot made to fiction is as great as her introduction of intellectual work as serious subject matter. It is essential, for an understanding of this quarrel, that we know Mr Casaubon's feelings, and it is essential for that that we understand his work. True, this quarrel is not directly about his work: that one took place earlier, when they were in Rome on their honeymoon, and arose out of Dorothea's unfortunately urging him to give his researches to the world, with an enthusiasm which his uneasy ear heard as reproach. This time the quarrel is about Will Ladislaw, the other subject on which Mr Casaubon is touchy, and this touchiness leads him to give her Will's letter accompanied by what she (not unfairly) hears as an anticipatory rebuke. The escalation of the incident, after that, is as could be expected: Dorothea's angry answer, Mr Casaubon's nervous 'Dorothea, you are hasty', her continued anger that he does not apologize, and his so predictable attempt at loftily dismissing the subject, 'though his hand trembled so much that the words seemed to be written in an unknown character'. All the force of George Eliot's realism is here: the accurate attribution of motives, the convincing dialogue, the eye for behavioural detail. The chapter has already announced its realism with one of those basic declarations of intent of the realist, the rejection of literary conventions. Mr Casaubon's motives for marrying included leaving 'behind him that copy of himself which seemed so urgently required of a man—to the sonneteers of the sixteenth century. Times had altered since then, and no sonneteer had insisted on Mr Casaubon's leaving a copy of himself.' It is not only the altered times that are responsible—George Eliot is quite capable of presenting someone from the sixteenth century who had unfortunately not received such insistence from a sonneteer: it is the fact of living in a world of prose that does not obey such poetic conventions. Such an indication prepares us for the nature of the dialogue that follows, true to the shapes of actual speech.

Actuality has been carried so much further since George Eliot that the episode may not, to us, seem all that close to nature. We see this on a technical level, her dialogue not having entered the broken, ungrammatical, elliptical series of mutual interruptions that modern realists (even modern poets) have learned from Hemingway and the tape-recorder; and even more on a psychological level, as we realize the nature of Dorothea's feelings. Rightly or wrongly, the techniques of naturalism have been associated with a reductive view of man: if that's all there is to human dialogue, then this is all there is to human nature. But George Eliot, despite her deliberate rejection of some of the conventions of uplift, does not want to see human nature as merely petty, and governed by the irritations of the moment. So though she shows us that she has the talent for a scene of modern bickering, her concern is the richer one of playing Dorothea's irritation against her deeper concerns. First, we are shown that her hand does not tremble: she is young and offended, not anxious and uneasy, and she writes better than usual, feeling she is now able to see the construction of the Latin she was copying: 'in her indignation there was a sense of superiority, but it went out for the present in firmness of stroke'. After being shown that she is the stronger of the two, we are then shown that she is the weaker: for when Mr Casaubon collapses (the plot obligingly enacting what self-pity always hopes for) she forgets her irritation in concern for him.

Two further remarks to suggest the full range of George Eliot's realism. First, she immediately opens outwards into the setting. Dorothea's violent ringing of the bell brings a servant, then Sir James Chettam, then Celia, then the questions about whether she should have married Casaubon that these others (though not she) can ask themselves explicitly. The domestic episode belongs in a larger social context, and for its full understanding we need that. But at the same time she moves inwards: the chapter would have been impossible without the privileged access she allows herself into the minds of both protagonists. The broken dialogue of modern naturalism is limited interpretatively because of its technical limitations. There are rewards for presenting dialogue only from the outside, but they are not so great as the complexity of understanding which is possible to the intrusive author.

After this marvellous realism, few modern readers are altogether satisfied with the bliss of passion between Dorothea and Will Ladislaw. Will seems too idealized, too poetic; Dorothea's trust in him too lacking in the complexity shown in the picture of her marriage. And instead of the probing analysis, the realistic dialogue and the wit, we have this:

> while he was speaking there came a vivid flash of lightning which lit each of them up for the other—and the light seemed to be the terror of a hopeless love. Dorothea darted instantaneously from the window; Will followed her, seizing her hand in a spasmodic movement; and so they stood, with their hands clasped, like two children, looking out on the storm, while the thunder gave a tremendous crack and roll above them, and the rain began to pour down. (Ch. 83)

Simply to find that inferior to chapter 29, as so many readers do, is to pass too crass a judgement: we need to recognize too that it is in a different literary mode. Suppose it came not from *Middlemarch* but from Charlotte Brontë, who despised Jane Austen precisely for her inability to write scenes like this, and whom we value for introducing passion into the sobrieties of the nineteenth-century novel—and who also uses the weather to symbolize it (as did so many before her, back to the medieval poets). Would we value it more highly if it came from the same novel as:

> But what had befallen the night? The moon was not yet set, and we were all in shadow: I could scarcely see my master's face, near as I was. And what ailed the chestnut tree? it writhed and groaned; while wind roared in the laurel walk, and came sweeping over us.[29]

The realism of *Middlemarch* is so far beyond the power of anything in *Jane Eyre* (parts of which, by realistic criteria, are absurd) that we can ask if George Eliot is suffering from the expectations she has herself raised, if the romance mode of this love scene is being compared to the realistic mode of the marriages. Well, it is always possible to answer that a difference in mode does not preclude a difference in quality, that George Eliot's romance is not as good as her realism. Using lightning is all very well, but calling it the terror of a hopeless love is too near cliché, just as the comparison with children would be all very well if it did not say 'with their hands clasped', turning them too easily to the babes in the wood of nineteenth-century sentimentality.

This answer would I think be correct, not only for George Eliot but for most nineteenth-century novelists, including Jane Austen and Elizabeth Gaskell. The point depends on a distinction between two modes, which I have already used and which is central to the argument of the whole book; and since it is a distinction which much modern criticism has attacked, it is now necessary to pause and defend it.

Excursus on Realism

Since the contrast between the poetic and the realistic has arisen from a discussion of *Middlemarch*, we can turn for theoretical backing to G. H. Lewes: for he combines a special relationship with George Eliot and a special relationship with realism. He more than anyone was the man who introduced the doctrine from France to England. For Lewes, the opposite to realism is not idealism but 'falsism': his criticisms of Dickens amount to a complaint that Dickens does not show us life as it is, just as his advice to Charlotte Brontë was to beware of the melodrama and adhere to the real: 'real experience is perennially interesting, and to all men', and though he recognizes the existence of other criteria, he makes it clear that he considers them inferior. The (now forgotten) novels of Miss Braddon are not to be considered literature, for they have plot interest but not the more important qualities of 'grasp of character, vision of realities, regard for probabilities and theoretical views of human life'. 'In a story of wild startling incidents such as *Monte Christo*,' concedes Lewes, 'it is absurd to demand a minute attention to probabilities;' and then goes on to make it clear that this consigns *Monte Christo*—and Miss Braddon—to a lower level than the 'incomparably more difficult' art that sets the story 'among scenes and characters of familiar experience'. '*Monte Christo* may talk a language never heard off the stage, but Major Pendennis must speak as they speak in Pall Mall.'[30]

There are two main objections to Lewes's case, one to his preference, and one to his distinction. Why should he be so sure that the language of Pall Mall is superior to the language of the stage? Lovers who move among the scenes of familiar experience do not talk like this:

> Now from head to foot
> I am marble-constant: now the fleeting moon
> No planet is of mine.

The language of Major Pendennis is a thin and brittle instrument compared with that: if the story of Antony and Cleopatra involves only the abstractions of life, then love is an abstraction of enormous exploratory power, and its expression opens up depths of the human spirit that are not mentioned in Pall Mall. Lewes has not seen the continuity between the popular stereotypes he despises and the imaginative power of the greatest literature.

This objection, though it reminds us of the limitations—the almost Philistine limitations—of Lewes's criticism, does not, in one sense, matter at all. Lewes is the spokesman for the new literary possibilities that have arisen in France, and his doctrine breathes the feeling that there are vast possibilities now opening up to the novelists. It is never a serious objection to one artistic mode that in their enthusiasm its defenders underestimate what can be done with others. Lewes's defence of realism is what matters, not his condescension towards romance.

A more serious objection to Lewes's argument is that his distinction is naive. His confidence about what reality is like is vulnerable to philosophic probing and epistemological sophistication; just as his confident deployment of 'realist' as a critical term ignores the semantic variation that modern metacritics engage in distinguishing. Roman Jakobson, for instance, distinguishes five main meanings of the term in critical practice.[31] First there is the distinction between what the author conceives and what the reader accepts as realistic (a distinction that can be made with any critical term); then there is the historical meaning—a particular movement in the nineteenth century; and finally two meanings concerned with the actual criteria imposed by realism on works of fiction—the thickening of the narrative with actual details, and the demand for consistent motivation. Distinguishing these is clearly a useful semantic exercise; but despite Jakobson's insistence that they must be kept separate, there is nothing inherently untenable in a follower of Lewes maintaining that he wants them all—or, more specifically, that the first two involve the last two, as the third maintained. Jakobson is a metacritic in the sense that he distinguishes terminology but never looks at reality or even at literature himself.

There is another kind of objection to Lewes, which involves a sophistication over literary history rather than over methodology. This is the view that realism is a set of conventions like any other, a perceptual grid applied to reality that, like all conventions, notices some things and not others, but can claim no privileged status as being closer to reality than romance, satire, fable or comedy. As spokesman for this view we can choose E. R. Curtius, who stresses the resemblance between realism and comedy, and insists that medieval attempts to speak as they do in Pall Mall belong to a tradtion that goes back to Euripides and Ovid. 'Where we can see "realism", what is actually there is a literary convention: the low style.'[32] This involves no rejection of the higher styles in other genres.

If this criticism is valid, it is a very serious one. To treat romance, fable or comedy in terms of a set of literary conventions, devices for noticing some things and not others, is to say nothing unacceptable to the practitioners of those modes; but to treat realism in this way is to knock the bottom out of its programme. Stendhal and Balzac, Lewes and George Eliot, could not possibly accept Curtius's view, since they saw realism as a way of emancipating themselves from the constraints of literary conventions, and presenting a world no longer subject to the selective vision these had imposed.

My discussion starts from an initial sympathy with Lewes's position, but tries to take account of the objections made in the subsequent debate. General appeals to 'reality' do not tell us enough about what Stendhal and George Eliot actually do in their fiction, so that the programme of realism must be translated into specific literary techniques.

A particularly useful criterion for realism is obtained by turning Curtius on his head, and looking for the rejection of pre-existing conventions in favour of an appeal to reality: that is, an awareness, in the novel, of how a situation would appear in the world of fable, satire or romance, and a quite deliberate refusal to do things that way—the co-existence, in short, of the mode that is rejected and the mode that is used. A simple example from the early George Eliot would be Hetty Sorrell, the most powerfully rendered character in *Adam Bede*. Hetty is the pretty milk-maid of folksong and ballad, the sort of girl about whom pastoral lyrics are written. Arthur calls her the pretty butter-maker, and describes her as 'a perfect Hebe; and if I were an artist I would paint her'. The assumption all men make—or all men outside her family—is that Hetty's nature is as delightful as her face. But George Eliot is not writing a ballad; outside ballads, the squire does not marry a milkmaid, and outside romance the pretty Hetty may be more self-centred, less delightful, than red-faced clumsy Molly. We have got to know Hetty as Hetty has to get to know the world, by removing the literary stereotypes.

That is a simple example: the later George Eliot, along with James, offers far more complex explorations in the course of not quite using the conventions; and it is by leaning against these that they remain, even at their most tantalizing, within the realist camp.

When all the theoretical arguments are over, there remains the inescapable appeal to literary experience. Almost all readers find that the great narratives, when we reflect on them, tend to fall into two classes. On the one hand, there is *The Golden Ass, Tristan, The Pilgrim's Progress, Candide, The Scarlet Letter, Sylvie, The Castle*; on the other hand there is *Moll Flanders, Clarissa, Le Rouge and le Noir, Effie Briest, Anna Karenina*. The second group are by authors whose ears are open to the tones of speech, whose eyes see the exact form of a gesture; who thicken the narrative with carefully observed detail; who believe in consistency of motivation in their characters; who inhabit a rationally comprehensible universe. The most familiar term for these writers is realists. There is far greater variety among the first group, and we have no convenient term to describe them all. In one way or another, they all remould reality, to bring it nearer to the heart's desire—or to the spirit's dread, or even to a theory. The diverse ways in which fantasy can reshape reality yield the rich diversity of literary *genres*—romance, allegory, satire, fable: only for verbal convenience shall I speak of them all as the romantic mode.

Realism sees a world under the control of reason: and reason and love keep little company together. The difference between romance and realism is exactly appropriate to that between love and marriage. Sober truthfulness will not do to render the transfiguring experience of love, nor will fantasy render the long complexities of married life. Somehow the view has got abroad (though it is perhaps less prevalent nowadays) that the Victorian novelists could not depict marriage; but the truth is more like the opposite. Both George Eliot and Elizabeth Gaskell are realistic writers who were constantly led away from realism, inevitably so when writing of love. Their writing in the romantic mode is usually competent, almost always conventional, and hardly ever has the full power of their genius. It is not marriage but love that they are not very good at.

2
The Paradoxes of Love

Why has the literary imagination seen love in contrast with marriage? Conflict makes for better stories than harmony, but we are here dealing with more than a device to keep the reader entertained. Love cannot accommodate itself to marriage because it cannot accommodate itself to society's demands, and to understand why is to explore the idea of love that has dominated European literature.

Before exploring the concept, I must name it; and here we have a lexical problem, for the only possible term is 'romantic love', and this is an anachronism. The main meaning of 'romantic' today, in popular usage, is probably 'connected with sexual love', but there is no recorded example of this before the eighteenth century, and no undisputed example—certainly no example without the accompanying noun 'love'—before the twentieth. The emergence of this meaning from the main eighteenth-century meanings of 'extravagant, far-fetched' and 'quixotic, over influenced by imagination' is difficult to chart because of the large area of overlap: thus when Francis Hutcheson observes in 1728 that 'a romantick lover has ... no notion of life without his mistress',[1] the usage sounds normal to modern ears, though the author probably felt it as synonymous with Fanny Burney's usage when she wrote, 'I am not romantic—I have not the least design of doing good to either of you.'[2] Hutcheson's is the earliest example I know where the modern sense is even possible, but it is not until very recently that it exists entirely on its own and the phrase 'true romance' ceases to be a paradox.[3] It is certainly anachronistic, then, to call the love of Romeo and Juliet 'romantic', and only correct to speak of the 'romance' of Tristan and Isolde by an etymological accident, but there is no other convenient term. And the anachronism is not without its advantages, for the lingering presence of the older meanings reminds us how extraordinary is the notion of love that sees it as irrational, anti-social and destructive of what it most values.

Love's Unreason

To say the truth, said Bottom to Titania, reason and love keep little company together nowadays. Like most of the really stupid characters in Shakespearean comedy he is ususlly right, and speaks for a tradition that is not only literary: 'affection aveugle raison' says the proverb.[4]

The movement of reason is piecemeal: a conclusion follows from two premises, and unless both are explicitly there, we are not reasoning. If love defies reason, then, it will operate instantaneously—as we know it traditionally does:

> It lies not in our power to love or hate
> For will in us is overruled by fate ...
> Where both deliberate the love is slight:
> Who ever loved that loved not at first sight?[5]

Love at first sight is so familiar a part of the story that a sophisticated writer may leave us uncertain of his tone when he introduces it:

> Your brother, and my sister, no sooner met,
> but they look'd: no sooner look'd but they lov'd;
> no sooner lov'd, but they sigh'd: no sooner sigh'd,
> but they asked one another the reason: no sooner knew
> the reason, but they sought the remedy: and in these
> degrees, have they made a pair of stairs to marriage,
> which they will climb incontinent, or else be incontinent
> before marriage.   *A.Y.L.I.* V.ii

Is this a parody? Shakespeare's comedies, we have seen, parody their conventions in a way that enriches the original. The original in this case runs as follows:

> Saladyne hearing this shepherdess speak so wisely began more narrowly to pry into her perfection, and to survey all her lineaments with a curious insight; so long dallying in the flame of her beauty that to his cost he found her to be most excellent: for Love ...[6]

The process is as quick, but the language is not so wittily conscious of the rapidity. Shakespeare's parallel sentences, following one another without conjunctions, form a kind of equivalent in syntax of the degrees (steps as well as stages) that Oliver and Celia are climbing incontinent: such a neat touch of concrete poetry makes us smile at the absurdity of the idea, but to mock so elegantly is, in a way, to take seriously.

An alternative to love at first sight is the love potion. In some versions Tristan and Isolde disliked each other at first, so that the love potion is solely responsible for their love (in Wagner, it brings to the surface a passion they had hitherto repressed).[7] More even than the convention of first sight, this emphasizes the essential irrationality of love. So of course do the familiar paradoxes: the lovers are one but also two, their love is fleeting but eternal, parting is their greatest evil but does not matter at all. Tristan and Isolde, says de Rougemont, 'lose no opportunity to be parted';[8] some of Donne's most powerful statements of love are valedictions. When the paradoxes involve the relation between mind and body, so that separation is not really separation, love becomes a philosophic puzzle:

> So they loved as love in twain,
> Had the essence but in one,
> Two distincts, Division none,
> Number there in love was slain.[9]

The extreme example of this is Marvell's *Definition of Love*, a poem that has the air of being written as a deliberate *tour de force*, an attempt to go further than any previous poet had yet gone:

> My love is of a birth as rare
> As 'tis for object strange and high;
> It was begotten by despair
> Upon impossibility.
>
> Magnanimous despair alone
> Could show me so divine a thing,
> Where feeble hope could ne'er have flown,
> But vainly flapped its tinsel wing.
>
> And yet I quickly might arrive
> Where my extended soul is fixed,
> But fate does iron wedges drive,
> And always crowds itself betwixt.
>
> For fate with jealous eye does see
> Two perfect loves, nor lets them close;
> Their union would her ruin be,
> And her tyrannic power depose.
>
> And therefore her decrees of steel
> Us as the distant poles have placed,
> Though love's whole world on us doth wheel,
> Not by themselves to be embraced;
>
> Unless the giddy heaven fall,
> And earth some new convulsion tear,
> And, us to join, the world should all
> Be cramped into a planisphere.

As lines, so loves, oblique may well
Themselves in every angle greet;
But ours so truly parallel,
Though infinite, can never meet.

Therefore the love which us doth bind,
But fate so enviously debars,
Is the conjunction of the mind,
And opposition of the stars.

The poem has Marvell's usual love of paradox, his wit, his perfect control of tone (is he smiling? is he despairing? is he mockingly confident?). As an example of its perfect polish, we can look at the sixth stanza, which describes the one set of conditions that might bring them together. It is obvious that any stanza beginning 'unless' will be followed by some kind of impossibility. Hence the deliberate ambiguity of 'giddy': unless the turning heavens get giddy and fall, unless the heavens (!) are light-headed enough to fall. The placing of 'us to join' invites an emphatic and so possibly ironic reading: would *that* be the reason? The stanza ends with a trick Marvell learned from Donne, the flaunting of an unusual technical term, and the effect of this is complex: an enjoyment of his own skill in getting it in, a suggestion that so obviously artificial a concept underlines the improbability. Marvell has a fair claim to be called the most perfect craftsman in English poetry.

An article by E. B. Greenwood[10] demonstrates how this poem drives the paradoxes of love further than anyone had yet done. There had been plenty of poems on the two-bodies-one-mind theme, on the exchange of hearts, on absence-no-separation, but here the paradox is a direct logical contradiction. Greenwood claims this poem is about 'the impossible project of overcoming impenetrability and thus becoming so united in mind, body and even position as to be mutually co-incident with a single self, and so utterly indistinguishable'. The idea of contradiction is taken from logic itself, so the claim that love is impossible is asserted with a new extremism.

> Marvell's poem, then, is not about a rare but possible union of lovers' souls … but is about an impossible union of two discrete existences themselves, a literal 'identification' of bodies.

The word in this comment to give us pause is 'about'. How can it be maintained the poem is about identification, or the overcoming of impenetrability? It is *about* love. Greenwood's account of the argument of the poem is illuminating, and probably correct, but he has inverted tenor and vehicle, so turning it into a poem about philosophy. F. W. Bateson takes issue with Greenwood for making the poem inhuman.

'Can a good poem merely be virtuosity or craftsmanship?' he asks. 'Must there not be a permanently relevant human core?' He then goes on to say that Marvell surely 'was attracted by women—just as women found him attractive', and wonders who *The Definition of Love* was addressed to.

> Did whoever it was supplied Marvell with the money he required for his five years on the Continent have a daughter? Did Lord Hastings ... have a sister?[11]

For these biographical speculations there is no evidence whatever; but when did lack of evidence prevent speculation about a poet's life, especially a poet who writes about love's impossibility? The most extreme example of this is the case of Jaufré Rudel, the twelfth-century troubadour, whose handful of poems all involve the idea of love at a distance. All the troubadours write about a love that does not lead to possession because of the aloofness, the social distance, the unattainability (for whatever reason) of the lady; in the case of Rudel, it seems to be physical separation that is the obstacle. One poem (no. II) celebrates the 'amors de terra louhdana', the love of (in?) a distant land, for which his heart grieves; the only remedy would be to find himself in an orchard or under hangings with his longed-for companion. Poem III tells us 'leunh es lo castelhs e la tors Ou elha jay e sos maritz: far is the *chateau* and the tower where she lies along with her husband' (the husband's place in this relationship must remain an enigma!). The poet's whole heart is there; when he lies asleep under the blankets, his spirit is there next to her. Poem V (*Languan li jorn son lonc en may*) begins: 'when the days are long in May, the distant song of the birds delights me, and when I have left there the memory of a distant love comes back to me. Then I go thoughtful, gloomy, head bowed, and neither song nor the hawthorn flower is any pleasanter to me than frozen winter.' In this poem the word *lonh* recurs like a refrain, at the end of the second and fourth lines of each stanza, five times in the phrase *amor de lonh* 'I shall never enjoy love if I do not enjoy this distant love ...' 'He speaks truly who calls me greedy and desirous of distant love ...' And poem VI ('No sap chantar') tells of his love for one who will never see him: 'I know well that I have never enjoyed her, that she will never enjoy me, nor will she consider me her friend (? lover—"amic"), nor of her own accord make me any promise'.[12]

No troubadour has haunted the imagination of later ages like Rudel. The legend of his love for the Countess of Tripoli began with his Provençal biographer, who tells the story of how he crossed the seas to meet her, fell ill, and arrived as if dead; how this was told to the countess, who came to his bedside and took him in her arms. He recovered consciousness, praised God for having kept him alive until he had seen her, and died in her arms. She caused him to be buried with great honour, and took the veil in her grief.[13]

There is no more basis in fact for this story than for Bateson's biographical speculations about Marvell, but it came to assume the same kind of status as Rudel's poems, so that the many poets who have written about him (Petrarch, Uhland, Heine, Browning, Rostand) have usually written of this legend rather than his writings. Making up stories about the private life of a love poet is biographically unjustified and theoretically unnecessary: the love-experiences that matter are those of the reader rather than the poet. But it is very understandable, for it expresses our conviction that the poetic devices of love poetry spring from the nature of love. Once we remove Bateson's point from the biographical basis it does not need, we see that it is correct. If distance did not idealize, if love were not an overwhelming experience fraught with paradox, Rudel would just be playing word-games, and *The Definition of Love* would join the forgotten philosophical poems of Henry Moore.

Religion and Love

If love is a transfiguring experience that can lead us to reject the world, and move us to the next higher plane, how can we fail to compare it with the supreme version of rejecting the world for something higher? All the claims that the lover makes in his eagerness to flatter or rejoice are made in earnest by the servant of God, who rejects the world for the sake of that *summum bonum* to which nothing else can be compared.

From the first, the love poets were aware of this; and medieval love-lyrics are steeped in religious analogies. Two stanzas by Walter von der Vogelweide ask for an explanation of love's mysteries:

I ask in wonder: can this be?
There she stands for me to see
Though out of sight. Is it my heart
Whose eyes behold her when we part?
It is a miracle has taken place.
How can it be that all this while
Without my eyes I see her face?

Shall I tell you what they are,
These eyes that see her everywhere?
They are my thoughts, that could look through
Stone walls to find her out. And now
Hearken to what I shall tell.
What sees as if with open eyes
Is only love, and the heart's will.[14]

How can it be that he sees his beloved so clearly when he has not seen her for so long? The answer is provided by the inner eye, the eye of the heart. This concept, Kolb explains, comes from post-Augustinian psychology, which provided the language of so much religious experience.[15] Or for an even more explicit use of religious vocabulary, we can turn to Marcabru:

> Fountain of beauty, perfect love,
> You light up all the world; and I
> For all us wretches plead for mercy.[16]

Christianity is a religion of paradox: he who saves his life shall lose it. Love too, as we have seen, has its paradoxes, and the poets have written of its bitter-sweet, of the savour that brings the highest joy, the pain one would not be without. Even if they did not consciously take this from the language of theology (though they often did), how can they have been unaware of the parallel? A particularly interesting example is provided by Kolb, in what must be the most systematically paradoxical poem ever written:

> Love is a madness mixed with sanity,
> Hope mixed with fear, and faith with perfidy,
> Quenched thirst, gay sorrow, reasoning that raves,
> Sweet shipwreck in Charybdis' welcome waves,
> Health that is sick, hunger that's satiate,
> Sweet mixed with bitter, peace that's mixed with hate,
> Bad virtue, evil good, leisure with haste,
> A tasty odour and a tasteless taste,
> Dead life, live dying and a false delight,
> A welcome storm, dark day and sunny night—[17]

Here is a quarry for every conceivable statement of love's contradictions. It is enough to make the metaphysical poets look like conventional songbirds, and reminds us that paradox cannot, any more than any other poetic device, of itself turn verse into poetry. The author remarks that he has taken the passage from *joculatoribus lasciviis*, who might be strolling players or the troubadours: its source is secular, but the parallel was also to be found in Holy Writ itself. *The Song of Songs*, one of the richest erotic poems ever written, was regularly interpreted as an allegory of the love of Christ and the Church, as it had been in pre-Christian times as an allegory of the love of Yahweh and Israel. No doubt any text can be allegorized, if the reader is determined enough; but if an allegorical reading needs to build on something in the text, then the rich sensuousness of the poetry, its complete absorption in the sexual associations of the images, surely discourage us from treating it as a poem that reaches beyond itself to another level of experience. For many centuries, men

learned to connect human and divine love, but only by doing violence
to what they read.[18]

To say that love and religion are compared does not tell us enough:
we need to ask whether the relation between them is one of analogy
or conflict. That is a question which involves the whole relation between
the realm of Nature and the realm of Grace, man's world and God's.
Guinizelli's famous lyric *Amore e Cor Gentile*, for example, after comparing love to the birds, to the sun's light, to the virtue of precious stones,
moves to a climax that compares his lady to God:

> God, in the understanding of high Heaven,
> Burns more than in our sight the living sun ...
> So should my lady give
> That truth which in her eyes is glorified ...

He then ends by asking if these analogies are acceptable to God:

> My lady, God shall ask, 'What dared'st thou?'
> (When my soul stands with all her acts review'd);
> 'Thou passed'st Heaven, into My sight, as now,
> To make Me of vain love similitude.
> To me doth praise belong,
> And to the Queen of all the realm of grace
> Who endeth fraud and wrong.'
> Then may I plead: 'As though from Thee he came,
> Love wore an angel's face:
> Lord, if I loved her, count it not my shame.'[19]

How are we to take this conclusion? He expects God to rebuke him for
the comparison: fancy reducing God to a simile ('desti, in vano amor,
me per semblante'). The poem ends, not with God's rebuke, but with
the reply he will be able to make ('dir li pero'). What is the effect of
the poet giving himself the last word? Not, surely, to make us feel that
he has answered God, that the rebuke was unfair: no one can in *that*
sense have the last word with God. His lady looked like an angel—but
we know she was a woman (assuming, as I do, that the poem is not
mere allegory). The last lines sound like an excuse, perhaps they even
remind us that the comparison with an angel is, after all, only a compliment. The poem is open-ended, but leaves the impression that the
whole series of analogies *was* improper.

We are here up against the main difficulty we now have in understanding the Middle Ages, and it is not surprising that the scholars disagree.
It is a commonplace that religion informed the medieval world view,
but what does that mean? It could mean that religion lay over everything
'like an all-embracing heavenly canopy, like an atmosphere and life-ele-
ment, which is not spoken of',[20] or that religion constantly invaded life

in the form of hectoring sermons, fear of domination, guilt and prohibition. Were the two realms in conflict or in harmony? A recent version of this controversy can be seen in Peter Dronke's criticisms of C. S. Lewis. Lewis in *The Allegory of Love* lays great stress on the cleavage between Church and court, and on the consequent hostility between Christianity and love poetry. The religious elements in the worship of *midons* (the lady), so far from showing the harmony of the two realms, may indicate that the religion of love is a parody or a rival of the real religion. Dronke in contrast stresses the belief of poets in the unity of the two loves, supporting his case by quoting a thirteenth-century *lai* on the harmony between God and sexual love:

> —Et por verite vos recort
> Diens et Amors sont d'un acort—

and (later) by a very learned account of the use by medieval theologians of human love to provide the material for talking about divine love; of the Aristotelian idea of the active intellect and how it can provide the basis for a belief in unity-in-diversity; and of the widespread image of *Sapientia*, a symbol that can unite human and divine love.[21]

In this controversy I find my sympathies are with Lewis, for several reasons. Dronke often examines a philosophic idea, shows how it could be used to support a particular view of human emotion, and then assumes that it was. Lewis is far more sensitive to the feel of actual poems, and I cannot easily imagine him commenting as Dronke does on the *alba* 'En un vergier'. The lady says:

> If only God let night stay without end
> And my beloved never left my side,

and the commentator, solemnly insensitive to the extravagance of wishing, says 'like so many lovers in medieval literature, she is convinced that God is on the side of human love'.[22]

In looking for a tension between love and religion, then, I do not believe we are chasing a shadow.[23] How can such tension manifest itself? The simplest way would be in the form of blasphemy: the rejection of God for the love of woman. One famous example, of irresistible impudence, comes in *Aucassin and Nicolette*. After being told that he will go to hell if he seduces Nicolette, Aucassin replies:

> What would I do in heaven? I have no wish to enter there. . . . For to heaven go only such people as I'll tell you of: all those doddering priests and the halt and one-armed dotards who grovel all day and all night in front of the altars. . . . To hell go the pretty clerks and the fine knights killed in tournaments and splendid wars, good soldiers and all free and noble men. I want to go along with these.[24]

It is not often possible, in a world that lives under the shadow of Christian teaching, to be as relaxed as that; yet in its far more sophisticated way, perhaps the Caroline lyric is also relaxed.

> When thou, poor excommunicate
> From all the joys of love, shalt see
> The full reward and glorious fate
> Which my strong faith shall purchase me,
> Then curse thine own inconstancy ...[25]

The tone here, on the surface, is light-hearted: whether because the speaker is airily indifferent, or because he is trying to seem casual to hide his humiliation at being jilted, is left to us to decide. The borrowings from religious vocabulary are shamelessly used to deck out a poem that is entirely about a sexual relationship, and only interested in it on the human level. The religious vocabulary is a poetic game.

Incorporating in the same work a belief in the value of human love, and a rejection of it in comparison with the firm exclusiveness of God's demands, produces the widespread device of the recantation: the love story or love lyric followed by its rejection as the poet's mind aspires to higher things, and says 'Leave me O love which reachest but to dust.' The treatise on love by Andreas Capellanus, after two books of intricate advice on how to overcome a woman's resistance, along with statements of the courtly code, concludes with a short third book exhorting the reader to take no notice of what he has read.[26] Chaucer's *Troilus and Criseyde* ends with the famous palinode that describes the whole moving story as 'Payens corsed olde rytes', and appeals to the God who is three in one to defend us from foes and 'make us, Jesus, for thy grace digne'.[27] And the atmosphere of penance and devotion at the end of the *Morte D'Arthur*, with the details of the expiation of Lancelot and Guinevere, ends the poem on a very powerful effect of judging the love that loomed so large in it.[28]

All who write about medieval love poetry mention the recantation, but in two subtly different ways. When Andreas or Chaucer ends by rejecting his own work, what is his 'real opinion'? In ordinary discourse, a rejection of what one said before is an attempt to cancel it, and to some critics, uninterested in the difference between imaginative literature and plain discourse, the recantation, coming at the end, should be taken as abolishing the poem. The answer to this position is that a palinode is part of its poem, not a comment from outside: our reading experience of Troilus and Criseyde is meant to conclude with the act of final rejection, playing against the tragedy we have experienced. Even the requests legend attributes to so many dying writers, from Vergil to Tolstoi, that their works be destroyed, may be a kind of palinode (they are never carried out): it is a way of rounding off our experience as readers with an awareness of the new perspective of old age. Even Aquinas is said to have had a vision that showed him that all his theology was worthless. The fact that a theologian too can have his palinode makes it clear that there is a theological basis for the fact that a clear choice—accept or cancel the work—is not made. That basis is the tension between nature and grace.

Who is Beatrice?

There is one case (according to some it is the only, even the only possible case) in which the tension is successfully-resolved, and in which a recantation would be impossible: that is the *Vita Nuova* of Dante. The love poems celebrate the virtues of Beatrice in religious terms, in a way that does not obviously differ from those of Dante's predecessors and contemporaries; but they are joined together in a prose text (copied out of the 'book of his memory') which glosses and explains them, and sets them in a rather minimal narrative framework. We are told how overwhelming was the first sight of Beatrice, when they were both nine; how he met her again nine years later and by her ineffable courtesy she greeted him; how accident led him to conceal his love for her by wooing another lady, and how this led to evil gossip and to her ceasing to greet him, to his great sorrow; how love then told him to drop pretences, and a conversation with ladies led to his resolving to write only in her praise; how during an illness he had a vision of Beatrice's death and how, later, she did die; how on the anniversary of her death he saw a lady watching him from a window, whose sympathy with his grief led to his receiving consolation from her, until a vision of Beatrice led to his being ashamed of his fickleness. That, more or less, is all; and the last paragraph hints at the role Beatrice is to play when he writes the *Paradiso*.

The fact that Dante went on to write the *Commedia* may be the biggest single reason for the special status that is given to the *Vita Nuova*: along with the existence of the prose text and (though this could be held to beg important questions) the excellence of the poems. The work is explicitly and prominently Christian, yet there is no recantation, no suggestion that his love for Beatrice must be laid aside for a higher love: this can only mean that Beatrice is granted a special status. She is now dead, and is among the saints in glory; when on earth her influence caused vile thoughts to perish and goodness to flourish; though a mortal creature she was not an ordinary human but a miracle. It is clear that she is being compared to Christ. How is this special status conveyed? The question is crucial, and I do not think there can be any doubt about the answer. Apart from a few details of a numerological kind (Beatrice's mystical connection with the number nine, the significance of the name of the lady Giovanna, who makes a John the Baptist to Beatrice's Christ) which to us now seem more dead than anything else in the Middle Ages, it is conveyed by just those poetic devices that we have been looking at, the traditional analogies between love and religion. Thus the overwhelming effect of his first sight of Beatrice is conveyed on the very first page as follows:

> At that moment, I say most truly that the spirit of life, which hath its dwelling in the secretest chamber of the heart, began to tremble so violently that the least pulses of my body shook therewith; and in trembling it said these words: Ecce deus fortior me, qui veniens dominabitur mihi. At that moment the animate spirit, which dwelleth in the lofty chamber whither all the senses carry their perceptions, was filled with wonder, and speaking more especially unto the spirits of the eyes, said these words: Apparuit jam beatitudo vestra.[30]

The God who is stronger than oneself most immediately, perhaps, suggests love; the appearance of his beatitude sounds primarily Christian; but both phrases belong to the traffic between the two vocabularies. They are in Latin not only because that is the language used by the spirit itself, and so recorded in the book of his memory, but also because Latin is the language of the Church. Or to turn to one of the poems, we can look at the Christian imagery of *Tanto gentile e tanto onesta pare*, in which Beatrice seems to have come down from heaven to earth, to show us a miracle:

> e par che sia una cosa venuta
> de cielo in terra e miracol mostrare.   (§ 26)

In the prose paragraph before the poem we do not even find the word 'seems' (*par(e)*), but the remarks of passers-by that 'This is not a woman but one of the beautiful angels of Heaven.' Of course *par* can mean the same thing as the fact that passers-by said it, but in order to grant Beatrice her special status we have to say that they were right. And once we say that, we have the same problem that faced Guinicelli at the end of his poem, as we can see in the *canzone Donne ch'avete intelletto d'amore*. When the angel in Heaven asks God to bring Beatrice up to them because Heaven has no other defect except the lack of her

> —Lo cielo, che non have altro difetto
> che d'aver lei—

and even tells Him that all the other angels are behind this complaint

> —e ciascun santo ne grida merzede—   (§18)

he is saying something theologically outrageous. How can there be a defect in Heaven? How can the angels tell God what to do? But God, instead of rebuking them as He rebuked Guinicelli, simply explains that He wishes Beatrice to stay on earth to comfort Dante and that they will have to be patient a while.

It does not matter how insistently the prose text drives us to take the religious images literally, and relates the overwhelming power of the experiences that led to the poems. No poet can persuade us, by a prose gloss, that his poem must be taken one way, if the images he has used open up another. That would be to submit the richness of poetry to the narrowness of announced intentions, and so commit the most basic of literary mistakes. No, if the reader takes the accounts of Beatrice as a miracle literally, if he grants a different status to the love–religion analogies from that he would grant them in other poets, it is because he is willing to read the text in a certain way.

There is no doubt that the reader who shows this willingness is rewarded by finding further levels of significance. The three stages of Dante's love, for instance, that which aimed at the greeting of Beatrice, that which turned to the happiness of his inward feelings of love, and that which accepted the death of Beatrice, corresponding to the division of the text by the placing of the *canzoni*, can be paralleled to the three stages of mystical experience in Augustinian tradition, locating the source of bliss *extra nos*, then *inter nos*, then *supra nos*.[31] But however much such parallels enrich the work, it is always possible for the reader who is not willing to grant Beatrice her special status to see them as sources of tension, and to enrich his reading in a different way.

What is the effect of this willingness? It is to control our reading strictly, and by offering us one kind of reward, to prevent certain questions being raised. And we should not underestimate the range and importance of these questions: they include all psychological curiosity about the relationship between Dante and Beatrice. The four thoughts with which Love harrasses him, for instance (the lordship of Love is good, the lordship of Love is evil, etc.) culminate in the thought that his lady is not like other ladies, whose hearts are easily moved.[32] The phrase (*che leggeramente si mouva del suo cuore*) is variously interpreted, but the differences are linguistic: they do not probe the question of what was going on, emotionally, in Beatrice. Nor do we know what was going on in Dante. The fact that he hardly knew Beatrice is obviously important, and distinguishes his love from more mundane love, but what, in terms of experience, did this distinction feel like? Was it like the experience of Hans Castorp, who loves a woman he never speaks to, and feels somehow closer to her than he does to the other guests he is friendly with at the sanatorium? This irrational feeling is given a perverse confirmation by the fact that he and Claudia never say 'Sie' to each other: either they do not speak at all, or they say 'Du', as if intimacy were closer to indifference than to friendliness. It is clear that this is a symptom of sickness. The consumption that is waiting to strike in Castorp as it is perhaps in all of us, and that is constantly being half-compared with repressed psychic material, issues in the traditional irrationality of love. Here is a modern novelist turning literary tradition into psychological exploration.[33]

Such exploration is not possible in the *Vita Nuova*: the special status of Beatrice would not survive it. This has often been pointed out by those critics who read the work biographically. We know that both Dante and Beatrice were married: is there any reference to this in the *Vita Nuova*? Dante attends a wedding feast in §14, at which he sees Beatrice among the other ladies, and is overwhelmed by her sight. Could this be her wedding? There is nothing in the text to suggest it, but that has not prevented some critics from regarding the silence as so striking that we might be intended to notice what is not said. And Dante's marriage? Could the lady of the window, who consoles him for the death of Beatrice, be Gemina Donati, whom Dante married about a year after the death of Beatrice (the fact that Beatrice had been dead a year when he saw her is mentioned in the text)? If this is so, it will make an enormous difference to how we read the episode. He tells us that he often went to look at her, and that the very sight of her brought tears to his eyes; that he saw her so often that his eyes began to take too much pleasure in seeing her; he struggled between his attraction to the lady of the window and his love for the dead Beatrice; and finally, after his vision of Beatrice, he thought only of her, telling us this in a sentence that does not even mention the lady of the window. The only possible remaining reference to her is in the remark that introduces the sonnet *Lasso! per forza di molti sospiri*, which was written to show that he had given up his evil desire and vain temptation. We shall read all this very differently, depending on whether he had never spoken to the lady, or had got to know her, or married her; and if she is his wife, it will make a big difference at what point they marry, and so whether these passages refer to uncertainty on whether to go on courting, or a change of heart when he is already married.

We are faced with the same argument that we encountered over *The Definition of Love*. The issue is raised by critics with biographical learnings, but their point does not depend on the biography: it arises once we allow our interest in the psychological dimension to be awakened, once we ask what the love for Beatrice, as a human experience, was like. And how can we refrain from doing this, if the *Vita Nuova* is genuinely figural? Once licensed to retain our interest in the literal, where do we stop? How can we fail, in a story like this (potentially quite as complex and as fascinating as Hans Castorp's love for Claudia) to ask what actually happened, to probe motives, to explore the relationship of these idealized feelings to sexual love? And once we start doing that, the special status of Beatrice disappears.[35]

I believe this problem is insoluble. When reading the *Vita Nuova* we either open ourselves to psychological curiosity or we do not. To do this with other medieval love poetry is to do it no harm, often to deepen it; but the special status of Beatrice depends on the absence of psychological exploration, for that would demand a concentration on the literal level that Dante does not invite. Does this mean that the *Vita Nuova* is now dead? In practice this may not be a problem, since readers of Dante today consist of enthusiasts for the poetry who will not make trouble over the ideas; medieval scholars naturally eager to exercise their historical imagination; and students needing to be told what to think. None of these has any reason to complain that Dante has not really answered God's question to Guinicelli. They will go on reading; but can we say that the *Vita Nuova* is a work that speaks to anyone's condition?

Sarah's Lover

All this was a long time ago, surely. Would we bother, as the sixteenth century did,[36] to trim the religious language of the *Vita Nuova*? Only a strong belief could be offended by the contest with human love. Or can this contest exist in a secular age, but in a new way: a way that will include the new fact of a secular universe, the new tension between religion and indifference?

To show that it can we shall need to find a novel whose author is aware both of the continuing life of religion and the godless world surrounding it; and who writes a love story within this context. The recipe may sound improbable, but it has been followed, in one of the most brilliant and disturbing of modern English novels. For Graham Greene is such an author, and *The End of the Affair* (1951) is such a novel.

Most of the aspects of love that we have so far discussed are found in *The End of the Affair*. Love is fundamentally different from marriage. Sarah's tempestuous and passionate affair with Bendrix has almost nothing in common with her dull marriage. The love affair produces quarrels, hatred and jealousy, of an intensity that no marriage could contain: marriage is a matter of the adjusting of habits and of loyalty. The contrast is made clear at the moment when Sarah finally decides to break her vow and run off with Bendrix. Henry comes home early, wretched after his lunch with Bendrix, and with more self-knowledge than usual, and appeals to her loyalty: without knowing that she was going to leave him, without really knowing that she had ever thought of doing so, he appeals to her to stay; and this activates a totally different set of feelings from those that were drawing her to run off. The point is made, earlier in the book, in the conversation Henry had with Bendrix that afternoon; in reply to Bendrix's 'I wanted love to go on and on, never to get less' he says, 'It's not in human nature. One has to be satisfied.' It is a husband's reply to a lover.

The End of the Affair: in the singular, as if there were one affair. But the title is ironic, for there is more than one. As well as Henry–Sarah–Bendrix, there is Bendrix–Sarah–Smythe: Sarah really belongs to Bendrix, Smythe wants her. Slowly we realize that behind these two triangles is another, Bendrix–Sarah–God. God is a lover, having an affair with Sarah, using the dirtiest tricks he can to win her from Bendrix. God has the sense to see that Bendrix is his real rival, not Henry, and His methods are more underhand than Bendrix's ever were: bringing Bendrix back to life for her, if she will promise never to see him again, carrying Sarah off (i.e. killing her) when she's in danger of relapsing. Against such unscrupulousness he has no chance, and by the time the book has ended He has seduced not only Sarah but Smythe too, and at the end He is starting on Bendrix.

God is quite explicitly presented as a rival—'a melodramatic word', Bendrix writes, 'painfully inadequate to express the unbearable complacency, confidence and success he always enjoys'. The private detective whom in a moment of panic Henry thinks of employing and whom Bendrix so grotesquely does employ tracks down the stranger who has 'certainly won in the end', winning Sarah from both husband and lover. What chance have they against a rival underhand enough to use miracles? The violent atheism of Smythe, the helpless fury of Bendrix's jealousy, are signs of their vulnerability: 'Hatred of God can bring the soul to God,' wrote Yeats. The worst thing of all about God's tricks is that they succeed.

Something like the same point is made in Poe's poem *Annabel Lee* (1850). This famous jingle tells how the speaker and Annabel Lee loved 'with a love that was more than love', so that 'the winged seraphs of heaven' envied them, and sent a wind out of a cloud chilling her.

> The angels, not half so happy in heaven,
>   Went envying her and me—
> Yes!—that was the reason (as all men know,
>   In this kingdom by the sea)
> That the wind came out of the cloud by night,
>   Chilling and killing my Annabel Lee.

It is the same idea: but how different. Where Greene does everything he can to show how outrageous the idea is, Poe does everything he can to soften it. Or rather—since I think Poe's intention was to keep the edge on his idea—the easy fluency with which he writes verse leads him to absorb everything into a musical flow that lulls when it should shock. The parenthesis (as all men know ...) serves no purpose except to make the general effect more poetic; the cause of her death is left uncertain, wrapped in a poetical phrase that could connote a miracle or a natural death; and Greene's careful references to 'he' are much more outrageous, even though he seldom names God, than Poe's more poetical 'angels'.

In the context of this plot, we can see that the love–religion parallel has to be taken with a particular kind of seriousness. It is prominently used, but not merely as a source of explanatory imagery for the description of love. It is a genuine parallel: Sarah having fallen in love is now falling in Love, and in a paragraph of Greenian brillance she develops the similarity:

> I've caught belief like a disease. I've fallen into belief like I fell in love. I've never loved before as I love you, and I've never believed in anything before as I believe now. I'm sure I've never been sure before about anything. When you came in at the door with the blood on your face, I became sure. Once and for all. Even though I didn't know it at the time. I fought belief for longer than I fought love, but I haven't any fight left. (V.i)

'I've caught belief like a disease': how much more powerful than the phraseology of the wind that blew out of the cloud by night. And the image is given a further reverberation when we learn that Sarah had been baptized as a child, and her mother had thought it might take. 'Like vaccination.'

If there is any way to show that the tension between love and religion is still active, this is it. For Greene has started from a world without Christian belief. None of the three main characters bothers with it, at first; Smythe, waging his campaign against God, is old-fashioned and embarrassing. To resort to miracles in such a world is—there seems no other way of putting it—underhand. It makes Greene's novel more tasteless, but also more brilliant, than the similar *Brideshead Revisited* of Evelyn Waugh. It is an underhand trick by the novelist to put them into a realistic story, and an underhand trick by God to use them as a weapon. Greene has realized that in a rational world, to which the realistic novel is the appropriate literary mode, the traditional devices that may have lost their power to impress will have gained a renewed power to shock. By this act of literary indecorum he has restored that tension that we might have thought was lost.

Love and Death

The supreme refusal of the world is death; and the supreme rejection of the bond of reason and one's fellow men would clearly be the coupling of love and death, the *Liebestod*. Everyone knows how common it is for lovers in literature to die together. When we ask ourselves what the nature of the connexion is between love and death, several kinds of answer are possible.

There could be a narrative answer, a psychological answer and a lyrical answer. The narrative answer would tell us whether the lovers die together, or separately, and whether or not they sleep together beforehand. That in turn would imply an answer to the psychological question, do they want to die, and do they see it as a surrogate for sexual experience? The lyrical answer will enact the same conceptions at the level of local verbal effects instead of plot.

In early literature the narrative answer is almost always that they do sleep together. Death is not presented as a surrogate for sexual experience, but rather as its fitting sequel. Neither Antony or Othello, Romeo nor Tristan, die virgin. The change comes with Racine, then with Wagner, who changed the story so that Isolde slept neither with Tristan nor with Mark. It is hard to be sure if this change makes the *Liebestod* more respectable or more pornographic.

Isolde's aria over the body of Tristan is the most famous *Liebestod* of all, though as it happens Wagner himself called it the *Verklärung* (transfiguration), reserving the term *Liebestod* (which he invented) for the Prelude. Unable at first to believe in his death, she insists that he is alive, and insists that the bystanders believe her ('Seht ihr, Freunde. Seht ihr's nicht?'). As she continues, the sense in which Tristan is alive becomes less and less personal, and her union with him more and more a pantheistic union with the elements:

Are they waves
Of fragrance flowing?
Odours coming
Odours going?
Should I gulp them
Till I'm sated
By the swell
Intoxicated?
Should I breathe
And melt in air,
With the odours
Disappear?[38]

She could be saying 'He is made one with Nature', but not in the measured pentameters in which Shelley mingles philosophic concepts with the sob of Nature's universal music; rather in something like a pure sobbing, a pure emotion of the surrendering of individuality. This is conveyed not only by the obvious incantatory effect of the short lines, but the synaesthesia, the bewildered loss of clarity that actually seems to take place in the self-questionings (*soll ich athmen, soll ich leuschen*), and the unattached words that float verbless (*ertrinken—versinken—unbewusst—höchste Lust*) at the end of the aria (and the opera). Both verbal and musical echoes connect this with the sexual ectasy of Act II, which constantly plays with the idea of courting, defeating, indulging in death. Sexual love and death both involve the dissolution of personality and Wagner is showing their identity.

It is easy to see why this is the classic example of *Liebestod*. In every sense, death is seen as the surrogate for love—in the narrative sense and in the psychological (the lovers constantly reject day and long for night), and the linking of death and union in the imagery is reinforced by the music: indeed, the music is primary (as befits Wagner's later theoretical position on the *Gesamtkunstwerk*), and there is something inherently inadequate in discussing the *text* of *Tristan and Isolde*. But though inadequate it need not be misleading.

If *Liebestod* is like this, we shall not find it before Wagner—one is tempted to say 'before Freud', since the idea of the lovers wanting death *instead of* consummation seems to presuppose unconscious wishing; and Wagner (writing in the very year of Freud's birth) had sniffed out what he needed of psychoanalytic theory. Gottfried's Tristan calls on death when his love is at its happiest: when Brangane tells him about the potion, and that it will be the death of them both, he answers:

> Whether it be life or death, it has poisoned one most sweetly! I had no idea what the other will be like, but this death suits me well.[40]

Is he speaking light-heartedly, or in delighted earnestness? If the former, it is dramatic irony; if the latter, it suggests that death has a sexual meaning. These are the two traditional forms of *Liebestod*, and both are important. A clear example of the first is Othello's invocation of death at the high moment of love: 'If it were now to die 'Twere now to be most happy.' Dramatic irony can be easy, even crude; or it can be subtle and moving. If we are not to feel that a simple point is being made at Othello's expense, then there must be a sense in which he is asking to die, even though the wish has not entered consciousness.

The other possible interpretation of Gottfried's passage—that Tristan is punning on 'die'—seems to be characteristically Elizabethan. The sexual meaning of 'die' is certainly found in Elizabethan poetry: it is frequent in Donne, and there are at least two incontrovertible examples in Shakespeare.[41] I do not find it easy to decide whether it is used in

Romeo and Juliet—what looks like the most likely instance[42] comes from the Friar! Romeo's dying 'Thus with a kiss I die' would be weakened if taken as word-play, for the clash between dying and sex, visually present to us on the stage, is best rendered verbally as a clash between 'kiss' and 'die' in which each keeps its own meaning. Whether this pun was based on popular usage or purely a literary device (I suspect it was the latter, since there is no evidence for a colloquial sexual meaning)[43] it merely implies the possibility of linking the two ideas. It does not suggest—word-play never can—what exactly the relationship is between death and orgasm.

The Wagnerian idea of death as a surrogate for sex is not explicitly present in *Romeo and Juliet* or *Othello*; but in their exploration of the complex connexions between the two they come very close to it. The lovers die together, in one case on their marriage bed, in the other in a tomb on which they lie together in a posture that could be a visual pun on the two metaphoric meanings of 'sleeping together'. And though death has not replaced sex, it is notable that both marriages contain only a single act of intercourse, as if sex were only a symbol and once is enough: the second sexual act is the joint death. And on the lyrical level both plays, and above all *Romeo and Juliet*, couple death and sex in their most moving imagery:

> Shall I believe
> That insubstantial death is amorous,
> And that the lean abhorred monster keeps
> Thee here in state to be his paramour.   (V.iii.102)

Personification is such a standard poetic device with the unoriginal, that it is striking to find it as a sign of such powerful originality. It enables Romeo to see death as a rival and thus to connect death and sex more explicitly than he could otherwise have done: and the resulting triangle, plus the physical repulsiveness of the usual representations of death, enable him to express disgust along with his love, so that the speech contains our ambivalent response to the connexion—that to die is to achieve perfect love, and that to die is a horrible substitute for love. Our knowledge that Juliet is not dead weakens the tension (her beauty is not a sign that death is supreme love, and the abhorred monster has not slept with her) but not much, since we can simply regard Romeo's point as proleptic (even the 'first night audience' has a shrewd suspicion that Juliet is going to die).

Shakespeare's third great play of love is different from these two, and for at least four of its five acts is not a play of *Liebestod* at all. The love of Antony and Cleopatra is defiantly associated with life, all the more defiantly for their being no longer young. Even in his first statement of the bliss of love and defiance of the world, when it would have been so easy to say, This is the moment to die, Antony does not:

> Let Rome in Tiber melt, and the wide arch
> Of the ranged Empire fall: here is my space ...   (I.i.33)

These are images of destruction, but of a destruction that will take place around them, leaving them unharmed. The image for their love is 'the nobleness of *life*'. They do not see themselves as dying: they 'stand up peerless'. And so although Antony dies in Cleopatra's arms, this is not seen as a consummation:

> I am dying Egypt, dying; only
> I here importune death awhile, until
> Of many thousand kisses, the poor last
> I lay upon thy lips.   (IV.xv.18)

If this was really *Liebestod*, that would be their finest kiss, not the poor last: death, which has to be importuned, is here getting in the way of their love. The point is even clearer when Cleopatra speaks:

> And welcome, welcome. Die where thou hast lived,
> Quicken with kissing: had my lips that power,
> Thus would I wear them out.   (IV.xv.38)

Could any protest be more intense? Every word suggests life, and the desperation that sobs in the last sentence expresses her helplessness because death is coming. Out of this intensity comes her lament—that greatest lament in poetry—when Antony does die, introduced by a line of marvellous simplicity, the wail of a betrayed child who had trusted Antony could not do that to her: 'Noblest of men, woo't die.'

When Cleopatra dies we have something different. Now love and death are associated, and perhaps there is no more profound lyrical expression of the *Liebestod* than her marvellous image:

> The stroke of death is as a lover's pinch,
> Which hurts, and is desired: (V.ii.295)

just as there is no more perfect expression of death as a sexual swoon than

> As sweet as balm, as soft as air, as gentle—
> O Antony!   (V.ii.311)

What has happened in the meantime is of course that Antony has died. The true *Liebestod*, we realize, is that of the lover who dies second. Only she (it is usually she) can really see dying in terms of *joining* the other.

And yet even this is not like the death of Isolde: for that, we need a new factor, that did not exist in the consciousness of 1607. We can call it pantheism, if we are clear that it is not the stiff intellectual pantheism of Spinoza and his followers, but an emotional experience that flows out of the Romantic movement. Isolde sees herself disappearing into impersonality: what she is going to do is summed up by the word *verhauchen*, to melt into a breath. Cleopatra's death involves no loss of identity. 'I am again for Cydnus to meet Mark Antony': she is setting out on a very specific experience, full of proper names:

> Methinks I hear
> Antony call, I see him rouse himself
> To praise my noble act.   (V.ii.283)

Such a remark is unimaginable from Wagner's Isolde. She is in a state of ecstasy, but Cleopatra is not; and this awareness of particular experience that Cleopatra retains gives even to this poetry of dying an impression of vitality. Did ever dead lovers intend to be as much alive as these two?

> Where souls do couch on flowers, we'll hand in hand,
> And with our sprightly port make the ghosts gaze: (IV.xiv.51)

It is the other souls who will couch on flowers, while the lovers walk by; and their 'sprightly port' makes it clear they will be keeping their individuality.

In Shakespearean tragedy, then, whatever longing there is for the ecstasy of annihilation is concealed. On the surface, death is resisted, or invoked only in irony. The post-Romantic, even the post-Freudian, world is there, but unconsciously.

How much of this view of love is still alive in the modern novel? I believe it is still with us, and will stay with us unless the literature of love grows almost unimaginably different; and as an example I have chosen an excellent but neglected novel by Jean Arnaldi, *Fausto's Keyhole* (published in 1962). The story takes place in Rome, and the normal life which provides the setting for the love story consists of the *pensione* run by Fausto's parents, his job as a woman's hairdresser, and his fiancée Letizia. The middle-aged parents have a marriage that is totally unattractive: the father is a womanizer subject to fits of furious self-righteousness, impotent but demanding with his wife; the mother has toothache and worry; Fausto has to sleep where he can in the crowded *pensione* and has no privacy even to be sick. His fiancée is a bitch and sexually a tease, and the slick modern Rome he lives in and drives through on his Vespa oozes with male lechery. All this is rendered in a stylish prose so accomplished it hovers on the edge of the vulgar:

> At the bus stop a small man with a mustache studied a tall foreigner as though he intended to make a topographical map of her. Once in the

bus he would see to it that he stood directly behind her, crushed against her, and she would wonder 'Is he really?'

Into this world comes the American girl who has lived for some time at the *pensione* before Fausto notices her, and with whom he has a sudden intense affair that lasts only a few hours. They make love near a fountain on the Via Appia, and that very evening he loses her: illness and plot complications take her from him, and a few days later she is dead. He never learns her name.

Here is the traditional contrast between the brief intimacy of love, culminating in death, and the vividly observed everyday life, sordid, comic and complex, into which Fausto is, in the end, sucked back in a moderately happy ending. And so to set against the descriptions of Rome and of Fausto's life that sound like the writing of a very good satiric journalist, another kind of prose is needed, in order to render the contrasting intensity:

> I remember spiralling downward, into another world, which had no colour and no time; I remember her body and my own swelling to immense proportions, and our movements so enormous that the earth itself scarcely seemed large enough to support them. My eyes were closed and I did not think. For once in my life, I had done with thinking. I *was* what I was doing, and that was perfect joy.

It is impossible for Jean Arnaldi to avoid the traditional paradoxes of love, though she plays variations on them. Love at first sight, for instance: the American irrupts suddenly into his life when he meets her coming out of the bathroom, and they both stand for a moment in their postures of recoil. From that moment she haunts him, and he later learns that she had been sure he was the sort of person she would like, though in the course of telling him this she is visited by the doubts of realism. As for death, we are aware all the time that the American is leaving Rome soon, and more or less aware that she is ill: the shadow of loss is over their affair from the beginning, and we are never sure if the grotesque assault by Fausto's father that evening caused her death or not. The American speaks mostly in semi-articulate colloquialism, but what she says has a long history:

> 'Funny,' she said. 'I want you to know me, and yet I don't want to talk about myself—my history. I'm hoping you will like me just by instinct. I guess that doesn't happen.'

Did Dante 'know' Beatrice, of whose history we learn nothing; did Romeo 'know' Juliet? The last brief sentence is a sceptical comment on the knowledge lovers have of each other, but it is near to Rosalind's scepticism, delivered by someone who more or less does believe it will happen.

The most striking variant in this story is that the American is at first sought by Fausto out of mere lechery and arrogance. He sets out to make a conquest of her, and she realizes this, poignantly. She wants to give herself to him, but only in love not in lechery, and the affair with her has to be disentangled gradually from the rest of Fausto's experience. At first therefore we are aware of the contrast between Fausto's gloating anticipation of how easy it will be, and what she represents in the book. It is of course the old contrast between love and lust: not the moral contrast between married love that respects the individual and the anonymity of passion, but something more like the opposite. It is love that approaches anonymity, it is lust that is part of the everyday reality of individuals. And so this love arises fully only after sex. This is no platonic marriage of true minds that scorns the body, but a marriage of persons who are unlocked to each other only after sexual consummation, even when that has not, at first, been wholly satisfying. Their second act of sex is therefore more deeply rewarding than their first. This (like much else in Jean Arnaldi's book) is found in Lawrence, and it constitutes, surely, a genuine change in the convention. Sexual intercourse, like other human experience, could improve with practice: to admit that is the sign of the realistic novelist, whereas the treatment of sexual love as unique and transfiguring often results in a story containing one single act of sexual union to symbolize perfection. In the love of Fausto and the American, as in that of Mellors and Connie Chatterley, we move through a form of realism to the expression of bliss. It has to be worked up to, but when it is achieved it is like this:

> I felt as though I had given something great, the
> greatest treasure in the world, and by a miracle, no one
> had been diminished in the giving. I too had given,
> and she had received this treasured thing, and I too was
> not diminished but was more.

The language of paradox: not explicitly religious, but with faint religious overtones. In that way this competent novelist, whose originality lies in her stylish New Yorker prose, shows her good judgement, falling back on traditional ways of rendering the transfiguring power of love.

The story so far has been that of a literary tradition. I have not yet asked what the social reality was like from which this tradition emerged, and how the two were related. It is time therefore that we turned not to what the poets have had to say about marriage, but to the institution itself.

3

Choosing a Mate

The popular view of the history of the family in our society sees it as a move from the extended to the nuclear family: from the large group of kinfolk, living together in a complex household, their lives involved with one another in every way, to the conjugal unit of husband, wife and their own children, nowadays without even servants, living in financial and emotional independence in their self-contained semi-detached dwelling. The theory derives largely from nineteenth-century writers on law, religion and society, and usually has a marked nostalgic or reactionary element; it is still widely believed in, but no longer by historians and sociologists who have specialized in the field. In the first place, new and more careful terminology has replaced the patriarchal family, *famille souche* and *famille instable* of Le Play.[1] Anthropologists distinguish broadly between nuclear, polygamous (in practice, almost always polygynous) and extended families, sometimes distinguishing the latter from complex (more than one married couple in the household). Patrilineal is distinguished from matrilineal, according to which sex the line is traced through; patrilocal from matrilocal (and other variants) according to where the couple settle on marrying; and an elaborate classification of kinship terminology enables us to describe how societies decide who counts as a relative and what he is called.[2]

More important, it is no longer held that the norm in European society used to be the complex or extended family, and that the nuclear family is the consequence of industrialism. It is not only that the nuclear family is universal, recognized as a unit in all societies, whatever more complex forms they also know;[3] it is also that scepticism is now widespread on whether the extended family[4] ever obtained in Europe. 'In England and elsewhere in Northern and Western Europe the standard situation was one where each domestic group consisted of a simple family living in its own house.'[5] In so far as the family was extended, this was so mainly in the upper classes.

Indeed, the old view has been turned on its head: there is now evidence to suggest that the extended family has actually strengthened its position in the last century or so. The arguments here are complicated. It may be that in the early days of the industrial revolution there was an increase in kinship ties, and in co-residence of married couples and parents. Today there are many ways in which the extended family operates as it could hardly have done in the past. Modern transport and communication have made contact easy, the increase of leisure has created free time in our lives that can be filled by contact with relatives; co-residence has probably increased, and financial help from parents to married children shows no sign of diminishing.[7] Although the nuclear family is usually thought to be especially suited to industrial society (the weakening of kinship constraints on mobility and career choice render possible the search for appropriate talent that industrialism demands), it may also be the case that those families which have been particularly successful in industrial society have been those whose kin network was strongest.[8]

Amid all this necessary scepticism, it is not easy to summarize what social scientists have to teach us about the structure and history of the family. And the aim of the sections that follow is not exactly (though I hope I have managed to preserve due modesty in front of the experts) to summarize: it is rather to remind us of what the family does, and then, by distinguishing between the various aspects of our lives that it controls (or did control, or was thought to have controlled), to put us in a position to ask piecemeal how it has changed. I shall mainly do the asking but I shall not be able to refrain from suggesting the lines that an answer might take.

What is the Extended Family?

The extended family can be thought of as an institution for the protection and handing on of property. When it is viewed primarily from a legal standpoint, this will appear to be its main function, and its operation will be concentrated in two processes, both of great interest to lawyers, inheritance and marriage arrangements. Inheritance patterns determine how the property will pass from one generation to another. It may be determined by fixed law or custom, or there may be considerable latitude allowed to the individual, in which case the making of the will is of great importance. Since it has always been extremely rare to leave property outside the family, the main differences are between primogeniture, the choosing of the heir by the father, and dividing up the inheritance among some or all of the children; the first two are both linked to the extended family, whereas the sharing of the property (widespread in Northern France and England even before it was made obligatory with the French Revolution) goes with the nuclear family.[9]

Marriage contracts are concerned with the financial situation of daughters and the basic arrangement is that the father of the bride pays the groom's family a portion, or dowry, in exchange for an agreement to support her and her children in the case of widowhood. They represent a willingness by one family to hand over wealth to another. This is not difficult to explain in general terms: economically it is a matter of swings and roundabouts, and even if the society is patrilineal, and allows property to pass only through the males, the sons need wives, and the father who pays for the marriage of his daughters will also be able to profit by that of his sons. This may seem hard on the couple that has daughers only, but it will not lead them to reject the practice: for the balance of swings and roundabouts applies to the typical, not to every family, and once a social custom is established, there is no right of opting out for those who seem to derive only disadvantage from it. And in fact there are advantages even in the case of daughters, for the portion entitles her to a jointure, i.e. to support if left a widow. The variations in portions and jointures, and in the ratio between them, that Stone has traced so carefully through the seventeenth century, make it clear that the functions of the family in controlling property were important and complex.[10]

Inheritance patterns, since they concern property, will naturally be most important among the wealthy; but we should not underestimate how far down in the society they matter. In agricultural communities the continuing livelihood of the next generation obviously depends on the land; who it goes to will determine who can marry. More generally, pre-industrial society had a far stronger concern for property, and less concern for earnings, than we have. This led Durkheim to observe that the decline of the extended family meant a decline in the importance of inheritance, and to suggest that the triumph of the nuclear family might eventually lead to the complete abolition of inheritance.[11]

We need not hesitate to say that the extended family as an institution for looking after property has declined, and to relate this to the enormous social change that now expects a man's prospects in life to depend primarily on his talents and his training. Yet there is some empirical evidence that the practice of receiving financial aid from kin is very widespread, perhaps more so than ever before. The parents (in-law) or grandparents expect nothing back (except, perhaps, the money) and claim no authority in return for their gifts.[12]

Property, then, is one aspect of the extended family. Another is co-residence. Instead of living alone with their children, the couple can live with one set of parents, perhaps an aunt or two, unmarried brothers and sisters (married ones too, in the case of the complex—Le Play's patriarchal–family), possibly more distant relatives, and a varying number of servants depending on their social status. Le Play even worked out that the most likely size of such a family would be 18.[13]

Of all aspects of the extended family, co-residence is the one which has come under the heaviest attack, above all by Peter Laslett and his school of social historians. Their research into household size has led to the conclusion that it was never larger than it now is. Laslett proposes an average size in England of '4.75 per household at all times from the late sixteenth until the early twentieth century';[14] and neither the Serbian *zadruga* nor the largest Japanese households remotely approach Le Play's figure.[15] These figures have been criticized, in particular for measuring the number of large households against the number of inhabitants instead of the number of households, and so underestimating their importance;[16] but the detailed statistical work behind them cannot be ignored, and for all we know about (for instance) the practice of an aristocratic couple spending their first few years with one set of parents ('my wife will hardly be persuaded to part with her daughter the first year till she be thoroughly settled and acquainted with her husband, which she knows will be for both their good'),[17] it is clear that the three-generation house was no commoner in earlier centuries than it is now. As Laslett caustically insists, our concern for 'the lonely old people who are becoming so lamentably common as the twentieth-century decades go by' usually takes the form of wanting a 'return' to a more natural and earlier form of the family that we have lost, but which in fact, has no claim to either of these epithets.[18] In this sense, the extended family was never really with us.

Thirdly, the extended family offers social contact: visits to grandparents, going on holiday with a sister's family, children who are cousins playing together. Historical comparisons in this field are particularly difficult, because of the extension of leisure.

Instead of leisured classes we now have leisure time (and activities) in all classes: where will we find, in the drab hard-working lives of the majority of our ancestors, opportunities like ours for social contact? Rites of passage—christenings, weddings, funerals—have long been thought of as family occasions, and it is sobering to find that even at these, gatherings of kinsfolk may not have been common.[19] There can be no real doubt that contact of this kind has increased in our time; if there is a widespread feeling to the contrary, this is perhaps easily explained by the fact that such contact usually involves an older generation, to whom it means more than to their children. The feeling that something is being done for the old will tend to become a feeling that it belongs to the past; whereas each new generation may, as it ages, come to value such contacts just as strongly, and receive them as frequently.

Fourthly, the extended family functions as an institution affecting the relations of the individual to the society, exercising control and bestowing advantages. It will exercise its responsibility in both directions: towards the society, by being held answerable for crimes that its members commit, and towards the members, by looking after their welfare. Both these have declined in our day, and the first has virtually disappeared: private justice has been almost totally replaced by public justice. If we think back to the Iceland of the Sagas, or to what is reported of Corsica before the French Revolution (and perhaps after), we find a situation in which the kin group is considered responsible for the crimes committed by any of its members and (the obverse of this) for the avenging of those done to its members. When one Michel Maury, peasant, 40, seduced Louise Thomas, 24, his servant, in 1751, her relatives threatened him with trouble—even with being killed—if he did not marry her:[20] clearly such clan responsibility had by no means disappeared from eighteenth-century rural France.

Responsibility for the welfare of members of the family took many forms: the marriage contract to secure provision for one's daughter and her children is just one example of this. It was in the course of the eighteenth century that banks and joint stock companies replaced kin as a source of borrowing for those needing to raise money (though even today the replacement is not complete).[21] Responsibility for welfare however involved much more than legal and financial elements: it was based on an emotional concern that left its mark on folklore. French children played a game called 'stepmother', which required four main actors—father, stepmother, orphan and maternal aunt—and which is vividly described by Retif de la Bretonne. The aunt, arriving from the neighbouring village, learns that her niece is maltreated by her stepmother (she makes her eat rotten bread, say the villagers; ritualistically, the aunt replies, 'Oh my poor niece: daughter of the poor sister I loved so'). Follows an elaborate drama in which the stepmother tries to pretend that the child is well treated, while continuing to force the rotten bread on her, and keep all delicacies for her own children; she is found out, the aunt tells the whole story to the father, and he beats his wife and hands over the child to the aunt, who takes her off chanting 'I'll feed her on white bread, fresh eggs and cream cheese....'[22] The cruel stepmother is a universal figure, far more significant at a time when mortality in childbirth was so high, and the widowhood and (often rapid) remarriage of fathers so common; the game reminds us of the continued interest that the dead woman's family needed to take in the welfare of her children. That aunt is the child-care officer of the eighteenth century.

Patronage too can be seen as an aspect of welfare. A wealthy or influential man carried a responsibility for the advancement of his (often distant) relatives. Richelieu raised all the members of his family to positions of importance, not only because he owed it to them and to his reputation, but also because his power was strengthened by the careful placing of those attached to him.[23] Anyone arriving at court without well placed relatives had great difficulty pursuing a career. As patronage declined it was replaced first by the purchase of offices—cash replacing influence; and then by the growth of our modern professional ethos, the meritocratic principle that appointment (and promotion) should depend only on competence. For the carrying out of all these various forms of responsibility, the family has now given way before police and judiciary, welfare departments and selection boards.

Finally, marriage. Along with co-residence, this is the aspect that seems most real, and has most vividly caught the popular imagination. Corresponding to the two kinds of family, there are seen to be two kinds of marriage choice: the *mariage de convenance*, an affair which concerns all members of both families and in which the couple are merely the principals, the focus of attention and pressure from several directions; and the free and unconstrained decision by two young people, apologizing to no one, to get married because they are in love. Common sense suggests (or has suggested) that the less a family interferes with one aspect of the individual life, the less it will interfere with another: so that the unconstrained choice of partner will be yet another aspect of the decline of the all-interfering family.

This chapter is about marriage choice: for of all aspects of the family and its activities, this is the one that literature has most concerned itself with. It will therefore be necessary to look at the social history of this one more carefully than the others. Before doing so, it is as well to establish consistent terminology.

Mariage de convenance does not, of course, mean marriage of convenience. There are two possible English phrases, depending on where our emphasis lies. If we want to emphasize the fact that the partner is chosen on grounds of personal, social and economic suitability, we will call it 'marriage of propriety': if the fact that the decision is not taken by the couple themselves, we will call it 'arranged match', and since this is the aspect that tradition has usually emphasized, this is the term I shall normally use. I say 'match' rather than 'marriage' when our attention is on the question of choice of partner. When the young couple take their own decision, we say it is because they are in love: I shall accept this belief for the moment (though it will be queried later) and shall therefore speak, in contrast, of the 'love match', or, to emphasize the debt which the ideology of the love match owes to literary tradition, I will speak, anachronistically, of 'romance'.[24]

The Arranged Match

The first thing to say about the two forms of marriage choice is that as they have appeared in Western society they do not include the full range of possibilities. Both exist within what Freeman calls a wide field of eligibles. It is possible to demarcate the field from which a mate can be chosen in various ways. There is always some demarcation: an incest ban is universal, and in our society there are fairly strong pressures towards ethnocentricity, though these may be weakening, along with other pressures to homogamy. What is almost completely lacking in our society is positive demarcation: that is, there is no designated field from which we are expected to make our choice, such as having to marry a cross-cousin. That sort of designation produces a narrow field of eligibles, within which it is still possible for the actual choice to be made either by the family or by the individuals. This narrowing of the field is unknown in England and America. The point is worth mentioning for the sake of anthropological perspective; but it is also important for understanding the significance of love. When the field of eligibles is narrowed, the arbitrariness of individual attraction will not matter much: the rules have already done most of the choosing. But when (as in modern Europe or America) there are literally millions of possible mates, the need for rational choice must be far greater: if it depends on the accidental squeezing of love-juice, the chances of disaster are enormously multiplied. The combination of the wide field of eligibles and a belief in the irrationality of love seems a recipe for disaster: one would expect a reaction against the doctrine of love. This reaction, as we shall see, can be either conservative or radical.[25]

A very convenient example of the contrast between the two forms of marriage choice is provided by a court case of 1666. One Elisabeth Bernard complained to a court in Troyes that she felt no *amitié* for her fiancé, Gross, to whom she had been betrothed by her mother, grandmother and relatives, and therefore wished to break her engagement. Gross replied that the said promises of marriage were made with the free and complete consent of the relatives above named.[26] One could hardly ask for a neater case of the two parties applying different criteria of whose consent was needed. As is usually the case with evidence from court records, we do not know the outcome.

Flandrin offers the following as a definition of the *mariage de raison*, as he calls it, which is not founded on love: 'an association by means of which two individuals or, even more, two families hoped to solve some of their economic and social difficulties'.[27] The first moves towards such an association are made not by the couple themselves but by their parents, and the bride's response may be primarily one of gratitude and obedience to her parents, rather than of affection towards the groom. Here is a dutiful daughter, aged 22, expressing her satisfaction with the arranged match in a way to delight the heart of the crustiest Capulet:

She stated that Thomas le Jolivet had hitherto paid her the honour of coming to her mother's house, where she lived, and that having heard from the said mother that the frequent visits of the said Jolivet were for the purpose of seeking her in marriage, that the said mother was agreeable and persuaded her to agree as well; this had caused her to study the feelings of this upright man; and that, finding nothing in him but uprightness, and virtues that suited her, she had agreed to the wish of her mother and conceived a personal liking for the said Jolivet, hoping that they would be able to live happily together in wedlock.[28]

Since the *mariage de convenance* is a family arrangement, the expected feelings on the part of the couple will not concern themselves only; the young man who is marrying into a family can even be seen as courting them. And so when Jean de Beauvan wanted to marry Françoise de Plessis, he wrote ardent love letters—to her brother! 'I want so much to change my relationship to you, my good cousin.'[29] A magnificent example is taken by Flandrin from the *Mémoires* of Saint-Simon. As it happens, it is an example that requires us to rearrange our contrast, for it concerns an arranged and unromantic match where the arranging is done by the groom himself. At the age of 19 Saint-Simon decided to respond to his mother's wish for himself to marry, and since his father was dead he had to make the proposals himself. He began with the Duc de Beauvilliers, to whom he explained his financial situation, assuring him that he and his mother would sign whatever marriage contract was proposed without examining it. Only then did they come to the question of which daughter it should be. The eldest, aged 14, was determined to be a nun; the second was deformed and not marriageable; and so on down—there were eight altogether. The duke protested that he would do his best, though he could not manage a large dowry:

I replied that he could clearly see, from the proposal I had made, that it was not material considerations that had led me to him, nor even his daughter whom I had never seen, but that it was he himself who had charmed me and whom, along with Madame de Beauvilliers, I wished to marry.[30]

Today we have reached the opposite extreme to this, as I realized on getting a note from a former student announcing her forthcoming marriage 'to a young man I was introduced to by my father: seems rather quaint in this day and age'. It is not easy to date the change even approximately, but in an important respect it had happened in early Victorian England. When Effie Gray was staying with the Ruskins (before there was question of a match between her and John) in 1847 she wrote home about his *affaire* with a woman she had not met (and who indeed may not have existed): 'I suspect from what is said that the lady has a fortune, and that love must come after marriage. Mr and Mrs Ruskin are always talking about marrying from reason, rather odd, isn't it.' This not the tone of a crusader for the love match, but of one who takes it for granted; and the same quietly puzzled contempt for rational (or moral) arrangements appears a week later:

> What you say about John's affair is very true, if he marry the lady it is from prudence and a false notion of duty, he has only seen the young lady six times at parties in his whole life and does not love her a bit, but believes they have each qualities to make the other happy were they married. Did you ever hear such philosophy?[31]

She is writing to her parents! Presumably she would fall into the third of the four phases that Laurence Stone distinguishes:

> In the first, marriage was arranged by parents with relatively little reference to the wishes of the children; in the second, parents continued to arrange the marriage, but granted the children the right of veto; in the third, the children made the choice but the parents retained the power of veto; in the fourth—which was only reached in this century—the children arrange their own marriages, with little open reference to—but under a good deal of subtle influence from—their parents.[32]

Stone places the shift from the first to the second in the late sixteenth and early seventeenth century; and from the second to the third between 1660 and 1780—though it is certain that some forms of the arranged match survived strongly into the nineteenth century. Indeed, the idea of four successive phases may be too much of a simplification to be helpful. Differences between classes are extremely important: in general, the lower orders were freer to make their own choice than the aristocracy.[33] Equally important, but fatally elusive, is the difference between what was preached and what was done: it is sobering to find Ralph Josselin's children, in what should be Stone's first period, apparently making their own choices.[34] Several issues in the theory of marriage may provide important milestones in this development. The end of marriage as a sacrament may accompany a belief that choice should be primarily the concern of the couple: 'emphasis upon the secular contractual bond tended to move the two individuals most concerned outside the range of extended familial connexion.'[35] This would suggest that free choice of partner was Protestant. But it could equally be argued that contracts, which concern property, are more likely to involve the kin, whereas a sacramental view of marriage concentrates on the couple themselves.

There was a striking difference between Catholic and Protestant positions on whether a marriage was valid without parental consent. The

Council of Trent ruled that it was, thus shocking both Protestant and a good deal of traditional lay opinion, including the French, whose delegation had pleaded for the contrary, and whose king did his best to keep the judgement from operating in France.[36] Who were the progressives and who the reactionaries in that argument? Common sense might see the Council as moving with the times, but it is at least arguable that they were defending traditional practice: the view that cohabitation without the blessing of the Church, though a sin, was also valid marriage, goes back at least to the twelfth century.[37] It is clearly a view that would be defended both by popular support of the right of a couple to choose,[38] and by the shrewd casuist anxious to reduce the amount of sexual transgression by reducing what was *called* transgression.

Once we look at these complications we can query not only the simple chronological sequence, but also the connexion between the extended family and the arranged match. For this, one of Stone's own arguments provides a starting point. This is the view that there was a strengthening of patriarchy in the sixteenth and seventeenth centuries.[39] A number of tendencies are grouped together to produce this view. The successful breaking of entails by lawyers increased in the sixteenth century, thus strengthening the power of an individual property-owner to dispose of his property as he saw fit. The authority of fathers over their children may have been strengthened, and was certainly talked about more: Bodin wanted fathers to have power of life and death over children, as did the Anglican convocation of 1606.[40] Flogging (by parents and by schoolmasters) became widespread, to a degree that must appal us today, and was associated with the Puritan emphasis on breaking the will of the child—as Stone crisply puts it, they needed, quite literally, to beat the Hell out of him. And in the sixteenth century at least the authority of husbands over wives seems to have been similarly strengthened (and also included beating). These can all be linked with one another; and with Protestantism ('the theology of Protestantism was patriarchal', says Christopher Hill) and with the strengthening of royal authority in the state. The analogy between the king as father of his people and the father as monarch in the household was a familiar one, and both were compared to the authority of God—'we must regard our fathers as Gods on earth', wrote one Guillaume du Vair in the sixteenth century.[41]

This could suggest that the arranging of marriages by fathers for their children can be seen as a function not of the extended family but of its decline: as the father's authority within the conjugal unit becomes more unquestioned, he exercises it increasingly in the choice of his son's wives or daughters' husbands. It may well be that the influence of the extended family, operating as a control over parental authority, made it more likely that a young man would be able to marry where he wished. If all this is true, it introduces a complication into the orthodox view that relates the rise of the nuclear family to individualism and the destruction of old traditions:

> The ideology of the conjugal family proclaims the right of the individual to choose his or her own spouse, place to live, and even which kin obligations to accept. . . . It asserts the worth of the *individual* as against the acceptance of others' decisions.[42]

At the least we would have to divide this change into two stages: the emergence of the nuclear family, with a weakening of traditional sanctions, an emerging belief in the thriving of the domestic unit, even at the expense of community stability; followed by (though there is an intricate overlap) the emancipation of the individual from all except the most essential authority structures. The analogy with monarchy is very illuminating. The first stage corresponds to the Divine Right of Kings: it might look like individualism (both king and father are individuals) but is better seen as the assertion of the authority of the ruler. The second stage corresponds to democracy, the self-determination of subjects as of offspring. First, kings began to seem old-fashioned or tyrannical; then the authority of the nuclear family began (like that of the kin before it) to seem an old-fashioned restrictive practice. Only then did individualism as we know it arrive.

One question about the arranged match must concern us, in some ways the most important of all. Its connexion with property is so obvious that to many its only purpose has seemed to be property arrangements. This is certainly Stone's view, and he even describes sixteenth-century marriage arrangements as 'slave-trading'; and there is (as we shall see later) no shortage of assertions among the critics of the arranged match that its iniquity consists in treating the young couple as if they were merely an appendage to their property, as if the concern of the match-making parents could be expressed by saying 'He is not to settle for less than ten thousand.'

I find such a view *a priori* implausible. However assiduously we are assured by historians that we must never assume our own values in the men and women of the past, it is difficult to credit that any society treated the quality of human relations as if it did not exist. Unless we grant the unimaginable—that there was no parental love before modern times— we must believe that parents cared about the welfare of their children. Stone cites a will of 1599 that notes 'curtly': 'To my daughter Margerie, 60 sheep, and I bestow her in marriage upon Edward son of Reynold Shaftoe of Thackeryngton.'[43] One longs to know how Margerie felt when she heard this. It is hard to accept that it would have felt normal to her. I do not find it at all difficult to imagine such a will in a Ben

Jonson play (almost exactly contemporary) where it would be offered as a shrewd bit of comical satire, not on the institution but on the father.

The next few pages will therefore set out to present evidence for the view that an institution which survived as long as the arranged match must have had a human face; that this would have consisted not only in consulting the child on his or her preferences (i.e. modifying the institution) but also in the belief that parents were the best people to look after their children's happiness.

Roman Catholic doctrine can be represented by the Brussels Catechism of 1685:

> It is right that a child who is not capable of discernment should not be free to bind himself, without the authority of his parents, by an indissoluble knot. It would be a revolting example of inhumanity on their part to abandon him to the rashness and temerity that are too common at his age, when it comes to deciding, by a marriage, the happiness or misery of his life. His natural guardians are able, without any reason for complaint on his part, to prevent him from engaging himself, or to break an engagement if they judge it unworthy of him or precipitate.[44]

The date of this is a good deal later than the worst examples of financially motivated high-handedness, and indeed it belongs to the time when Stone's second phase was moving into the third (choice by children, veto by parents). It is therefore all the more striking that it says nothing about granting the offspring either choice or veto, which it would see as a dereliction of parental duty. The happiness of the child and the arranging of his match are not seen as opposites but as going together.

Indeed, the very contrast we are using—between property and happiness—is an oversimplification. Even when the injunction to parents pays little attention to personal happiness, it is still likely (especially in Protestant countries) to put aside property in favour of piety as the prime consideration. Increase Mather, writing in Salem at the end of the eighteenth century, urges his Puritan readers:

> Take heed how you dispose of your Children. ... It may make us dread to think what's coming, in that it is with us as it was with the old World, the Sons of God are marrying with the Daughters of men, Church Members, in disposing of their Children look more at Portion than at Piety.[45]

—not very different, in general intent, from the injunction of Jean Benedicti in 1584, that children are especially obliged to obey their parents over marriage choice when the profit of the house was concerned: 'for instance, in contracting a valuable alliance, extirpating heresies or soothing old enmities and quarrels between houses'.[46] Even public reasons for arranging marriages concern more than property.

Stone suggests that letters of advice from fathers to their sons can tell us a good deal about the attitudes to marriage, since these often include instructions on taking a wife—presumably in case the father dies and the young man, like Saint-Simon, is left to arrange his own match. Lord Burghley's *Ten Precepts*, written before 1615, insists on the necessary continuation of parental control ('marry thy daughters in time, lest they marry themselves'), and his advice on the taking of one's own wife balances three considerations, property, physical attractiveness ('nor choose a base and uncomely creature altogether for wealth') and good sense ('there is nothing more fulsome than a she-fool').[47]

Complaints over the wildness of youth can often tell us a good deal about attitudes to marriage. Here for instance is Etienne Pasquier, writing in sixteenth-century France:

> I cannot believe that when headstrong youth has no other guide than inordinate passion, God has any part in it. ... I wish that without glossing over the subject, a good stable law be instituted, whereby a marriage between children which parents have not sealed with their authority be declared null and void.[48]

The reasoning here seems to have nothing to do with property, simply with piety and marital stability: the children will make mistakes, and so should leave it to the parents, who know better. Remarks of this kind will often be found in the lamentations of the *laudator temporis acti*, the celebrator of the past, as he shakes his head over the decline in moral standards. It should be obvious (though there are many sophisticated historians to whom it is not) that such laments are not evidence that moral standards are declining: they are caused by the temperament of the lamenter, not the objective state of society around him. But they can be very revealing evidence for what he (and, therefore, those of similarly conventional minds) assumes ought to be the case. Thus Richard Allestree laments in 1673:

> Nowadays she that goes with her Parent ... thinks she does but walk abroad with her Gaoler. But the right of the Parent is so undoubted, that we find God himself gives way to it, and will not suffer the most holy pretence, no, not that of a vow, to invade it. ... How will He then resent it, to have this law violated upon the impulse of a gay passion, and an amorous fancy.[49]

There are surely two assumptions here that must have been widespread. The first is the absoluteness of parental authority, against which no counterforces are recognized; the second is that controlling the marriage choice of one's children is a moral question, that concerns not the family property but their own welfare.

Finally—as a Protestant equivalent to the Brussels Cathechism already cited—here is an extract from the Massachusetts Statute of 1647:

Whereas it is common practise in divers places, for young men irregularly and disorderly to watch all advantages for their evil purposes, to insinuate into the affections of young maidens, by coming to them in places and seasons unknown to their parents for such ends, whereby much evil hath grown amongst us, to the dishonour of God and damage of parties. . . . For prevention whereof for time to come: it is further Ordered, That whatsoever person from henceforth, shall endeavour directly or indirectly, to draw away the affection of any maid in this jurisdiction under pretence of marriage, before he hath obtained liberty and allowance from her parents or governors (or in absence of such) of the nearest magistrate, he shall forfeit for the first offence five pounds.[50]

The 'much evil' is presumably not the marriage of the young maidens (mention of 'first offence' seems to preclude that) but the winning of their affections (and presumably, on occasion, of their virginity). Once again, the concern is moral: not property but spiritual welfare is at stake.

I believe that to equate parental control over choice of mate with primarily economic matters is a libel on many generations of concerned parents. Nor is it difficult to see how such a libel came about: a considerable grain of truth, plus the eagerness of those who believe in romance to blacken the alternative view.

One final point. I have so far assumed, as European society for many centuries assumed, that when a marriage is arranged, the arranging is done by the parents. Insofar as property is the criterion, this assumption is correct, since the family as an institution is concerned with the transmission of property from one generation to another; but insofar as the arranging is done for the happiness of the couple, why should it not be done by anyone concerned about the welfare of the partners (or one of them), and able to interpose a shield of reason against blind Cupid and his arrows? Why should it not be done by the couple themselves?

In the case of widows and (especially) widowers it often was. Here for instance is M. Wigglesworth, in seventeenth-century New England, setting forth ten reasons why Mrs Avery should marry him.

2ly. That upon serious, earnest and frequent seeking of God for guidance and Direction in so weighty a matter, my thoughts have still been determined unto and fixed upon yourself as the most suitable Person for me.

3ly. In that I have not been led hereunto by fancy (as too many are in like cases) but by sound Reason and judgment, Principally Loving and desiring you for those gifts and graces God hath bestowed upon you, and Propounding the Glory of God, the adorning and furtherance of the Gospel. The spiritual as well as outward good of myself and family, together with the good of yourself and children, as my Ends inducing me hereunto.[51]

He did not need, surely, to assure her that he was not led by fancy; for romantic fancy does not classify under ten headings, like a book-keeper. None of the reasons has even a touch of social irresponsibility: they are all variants on religion and family interests, and no one had squeezed the juice of love-in-idleness on his eyes.

But the widowed can fall in love; and for an instructively complex example, I turn to the marriage of Hester Thrale to Gabriel Piozzi. Mrs Thrale was a wealthy widow in her early forties, with five daughters, when she fell in love with an Italian musician and, after a good deal of agonized indecision, married him. Virtually everyone she knew opposed the match, above all her children and her dear friend Fanny Burney. Eventually she laid her case before her eldest daughter, in a scene which touchingly reversed the usual situation:

> I told her the strength of my passion for Piozzi, the impracticability of my living without him. . . . I confessed my attachment to him and her together, with many tears and agonies.[52]

Here she was, 'requesting of my child that concurrence which at my age (and a widow) I am not required either by divine or human institutions to ask even of a parent'; and sufficiently aware of the irony to comment:

> I married the first Time to please my Mother, I must marry the second Time to please my Daughter—I have always sacrificed my own Choice to that of others, so I must sacrifice it again:—but why?[53]

There is no reason to suppose that the daughter's objections were any different in content to Fanny Burney's, who sympathized but insisted—

> that while She possessed her Reason, nothing should seduce her to approve what Reason itself would condemn: that Children, Religion, Situation, Country and Character—besides the Diminution of Fortune by the certain Loss of 800£ a Year were too much to Sacrifice to any One Man.[54]

There is however one crucial difference, that Fanny's objections were disinterested (as were Dr Johnson's) whereas the daughter felt her own interests at stake. Hester herself set down the reasons for and against her marriage in her journal at some length:

> But if he is ever so worthy, ever so lovely, he is *below me* forsooth: in what is he below me? in Virtue—I would I were above him; in Understanding— I would mine were from this Instant under the Guardianship of his:—in Birth—to be sure he is below me in birth & so is almost every Man I know, or have a Chance to know;—but he is below me in Fortune—is mine sufficient for us both? more than amply so.[55]

She was in love with Piozzi, but the union can hardly be seen as a romantic match, in view of this careful reasoning: it is as if both kinds of marriage are here combined, with Hester playing the part both of the girl who is swept off her feet and of the sober parent weighing up the arguments. And it is striking that the arguments above—the usual ones when a prudent match is being arranged—are followed by a further paragraph beginning 'now for more solid objections', and dealing with the difficulties of marrying a foreigner and a second husband. These 'more solid' points do not concern the external factors of birth and fortune at all, but are entirely a rational calculation of happiness.

The case of Hester Thrale shows the possibility of destroying the contrast between the match that is arranged by parents and the romantic love match seen as the ideology of free partner-choice: for here is someone arranging her own match in rational discussion with her daughter, her friend and herself. This is an anticipation of the twentieth century, in which the discussion can be done by computer. The obvious use of a computer is to codify the requirements of customers so that they are more likely to meet the partner they want than if they relied on the chance opportunities provided by parties and accidental meetings. Distaste for computerized marital agencies as inhuman is likely to come from the romantic: believers in rational choice ought to find them the logical outcome of free but unromantic self-selection, and never fail to point out that no client need actually marry, unless he/she wants to, the partner who is proffered as fitting his specifications.

The computerized agency may represent free choice, but not the computerized researcher. Social scientists do not begin from what the partner is asking for, but from past experience. Feeding in data about date of birth, race, education, occupation, income and so on, they can discover what combinations have fared well or badly; and can tell you that your composite prototype did or did not find the girl you want to marry a suitable mate. Once again, you can ignore the advice, and only the most timid will be so blinded by science as to feel the same need to obey the computer as used to be felt to obey parents. For this computer is carrying out systematically exactly the same function as family (or Fanny Burney) once carried out intuitively.

Free choice, then, means emancipation from the constraints not only of parents but of daughter, friends and social scientists; and rational free choice means replacing them not by blind Cupid but by discussion—including presumably a willingness to hear their arguments. This means the termination of the contrast on which this chapter is based, and in strict logic should be discussed here; but I shall leave further discussion of it for chapter 5. For though (in strict logic) the idea of rational free choice can be put forward by men or women, it has in practice come mainly from women, backed by all the force of feminism. For the time being, we shall stay with our contrast, as did European society.

Propaganda for Romance

After urging historians not to travesty the arranged match, I have to
say this is just what the poets have done. Literature is full of love stories
involving extravagant and improbable (i.e. 'romantic') adventures, in
which our sympathies are wholly on the side of the true lovers whose
course does not run smooth. When Aucassin is put into prison by his
father, and Nicolette into another prison by her guardian, we are meant
to feel, quite simply, that the parents are crusty old men trying to interfere with the course of true love. The tone of *Aucassin and Nicolette* is
lighthearted, but there can be only sympathy for the son saying to his
father 'May God never grant me anything I ask Him, if ever I take up
arms, or mount a horse, or go to do battle in the press where I might
strike some knight or he me, unless you give me Nicolette, my own
sweet love, whom I love so dearly.'[56] All the world loves a lover, and
loves him all the better for a little difficulty with his parents. It is easy
to understand the view that such romances are unsuitable reading for
flighty youngsters: as a contribution to the debate on marriage choice,
they are regularly hostile to parents, and constitute a steady propaganda
for the love match. Dare we use so reductive a word as 'propaganda'
for *Aucassin and Nicolette* or *Romeo and Juliet*, *A Midsummer Night's Dream*
or *The Eve of St Agnes*? The term belongs better, surely, with the stuff
that Sheridan's Lydia Languish loved to read, and that filled her with
a taste for midnight elopements ('so becoming a disguise! so amiable
a ladder of ropes! Conscious moon; four horses; Scotch parson'). Yet
the masterpieces often seem to belong as clearly on the side of the distressed lovers as 'The Fatal Connexion', 'The Mistakes of the Heart' and
'The Delicate Distress'; and to emphasize this point I shall defiantly call
them propaganda. We need to see, and admit, that the immeasurable
superiority of *Romeo and Juliet* need not consist in its being any less unequivocally on one side.

After Tybalt's death, Juliet is placed in a situation of potential dramatic
conflict. Romeo is more than ever the family enemy, and her father has
decided to hurry on the marriage with Paris. In one kind of play, this
could lead to an inner struggle in Juliet: her love for Romeo against
her duty—and affection—towards her parents: surely out of such
struggles, with the character pulled in both directions, the stuff of drama
is made. But Shakespeare has not only avoided this situation by making
it plain that Juliet only considers one possibility; by placing the wedding
before the fight with Tybalt, so that Juliet is already married when she
hears the news, he makes no other outcome possible. True, Juliet has
a kind of struggle when the Nurse tells her what has happened, in III.ii:
she bursts into a violent denunciation of Romeo ('O serpent heart, hid

with a flowering face'), only to change, as soon as the nurse joins in, into an equally passionate defence. This produces two of the most moving lines in the play:

> Ah, poor my lord, what tongue shall smooth thy name
> When I, thy three-hours wife, have mangled it?   (III.ii.98)

This is perhaps the only moment (at any rate since 'O be some other name' five scenes and a world of experience ago) at which Juliet is struggling internally between two attitudes to Romeo: it is so moving because its simple repentance contrasts so strongly with the unhesitating commitment to love that is otherwise so irresistible. In the scene with her mother which follows, Juliet's desperate word-play

> —I will not marry yet; and when I do, I swear
> It shall be Romeo—whom you know I hate,
> Rather than Paris—   (III.v.121)

is an attempt to release her feelings while concealing them from her mother, not the sign of any conflict in her. And neither the dispute with her mother, nor even the brief inner struggle preceding it, are allowed to have the slightest influence on her decision. The celebrated ending of the scene makes this clear. After the Nurse has made her shocking proposal to forget Romeo and marry Paris, Juliet saves her outburst of indignation until she is left alone; to the Nurse she merely says 'Well thou hast comforted me marvellous much', and immediately sets in motion her dissimulation. There is no need to answer the Nurse, because she is not interested in any advice except to stick to Romeo. She will kill herself or take the potion, she will enact for us her dread of lying in the vault 'to whose foul mouth no healthsome air breathes in', but the struggle in that marvellous speech is with fear, not a struggle over what she intends to do. Juliet, like the play, is unequivocally committed to the choice she has made, and to the love match.

Yet the arranged match, which is prominently treated in the play, is not in itself shown as either comic or cruel. It is proposed by Lady Capulet in her first conversation with Juliet:

> Tell me, daughter Juliet,
> How stands your dispositions to be married?   (I.iii.64)

The whole of this early scene breathes normality. The Nurses's garrulousness and affection, Juliet's modest obedience, the mother's concern to persuade her, all belong in the ordinary way of family life. Critics have seen Juliet's unquestioning obedience in this scene as a sign of her immaturity: she is not yet the Juliet who so instantly decides to ignore the Nurse's advice and cease to confide in her. Certainly it is true that there is a kind of formal parallel to the immaturity of Romeo's love for Rosalind, and certainly it is true that this early Juliet is not yet a person, as she becomes under the influence of love: but immaturity is not folly, and her mother is not tyrannizing over her by proposing the match. Her aim is to persuade, not to command: Capulet himself has already said to Paris:

> But woo her, gentle Paris, get her heart.
> My will to her consent is but a part.   (I.ii.16)

And what arguments does Lady Capulet use to persuade her daughter? There is nothing about Paris's estate, nothing about wealth and property: all the praise is of his person ('Verona's summer hath not such a flower') and of his love for Juliet. Even Capulet, when raging in III.5, recites Paris's virtues in a way that suggests that what really matters are his personal attractions:

> And having now provided
> A gentleman of noble parentage,
> Of fair demesnes, youthful, and nobly train'd,
> Stuff'd, as they say, with honourable parts,
> Proportion'd as one's thought would wish a man. ...   (III.v.178)

First comes the assurance that he belongs, of course, to the right social class; then comes the praise of Paris himself. Shakespeare has not tried to suggest, as he would have if the aim was to present the arranged match as tyrannical, that it is purely, even mainly, a matter of money.

Paris himself is everything that he is cracked up to be. Eager, deferential, with no ill will, he does not wish to bully Juliet, or hurry her during the time of grief: it is he who says "These times of woe afford no time to woo', and it is Capulet who decides to hurry the marriage. Paris is a victim of circumstances: he was more than ready to love Juliet, he will strew flowers on her tomb, and when, without ever discovering why, he is killed while doing so, he asks to be treated as if he had died for love. Paris knew nothing of love as the tempestuous destroyer of social institutions: he wanted to love within the rules, and if he had not been caught up in this story he would have done so—though it would not really have been what we call love. He would have been a good husband and trained Juliet to say, in her turn, 'How stands your dispositions to be married?'

There is nothing wrong, then, with the arranged match: yet once Capulet has got hold of it, how ridiculous—and how appalling—it becomes. Gone is the considerateness that tells the young man to win her heart first: gone is everything except the bullying and haste that turns it into a mere contest of will between father and daughter—with the

mother standing helplessly by. We have already looked at Capulet ram-
paging: there is nothing normal, no sense of the pleasant interaction of
family life when he loses his temper:

An you be mine, I'll give you to my friend.
An you be not, hang, beg, starve, die in the streets. (III.v.191)

When we add to this the Nurse's calm proposition of bigamy, it is clear
that not only our emotions but also our moral sense put us on Juliet's
side: it is not only the splendour of her love for Romeo, but also the
integrity that simply brushes aside counsels of expediency and lying,
which make it plain where sympathy lies, which put (or keep) our hearts
with the star-crossed lovers.

Is there a contradiction here? I do not believe there is. We are wholly
on the side of the love match, yet we recognize the normality of the
mariage de convenance. After love has intervened, what was normal turns
to tyranny: and we see it turning as the play proceeds. Though there
is never any doubt where sympathy lies, there is a good deal of doubt
about the relation of the play to the norms of society. The audience at
Romeo and Juliet had married or expected to marry as their parents
arranged: their sympathy existed in a tension with the values they
brought to the theatre. The play's awareness of this consists in the fact
that the marriage with Paris is not cruel but is made cruel.

If Lydia Languish saw *Romeo and Juliet* (as she no doubt did) she would
not have felt it let her down ('such becoming oaths! such admirable
swordplay! poetic moon; dangerous potions; charming friar'). It is
reductive to call it propaganda yet, read in the appropriate spirit, it can
serve as propaganda. Though it has the complexity of great art, it shows
us that in one kind of great art complexity can exist alongside very simple
commitment.

But if she had lived to read the nineteenth-century novel, Miss Languish would have been truly disappointed: for it treats romance with in-
eluctable complexity, and if there is commitment it is often elusive.
Before turning to some of these complexities, I want to ask if the propaganda simplicities lived on. Of course they lived on, as stereotypes do,
in the crudities of popular fiction: but this book is not a history of best-
sellers and popular conventions. Instead of slumming among the descend-
ants of 'The Mistakes of the Heart' I want to ask where these stereotypes
survive in the great writers. In brief, the answer is: not in the realistic
novel, but in those alternative forms that retain the shape of fantasy, that
use the extravagant situations and clear contrasts of the old romances.
Where else should romance belong but in romances?

80 *Choosing a Mate*

Alternatives to Realism

The one great novelist in the nineteenth century who never lost touch with popular melodrama was Dickens. His early novels draw unashamedly on plot-stereotypes that he obviously enjoyed with enormous gusto—a gusto that we can see, in retrospect, was that of genius.

Perhaps no marriage in English fiction was ever arranged with the mad tyranny of Madeline Bray's in *Nicholas Nickleby*. The most devoted of daughters, she obeys the slightest whim of her sickly, selfish father, who lives on her industry, insults those who try to help her, and intends to marry her, for money, to Arthur Gride, 'a little old man of about seventy or seventy-five years of age ... in whose face there was not a wrinkle, in whose dress there was not one spare fold or plait, but expressed the most covetous and griping penury'. Madeline, swallowing her distaste, will not hear a word against the plan, since she considers it her duty to do everything for her father; and she is saved only by his magnificently melodramatic death after everybody is gathered for the wedding. When Nicholas turns up at the wedding, in the hope of preventing it, his Uncle Ralph, who has arranged it all, is thunderstricken. 'His hands fell powerless by his side, he reeled back; and with open mouth and a face of ashy paleness, stood gazing at them in speechless rage.' When the sound of the body falling is heard, followed by Madeline's scream, Nicholas cries: 'Stand off! If this is what I scarcely dare to hope it is, you are caught, villains, in your own toils.' There is no popular melodrama in Victorian times which uses the formulae more crudely than the early work of Dickens. And so all the elements in the arranged match are pushed here to the point of parody. The feelings of the bride are not consulted: to underline this she is given a lover who dares not even declare himself, and the groom is made ludicrously unattractive—avaricious, old and lecherous. The sexual feeling which is carefully not mentioned in Nicholas's attraction to Madeline is allowed to emerge in distorted form in Gride: 'Is she not a dainty morsel ... Such long lashes, such a delicate fringe.' The marriage is a family concern: to exaggerate this, 'family' is concentrated into the one figure of the petulant, self-pitying father, and filial duty entails a degree of physical loathing to be overcome that turns the good daughter into a martyr.[57]

Nicholas Nickleby is in prose: but it has none of the prosaic virtues. We have seen it constantly dropping into stereotypes, constantly pushing towards lurid exaggeration, until we might wonder why it conforms to the sobriety of continuing each line to the right-hand margin of the page. To find a story of romantic love in verse I turn to Tennyson, and choose *Aylmer's Field* (1864)

Sir Aylmer Aylmer, that almighty man,
The country God—in whose capacious hall,
Hung with a hundred shields, the family tree
Sprang from the midriff of a prostrate king. ...   (l.13ff)

It is clear from the first what the elements of this story will be: family tradition and family pride, Sir Aylmer's only daughter Edith, her love for the parson's brother Leolin Averill, the father's anger when it is discovered. And it is clear from the beginning that the attitude to family tradition is critical. 'Sir Aylmer Aylmer': the name is so important that they use it as a Christian name too, and the ring of the repetition is imposing but also, somehow, impoverished, as if they can't manage more than one name. 'Almighty' and 'country God' sound more like the critical outsider than the true admirer, 'capacious' is not quite the word if you really admire the house, and the quaint old detail that the family tree 'sprang from the midriff of a prostrate king' is nicely poised between amusement and respect—it has the tone of an academic showing us round because the more deferential National Trust guide is away.

Sir Aylmer is a parental tyrant of the most savage kind. He had encouraged the friendship between the lovers, being too unimaginative even to think what it might lead to:

He like an Aylmer in his Aylmerism
Would care no more for Leolin's walking with her
Than for his old Newfoundland's: (123)

we can easily imagine an Aylmer lady on a medieval tapestry taking her bath in front of servants and yokels, caring no more for them than for her old Newfoundland. It is already clear that parental authority and the family name belong with the splendid but inhuman past. And so in the scene in which Leolin is told to give up Edith we are shown a sick pride. They do not value Edith in love but as

The sole succeeder to their wealth, their lands,
The last remaining pillar of their house,
The one transmitter of their ancient name,
Their child.   (294)

Leolin reacts heroically, and when told to write a letter saying that he meant nothing, his 'horror-stricken answer' is

So foul a traitor to myself and her,
Never oh never.   (319)

Whereupon he is told that he will be lashed like a dog if found near the doors again. There is a last meeting and a last pledge between the lovers, and then the campaign of separation and attrition begins. Sir

Aylmer has one moment of tenderness ('that one kiss Was Leolin's one strong rival upon earth') but soon reverts to bullying, and the ordeal is too much for Edith, who

> slowly lost
> Nor greatly cared to lose, her hold on life.   (567)

The poem's commitment to the lovers and against parental interference is as complete as any of Miss Languish's favourites. The parents try to find another husband for Edith, in what is virtually a parody of the arranged match:

> Whatever eldest-born of rank or wealth
> Might lie within their compass, him they lured
> Into their net made pleasant by the baits
> Of gold and beauty, wooing him to woo.   (484)

It is merely a desperate reaction against the love match they have forbidden, not a true concern for Edith's welfare: the desperation emerging most clearly in the word 'whatever'. Leolin has a long denunciation of 'this filthy marriage-hindering Mammon', in which he runs together the love of money and the love of lineage in a way that is hardly fair to the family tree springing from the prostrate king: Tory Squires like Sir Aylmer, in nineteenth-century England, were lavish enough with their own denunciations of the Mammon of industrialism and the money-seeking of the 'millocracy'. For Tennyson, however, parental interference is always associated with money as, in the eyes of critics of the arranged match, it inevitably is: the same situation is found in *Maud*, in *Edwin Morris*, where 'they wedded her to sixty thousand pounds', and in *Locksley Hall*, where it is gold 'that gilds the straitened forehead of the fool'. *Locksley Hall* uses many of the traditional devices of the love story, including an almost Wagnerian longing for *Liebestod*:

> Better thou and I were lying, hidden from the heart's disgrace,
> Rolled in one another's arms, and silent in a last embrace.   (57–8)

When it comes to interference with the love match, Tennyson is an extremist: and *Aylmer's Field* is his most extreme poem. This is mainly because of Leolin's elder brother, the local parson, who adds the commination. He sees things in religious terms, and he is completely on the side of the lovers. He therefore tells Leolin 'The very whitest lamb in all my fold loves you'; and when Edith's death has been followed by Leolin's suicide, he preaches the astonishing sermon that gives the poem its long climax. His text is 'Behold, your house is left unto you desolate,' and he recites the praises of the dead Edith with an extravagance that almost recalls Donne's *Anniversaries*. Turning then to his own

brother (who had virtually been a son to him) he comes to his own loss as
climax:

> Nor mine the fault, if losing both of these
> I cry to vacant chairs and widowed walls,
> 'My house is left unto me desolate'.   (719)

This assault on the feelings of his congregation is terribly effective. Some
of his hearers weep; some scowl at Aylmer. Whereupon Averill turns
to the squire and his wife and preaches directly at them.

> Who wove coarse webs to snare her purity,
> Grossly contriving their dear daughter's good—
> Poor souls, and knew not what they did but sat
> Ignorant, devising their own daughter's death!   (780)

It is no wonder that Aylmer's wife finds this too much for her, swoons
shrieking at her husband's feet and has to be carried out of church. Averill
has preached them both to death: 'Nevermore did either pass the gate
Save under pall with bearers.' We are not meant to feel any censure of
Averill's sermon: such public denunciation from the pulpit is presented
as the overflowing of his own grief, not as the aggressive act it also is.
Tennyson set the poem in 1793, and sprinkled it with references to the
horrors taking place across the channel: this adds a *frisson* to the moments
of high emotion, and spice to the sermon. After a lurid description of
the Terror

>   —ever murdered France,
> By shores that darken with the gathering wolf,
> Runs in a river of blood to the sick sea—   (766)

the preacher returns to his subject, appropriating the horror he has stirred
up to his own side of the case:

> Was this a time to madden madness then?
> Was this a time for these to flaunt their pride?   (769)

This is political rhetoric of the most unscrupulous kind. Horrible things
are taking place somewhere else: therefore, in the argument at hand, the
others are more wrong, we more right. In logic, it would be as consistent
for a pro-Aylmer preacher to say

> Is this a time to stir up trouble here?
> Was this a time to steal our daughter's heart?

Averill's treatment of Aylmer and his wife in the sermon has much in
common with their treatment of Edith: an emotional bullying, taking
advantage of the authority he enjoys. That Tennyson did not see it this
way, but only as the expression of grief, the unloading of a weight of

emotion, is clear from the lines that introduce it: after announcing the text, he

> lapsed into so long a pause again
> As half amazed half frighted all his flock:
> Then from his height and loneliness of grief
> Bore down in flood, and dashed his angry heart
> Against the desolations of the world   (629)

Tennyson's allegiance to the Romantic belief in expression is complete: for the preacher as for the poet, such intense sincerity is a guarantee of the moral value of the product. And the plangent overtones of that last line make it the most Tennysonian in the poem. I doubt if Tennyson was capable of ending a line with 'world' without investing it with a heart-warming resonance: there are the 'glories of the broad belt of the world' seen by Enoch Arden on his tropical island, and the 'deep pulsations of the world' felt by the poet in his Lincolnshire garden.

Averill's sermon is an astonishing mixture of Tennyson at his most sensitive and his most insensitive. The reason such an eloquent expression of grief can also be such a callous piece of bullying is that the poet's allegiance to the love match is so complete that he simply does not see what he is stooping to in order to put us against the tyrannical parents.

Nicholas Nickleby and *Aylmer's Field*: two acts of propaganda in the war against *mariage de convenance*. Viewed in terms of attitude towards a social issue, they are very similar: yet how different the experience of reading them. The reason why modern taste cannot, I believe, accept the story of Madeline and Arthur Gride is that it seems written in such total unawareness of how much its melodramatic techniques resemble the comic. How did contemporaries know—as they clearly did—when to feel indignant, and when to laugh? They cannot have distinguished in terms of technique, for here there is virtually no difference. The answer must depend on the moral assumptions they brought to their reading: there are some things one does not joke about, such as sex, or the devotion of daughters to their fathers. Yet even here there are borderline cases:

> 'Precisely what I told you,' said the artful Ralph, turning to his friend, old Arthur. ... 'There is no obligation on either side. You have money, and Mrs Madeline has beauty and worth. She has youth, you have money. She has not money, you have not youth. Tit for tat, quits, a match of Heaven's own making.'   (Ch. 47)

Ralph is invested with so much moral melodrama that we are clearly not allowed to respond to what he says with anything except indignation; yet out of context the epigrammatic balance of this would suggest a witty summary of the *mariage de convenance*, made perhaps by a comical marriage-broker in an aside, or a choric commentator summing up for the audience.

Dickens is so brilliantly capable, in this very book, of drawing comedy out of the stereotypes of melodrama (amiably in Crummles, savagely in Squeers), that his insensitivity to the comic potential of Madeline's story seems astonishing. The unscrupulous heaping up of excess, the theatrical phrasing, the surfeit of stereotyping, simply can no longer be taken seriously (by some Victorian readers, Lewes or Mill for instance, they never could be). Is Tennyson, then, any less stereotyped, any less theatrical? The answer has to be no: yet in *Aylmer's Field* it is all more acceptable. Why?

There is Tennyson's poetic genius. We will take anything, surely, from the poet who describes a dagger

> Sprinkled about in gold that branched itself
> Fine as ice-ferns on January panes
> Made by a breath.   (221)

There is nothing like this at the Brays', where all description is predictable in its detail: 'the perfect pallor, the clear transparent whiteness, of the beautiful face which turned towards him'. Tennyson's marvellous language is not mere decoration: it adds a resonance to the story itself, so that it is hard to say if the effect of the concluding lines is a matter of style or of the very conception of the story. The Aylmers having died out, the Hall is broken down, and by now

> The hedgehog underneath the plaintain bores,
> The rabbit fondles his own harmless face,
> The slow-worm creeps, and the thin weasel there
> Follows the mouse, and all is open field.   (850)

We are taken back to the title of the poem by its conclusion: the ability to write so compellingly of the reconquest by nature sets the story in a context of inevitability, universalizes it, and justifies the use of stereotypes in a way that only poetry can. Of course the individual poetic mastery is important here: the marvellous rhythmic control, the placing of the monosyllabic verbs, the choice of the two dissyllabic verbs, even the fact that they alliterate—all this bears the insignia 'Tennyson' as unmistakably as the image of the ice-ferns. Yet in another sense our response does not depend on such individual effects: they are confirmation of an awareness we already bring to our reading. Before we respond to the poetic quality, we respond to the fact of poetry: the blank verse is a licence to enjoy the language in a way Dickens only allows himself when he is being comic. There is nothing comic in *Aylmer's Field*, just as there is nothing Dickensian in the style, but there is a gusto, a delight in the power of the writing, in the extracting of splendid phrases from the situation, that would have saved the story of Madeline. In *Nicholas Nickleby* a comic masterpiece was clamouring to be written, and Dickens would not admit it; the (unauthorized) enjoyment we can only take by ignoring this and pretending that it *is* funny corresponds to the enjoyment that is authorized in *Aylmer's Field* by the fact that we are reading poetry.

To complete the argument, we now need a work of comic melodrama, a defence of young lovers against marital arrangements that is unashamed of theatricality, and goes on to derive comic possibilities from this. Where better can we find this than in the plot of an opera: for opera by its nature, believes in the theatrical, and makes the most of stereotyped situations. The lines of characterization in opera are necessarily simple; the enjoyment of a comic opera derives from contented acceptance of that simplicity, of uncomplicated narrative as the basis for music.

So for the most straightforward example imaginable of the romantic love story I take the text which Karla Sabina wrote for Smetana's *Bartered Bride* in 1866. In a general atmosphere of carefree youth and pastoral holiday, we are shown a couple who have fallen in love without their parents' knowledge. Marenka, the girl, is about to be married off: not simply by her parents but (so that the arrangements will be felt as interference) by a marriage-broker, Kecal—who is a figure of comedy, an overdressed bass with (he pulls a face) a wife at home, worse luck. And Vasek, the intended groom, too, is a comic figure, a stammering, ineffectual mother's boy, easily frightened off. His appearance is saved for the second act so that we may savour its full absurdity.

> If I cannot get a wife
> The whole village will laugh me to scorn.

Jenik the hero tricks Kecal with the simplest of devices: he sells Marenka to 'the son of Micha', and even the inattentive listener who missed the reference to Micha's runaway son by his first marriage has no difficulty in realizing what is happening. The trick enables us to have another stereotype—the cruel stepmother who caused Jenik to run away—and to smile further at the gullibility of the marriage-broker. After the expected tears from the 'betrayed' Marenka, and her delight when she realizes the truth, all ends happily. Because it is comedy, the parents come round to accepting the *fait accompli*.

Here is propaganda for romance at its simplest. We know nothing about the lovers except their youth and their love; nothing about the arranged match except that arranger and groom are ridiculous, and that it is an interference with the course of true love. When her father and the broker show her the contract signed with Micha, the groom's father, she replies indignantly that it does not count, because she and Jenik knew nothing of it: exactly the argument that Elisabeth Bernard[58] advanced in all seriousness. The obstacles melt away in a riot of harmony, as is wholly proper in comic opera, and the chorus sings in conclusion that faithful love has won the day.

All three of these examples rely on a simplified situation and a clear preference; and for all that brilliance, one can see why they would leave some readers—and writers—dissatisfied. These are the realists: marriage, as I suggested in the first chapter, belongs to them, though love doesn't. What about getting married?

The realist is aware that midnight elopements and cunning friars are neither frequent nor effective. Mr Gascoigne in *Daniel Deronda*, planning to get his fatherless niece married, knows this perfectly well:

> And in considering the relation of means to ends, it would have been mere folly to have been guided by the exceptional and idyllic—to have recommended that Gwendolen should wear a gown as shabby as Griselda's in order that a marquis might fall in love with her, or to have insisted that since a fair maiden was to be sought, she should keep herself out of the way. Mr Gascoigne's calculations were of the kind called rational, and he did not even think of getting a too frisky horse in order that Gwendolen might be threatened with an accident and be rescued by a man of property. He wished his niece well, and he meant her to be seen to advantage in the best society of the neighbourhood. (Ch. 4)

George Eliot lays the question of marriage choice before us with fierce clarity in the subplot. Mrs Arrowpoint is a writer of romances that lean heavily on the exceptional and the adventurous; she has written one on Tasso, who has the charm of having loved a woman against the wishes of her family, and whose life is more interesting than his poetry, because it can be made more romantic. But Mrs Arrowpoint is also very wealthy, and when her own daughter tries to follow the Tasso model and marry an artist for love, she is shocked, and will not tolerate this attempt to insert romance into the actual; and George Eliot, observing her with the steely eye of realism, catches the hard hostility of her voice with a shrewdness that (we may be sure) was wholly absent from Mrs Arrowpoint's own works of fiction. Catherine Arrowpoint does not elope with Klesmer, and there is no conscious moon: she tells her parents, in a carefully depicted family quarrel, that she intends to marry the man she loves, and does not accept that it is her duty to marry in a way that will 'place the property in the right hands.' 'People can easily take the sacred word duty as a name for what they desire any one else to do.'[59]

Realistic treatments of choosing a mate are concerned with the tension between the two systems; they may come down on the side of romance, but not with the propagandist fervour we have so far looked at, and not with unquestioning use of the stereotypes. I have chosen three examples from the nineteenth-century novel, by three of the great realists. First, *The Newcomes* (1853–5), since no novelist is more concerned with marriage choice than Thackeray; then *Bleak House* (1852–3), to show what happened to Dickens after he abandoned the simplicities of *Nicholas Nickleby*; and finally *Irrungen Wirrungen* (1888), in which Fontane treats a dimension of the problem which the English silently ignore.

The Newcomes

That the subject of *The Newcomes* is two kinds of marriage is announced from the beginning. The main characters of the story spring from the two marriages of old Thomas Newcome, who is dead before it begins. His first marriage, with a simple country girl from his village, was a love match, and produced Tommy (Colonel Newcome) and his son Clive, the hero; this side of the family has all the warmth, impulsiveness and generosity. His second was with the boss's daughter, Sophia Alethea Hobson, a pious and formidable businesswoman—'bravely he went in and won the great City prize, with a fortune of a quarter of a million'—and produced Brian and Hobson: this side has all the piety, snobbery, coldness and success. The essential point about the consequences of marriage is made, implicitly but prominently, in the genealogical structure of the book. It is confirmed explicitly by Mme de Florac, who speaks in favour of marrying for love, though she herself did the opposite.

> Do you know that the children of those who do not love in marriage seem to bear a hereditary coldness, and do not love their parents as other children do? They witness our differences and our indifferences, hear our recriminations, take one side or the other in our disputes, and are partisans for father or mother. (Ch. 47)

All the marriages can be fitted into this scheme: that of Barnes Newcome, for instance, who marries Clara as a commercial transaction (he has the money, she has the rank), bullies her, and then is abandoned when she runs off with the man she had always loved. Ethel Newcome too is intended for a fine match, though in her case this never comes off, since Thackeray develops the device he had already used with Beatrix Esmond—the proud beautiful girl who keeps losing her chance of a fine husband, partly through cruel bad luck. It is not always easy to distinguish bad luck from the girl's own rebellious urges (there is some subtle plotting here), and in the light of the book's values it is equally difficult to distinguish bad luck from good. The superficial explanation of Ethel's broken engagements is that she must be saved for Clive and a happy ending, but to say that would be unfair to Thackeray's complexity. In *Henry Esmond* Beatrix, after her series of missed chances, is left single at the end, and even in this more conventional novel Clive and Ethel are allowed only a chastened, mature union after Clive's disastrous marriage. Above all, such an explanation in terms of mere plot ignores the subtle and intelligent exploration of Ethel's own very mixed feelings about whether she wants to marry these men. Her consciousness of 'the wretched consequences of interested marriages' builds up steadily, and makes one brilliant appearance when she is still engaged to her cousin, Lord Kew. Taken to an exhibition of paintings, she remarks on the little green ticket to show that a painting has been sold:

> 'I think, grandmamma,' Ethel said, 'we young ladies in the world, when we are exhibiting, ought to have little green tickets pinned on our backs, with "Sold" written on them; it would prevent trouble and any future haggling, you know. Then at the end of the season the owner would come to carry us home.' (Ch. 28)

We can find the same contrast in *Pendennis*. Arranged marriage is shown through the Beatrix-figure, Blanche, who has money and whom Pen can have, along with a seat in Parliament; and romantic marriage through the conventional heroine, Laura. Now since it is part of the romantic convention that the hero meets the heroine for himself, even in some way that involves opposition to the family, it is wholly inappropriate that Laura is Pen's adopted sister, and that the match has long been planned by his mother. Thackeray therefore uses two ingenious tricks to show his loyalty to the romantic theme. First, Laura is the daughter of Helen Pendennis's cousin whom she had loved and renounced, later making a sober match with a successful man much older than herself; so that the very existence of Laura symbolizes marrying for love, however foolishly in the world's eyes. And second, the match between Pen and Laura must be, as it were, disarranged. Pen proposes to her early in the book, saying to himself:

> I am going to tie myself for life to please my mother. Laura is the best of women ... [and] as both the women have set their hearts on the match, why, I suppose I must satisfy them. (Ch. 28)

And during the proposal he calls her sister and explains that he is so broken down and disillusioned (at 23) 'that I have hardly got a heart to offer'. Laura is one of Thackeray's most insipid heroines but she has at any rate enough spirit to object to this and she refuses him. Only after his mother has died and he has lost Laura by his own folly is he allowed to have her after all. The arranged match has thus been turned into a pure love match.

Is there any correlation between the two kinds of marriage, and Thackeray's two kinds of heroine? This contrast is well known to all his readers: between the submissive angel for whom there is only one man, whom she wishes only to love, honour and obey, and the spirited, unscrupulous seductress, self-interested, intelligent, untrustworthy and with enormous vitality. It is the contrast between Amelia and Becky in *Vanity Fair*, Laura and Blanche in *Pendennis*, Clara and Ethel in *The Newcomes*. There are variants (*Lovel the Widower*, for instance, ends with a marvellously comic glimpse of a Becky inside the Amelia), but the contrast is central to Thackeray's fiction. Now the submissive angel, since she is essentially unquestioning, is essentially conservative; and we might therefore expect her to accept her parents' arrangements when it comes to marrying. But both Amelia and Charlotte Baynes marry in defiance of their parents, and in *Philip* Thackeray tells us explicitly that Charlotte's parents have gone too far in trying to prevent her from marrying Philip, and have lost their authority over her. The fact that the submissive heroines make love matches (or, as in the case of Clara Pulleyn, clearly ought to have) reveals how hollow parental authority has become for both Thackeray and his readers. Romantic marriage is seen as natural for the meek little woman: if that involves defying her parents, no reader will feel this to be subversive of any authority he respects. The authority she does not defy is that of the husband, and the acceptance of male dominance in marriage is actually reinforced by the romantic conventions. 'Oh what a blessing it is to see him so happy,' says Charlotte of her husband. 'And if he is happy I am.' In contrast to this, the Beckys are neither naturally submissive nor able to surrender their independence of spirit sufficiently to fall deeply in love: they are too calculating for romance.

The angels, then, can be associated with marrying for love. True, Amelia's match is arranged at the beginning of *Vanity Fair*, but like Laura's it has to be disarranged, and after her father's ruin it turns into a love match (though a one-sided love match). Becky, in contrast, has to scheme for a husband: she has to do her own arranging.

That then is the simple contrast, and the simple preference is for the love match. Jack Spiggot in *The Book of Snobs* was prevented from marrying Letty Lovelace by their two mercenary fathers:

> 'My father and hers couldn't put their horses together,' Jack said. 'The General wouldn't come down with more than six thousand. My Governor said it shouldn't be done under eight. Lovelace told him to go and be hanged, and so we parted company. They said she was in a decline. Gammon! She's forty, and as tough and as sour as this bit of lemon peel.'
>
> (Ch. 33)

The snobographer reflects that he's seeing the wreck of two lives, and denounces the creed that ruined them—'Thou shalt not love without a lady's maid; thou shalt not marry without a carriage and horses.' The next chapter describes the family life of Mr and Mrs Gray who married without money, to the distress of the bride's mother, and are quite happy in their modest circumstances. The contrast is clear, between marrying (or not marrying) for money, for which the fathers are held responsible, and marrying to please yourself, that is, for love. It is the age-old contrast of romance.

If Thackeray held consistently to this simple contrast he would be a much less interesting novelist: the conventional framework I have described underlies but does not dominate his fiction, and to move (now) to the qualifications is to show the subtleties of his realistic vision.

Though the main plot of *Pendennis* is propaganda for romance, there are two episodes to set against this. The first is the opening story, almost self-contained, of Pen's first romantic involvement—with the actress, Miss Fotheringay (real name, Milly Costigan). The girl is ten years older than Pen and has other fish to fry even when listening to his advances. He sits with her hour after hour, spouting Byron and Moore, while

> the lovely Emily, who could not comprehend a tenth part of his talk, had leisure to think about her own affairs, and would arrange in her own mind how they should dress the cold mutton, or how she would turn the black satin. (Ch. 6)

Pen is rescued by his uncle, Major Pendennis, who brings him to his senses, by telling him a few home truths about Milly and—more effectively—telling Milly that Pen has no money. Maternal uncles are, in some societies, the accepted guardians of their nephews' welfare. The Major pours scorn on his passion ('What! a woman who spells affection with one f?')—as does Thackeray, who leaves Pen gloomily sitting in an almost empty theatre, watching the Fotheringay act. 'We are not going to describe his feelings,' says Thackeray,

> or give a dreary journal of his despair and passion. Have not other gentlemen been balked in love besides Mr Pen? Yes indeed; but few die of the malady. (Ch. 13)

This is not Thackeray at his best: it has the facetiousness of his early sketches, and its relation to the later, romantic plot is that of a rather crudely juxtaposed opposite. But there is no doubt that it is an opposite: 'few die of the malady' is one of the anti-romantic commonplaces. Major Pendennis interferes (with some shrewdness) to prevent the wrong marriage: this can be regarded as a variant on arranging the right one. And later in the novel we are shown what would have happened if he had not interfered. Pen's kind friend Warrington had no uncle to save him from a similar entanglement and ended up married to 'a woman of a much lower degree and a greater age than my own'. This marriage has ruined his life. She turned out to be a boor who 'could not comprehend one subject that interested me' and anyway she had always loved some-one else—'a person of her own degree'. Warrington's story is cursory (two pages) and it too does not show Thackeray at his best: reading it with a modern democratic eye, we can see that he bears more responsi-bility for the disaster than his author is willing to admit. He was trapped into an unsuitable marriage, but his inability to adjust his conventional views on the roles of husband and wife helped to keep it unsuitable. Both tales tell us that romantic young men will make fools of themselves, and so should not, as the Brussels Catechism had it, be abandoned to the rashness and temerity too common at their age.

This counter-attitude is less obvious in *The Newcomes*, but more subtly and powerfully used. The case for *mariage de convenance* is presented by Lady Kew, Ethel's grandmother. In one of the most interesting conversa-tions in the novel, Ethel protests against the 'mammon worship' that sells daughters like Turkish women.

> I would, if I loved a man sufficiently, loved him better than the world, than wealth, than rank, than fine houses and titles—and I feel I love these best—I would give up all to follow him.

She would rather be at the plough, she declares, than dealt with as she is now; to which the old woman replies, 'No, you wouldn't, Ethel.'

> These are the fine speeches of school-girls. The showers of rain would spoil your complexion; you would be perfectly tired in an hour, and come back to luncheon. You belong to your belongings, my dear, and are not better than the rest of the world—very good-looking, as you know perfectly well, and not very good-tempered. It is lucky that Kew is. Calm your temper, at least before marriage; such a prize does not fall to a pretty girl's lot every day.

Here is the first reason for accepting the world's arrangements—that you love the world's good, as Ethel does (a fact she admits in calmer moments and even, in passing, here). The other reason comes up later in the same conversation. Ethel asks her grandmother why she desires the marriage so much. The answer is interesting—and moving:

> Because I think it is high time that Kew should *ranger* himself; because I am sure he will make the best husband, and Ethel the prettiest Countess, in England.' And the old lady, seldom exhibiting any signs of affection, looked at her grand-daughter very fondly. (Ch. 32)

It is not just an abstract conception of family honour that motivates the old lady, we see, it is Ethel's welfare, and she cares for Ethel. All Thackeray's fierce old women (Lady Kew, the Baroness de Bernstein, Miss Crawley) love matchmaking—and matchbreaking—for they love wielding authority over the love life of their young protégés; and the mingling of power and shrewdness, concern and selfishness, in their affectionate bullying is observed with an insight that makes the simple reductivism of *The Book of Snobs* look like a parody of the arranged match.

Romance has a parody too, which is infatuation, and Thackeray offers a great deal of that. It is not only young men who make fools of themselves for love: women can lay themselves open, through their infatuation, to sexual (and in consequence to financial) exploitation. The best illustration of this is *Barry Lyndon*. Barry is an Irish scoundrel who makes a career for himself by his vitality, his gambling skill, his sexual aggression and his unscrupulousness. The climax of his career is his marriage to Lady Lyndon, whom he starts courting when her husband is still alive (to the vast amusement of that old cynic). Once she is widowed he succeeds with cool impudence in making her utterly infatuated with him. Without this infatuation he could not have robbed her, and in a situation where infatuation does not lead to marriage he would not have succeeded—as he himself realizes in an earlier reflection. He is telling us how he failed in all his attempts to consolidate his fortunes by marriage.

> Ladies are not in the habit of running away on the Continent, as is the custom in England (a custom whereby many honourable gentlemen of my country have much benefited!); guardians, and ceremonies, and difficulties of all kinds intervene; true love is not allowed to have its course, and poor women cannot give away their honest hearts to the gallant fellows who have won them. Now it was settlements that were asked for; now it was my pedigree and title-deeds that were not satisfactory: though I had a plan and rent-roll of the Ballybarry estates, and the genealogy of the family up to King Brian Boru, or Barry, most handsomely designed on paper; now it was a young lady who was whisked off to a convent just as she was ready to fall into my arms; (Ch. 10)

'True love is not allowed to have its course': and quite right too, we can hear Lady Kew saying, for true love is the phrase silly young girls use when they are making fools of themselves.

If Lady Lyndon was silly, poor Matilda Griffin was sillier. *Mr Deuceace at Paris* is the story of a contest between two rogues, father and son, for the hand of a widow or her stepdaughter—'or' because each of them naturally wants the one with the money, and the son, outwitted, ends up with the daughter but no money. The daughter is crooked, and squints; her love-letters are pathetic in their fulsome affectation; and Deuceace treats her with totally cynical indifference. It is all intended as a facetious sneer, but the story is nasty enough to have a certain raw power, and the final glimpse of Matilda, left with the maimed and bitter husband who hates her, is too savage to be simply funny.[60]

The Newcomes may not be Thackeray's best novel, but it is central to his work: the contrast between *mariage de convenance* and the romantic match is more subtly treated there than anywhere else. Both *Barry Lyndon* and *Mr Deuceace* support Lady Kew: marriage arrangements and family control would have saved these two stupid but not wicked heroines from the scroundrels who manage to get hold of them. *Mariage de convenance* can protect against exploitation.

Esther's Suitors

In the later Dickens there is a complexity of social awareness almost at the opposite extreme from the jolly crudities of *Nicholas Nickleby*— even though the crudities continue to be present, as the case of *Bleak House* will show. Esther Summerson, with her constant unselfishness, her professions of simplicity and her household keys clinking at her waist, is not at first glance a heroine to appeal to modern tastes—until we look more closely at her repressed personality and her not quite conventional story.

Esther receives three proposals: from Mr Guppy, from Jarndyce, and from Allan Woodcourt. The first would be pure comedy if it was not addressed to Esther:

> I am aware that in a worldly point of view, according to all appearances, my offer is a poor one. But Miss Summerson! Angel!—No, don't ring— I have been brought up in a sharp school. . . . I have walked up and down, of an evening, opposite Jellyby's house only to look upon the bricks that once contained Thee.   (Ch. 9)

It is a parody of romance. Seen in himself, Mr Guppy (Kenge and Carboy's clerk with 'an entirely new suit of glossy clothes on, a shining hat, lilac-coloured gloves, a neckerchief of a variety of colours, a large hot-house flower in his button-hole, and a thick gold ring on his little finger') is merely ridiculous; in relation to Esther he is somehow offensive, and after she has dismissed him with a mixture of contempt and anger she goes upstairs to her own room 'where I surprised myself by beginning to laugh about it, and then surprised myself still more by beginning to cry about it'. Mr Guppy's offence is that he did not stay in his part of the book. He belongs among the Dickensian humours, the comic characters on whom Dickens lavishes his linguistic inventiveness; Esther is the heroine, whom one writes and thinks of with respect, and a proposal like this threatens to draw her into the comedy, where respect gives place to gusto. She must be protected from such contamination, just as Amy

Dorritt must be protected from John Chivery, leaving him to compose his epitaph with a comic spirit ('Here lie the mortal remains of John Chivery, never anything worth mentioning...') that is not allowed to touch her. But Dickens treated John Chivery better than Mr Guppy, leaving him to pine entertainingly in his section of the book, whereas Mr Guppy, in great embarrassment, feels it necessary to extricate himself from his offer when Esther loses her looks, in an episode that is not at all funny, because he is over-anxious to make it plain that he did not 'really' love her. What does 'really' mean? If it is a moral point (he loved her looks not her person) it has nothing to do with the aesthetic gap between the comedy and the pathos, and Dickens shows distrust of his own powers by putting him down in that way. It is as if he feared that to parody romantic love was to suggest that he was not on its side even in the main plot, so Guppy has to be a parody of only the most superficial kind of romantic love.

Esther's final proposal, the successful one, is the pure convention of romantic fulfilment: handsome but poor lover, heroic adventures in the Far East, return home to find her Another's, sad confession of his devotion when he thinks it Too Late, and then, to the readers predictable delight, the Happy Ending after all. If George Eliot and Elizabeth Gaskell grow more ordinary, less profoundly complex, when handling such a story, Dickens grows commonplace to the point of tedium. It is no service to Dickens to linger on this part of the story, or to quote any of its speeches beginning 'O, Mr Woodcourt, forbear, forbear', or 'Heaven knows, beloved of my life.'

Between these two—the parody romance and the romance we long to parody—comes the proposal of Jarndyce, and on that there is more to say. For most of the book, Jarndyce is her guardian, uniformly kind, grumpy only when others behave badly, reliable both morally and (in clear contradiction to all we're told of the Chancery Case) financially. Esther accepts him; and only by his own magnanimous withdrawal at the end does she marry the man we naturally expect her to marry.

Marriage to Jarndyce would have been of the highest *convenance*. Esther has (effectively) no parents, so her guardian must arrange things for her, and he does this with himself. The greatest possible care is taken to protect their engagement from both romance and sex. The proposal does not declare passion, run to poetic metaphor, or even use the words love or marriage: it asks her—by letter—whether she will become mistress of Bleak House. It is as fatherly as any act of Jarndyce's: 'I saw his face, and heard his voice, and felt the influence of his kind protecting manner, in every line.' There are constant assurances that her acceptance will make no difference to their relationship—and since Esther is already his trusted housekeeper, the one difference would be sexual. The care which Jarndyce takes not to hurry things almost suggests that he dreads consummation.

This marriage so carefully reduced to the domestic is appropriate to Esther, the most domestic of heroines. We are right to see her as conventionally Victorian, but not as a conventional Victorian heroine. The example of that in the novel is Ada—'such a beautiful girl! With such rich golden hair, such soft blue eyes, and such a bright, innocent trusting face!' Compared with Ada's winsome charm, her devotion to Richard, her golden hair, Esther seems not virginal but sexless. Dame Durden, Dame Trot, are her tediously reiterated nicknames, the housekeeping keys her emblem. Contemporary reviewers did not always take to Esther: 'A wicked wish arises', said the *Spectator*, 'that she would either do something very "spicy" or confine herself to superintending the jampots in Bleak House.'[61] When they praised her, it might be in defensive italics: 'Among all the amiable and interesting female characters that the pen of Dickens has portrayed, we venture to assert that there is not one so perfectly *loveable* in every way as Esther Summerson.'[62] I take the italicizing as an admission that Esther has not got the amiability and interest we expect of a heroine; she has something else, that perhaps we don't expect, that perhaps we don't associate with heroines, but rather with mothers, or with the wives of other people.

The response of contemporary readers to *Bleak House* must have involved a shift from literature to life. Esther is not the stuff heroines are made of—to ram the point home, she has to be deprived of her good looks halfway through—but, loveable Dame Durden, she is the stuff of Victorian motherhood. Marriage to Jarndyce fulfils none of the romantic expectations, but how like it would be to marriage as many nineteenth-century women looked forward to it—to a man considerably older than themselves, who would treat them like his daughter. Jarndyce's constant postponement of the wedding, which I have suggested is an avoidance of sex, would add to his attraction for female readers not caring to think about that still mysterious, not altogether pleasant element in marriage. When Jarndyce has finally handed Esther over to Woodcourt, we are given this:

> I clasped him round the neck, and hung my head upon his breast, and wept. 'Lie lightly, confidently, here, my child,' said he, pressing me gently to him. 'I am your guardian and your father now. Rest confidently here'.
>
> (Ch. 64)

The emotion behind this is clearly relief. There is an obvious explanation for this relief, that she is now going to marry Woodcourt after all, but we would be deceiving ourselves if we thought that was the reason here. For it is felt by Jarndyce as well as Esther, indeed it is an emotion *between* them. It can only be relief that their relationship really is not going to change, that nothing so unseemly as the marriage bed will interfere with her reliance on his wisdom and strength. And only now that this is clear can they clasp each other in such intense physical contact.

The power of literary conventions is very great. I am sure that contemporary readers wanted Esther to marry the wooden hero Woodcourt, and felt betrayed at the thought that she might marry Jarndyce. The fact that they could recognize a real-life situation in what they hoped she would be rescued from did not alter this wish, though I am sure it determined the nature of their discontent, perhaps gave them a bad conscience about it. (I put all this in the past tense, since older husbands, and—even more—fatherly husbands are now so much less common; yet emotions are so conservative that much of this may obtain today). The intense relief with which Esther is finally clasped in Jarndyce's arms may then awaken in the reader a relief that he is going to be given the kind of ending he feels entitled to, that not life but literature is in charge.

One final comment. We have not been looking at the best of *Bleak House*. Perhaps the most successful of Esther's suitors, aesthetically, is Mr Guppy, but he is the most peripheral to her story. The psychological complexity of the relationship with Jarndyce gives that a good deal more interest than the happy ending with Woodcourt, but it is a complexity that does not issue either in appropriate symbol or in explicit understanding, nor does it save Jarndyce from a good deal of simplified sentimentalizing. He never, alas, fulfils the glorious promise of his first appearance, riding unannounced opposite Esther in the couch, offering her two pies and, when she politely refuses, saying 'Floored again', and throwing them out of the window. Yet although he loses that inimitable Dickensian life, he does keep a certain uncomfortable interest through his relationship with Esther. Psychological complexity is better than the tame following of convention, but is not enough in itself for true literary power.

Botho's Dilemma

In the lives of many young men in the nineteenth century, the rival of the arranged match was not the love match but the liaison. We naturally have no statistics, but it is clear that, for many who were not rebels, conforming with the marital plans expected of them meant giving up their mistresses. English fiction, in its respectability, has little to say on this situation; so I turn to Theodore Fontane.

Irrungen Wirrungen is a touching short novel about a young Berlin aristocrat, his mistress and his wife. We start from the mistress, Lene, and the small circle she lives in—Frau Nimptsch, her adopted mother, who is a washerwoman, and the gardener's family next door. It is a warm, humane group, where her lover, Botho von Rienäcker, is made welcome. There can be nothing permanent between them, but the two are, for the moment, deliciously happy. Their most perfect day is an outing to a charming rural spot called Hankels Ablage (Hankel's Dump: the unromantic name is deliberate, and is discussed), an outing which changes its nature when three of Botho's fellow officers turn up with their ladies, leaving Lene with the feeling that their happiness was spoilt, though no one was to blame. The very next day comes the news that Botho is to marry his cousin. The marriage is not unhappy, but the cheerful chattering Käthe can never mean to him what Lene meant.

Some years later later Lene receives a proposal from a respectable and pious factory foreman, and feels obliged to tell him about her past; he calls on Botho, who gives him what I suppose we must call a glowing testimonial. The story ends with Lene's marriage and Käthe's half-discovery of Botho's past, which is clearly not going to upset her unduly.

Botho's marriage to Käthe is a classic *mariage de convenance*. It is arranged by his mother and his uncle, and urged on him in a letter that begins with financial difficulties, then goes on to remind him of the understanding he has long had with Käthe, whose mother is now showing signs of impatience. What she has said reaches Botho very indirectly, but its tone gets through and that is unmistakable:

> If Herr von Rienäcker pleases to abandon what was planned and agreed by the family, and to regard undertakings which have been entered on as mere child's play, she has no objection. Herr von Rienäcker may consider himself free from the moment he wishes to be free. But if his intentions are, on the contrary, not to make use of this unconditional opportunity to withdraw, then it is high time to make *that* plain.   (Ch. 14)

Botho has to make up his mind. 'You know what I wish,' his mother writes, 'but my wishes need not bind you.' Fontane's point is that despite this surface freedom Botho is as bound as the young men of earlier centuries who were obliged simply to accept their parents' choice. For he is the prisoner of his social situation:

> Who am I? An average member of the so-called top layer of society. And what can I do? I can manage a horse, carve a bird and gamble. That's all: so my choice is between circus rider, head waiter and croupier.   (Ch. 14)

Bred to no career but the conspicuous display of the regiment, conformist by nature, attached to his family, he has no choice. The completeness of his conformity is revealed to us even in his affair: his politeness to the garrulous Frau Dörr, Lene's neighbour, his tenderness to Frau Nimptsch, his playful imitation of polite conversation when they are gathered round the fire, all show him being accepted as one of the family.

Wherever he is, he feels most at home as part of a circle: he and Lene need a framework for their solitude. The visit that Botho pays to Frau Nimptsch's grave, to place the wreath of everlastings he had promised her, half-tenderly, half-playfully, is a parody of family obligation—but a parody more touching than the original. The more we see Botho at home in Lene's circle, the more clearly we see why he has to marry Käthe. His own summary is a phrase that could serve as epigraph to any of Fontane's novels: *Das Herkommen bestimmt unser Tun*: social origin determines our actions.

All Botho's friends have mistresses; all the mistresses understand the situation, and if they are realistic they plan accordingly. During the outing to Hankels Ablage, the women have a couple of hours to themselves, and as they walk in the woods Lene finds herself with Isabeau, mistress of Botho's friend Balafre. (But in fact her name is not Isabeau, and we never learn what it is: the men have given their womenfolk names out of Schiller, this in itself tells us how they regard them—poetically but with a kind of contempt.) Isabeau finds her affair tedious (she is 15 years older than the others); but she is saving up, and intends to marry a widower ('and I already know who'). When she realizes that Lene is in love with her Botho, she shakes her head sadly: that's bad. We have already had this warning: Frau Dörr, the neighbour, who also has a 'past', has already insisted *nichts von Einbildung*—'don't delude yourself'. Lene realizes this but she is nonetheless involved emotionally, as is Botho. Fontane has written a story about a liaison which is also a love affair, thus combining the theme of love versus marriage with that of conflicting choice of mate: there are surprisingly few examples of this in realistic fiction, and no other, I think, even in Fontane. His marvellous power of representing intimate emotion by external descriptions of events (he is a very reticent writer) depicts the idyllic happiness of the lovers through the quiet of the Dörrs' garden, or the secluded calm of Hankels Ablage—to which, however, steamerloads of tourists come in their hundreds, and only Botho's wealth, we realize, takes them there on their own.

Botho's social position is present even in the most idyllic, the most intimate moments. Of course this is a personal story, in the sense that all novels are personal stories, but the persons have no autonomous existence: social forces operate through them. And when the inevitable happens, and marriage and respectability call, what then happens to the mistress? Marriage, we must realize, is no mere form in this world: the wives expect to be treated like companions, and simply to continue the affair would demand a degree of hypocrisy (even of skill) that men like Botho do not possess. To defy society and marry is not seriously considered: that would be one kind of story, but it is not the kind that interests Fontane, sober chronicler of how 'the so-called top layer of Society' actually behaves.

Is a compromise possible? Very carefully—even schematically—Fontane inserts a conversation towards the end of the book to show that it is not. Botho's friend Rexin loves his mistress Henriette—'or, to show you just how I feel about it, I love my black Jette'. By temperament (and for moral reasons too, though he is too modest to lay claim to these) he is monogamous; but he knows he could not marry her. 'I couldn't do that to my parents; and I have no wish to leave the service at 27 to be a cowboy in Texas, or a waiter on a Mississippi Steamboat.' *Das Herkommen bestimmt sein Tun*. And so he proposes a compromise: a union without marriage, a permanent liaison. Botho, who's begun by laughing at him, is by now thoroughly in earnest, and urges him against this. It will not work: he will be pulled in one direction or the other, his career and family will be ruined or become intolerable to him, or else he will have to give up his black Jette. Relationships in which binding and loosing come in the same hour are not the worst; the worse are these disastrous attempts at compromise.

So there is only one solution: when the time comes, to put an end to one's 'relationship', as society expects, as most of the young men do without a qualm, but as Botho, and now Rexin, so desperately do not want to do. If this is the end of their happiness then, as Lene says, we'll have to live without happiness (*Dann lebt man ohne Glück*). 'Nothing that has happened,' says Botho to Rexin, 'can be annihilated; a picture that is buried in the soul never fades completely, never completely vanishes.' The careful account of just what is left for Botho and Lene, each married to an affectionate, a much more 'suitable' partner, gives the book its quiet firm honesty. Fontane the realist has not joined the marvellous propaganda war for romantic love.

All this makes Fontane sound an extremely conservative novelist. Since he was a man of liberal views who (especially in later life, when the novels were written) showed strong democratic, even radical, sympathies,[62] this would suggest a tension between author and tale that is, after all, not unknown in literary history. It will be useful to look at another example, and I choose his most admired novel, *Effi Briest*. It too is the story of a *mariage de convenance*. Effi is married at the age of 20 to Baron Instettin—called in from romping with her girl friends to be introduced to this stiff, courteous suitor—'older than you' her mother explains, 'which on the whole is fortunate'. What she does not mention to Effi, what Fontane adds to give an ironic dimension to this very proper marriage, is that he had been an unsuccessful suitor of her own, who has waited docilely until her daughter is ready for him. The parents had the best of intentions in giving their daughter to 'an upright man, of character and position', but they brushed aside too easily the impulsive, affectionate temperament, the longing for warmth and distraction, that the correctness of a well-bred Prussian civil servant could not satisfy. If Fontane had chosen to join the propaganda war, he would have found her a romantic young lover—as for instance Meredith did for his heroine in the partly similar situation of *Lord Ormont and his Aminta*; Fontane, who like a good realist took his plots less from tradition and more from life, found her a middle-aged rake, a good comrade whose sense of honour enabled him to help a friend and, five minutes later, to deceive him, all with delightful bonhomie. With his usual reticence, Fontane tells us virtually nothing of the affair, but its emotional importance to Effi, along with her hatred of what she is doing, are evident. What we are told a good deal about is the subsequent discovery, through a pure accident, by Instettin, and his decision to disown his wife and fight a duel with her seducer. It is this decision that we are meant to see as parallel to Botho's decision to marry Käthe. Instettin feels no wish for revenge; it all happened six years ago, and commonsense as much as compassion might lead him to let the matter drop. But in a long debate, first with himself, then with his friend Wüllersdorf, he finds that he cannot. *Das Herkommen bestimmt unser Tun*, Botho said: *man gehört einem Ganzen an*— we are part of a whole—is the corresponding remark in *Effi Briest*. Instettin's life will be full of situations in which people will know what he did—or didn't do—and judge him for it; if he doesn't fight Crampas, every time he finds himself in the same company as Wüllersdorf he will feel obliged to glance at him to see if he is smiling wryly. It leaves his life joyless, but he has to follow his *Herkommen*.

Fontane would not have been surprised to learn that by the 1970s both the duel and the arranged match have totally disappeared; he knew that even in his own time he was depicting social processes that did not apply to the whole society. Much of the power of his novels lies in their account of the defence mechanisms of an apparently secure privileged group, that will not let Botho marry Lene, that pays lip-service to romance but (in *Frau Jenni Treibel*) insists that a merchant family must marry money. The stratagems succeed, good society is safe, but the existence of such powerful mechanisms imply the reality of the threat.

Romance and Real Life

This chapter has argued that the clash between the two forms of marriage choice is mirrored in the contrast between the two main literary modes, romance and realism: the former taking sides clearly, the latter incorporating an uncertain and divided preference. The argument is complete, but the chapter needs an epilogue.

Wooing and wedlock in literature differ in two ways from what the historians tell us: not only in being fictitious, but also in treating individual cases fully. The historian whose aim is to perceive social patterns will treat particular instances cavalierly, collecting as many as possible and taking from them only what is relevant to his analysis. To set literature against life, do we not need to see actual wooings unfold in front of us with something of the fullness of a novel?

The material, for earlier centuries, is not easy to find, but I have two examples to offer. Anne Lady Halklett, who died in 1699, left an autobiography containing a triple love story.[64] John Constable's wooing of Maria Bicknell lasted from 1800 to 1816, and is well documented in his correspondence. Here are two stories that really happened, which contrast chronologically and in the protagonist's temperament—and, if they were fiction, we would also add, in *genre*.

There were three men in Anne Murray's life: Mr Howard, son of Lord Howard, who courted her when she was 22; Colonel Brampton, a royalist agent, whom she was drawn to for his loyalty to the king and his constant flirting with danger, and whom she considered herself engaged to for some years; and Sir James Halklett, a widower with two children, whom she finally married at the age of 34. The three affairs have their romantic elements, most of all the first.

Mr H. (as she calls him) did not fall in love at first sight ('he was half a year in my company before I discovered anything of a particular inclination for me') but, as if to make up for that, there were premonitions: 'before ever I saw him severalls did tell me that there would be something more than ordinary betwixt him and me'. He wooed her in secret, then was able to talk his father round, but her mother (a widow) was violently opposed to the match. It is not easy to see why: it represented a social rise for Anne, Lord Howard was willing, and her objection that Lord Howard's fortune was small enough for him to need to find a wealthier bride for his eldest son sounds implausible from her. It looks as if she was piqued because she 'had absolutely discharged my having a thought of allowing such an address'. Whatever the reason, she was not only implacable but also vindictive. Anne was not allowed to sleep alone: 'my sister's woman was to be my guardian'—just like Clarissa. When Lord Howard renewed his proposals 'my mother's anger against me increased to that height, that for fourteen months she never gave me her blessing, nor never spoke to me but when it was to reproach me; and one day said with much bitterness she did hate to see me'. That Capulet's fury with Juliet is partly caused by his realization that she has an independent will (even, simply, an independent life) that he had not been aware of, is a plausible though rather modern suggestion; here, in a story from real life, it seems the obvious explanation.

Anne had not (she claims) encouraged Mr Howard, for she did not believe children should defy their parents. Indeed, she feels she must respect even Lord Howard's wishes: he had sent for his son out of France, hoping to find him a rich wife, and 'it would be high ingratitude in me to do anything to hinder such a design'. She was clearly a devout and submissive child, and there is no doubt of the genuine distress she felt at her mother's treatment of her. Yet at the same time she had a romantic streak worthy of a ballad heroine. Her mother having threatened her with dire consequences if she saw Mr Howard again, she granted him an interview blindfold! Even ten years later, when Colonel Brampton insisted on knowing whether she was married to Sir James Halklett, she got out of an awkward situation by saying out loud 'I am' and secretly adding 'not'. There is no contradiction between her respectable piety and this sort of equivocation: in the individual as in society, romance is the reverse side of filial obedience.

It is sad to report that the affair with Mr Howard ended as the cynics would have predicted. He persisted for a while, despite the difficulties, and even told her that he was visiting all the young ladies about the town in order to make his friends think he had forgotten her, but swore he would never marry anyone else. Four months later came the news that he was married. She reacted with dignity. 'Is this the man for whom I have suffered so much? Since he hath made himself unworthy my love, he is unworthy my anger or concern.' Her greatest distress was her mother laughing at her. Yet poetic justice was not absent after all. Her maid Miriam cursed Mr Howard's bride in language that could come from *King Lear*: 'Give her, O Lord, dry breasts, and a miscarrying womb,' and 'it seems the Lord thought fit to grant her request'. Not only were her children stillborn, but the marriage was not happy: I do not think there are any traces of satisfaction in the words with which Anne records this fact.

If her first affair was romance in the modern sense, her second was romance in the older. Colonel Brampton enlisted her help in the rescue of the Duke of York from prison (game of hide-and-seek as decoy; woman's dress as disguise). He was imprisoned under the Commonwealth, and escaped by pouring aqua fortis on his prison bars and letting himself down with a rope of bedclothes—which broke. Later he became a double agent. There seems no doubt that Anne was strongly attracted to him, and the cloak-and-dagger style of adventure must have been part of his charm. Her mother was dead by now, but there was still an obstacle to their marrying, for Colonel Brampton had a wife alive, from whom he was estranged.

He kept discovering (or pretending) that she was dead, then discovering (or admitting) that she was alive after all. Anne kept her faith in his sincerity, and thought her family and friends prejudiced against him, and it is impossible to make out the truth. There was even a duel between Brampton and her brother-in-law, in which the latter was badly wounded. This naturally distressed her, and she records that she never approved of duels, but all the same 'I had a satisfaction to know so worthy a person as my brother owned a concern for me'. In the end, it seemed clear that the wife was alive, and her little equivocation (which took place at their last interview) cut short what was perhaps going to be a proposal for an irregular union. She was better informed about the situation than Jane Eyre.

Her third lover, Sir James Halklett, must have been older than she was, and Lawrence Stone sees this as a sober conclusion to her romantic life: he describes him as 'her patient elderly suitor'. This is not the figure he cuts in her autobiography. What is most striking in her account is his persistence. When she told him that she considered herself engaged to Colonel Brampton he did not, as she expected, lose interest in her: 'I was in an error when I believed he loved me at an ordinary rate, for it was never more visible than when he had least hopes of a recompense.' He changed to 'virtuous friendship', then back to a wooer when he discovered that Brampton's wife was alive. It took him a long time (about four years) to break down her resistance: it is not clear how far this was a reluctance to marry, how far it was religious scruple (Sir James made a marked step forward when he got a clergyman they both respected to tell her she ought to yield), and how far she was emotionally involved with Brampton even after she had given him up: two pages are missing from the manuscript at what might be a crucial point in the story— just after she has been told it is now public knowledge that the wife is living. 'Oh! (said I, with a sad sigh,) is my misfortune so soon divulged.' If she tore out any pages herself, surely these would be the ones.

Since Anne married Sir James, and appears to have lived happily with him, she may have presented his wooing with more enthusiasm than it aroused (or sprang from) at the time. She does not even tell us that he was a widower, and the mention of his daughters comes as a shock to the modern reader. It would be tempting to see her third affair as *a mariage de convenance*, a settling into middle-age contentment after the two versions of romance. The hagiographical life of Lady Halklett[65] suggests such an interpretation, since it omits Mr Howard completely and Colonel Brampton almost completely (mentioning that Anne's visits to him on business of intrigue aroused unjustified scandal, but breathing no word of any attachment), and is very fulsome on the piety and mutual affection of Sir James and his lady; but she does not tell the story that way: Sir James's persistence is not made to sound very different from Mr Howard's. Perhaps she had not read enough romances to know that true lovers must neither grow old nor turn into husbands.

We naturally assume that the adventures of romance are part of the propaganda: all those coincidences and all that excitement—are they not literature's twopence-coloured tribute to the love match, a lurid pattern imposed on drab reality to make marrying more interesting? It gives us pause to see that Lady Halklett's story compares, for adventure, very creditably with that of Juliet.

Have we moved into a more sober age by 1800? Or are we, with Constable, among the sobrieties of bourgeois culture? Or is it just a contrast of temperaments, or simple accident, that makes his love story so different? He met Maria Bicknell at the house of her grandfather, Dr Durand Rhudde, rector of East Bergholt, where the Constables lived, in 1800: he was 24, she was 12. In 1809 he 'avowed' his love for her and then followed a courtship of 7 years. The Bicknells were prominent in the Law (Charles Bicknell, Maria's father, was solicitor to the Prince Regent) and the Rhuddes were prominent in the Church (Dr Rhudde held two livings, was Chaplain to George III, and lived in grand style). To that family an unsuccessful painter (and a landscape painter to boot, who disliked the more dignified and remunerative genre of portraiture), son of the local miller, did not seem a good connexion; and the match was opposed on the grounds that Constable was too poor to support her adequately. Maria returned his affection but refused to disobey her father. They met, but not too clandestinely; they corresponded, but not too often. Sometimes she rebuked him for not writing; more often, for writing too much. Mr Bicknell varied between vague disapproval and forbidding Constable the house. In 1816 Constable's patience was exhausted, and since they were making no progress towards acceptance by Maria's father and grandfather, he insisted on getting married forthwith. Maria continued to suggest that it was not too late to be prudent and wait longer, but on 2 October 1816 they were married by Constable's friend Fisher, with no members of either family present. The groom was 40, the bride 28.[66]

Here is the stuff of novels: the course of this true love did not run smooth, and we can study the obstacles. And here too is the stuff of social history: one example, useless for the general picture, like all single examples, but essential if we are to put some flesh on the bones of history.

We can begin by noticing a variation on the stock situation. The main opposition to Constable came not from Maria's father but from her grandfather. This is a variant that any novelist might have been pleased with: the normal distribution of power is, as it were, elongated. Dr Rhudde is powerful, domineering and old: he was 80 when the quarrel was at its height, and lived to 85. The age difference between him and

Maria is as great as between Capulet and Juliet, but there is a buffer generation in between. His behaviour is very like Capulet's, even to saying that he 'considered Maria no longer his grand-daughter'. His wealth and his authority in the village had clearly produced an authoritarian character who enjoyed exercising power, and even enjoyed keeping others waiting for his decisions. Under his shadow, his son-in-law appears a pathetic figure, stern towards his daughter but compliant to the old patriarch with legacies to dispense (a complication for poor Bicknell was that one way for Dr Rhudde to exercise his displeasure was to leave his money to the family of his other daughter, so that not only Maria but her sisters would suffer). Constable seems to have felt some contempt for the 'stupid apathy' of his father-in-law, and for his lack of dignity in his dealings with Dr Rhudde; and it may well be that Maria, for all her affection and respect for her father, saw it too. It is she who provides the most vivid detail: after she had agreed to go ahead with the wedding she made another effort with her father, but 'he merely says that without the Doctor's consent, he shall neither retard, or facilitate it, complains of poverty and so on—but I will hasten to a more pleasing scene'.

Next, we can notice a perhaps half-conscious assumption by all those taking part. Maria's family, though trying to prevent the marriage, do not seem to have had any other suitor in mind; if they thought of producing one when Maria was cured of Constable they were surely leaving things rather late. And Constable had no other woman in mind: he did not fall in love with Maria till he was in his thirties, there is no suggestion of a previous love, and he described her (in a letter that sounds urgent enough—even angry enough—to be truthful) as 'the only woman I ever loved in the world'. If they had not married then John almost certainly and Maria quite probably would have stayed single. Of John's two brothers and three sisters, only one married; of the six of his seven children who reached adulthood, only one married; too many of Mr Bicknell's children died young to make a corresponding calculation meaningful for them, but this brief dash of statistics seems to confirm what the story suggests, that we have here a subculture that does not necessarily expect marriage.

Novel-readers, however, do expect it. We may be kept guessing who Emma Woodhouse and Esther Summerson are going to marry, but we never doubt *that* they are. The cases when a novelist disappoints this expectation are rare, and have a special flavour. There is a good example in *The Virginians*. Why does only one of the Warrington brothers marry? They each fall in love with one of the daughters of Colonel Lambert. George marries Theo but Harry, who had earlier met and loved Hetty, is not allowed to have her. He has to make his career, of course; but why, as he does this, should he have to make his way back to

America, and then marry Fanny Mountain, daughter of his mother's companion, more or less out of pity? It is clear that Fanny is not really good enough for him; and even when he is left a widower and the young female reader feels that at last her thirst for romance will be quenched— there is Hetty, who has stayed obligingly and sadly single to wait for him, and to be a second wife of your now middle-aged lover is at any rate better than nothing—even then Thackeray does not let them marry.

The case of Trollope's Lily Dale is similar. Jilted by Adolphus Crosbie in *The Small House at Allington*, she ends the novel a spinster. When the worthy Johnny Eames makes a further effort to win her in *The Last Chronicle of Barset* his suit is supported by all the members of her family, who share the reader's expectation that her unfortunate experience must be, if not wiped out, at any rate appeased by marrying the other man— almost as if the plot function of being jilted by the cad is to reward the devoted admirer. Lily has a kind of justification—she still, in some sense, loves Adolphus (though in a very mild sense, in this respectable treatment); but the reader is disappointed, sad, and even frustrated, and that was Trollope's intention:

> I know in what college I'll take my degree, and I wish they'd let me write the letters after my name, as the men do.... O.M. for Old Maid.[67]

In both these cases we have not so much the rejection as the abandonment of the convention. No fresh factor, no intrusive knowledge or feeling from the real world, enters the novel and thrusts the convention aside. Both novelists are thinking primarily in terms of the effect on their readers. To build up the expectations of romance and then decide, for a change, to disappoint them is (really) to remain within the convention, using its impact as a way of controlling (though differently) your reader's responses.

> He did not break his heart. Cupid's arrows, ladies, don't bite very deep into the tough skins of gentlemen of our age; though, to be sure, at the time of which I write, my brother was still a young man, being little more than fifty. Aunt Het is now a staid little lady with a voice of which years have touched the sweet chords, and a head which Time has powered over with silver.[68]

This pathos reinforces the convention of romance, for it depends on it. When there is a feeling abroad that too many love stories have ended happily, then the intelligent rather world-weary novelist (like Thackeray) or the craftsman looking for variations (like Trollope) might decide it is time for a change. Hence the feeling that he is taking an almost perverse pleasure in disappointing his readers.

This seems to be a change wholly explicable in terms of the development of the *genre*; and for a long time I regarded it as a piece of self-contained literary history, a useful illustration of how conventions could be manipulated for reasons that have nothing to do with social forces. The case of Constable has reminded me that this view is oversimplified, for some readers at least would have been aware that the convention never had corresponded fully to reality. Constable's sister Mary, who died unmarried in 1865, could have read *The Virginians* and (just) *The Small House at Allington*; plenty of other staid little ladies with heads which Time had powered over with silver must have read both. Their disappointment at the endings must have consisted of a mixture of feelings it is now hard for us to recapture: frustration of their expectation as novel-readers, plus something more like satisfaction at the recognition that the affectionate and well-meaning could end up graduating O.M.

What did John and Maria think about love? Here we have a situation in which the clash between love and marriage emerges in the clearest way possible: a quarrel between the bride and her father the night before the wedding, and a ceremony with none of the family present. Yet when we turn to what the couple believed we do not find any of the extreme romantic positions. Not only does Maria begin with conventional expressions of filial obedience, and show a constant dislike to arranging meetings in a way that might look like scheming, they both held a view of love that saw no contrast with reason and social responsibility. Thus Constable writes:

> How much I regret the absence of her who never sees me (even in this unpropitious scene) without a smile of affection and kindness—surely that heart which never meets me without benignity and love must prove a lasting solace and comfort to me in future.[69]

This is not the irresponsibility of ecstasy but a sober expectation of happy life together. With a sobriety that would be striking even in Jane Austen, he congratulates himself 'on being capable of loving one who is so virtuous, wise and just'. He shows her letters to his mother, assuming (rightly) that she will not mind; and indeed his mother was an active ally in the long (unsuccessful) effort to bring Dr Rhudde round.

Both lovers accept the responsibilities of marriage, and see it not only as the climax of wooing (which we have seen to be the romantic view) but as an event in the history of the larger family. John decides to inform the intransigent Dr Rhudde in the most respectful manner about the wedding because 'the very idea of a sneak into the family is shocking'. It is important that they enter on their life together with clear consciences. Constable finds himself jealous of the happiness of his friend

Hurlock who 'told me of the great joy he has experienced from the moment of his wedded life, and of the respectable member of society he had consequently become'. And there is one very revealing indication of how the couple (if they had lived long enough) would have behaved to their own children. When Dr Rhudde eventually died and did despite everything leave Maria her share, Constable wondered whether to settle it on her and the children. Evidently Maria 'had expressed a dislike to settling anything upon children as it went to render them independent of their parents'.

The case for the marriage of propriety is linked with financial realism. The heroine who sweeps it aside makes fine speeches on how she would rather starve than not obey her heart, either with the author's approbation (Florence Dombey) or mockery (Marianne Dashwood) or ambivalence (Ethel Newcome): someone standing by puts the case for a little shrewdness, as we have seen Lady Kew did to Ethel. With the Constables that was not necessary, since the shrewdness came from Maria.

> I had better not write to you any more, at least *till I can coin*, we should both of us be bad subjects for poverty, should we not? Even Painting would go on badly, it could not survive in domestic worry.[70]

The elegant realism of that is unmistakable, and the rest of the letter suggests that she is fighting back her tears as she writes. It is harder to be sure of the tone of what may be a very revealing remark three years later: 'indeed, my dear John, people cannot live now upon four hundred a year'.

What we find in the Constable story is the situation for romantic love but surprisingly little of the sentiment. There is however one sentiment present that could also follow from the situation: not defiance, but ecstasy, not irrationality, but sadness. At times Maria strikes a note of *tristesse majestueuse* that is more moving than anything else in the correspondence. She is not a Marianne but an Elinor, almost a Bérénice.

And even the situation is only there in outline: for there is one other element missing from this story, and that is plot. Why did they get married, after waiting seven years? It is not easy to find an answer to this, except to say that Constable had had enough. The feeling that time was passing and they had been fools to leave things too long does not appear until 1816, the very year of the marriage; and nothing in particular precipitates it. To see the comparative shapelessness of a real-life story like this is to see the case for plot, as a way of pointing up the essentials of a situation. A novelist would have devised an act by Mr Bicknell or Dr Rhudde that would (ironically) provoke the marriage it was intended to hinder; or set in motion far earlier an attempt by Constable that eventually overcame the obstacles; or (depending on the kind of novelist) deliberately make it the result of accident when design had foundered. All these would be ways of reading the situation that remain silent in the actual story. History is not as shapely as fiction.

4

Married Love

This chapter is concerned with the high view of married love that is evident in English society from the sixteenth century, and its relation to the literary tradition: particularly with whether it brought into being a counter-tradition to that which saw love and marriage in contest. The subject is vast, and I shall concentrate on three historical moments: the seventeenth century, the Victorian age, and a particular moment in the twentieth century represented by Lawrence, in each case setting against each other the ideological statements on married love, and the evidence of imaginative literature. I hope this method will lose less in thoroughness than it will gain in particular illumination.

Protestant Marriage

The Anglican Prayer Book proposes three purposes of marriage: the procreation of children, the avoidance of fornication, and mutual society, help and comfort. No view of marriage can omit the first two, which follow from the fact that human beings have sexual drives, and sex produces children. A particular conception of marriage therefore depends on the third: the more importance is given to it, the higher the expectations of what marriage means. Historians of Puritanism are agreed that the Puritans regarded marriage with a new warmth and set especial store on fellowship and mutual comfort.[1] Stone even suggests that their zeal for matrimony softened their firm insistence on paternal authority.[2] Here is William Perkins:

> Marriage was made and appointed by God himself, to be the fountain and seminary of all other sorts and kinds of life, in the Commonwealth and in the Church.[3]

Thomas Becon, instead of insisting that there is no marrying or giving in marriage in Heaven, describes matrimony as ordained of God 'and that not in this sinful world, but in paradise, that most joyful garden of pleasure', and continues with a very full account of the high delights of mutual consolation:

> Wherein one man and one woman are coupled and knit together in one flesh and body in the fear and love of God, by the free, loving, hearty and

good consent of them both, to the intent that they two may dwell together, as one flesh and body of our will and mind in all honesty, virtue and godliness, and spend their lives in the equal partaking of all such things, as God shall send them with thanksgiving.[4]

This celebration of marriage involved an explicit rejection of Popish austerity. Thomas Gataker attacks the Church of Rome for considering marriage dishonourable. Priestly celibacy involves not only a contempt for (or at best a toleration of) sex, it leads, in a world where men (including priests) are imperfect, to preferring whoredom to wedlock; and the Puritans like to tell stories such as this:

> Witness Pope Honorius his Legate, who in a synod here at London, having inveighed most bitterly against Priests' Marriage, and made a solemn Decree against it, was the very next night taken himself with a Whore.[5]

Gataker's account of what a good wife brings lengthens the list from three items to five: 1. Society: 2. Assistance ('a help meet for him'): 3. Comfort and Solace: 4. Issue: 5. Remedy against incontinence. The last two are familiar: here they are not only relegated to the last places, they are preceded by an expanded version of 'mutual society, help and comfort', divided into three separate headings.

What is the place of sex in this high valuation of marriage? It is hard to be sure if the comfort and solace are physical; as it is hard to know what Gataker means when he qualifies the fifth gift, remedy against incontinence: 'a benefit likewise that before Man's fall was not, because then there was no need for it'.[6] If there was no sex before the Fall, then Gataker is of the school that regards it as a concession to man's fallen nature; but he may of course merely be reminding us that there was no fornication before the Fall because there were no other women. Elsewhere Gataker maintains that it is the purpose of Satan to persuade us that 'in the kingdom of God there is nothing but sighing and groaning and fasting and prayer', whereas 'in His House there is marrying and giving in marriage, ... feasting and rejoicing'.[7] It looks on the whole as if married love was physically as well as spiritually delightful: the Puritans were not puritanical about sex.

None of the Puritans has left us a more eloquent statement of the blessing of married love than Milton. In his four divorce tracts, he sets forth his belief in 'meet and happy conversation' as the chiefest end of marriage:

> God in the first ordaining of marriage taught us to what end he did it, in words expressly implying the apt and cheerful conversation of man with woman, to comfort and refresh him against the evil of solitary life, not mentioning the purpose of generation till afterwards, as being but a secondary end in dignity, though not in necessity.[8]

Milton likes to list the purposes of marriage, arranging them in order of importance. On one occasion he lists three: 'godly society; next, civil; and thirdly, that of the marriage bed'.[9] On another there are five:

In matrimony, there must be first a mutual help to piety: next, to civil fellowship of love and amity; then, to generation; so to household affairs; lastly, the remedy of incontinence.[10]

There is no important difference between the two lists: what they have in common is giving first place to companionship—first in godliness, then in civil, or secular, fellowship.

We cannot miss the irony that this high ideal of marriage is found in a defence of divorce. Milton's reputation has never recovered from the fact that he began writing his first divorce pamphlet six weeks after his marriage to Mary Powell; and the note of personal involvement is unmistakable in his account of 'what a violent cruel thing it is to force the continuing of those together whom God and nature in the gentlest end of marriage never joined':

Then enters Hate; not that hate that sins, but that which only is natural dissatisfaction, and the turning aside from a mistaken object.[11]

'Not that hate that sins'. Milton is very sure that it wasn't his fault, that the husband who is disappointed in his wife (and he was disappointed with the intensity of all his enormous idealism) is to be commiserated, not reproved. And so, corresponding to the listing of the ends of marriage in order of importance, comes a reverse listing of the reasons for divorce: it is quite wrong to grant divorce only for adultery or 'frigidity' (which I take it means impotence)—the incompatibilities of the body—and not the incompatibilities of the mind, which are of far more weight.

It is an irony, in terms of Milton's biography, that his plea for divorce produced his defence of marriage, but in a broader sense it is not ironic at all: we can even say that he was ahead of his time. It is only in the twentieth century that we have come to associate the idealization of monogamy with a high frequency of divorce, but the connexion now seems almost inevitable: the greater the emotional investment made in marriage, the higher the chance of disappointment. It took society three hundred years to realize this and embody it in permissive legislation: Milton's combination of egoism, sophistry and individualism led him to see it in a way that shocked his contempoararies.

Milton's views on marriage are interesting enough for their own sake; but their interest is of course immeasurably increased because he wrote the first great imaginative expression of the new ideal. *Paradise Lost* is known to be a poem about sin and temptation, about God's Providence, man's free will and Satan's heroic defiance; what is not so often remembered is that it is the great English poem of marriage.

Adam and Eve

What was it like in Eden? There is an inescapable paradox in the attempt to think about unfallen man: to describe Adam in Paradise it is necessary to use the language we understand, to draw comparisons and terminology from the post-lapsarian world. If the bliss of Paradise is fully comprehensible to us, how does it differ from ordinary, post-lapsarian happiness: if it was beyond any joys we can now know, how can it be described?[12]

The union of Milton's Adam and Eve is the model marriage of the seventeenth-century Protestant, yet it is also a union such as no fallen mortal can attain. Fortunately Milton leans more to the first half of this paradox than to the second; otherwise, *Paradise Lost* would be a shadow-poem, never speaking to our condition, and would have to be written in hints and guesses. There can be a poetry of hints and guesses, but no one was less fitted to write it than Milton.

So if we approach this marriage with the prayer book in hand, or Perkins, or Gataker, we can see it as for the procreation of children, the avoidance of fornication, and mutual society, help and comfort. Procreation is present from the beginning: they address each other, or are named by Milton, as 'Mother of Mankind', 'Our primitive great Sire', and they look forward to the time when more hands will aid them in their gardening. Avoidance of fornication is clearly not a problem, but its pre-lapsarian equivalent, the satisfying of sexual desire, is presented in positive terms as the 'Rites Mysterious of connubial love'; and in his hymn to wedded love Milton, forgetting for the moment that we are in Eden, writes

> By thee adulterous lust was driv'n from men
> Among the bestial herds to range.   (IV.753)

It was a conscious decision on Milton's part to make the love of Adam and Eve sexual, rejecting the tradition that saw sex as the consequence of the Fall. Unless he had done this, he could not have offered it as an ideal of marriage that meant anything to fallen readers. In one of his angry intrusions of personal opinion he dismisses the opposite view with contempt:

> Whatever Hypocrites austerely talk
> Of purity and place and innocence ...
> Our Maker bids increase, who bids abstain
> But our Destroyer, foe to God and Man?   (IV.744)

This is Gataker's point. It is the devil who suggests that in the kingdom of God there is nothing but sighing and groaning, fasting and prayer: in Paradise there was marrying, feasting and sexual delight.

But it is the third purpose of marriage, mutual comfort, that, in the best Puritan tradition, is the most important. When Adam pleads with God for a companion, he does so not because he feels the bodily need of a sexual mate, but because no complete happiness is possible in solitude; his dominion over all the living creatures is insufficient to relieve his solitude, not because he cannot couple with them, but because

> Of fellowship I speak
> Such as I seek, fit to participate
> All rational delight, wherein the brute
> Cannot be human consort.   (VIII.389)

The relation between such fellowship and sexual union is not one of contrast but of hierarchy: they function together, as higher and lower. The lines that state this most clearly are not very happy poetically, since they hover on the edge of being coy:

> he, she knew, would intermix
> Grateful digressions, and solve high dispute
> With conjugal Caresses, from his lip
> Not words alone pleased her.   (VIII.54)

This is from the explanation of why Eve chooses to retire when Adam and Raphael begin their discussion of astronomy: not because she is not interested, but because she prefers to hear it all from Adam. Their intellectual companionship is not that of equals, but is based on clear (and reiterated) male supremacy.

> My author and disposer, what thou bidst
> Unargued I obey; so God ordains,
> God is thy law, thou mine: to know no more
> Is woman's happiest knowledge and her praise.   (IV.635)

I take it that for Milton's contemporaries this, though clearly not a high point of the poem, was a dignified piece of exposition, whereas I doubt whether any attentive modern reader, unless in a state of male chauvinist nostalgia, can enjoy it much. That genuine companionship can be based on a hierarchical relationship is, after all, inescapable even in our democratic culture and it is a parody of democratic ideology to deny it: parent and child, pupil and teacher, are ineluctably hierarchical. But that some relationships, previously hierarchical, can be equal, is of course the achievement of democracy, and the husband–wife relationship is the supreme example of this. This is part of the theme of the next chapter; for the moment, reading *Paradise Lost*, we can notice that it presents a poetic problem: how do we respond to the dignified exposition of a dead doctrine? There are three main answers: that we respond to the 'poetry' by ignoring the

116   *Married Love*

content, that such poetry can mean nothing to us today, or that we respond by applying the feeling to a parallel content that we still accept. All three have some truth in them. The first can be formalist to the point of preciosity, the second gives away too much, the third (to which I incline) is too prone to rewrite the poetry.

The union of Adam and Eve is a Protestant marriage in the best sense, setting high value on the human relationship which is one of 'godly society, next civil, and thirdly that of the marriage bed'. How is this union actually shown to us? To understand this, we will do best to relate the presentation to the three central ideas of Nature, Reason and Tradition.

Marriage is natural because all creatures couple. Sex is not unique to mankind, therefore a full acceptance of sex (and the acceptance in *PL* is, we have seen, full—fuller than in the divorce tracts) is likely to have implications of naturalism: the view, that is, that man is essentially no different from the rest of nature. Even to us naturalism is reductive— how much more to the hierarchical thought of the seventeenth century. It is therefore necessary to give human sexuality a special and superior place. Of course this can be done by the doctrine we have already mentioned, that for us sex is not the highest aim of marriage, and Milton does maintain this

> —Neither her outside formed so fair, nor aught
> In procreation common to all kinds ...
> So much delights me as these graceful acts
>   ... which declare unfeigned
> Union of mind, or in us both one soul.   (VIII.595)

Yet it is out of the naturalism that much of the finest poetry is made:

>   or they led the vine
> To wed her Elm; she spoused about him twines
> Her marriageable arms, and with her brings
> Her dower th'adopted clusters, to adorn
> His barren leaves.   (V.215)

How do we read these extraordinary lines? In some poets, we would treat them as a conceit: an opportunity to enjoy the dazzling skill of the poet by pretending to regard the vine as married to the Elm, enjoying it all the more as he spins out the metaphor ever further. This is to see the poetry as a game, and that, for such a committed work as *Paradise Lost*, is impossible. Milton does not play games with doctrine. We have then to read the lines as saying that marriage is found in nature, that all these parallels are possible because the human institution is based on our resemblance to the creatures—and that is naturalism, even (perhaps) reductive naturalism.

It is, however, counterbalanced, poetically as well as doctrinally, by the fact that nature itself understands hierarchy: the creatures themselves know that man is their superior. This is clearest in the account of the nuptial bower:

> other creature here
> Beast, bird, insect or worm durst enter none;
> Such was their awe of man. (IV.703)

Here is the basis for the symbolism of nature. If the plants and animals are imbued with an awareness of the special place of man, then they do not exist just for themselves but to serve or celebrate what is higher. This is so important that it is not possible to conceive of lower creatures existing for themselves alone. Eve looks at the stars and asks

> But wherefore all night long shine these, for whom
> This glorious sight, when sleep hath shut all eyes. (IV.657)

To the biologist, beast, bird, insect, or worm have as much existence as we have; to the astronomer the stars go on shining, for reasons that have nothing to do with us. To call them 'glorious' however is to presuppose a spectator, and so anticipate the answer: which is that 'millions of spiritual creatures walk the earth' even when we are asleep, that the stars are part of a nocturnal service going on all the time.

The relation between marriage and nature in *PL* is, then, ambivalent. Human matrimony is certainly a higher institution than the mating of the beasts, but is most powerfully presented when it is assimilated to natural processes. In a modern poet the effect of this would certainly be reductive; but for Milton nature itself is, as it were, not naturalistic.

This is, in effect, to say that nature is rational; so that it is not possible to distinguish the relation of marriage to nature from our next question, its relation to reason. In theory, this is no problem: unfallen, Adam is a rational creature, and in loving Eve he is carrying out God's plan. Sexual enjoyment is approved by reason, so it will neither excite shame nor threaten to exceed its due place. But for us, who are fallen, sexual feeling is associated with shame, or ungoverned passion, or both. That is why the fallen sexuality of Adam and Eve in Book IX is so much more intense, more powerful, more *real* than that in Eden. A lover whose adoration is governed by reason is traditionally no true lover, as Adam is soberly reminded:

> In loving thou dost well, in passion not,
> Wherein true Love consists not; love refines
> The thoughts, and heart enlarges, hath his seat
> In Reason. (VIII.588)

There is no denying that the unfallen love of Adam and Eve must seem cold to us: the elaborate speeches they make, as befits their station as

universal parents, are clear reminders to the twentieth-century reader
of a stylistic formality no longer with us, and one which certainly
assumes a rational ordering of our relationships. All I would like to point
out is the existence of one surprising anomaly.

Adam and Eve are naked because they do not know shame:

Nor those mysterious parts were then concealed,
Then was not guilty shame, dishonest shame
Of nature's works.   (IV.312)

This is a point in the poem at which Milton is very insistent on the contrast between fallen and unfallen man: launching himself into a long
denunciation of how 'sin-bred' shame has dishonoured all mankind,

And banished from man's life his happiest life,
Simplicity and spotless innocence.   (IV.317)

Why then does Eve blush? Simplicity and spotless innocence should produce none of the inner psychic tension that issues in a blush. The very
fact that Milton can see the blush as part of Eve's charm is testimony
to his own fallen state, but undermines the necessary contrast. Indeed,
the very reverence that describes the sexual organs as 'those mysterious
parts' is fallen: where right Reason governs, there will be no sense of
mystery. In Book V Milton remembered that Eve should not blush. She
is welcoming Raphael, and

Undeckt, save with herself more lovely fair
Than wood-nymph, or the fairest Goddess feigned
Of three that in Mount Ida naked strove,
Stood to entertain her guest from Heaven; no veil
She needed, virtue-proof, no thought infirm
Altered her cheek.   (V.380)

The reason Milton can remember here that she should not blush is
stylistic. He has used one of his similes from classical mythology in a
way that is a favourite with him: delighting in an account of the beauty
of Venus, then telling us how much finer Eve was. Did the three god-
desses blush in front of Paris? I am not sure: at the very least, Milton
is saying that they ought to have, that perhaps they'd have been the
better for a veil—whereas Eve needs no such thing. It does not matter
now if Eve is presented in terms that seem cold, or negative, since the
positive effect of the simile is working in her favour. It is certain now
that Eve is above blushing, not that she is too feeble to blush.

I am delighted that, when not using a simile, Milton made Eve blush:
it is an inconsistency that fallen readers can be grateful for. But it is unfortunate that he made Raphael blush too. Asked whether heavenly spirits

love, and how they express it, he replies 'with a smile that glow'd celestial rosy red'. It was nice to know that there were psychic tensions in unfallen Eve, but why in an angel? To tell us that red is 'Love's proper hue' is totally question-begging: proper to us, yes, but only proper to a wholly rational creature if the blush is quite unlike a human blush. If Raphael is embarrassed about love, are we to grow sceptical of his firm insistence (already quoted) that love hath his seat in Reason?

Those lines were delivered to Adam in rebuke for his excessive praise of Eve, and since that praise was a compliment, of a traditional sort, we can see that the relation of love to Reason is connected to its relation to tradition. Compliment is the art of elevating the person praised to a higher level than we know she ought to occupy. It is the very type of a compliment to say 'Authority and Reason on her wait.' The whole passage is among Milton's most delicate writing—the sort of delicacy we do not normally expect of him.

> Or Nature failed in me, and left some part
> Not proof enough such object to sustain,
> Or from my side subducting, took perhaps
> More than enough: (VIII.534)

after his apology he explains that he knows quite well that she is the inferior, but

> when I approach
> Her loveliness, so absolute she seems
> And in herself complete, so well to know
> Her own, that what she wills to do or say
> Seems wisest, virtuousest, discreetest, best.   (VIII.546)

Lovers who pay compliments are not usually unfortunate enough to have an archangel standing by, to tell them sternly that custom might stale her infinite variety, that she is not really divine, that if

> Wisdom in discourse with her
> Looses discountenanced and like folly shows,   (VIII.552)

then the speaker's judgement is unhinged. It is the nature of a compliment to transgress strict truth; it is the nature of an archangel to assert reason, and insist on truth. Adam's aberration (an anticipation of course of his allowing Eve to persuade him to the Fall) is presented in the language of compliment because that is the traditional language of lovers as we know it; all Raphael needs to do is to draw attention to its extravagance. We may feel on Adam's side (as we may even when he eats the apple) but there is no doubt that Reason is on Raphael's: it has to be, for Adam has been expressing the love we all know, that keeps little company with reason.

There is one other reference to traditional love making, in which the rejection is even clearer and firmer. The hymn to wedded love, after praising the 'perpetual fountain of domestic sweets', contrasts the joys of wedded love with those relationships where true love does not dwell.

> not in the bought smile
> Of harlots, loveless, joyless, unindeared,
> Casual fruition, not in Court *amours*
> Mixed dance, or wanton masque, or midnight ball,
> Or serenade which the starv'd lover sings.   (IV.765)

Here is the whole traditional apparatus of love making, bluntly lumped together: sophisticated courtship and the *amor de loinh* belong with harlotry, all of them contrasted with wedded love. So much for the Troubadours, so much for courtly love.

For Milton, marriage is the opposite to the literary tradition of love—and is preferred to it. In terms of literary history, this is a plain rejection: instead of love's tortured paradoxes, the simple joys of marital consummation. That this is seen as a complex and growing relationship follows from one detail that we might hardly notice until we stop to think: that Adam's description of the wedding ceremony is in the past tense. He describes to Raphael the nuptial bower, the fresh gales and gentle airs, and the song of the nightingale, that were their ceremony and organ music, concluding:

> Thus have I told thee all my state, and brought
> My story to the sum of earthly bliss
> Which I enjoy....   (VIII.521)

Literature is full of weddings: but looking back upon a wedding, from the happiness of married bliss? In this, *PL* was truly innovatory, rejecting tradition and celebrating a different kind of love.

Marrying Laura

In presenting married love as the opposite to the literary tradition, Milton is perfectly orthodox. Damaris Marsham, for instance, in her *Reflections upon Marriage*, propounds a view of marriage choice that avoids the mercenary on the one hand, and the romantic on the other. Questions of money and acres are necessary questions, and those who marry for love find time enough to 'repent their rash folly', but 'he who does not make fellowship the chief inducement of his choice does not deserve a good wife'.[14]

Petrarch loved Laura, and Thomas Gataker, like a good Puritan, loved the wife he was joined to in holy matrimony. Does the second sentiment incorporate any of the first? Is there any connexion between them, except that of simple contrast?

Put in that form, it is not an easy question to answer, for the Puritans were not literary men: Thomas Gataker and William Perkins did not care about Petrarch, perhaps did not even know about him. But we can pursue the connexion, and it amounts to asking about the connexion between society's ideal of marriage, and the literary ideal of love.

To William Gouge love is a duty. It is required of wives,

> and they are required to be lovers of their husbands, as well as husbands to love their wives: so as it is a common mutual duty belonging to husband and wife too: and that is true wedlock, when man and wife are linked together by the bond of love.[15]

Isolde and Phèdre knew this: but their love was not of that kind. It is obvious that Gouge would not have tolerated court amours, but nor would he have felt any enthusiasm for a view of marriage concerned only with child-bearing, sexual satisfaction and domestic duties:

> Under love all other duties are comprised: for without it no duty can be well performed.... It is like fire, which is not only hot in itself, but also conveyeth heat into that which is near it: whence ariseth a reflection of heat from one to another.[16]

Married love is intense and essential, but it is nothing like the drinking of a potion, or a flash of lightning, or the squeezing of a little purple flower. One is tempted to say, in defiance of the most important element in Puritanism, that Gouge does not believe we are fallen: such deep feeling so perfectly controlled by Reason and Duty suggests a pre-lapsarian balance in our nature.

The Puritans are not wholly consistent about this: Gataker's account of married love reintroduces some of the mystery. 'As Faith, so Love cannot be constrained,' he writes: Reason is not after all in control, and this statement would not be out of place among the traditional paradoxes of the love–religion parallel. Gataker continues:

> As there is no affection more forcible; so there is none freer from force and compulsion. The very offer of enforcement turneth it oft into hatred. There are secret links of affection, that no reason can be rendered of: as there are inbred dislikes, that can neither be resolved, nor reconciled.[17]

This is subversive stuff: no wonder it goes on to warn parents that though they may find out a fit wife for their children, they may not be able to direct their children's affections. Had the worthy Thomas Gataker been reading *Romeo and Juliet*, where he would certainly have found out about secret links of affection?

It is touching to find subversion in the Puritan ranks, but for the most part Gataker holds the orthodox view, that married love is a blessing and a duty. Smith, reminding us that women have many faults, asserts

> he which chooseth of them, had need have judgment, and make an Anatomy of their hearts and minds, before he say, 'This shall be mine.'[18]

No love at first sight here, for not all a woman's qualities, Smith insists, are likely to be learned at three or four comings.

How do we distinguish married love from romantic love? It will help to set forth the contrast systematically:

Romantic Love	*Married Love*
Irrational	Rational
Idealizes	Individualizes
Sublimates sex (sometimes)	Accepts sex
Is intensely private, and so	Is publicly known, and so
Seeks solitude or flees Society	Integrated into Society
Rival of Religion	Approved by Religion
Static (and instantaneous)	Developing
Precedes (or is outside) marriage	Follows marriage

To find examples of the first, we will look to literature: but not exclusively, for people believe what they read, and begin to look for (and find!) romantic love in their lives. To find examples of the second we will look to orthodox ideological statements, and to actual behaviour: but not exclusively, for the poets and story-tellers begin, slowly, to depict that too. This depiction will be the subject of the later part of this chapter.

When Benjamin Colman looked round him for a wife he wrote:

> It soon appeared to me that among the many virtuous single gentlewomen of the Town, Madam Sarah Clark, Relict of John Clark, Esq., must be the person to make me and my children happy, if married again. Her Piety, Gravity, Humility, Diligence, Cheerfulness, natural Love (long since) for my children and theirs to her: besides her retired way of living and a small worldly Estate free from all incumbrances, all concurred and moved me to make my Addresses to her.[19]

It is clear which kind of love we are here concerned with. No reader of romances, this—or, if so, he kept them firmly out of his life. His choice is rational, and he knows the reasons: they include, but are not dominated by, considerations of estate. There is no contrast between public and private, none between reason and emotion. Benjamin Colman was a widower, and perhaps had passed the age of romance: we do not, unfortunately, know how he chose his first, but there is no reason, in that sober New England community, to believe that it was very different.

Piety was important to Colman, but it is not difficult to secularize this view of love—as is done, for instance, by Cobbett, whose *Advice to Young Men* offers a sturdy no-nonsense view of marriage that has little truck with romance. He has no time for 'mopers': 'the gaiety is for others, and the moping for the husband'.

> One hour she is capering about, as if rehearsing a jig; and the next, sighing to the motion of a lazy needle, or weeping over a novel: and this is called sentiment! Music indeed! Give me a mother singing to her clean and fat and rosy baby, and making the house ring with her extravagant and hyperbolical encomiums on it. That is the music which is the 'food of love', and not the formal pedantic noises, an affectation of skill in which is nowadays the ruin of half the young couples in the middle rank of life.[20]

This is a bourgeois equivalent to the scorn of Court amours, mixed dance or wanton masque. Cobbett despises women who allow romance and its conventions to influence their conduct: marriage must embody the rational norms of society, not the extravagances of art. Even when it does begin from romance, it can be rescued: he tells a story of a woman who made a runaway match, whose husband went to prison for debt, and who then rose to the occasion:

> I there found also his wife, with her baby, and she, who had never, before her marriage, known what it was to get water to wash her own hands, and whose talk was all about music, and the like, was now the cheerful sustainer of her husband, and the most affectionate of mothers. All the music and all the drawing, and all the plays and romances, were gone to the winds![21]

Life can at any rate rescue us from literature.

If there is a single item, in the lists above, which can serve as a touchstone for the others, it may be the last. Married love does not arrive fully formed: being an individual relationship, it grows and changes. It may therefore be seen as the result rather than the cause of marriage. Mary Astell asserted in the seventeenth century:

> That a woman should not love before Marriage, but only make choice of one whom she can love thereafter; she who has none but innocent affections being easily led to fix them where Duty requires.[22]

The point is important when the partner is still chosen by the parents. No one else can tell us who to fall in love with at first sight: so if romance is the basis of marriage, it must involve self-choice. Rational choice, however, as we saw in the last chapter, can be made by anyone: if the young read too many romances, it had better be done by the parents. This will do no harm to love, if it is the love that grows with marriage.

One of the strongest assertions I know of the contrast between romance and marriage is that of Denis de Rougemont. His argument is vigorous and simple:

> We are in the act of trying out—and failing miserably at it—one of the most pathological experiments that a civilized society has ever imagined, namely, the basing of marriage, which is lasting, upon romance, which is a passing fancy.[23]

Romance and marriage are incompatible because 'it is the very essence of romance to thrive on obstacles, delays, separations and dreams', whereas marriage is designed for 'constant physical proximity to the monotonous present', Hence the high divorce rate. De Rougemont claims that romantic love as the basis for marriage choice is the product of freedom, of the decline of the traditional constraints imposed on individual choice by family and rules: and he sees this situation as exceptional, even unique, among the world's societies. He does not deny to love and romance any function at all in a healthy social order: but it should be only 'the minor and final role of a catalyst, which can disappear with no damage ensuing once the combination has worked by virtue of its presence.'

Much of this case had already been stated in de Rougemont's book on *Passion and Society*[24] under the scornful heading of 'marrying Iseult'. Twentieth-century evasiveness has produced 'a wish to *enjoy* the myth as *cheaply* as possible', to have one's cake and eat it. Its clearest manifestation is seen in American films of the 1920s where 'every plot had to lead up to a final lingering kiss against a background of roses or rich hangings'. Such happy endings are a betrayal of the myth of passion, for love stories need insuperable obstacles to the fulfilment of love; and the point forms part of de Rougemont's large indictment of the spiritual emptiness of our age.

De Rougemont's case clearly has much in common with that argued by this book; but it includes a number of short-cuts and oversimplifications. In the first place, he presents as a historical contrast what is really a generic one. The difference between seeing romantic love as tragic and as leading to marriage is not the difference between the Middle Ages and our own time, nor between the honesty of great literature and the evasiveness of Hollywood films (de Rougemont somehow equates these two differences); it is simply that between two *genres*, that is, two ways of patterning experience. We did not have to wait for Hollywood to see the lovers marry: Rosalind and Orlando are following an ancient pattern of folktale.

Second, de Rougemont's view of the ideology of love is static. Like any *laudator temporis acti* he sees the present in terms of the breakdown of old institutions, rather than their adaptation. When the interlocking kinship roles have weakened, it will be necessary for the couple to find new ways of adjusting to the requirements of marriage, and love, which was once the enemy of those roles, may now take on this function. This is the argument of W. J. Goode's article on 'The Theoretical Importance of Love.' Goode quotes examples that emphasize the irrationality of romantic love, and the inability of other cultures to accept it or even to take it seriously (Samoans laugh at *Romeo and Juliet*: 'why didn't he get another girl?');[25] but at the same time he maintains that it is now an integral part of our cultural values, bound up with 'individualism, freedom and personality growth'. This view is only tenable if romantic love has changed, so that it can perform the function of 'holding a couple together long enough to allow them to begin marriage'. It has now, in other words, become a kind of splint, binding the couple together during the necessary tensions that enable them to grow into a mature relationship.[26]

Let us then make the comparison that de Rougemont considers impossible, and see how much of romantic love can be incorporated into marriage—that is, how far one can marry Iseult. Or, rather, since we are now concerned with the lyric tradition rather than the romances, marry Laura. In the case of love poetry, the relation between the two experiences might, we would expect, be very close: can the love poet drop all his serenading habits when he sings to his wife?

Spenser or Shakespeare?

Spenser's *Amoretti and Epithalamion*, published in 1595, are the first love poems that we know to have been written by a poet to his bride. This ought to make them a crucial event in the transition from the Petrarchan love of the sonneteers to the married love of later times. And yet how could such thoroughly conventional poems be crucial in any transition?

There is no doubt that the poems use all the stock devices, and use them in expected ways. The beloved is a tyranness, the poet humbles himself before her, begging for the favour she is too cruel to grant; he spends his days in 'pining languor'; his rude music cannot 'the dreadful tempest of her wrath appease'; she takes delight in inflicting woe on him; over and over he calls her 'cruel': 'Fair cruel, why are you so fierce and cruel?' He used the love–war conceit, once again in completely conventional form: she is 'sweet warrior', he sues for peace, his powers are weak, her eyes shoot a thousand arrows. He takes images from religion: she is 'divinely wrought', 'of the brood of angels heavenly born', and her eyes are 'likest to the Maker's self'. There is nothing in all this not already addressed to Stella and Delia, or to Petrarch's Laura and Dante's Beatrice.

What then is Spenser doing that is new? 'Spenser's originality,' writes Legouis, 'was this: that he dedicated this verse to a maiden he could and *did* marry in the end.'[27] We know that he married Elizabeth Boyle in June 1594: is the publication of this collection shortly afterwards an invitation to the reader to link the poems to that event? One or two of them suggest links: Sonnet 74 tells us that the lady is named Elizabeth; no. 60 tells us his age; several references tell us that the whole courtship lasted a year and a half. And that is all. If Spenser has made any attempt to attach the book to external events, by means of factual links, it is highly elusive. The shadowy narrative that lies behind the sonnets is even less definite than those behind Sidney's sonnets, or Shakespeare's: there will never be agreement on what the quarrel is which is referred to in sonnet 86 and whether it has anything to do with the separation of sonnets 87–89 (and that with the separation of no. 78). How many contemporary readers can have known (what modern scholars only know thanks to Grosart's researches) whom he married and when? The originality which Legouis attributes to him may be a matter of the dedication only.[28]

There is a second sense, however, in which Spenser has moved from Petrarchanism to marriage, and which does not depend on external evidence at all: that is the fact of publishing them along with the *Epithalamion*. By doing this he has joined two *genres* which, as far as I know, had not been joined before. A wedding song has its own conventions, which go back to Pindar and Catullus (to which Spenser adds some rich Biblical recollections). It is impersonal, celebratory, richly solemn; it has none of the extravagant conceits, none of the posturing, none of the self-abasement of the Petrarchan sonneteers. There is a huge distance between, say:

> Is it her nature or is it her will,
> To be so cruel to an humbled foe?
> If nature, then she may it mend with skill,
> If will, then she at will may will forego.

—with its ingenuity, its mock-lament, its semblance of psychological probing; and the majestic organ-music of

> Open the temple gates unto my love,
> Open them wide that she may enter in,
> And all the posts adorn as doth behove,
> And all the pillars deck with garlands trim ...

'As doth behove' would be a clumsy fill-up in the sonnets; its solemn insistence on decorum is perfectly in place here. *Epithalamion* is not the kind of poetry that most immediately appeals to modern taste: next to the dazzle of Donne, its movement seems stiff, and the solemnity is remote from a public that gets married in registry offices. But next to the over-used conceits of the sonneteers, it rings out clear and true like a bell. It is written to celebrate an occasion, not to show how clever the poet is.

Now cease ye damsels your delights forepast;
Enough is it, that all the day was yours:
Now day is done, and night is nighing fast:
Now bring the bride into the bridal bowers.
Now night is come, now soon her disarray,
And in her bed her lay;
Lay her in lilies and in violets,
And silken curtains over her display,
And odoured sheets, and Arras coverlets.
Behold how goodly my fair love does lie
In proud humility;
Like unto Maia, when as Joue her took,
In Tempe, lying on the flowery grass,
Twixt sleep and wake, after she weary was,
With bathing in the Acidalian brook,
Now it is night, ye damsels may be gone,
And leave my love alone,
And leave likewise your former lay to sing:
The woods no more shall answer, nor your echo ring.

The *Epithalamion* has a unity which no sonnet sequence can have, as we can see from a stanza like this. It is imbued with a sense of movement, of passing from one stage of a ceremony to another. This enables it, too, to have a personal quality beyond anything in the *Amoretti*, for the very fact that it is a public poem, celebrating something so public as a wedding, renders possible the step from public to private, the departure of the attendants, that this stanza so marvellously enacts, moving from the laying of the bride (the last public touch) to the richness of the bed (gifts from the public world) to the tender excitement of 'Behold how goodly my fair love does lie,' in which *the* Bride (still public) can now be seen as *my* love. Back for a moment to the public role of the poet, as he adds the classical similes that are for himself, but for the attendants to overhear; then, polite but firm, telling them it is time to go, 'and leave my love alone', and then finally back to the refrain that ends every stanza, but now in the negative, as if they are straining to hear the woods echoing with the song but all, in their at last achieved intimacy, is now silence.

Here then is the true originality of Spenser's book: a point immediately clear to the reader who knows (and cares) nothing about the poet's life. The sonnets are conventional, but to follow them with so magnificent a wedding song is to place them in a fresh context, to invite

us to reflect that here is a poet who goes through the Petrarchan motions
and then turns out—somehow—to mean it.

This is to change the context in which we read the *Amoretti*, but what
of the sonnets themselves? Do any of them deal with a new kind of love,
made up of complex interrelations rather than conventional adoration?
The best candidate, it seems to me, is no. 86, which is about a quarrel.
Here surely is the stuff of reality: married folk quarrel, Petrarchan lovers
don't. It is not very clear what the quarrel is about: a 'venomous tongue'
has stirred up 'coals of ire' in his love by means of 'false forged lies';
and the more we read the poem, the less we seem to know about it,
for it becomes clearer that it is not dealing with what happened between
the lovers at all:

> Venomous tongue, tipped with vile adder's sting,
> 　of that self kind with which the Furies fell
> 　Their snaky head do comb, from which a spring
> 　of poisoned words and spiteful speeches well. . . .

The poem is a curse on the unnamed third party for stirring up trouble.
It is not concerned with what he said, but with cursing him. It tells us
nothing about him except (once again) in analogies: adder's sting, the
Furies, poisoned spring. The images spring from the poet's indignation,
not from what happened. When it comes to a situation—like a quarrel—
for which understanding depends on information, the poet has no way
of really dealing with it.

This is true of all the poems. If we ask whether Spenser has managed
to write about a love which grows and develops instead of the marvellous
romantic stereotypes, there is no way of answering yes. He may have
wished to: but we cannot know this, for the poetic tradition he is using
does not provide him with the equipment. It is a tradition that deals
in paradoxes and Platonic analogies, similes and conceits, the emotions
of worship, bliss and despair; not in experiences which grow and adapt
to other individuals. To write about these needs a poet who is able to
free himself from the tradition.

What would such a poet be like? We do not have far to look for an
answer, for he was writing at almost exactly the same time:

> Being your slave, what should I do but tend
> Upon the hours and times of your desire?
> I have no precious time at all to spend,
> Nor services to do, till you require.
> Nor dare I chide the world-without-end hour
> Whilst I, my sovereign, watch the clock for you,
> Nor think the bitterness of absence sour
> When you have bid your servant once adieu;

Nor dare I question with my jealous thought
Where you may be, or your affairs suppose,
But, like a sad slave, stay and think of nought
Save, where you are how happy you make those.
  So true a fool is love that in your will,
  Though you do any thing, he thinks no ill.[29]

Shakespeare's sonnets owe as much to tradition as Spenser's. They too are packed with conceits and paradoxes, they make more use of word-play, they use Platonic analogies and logical ingenuities, they arrange their quatrains in series and end with a fine rhetorical effect in the couplet. All Elizabethan readers must have felt that this poet was one of them, that he had read the same rhetoric books, heard the same tunes, sucked in the same analogies from his schoolmaster. Yet in the crucial points that divide one kind of love from another, he is able to render the complex tension of two individuals interacting.

In this sonnet, for instance, we have the stock situation of the beloved as the sovereign, the poet as the slave, the servant; we have the 'bitterness of absence', as we have in Spenser; we have alliteration, in line 11, and we end on a flourish of word-play (*true* = 'genuine' or 'loyal', and 'will' is the beloved's will or the poet's name). Yet for all this, the first three words are enough to announce a kind of poetry we have never known before: they announce, in a level voice, what the conventional situation is—cooly, perhaps aggressively, perhaps protesting, perhaps resigned. The voice is so genuine we cannot be sure how to take it.

The poem turns the conventional situation on its head. Like so many of Shakespeare's sonnets (not the anthology pieces, the golden compliments, but the probing, complex poems of psychological analysis) it is impossible to say whether it is ironic or not. These assurances that he is not going to make the expected complaints, that he is content to watch the clock (did Shakespeare invent this brilliant phrase?), that he will have no thought 'save where you are how happy you make those'—is this the truest humility or the bitterest reproach? We would hardly hesitate over the answer if it were written today, but Christian submission and social deference have both declined so much in our century that the irony we would automatically assume may be a sign of our times. Shakespeare's poem seems to me to be poised between the genuine and the ironic assurance, calmly allowing either possibility, and by doing so allowing an almost infinite subtlety in the exact relationship between speaker and subject. This surely is the stuff of which married love is made—and Shakespeare knew it.

So shall I live, supposing thou art true,
Like a deceived husband; so love's face
May still seem to love me, though alter'd new;

Thy looks with me, thy heart in other place:
For there can live no hatred in thine eye,
Therefore in that I cannot know thy change.
In many's looks the false heart's history
Is writ in moods and frowns and wrinkles strange,
But heaven in thy creation did decree
That in thy face sweet love should ever dwell;
What e'er thy thoughts or thy heart's workings be,
Thy looks should nothing thence but sweetness tell.
   How like Eve's apple doth thy beauty grow,
   If thy sweet virtue answer not thy show.   (Sonnet 93)

This poem, too, is in touch with the tradition of flattery. It is addressed to one of perfect beauty, one in whose face 'Sweet love should ever dwell.' The poetry loses none of its conventional eloquence in saying this, but the purpose is not to flatter. The fact you have changed will not be seen in your face; this natural charm is a comfort, but one to be bitterly enjoyed, for it enables the poet to go on deceiving himself— 'like a deceived husband'. Yet the situation is not that of marriage; it is not even erotic. Shakespeare is writing to a man; the man is his patron, his friend and his social superior—almost certainly his sexual rival as well. It is a rich and complex situation, but not of the kind the sonnet was supposed to deal with. But in the handling of this situation, we can see the language being forged for the handling of many others. The relation of Spenser and Shakespeare to poetic tradition is simply stated: Spenser follows it, Shakespeare uses it. Who then is the revolutionary poet? Spenser appears to have set out to do something revolutionary: to attach Petrarchanism to marriage. But that is all he has done—to attach one thing to another. For any corresponding transformation of the poetry itself, he would have needed to be Shakespeare.

The Angel in the House

The best starting point for looking at the Victorian ideal of wife and mother is the solemn eloquence of Ruskin. *Of Queens' Gardens* (1865) begins by rejecting on the one hand the wild words about the mission and rights of Woman, and on the other the idea that women is only the shadow and attendant image of her lord. Between these comes the ideal of womanly mind and virtue: 'the centre of order, the balm of distress, and the mirror of beauty'. Woman's power is for rule not for battle; wifely subjection, so far from depriving her of influence, gives her enormous responsibility:

> There is not a war in the world, no, nor an injustice, but you women are responsible for it; not in that you have provoked, but in that you have not hindered.

The whole account is seasoned with laudatory and idealizing adjectives—
'harmonious', 'wise', 'pure', 'exquisite', 'true', 'good'—often in the
superlative. Few other writers matched this high style but the sentiments
were widespread. The contrast with the outside world is central to the
ideal: the influence of Wife and Home counteracts that of the world's
arena, where selfish passions reign, and the husband must come home
to be decontaminated. *The Edinburgh Review* said in 1841:

> It is of the utmost importance for men to feel, that in consulting a wife,
> a mother, or a sister, they are appealing *from* their passions and prejudices,
> and not *to* them, as embodied in a second self.[31]

Forty years later, when Eliza Lynn Linton stated the ideal in *The Girl
of the Period*, a touch of nostalgia has crept in: 'Time was when the phrase
"a fair young English girl" meant the ideal of womanhood':

> a girl who, when she married, would be her husband's friend and companion
> but never his rival; ... one who would make his house his true home and
> place of rest, not a mere passage-place for vanity and ostentation to pass
> through; a tender mother; an industrious housekeeper, a judicious
> mistress.[32]

Mrs Linton's method of asserting the ideal is to lament the fact that
England is now full of women who (through frivolity as much as
feminism) no longer live up to it. This may be because it is now 1883,
and the image is misting over; but complaint of that sort is so common
that perhaps we should simply see it as a rhetorical device for asserting
her belief.

It is important not to illustrate the ideal only from the pious, the unquestioning and the stupid. To show how profoundly it had permeated
the society we need to look at those who were perceptive about social
issues and prepared to criticize orthodoxy. Anna Jameson, for instance,
attacked the view that women should be tender, shrinking and sensitive:
women now need character, they need 'the self-governed, the cultivated,
the active mind' to protect and maintain themselves, and she points out
that thousands of women are not happy wives and mothers. Exempting
women from toil is all very well, but not 'if it be merely a privilege
of station': that would give us no right to look down on the Indians,
who make images of their women, and without hypocrisy.[33]

Mrs Jameson has her modest place in the history of woman's independence, though not in that of feminism. Her 'Memoirs of Women loved
and celebrated by poets', is written in the belief that 'truth is the basis
of all excellence in amatory poetry, as in everything else'. It is nonsense
to claim that Petrarch's Laura is an invented figure—she was real, she
loved Petrarch, she stayed chaste. The interest of all this as literary criticism is small, but it tells us a good deal about images of woman. When

it comes to conjugal poetry, modesty restrains men in speaking of their wives, but

> a woman is not under the same restraint in speaking of her husband; and this distinction arises from the relative position of the two sexes. It is a species of vain-glory to boast of a possession; but we may exult, unreproved, in the virtues of him who disposes of our fate.[34]

There is no irony or reluctance in the way this independent-minded woman uses those now terrible words 'possession' and 'disposes of'. Of course she is writing in a literary glow, about the far past. To ask if she thought the same about contemporary marriage we can turn to her last chapter, on Heroines of modern poetry; and what we find, sure enough, is indistinguishable from Ruskin. Women are responsible creatures, and idealizing them ought not to convert them into functionless deities. The ideal is service, distinguished from a cloud of poetic worship on the one hand, and on the other from an aristocratic frivolity that sees them as playthings.

A similar middle course is taken by the tough-minded W. R. Greg, stalwart of the *Edinburgh Review*. His essay on 'The False Morality of Lady Novelists' (more interesting than Mrs Jameson as literary criticism) is very similar as a social document. Greg is equally against two extremes in marriage: on the one hand, sexual passion which sweeps all before it, and which is so irresponsibly idealized by the poets, and on the other family-arranged marriages in which love has no part. Between them lies the possibility of true married love.[35]

If now we turn to social reality, do we find that the actual marriages of the Victorians lived up to their ideal? Not, unfortunately, if we go by the eloquent spokespersons just cited. Ruskin's marital fiasco is known to all; Mrs Jameson was one of those formidable nineteenth-century women who got rid of an ineffective husband and earned her living by her pen; and Mrs Linton married a Bohemian artist who preferred helping humanity to paying the butcher, and was disappointed that her views were not radical enough ('It is true that she is enthusiastic about Garibaldi; but then she is just as enthusiastic about Lord Palmerston').[36] They separated after a few years, and she left a version of the fiasco in her autobiographical novel *Christopher Kirkland* (1885). It sticks closely to the facts but—crucial change—reverses the sexes. When Christopher Kirkland marries the widow of his friend Lambert in order to look after her and the children, and finds that she is a 'Women's Rights woman from head to heel' who considers it petty to want a clean tablecloth, even the most liberal reader must have been tempted to shudder and think of Mr Jellyby; but since it was in fact the man who despised tablecloths, and the woman who decided that she could not put up with the children carving arabesques on the sideboard, we might feel that her decision to give up is more modern and liberated than was altogether seemly from the author of *The Girl of the Period*. But at least there was nothing liberated about her distress: 'And yet I long for love and I pine for a home.'

Perhaps it would be right to attend not to what these moralists did but to what they said; for there certainly were plenty of Victorian families where the wife was valued for moral influence in the home, and looked up to not in a Dantesque cloud of unknowing, but as a responsible and intelligent guide. We catch a glimpse of one in Catharine Tait's memoir of her five little daughters. As befits the family of the Dean of Carlisle, there was an atmosphere of strong piety, and she helped her children learn hymns and psalms, read the Bible and prayed with them, and took them on certain days to the Cathedral. She was a busy woman ('I had either home business to do, or school, infirmary, workhouse or poor to attend to') but always found time for the children, and on Saturdays she would examine them in their lessons ('question closely on history, which I had read on purpose'). Sundays were days of great happiness, in which family feeling was mingled with devotion

> ... After dinner was their time with their Father; each one in turn would climb on his knee and say the Hymn and Psalm they had learned for Sunday. When the little ones were gone to bed, the elder children would sing Hymns and chant Psalms until their bedtime came.[37]

To find a contrast to the Taits within the range of Victorian orthodoxy it would be satisfying to look at the family life of W. R. Greg. Unfortunately we know little of this, but we do know something about his mother, and about the atmosphere in which Greg grew up. Morley describes the 'grave simplicity' of the home,

> their intellectual ways, the absence of display and even of knick-knacks, the pale blue walls, the unadorned furniture, the well filled bookcases ...[38]

Mrs Greg had some literary capacity of her own, compiled a book of Maxims, and wrote two volumes of *Practical Suggestions towards alleviating the Sufferings of the Sick*. Two descriptions by family friends tell of the happiness and intellectual liveliness of the household. 'They actually do not know what it is to be formal or dull' wrote Catherine Stanley: 'each with their separate pursuits and tastes, intelligent and well-informed.' And Mrs Fletcher, who thought them the happiest family group she had ever seen, attributed to the wife the main Ruskinian function of countering the degrading effect of the outside world of money-making:

> We stayed a week with them, and admired the cultivation of mind and

refinement of manners which Mrs Greg preserved in the midst of a money-making and somewhat unpolished community of merchants and manufacturers.

Here we are in a very different segment of society from the Taits: business, not the clergy, and Unitarians of Puritan stock, not High Anglicans. The common element between the Tait and Greg families is the nineteenth-century domestic ideal.

It would be easy to go on describing and illustrating; but I want now to move beyond description. The best way to explore the idea is historically, by comparison with earlier and later images of the wife, and analytically, by asking what its essential elements are. Every marriage includes a sexual relationship, involves the distribution of authority, and is explained by means of analogies, of which much the commonest are with religion. We therefore need to look at attitudes to sex, at the degree of male authority, and at the use of religious imagery, all of them, as far as possible, comparatively.

The most elusive of these is the first, both because of the conventions of reticence, and because it was supposed to be a non-subject in the case of women. The orthodox view is stated with 'scientific' bluntness by Acton:

> I should say that the majority of women (happily for them) are not very much troubled with sexual feeling of any kind. . . . The best mothers, wives, and managers of households, know little or nothing of sexual indulgences. Love of home, children and domestic duties, are the only passions they feel.[40]

The sexless wife and mother is not an image that the Victorians invented: not only is it very old, it is embodied in the most famous of all images of woman, that of the Virgin Mary.

That Jesus was born of a virgin is an article of faith for all Christians; but there have been disputes about whether his mother had any other children. The scriptural references to his brethren and (once, in Mark) to his sisters might seem to make it obvious that she did, but tradition has been very reluctant to admit this. The two main explanations have been that of St Jerome, generally accepted in the Western church, that the brethren were his cousins, and that of Epiphanius that they were the sons of Joseph by a former wife, which has been accepted by the Eastern church. It is obvious that support for these views comes from the wish to believe that Mary (or, in Jerome's case, both Mary and Joseph) remain virgins. Preference for virginity over marriage is of course clear in St Paul (*1 Corinthians VII*) and is found in Jesus too (*Matthew XIX 12*). The doctrine of the Incarnation requires the Virgin birth, but has no need to postulate the subsequent virginity of Mary; but if we place Mary in the centre, then it can be important to believe that her virginity must be preserved, for only then can she represent the compatibility of sexual purity and motherhood.

The Virgin Mary not only symbolized the non-sexual wife and mother, she did so in a way that avoided some of the psychological problems, because she was not an ordinary woman. But when the insistence on the lack of sexuality is transferred from Heaven to Earth, from the far past to the present, and from religious iconography to the domestic situation, problems can arise. It is striking how well they were avoided in the nineteenth century, that is, how well the admiration for purity was secularized and domesticated. The best illustration of this which I know comes from Cobbett. Defending the view that adultery is worse in women than in men, he first mentions the possibility of illegitimate children, then adds, 'besides the deeper disgrace inflicted in this case than in the other'. Why is the disgrace deeper? Because of the total want of delicacy:

> Women should be, and they are except in a few instances, far more reserved and more delicate than men: nature bids them be such; the habits and manners of the world confirm this precept of nature.[41]

'Delicacy' here clearly has a sexual meaning. He dislikes the thought of widows remarrying, for

> after the greatest of ingenuity has exhausted itself in the way of apology, it comes to this at last, that the person has a second time undergone that surrender, to which nothing but the most ardent affection could ever reconcile a chaste and delicate woman.[42]

In view of his high praise of his wife, his pride in his sons, his happy marriage and his obvious virility, these passages throw an interesting light on Cobbett's attitude to marital sex.

Fully to understand the Mary-ideal we must remember that it has constantly been offset by a contrary image, that of woman as representing the sensual qualities, in contrast to man, who represents the martial and the intellectual, so that women are dangerous (and despicable) because of their insatiable sexual appetite: woman, said Bernard of Cluny in a voice that echoed throughout the Middle Ages, is 'a ditch of lust, a swirl of the whirlpool, a fountain of vice'. The best image for this view is Dalilah, the harlot who tricks the hero into revealing the secret of his strength. If we use a psychoanalytic interpretation and say that the cutting off of the hair is a symbol for the expenditure of semen the point is clear; but it is clear even without that, for there is no doubt that Dalilah uses her sexual attractiveness to get Samson's secret. The fact that he told her a false secret three times, and was betrayed each time yet still could not resist her coaxing, shows us that men know well what the danger is, but so powerful is the lure of sensuality that neither will nor judgement can make them refrain. Milton read the story this way, and his Dalilah says

> I knew that liberty
> Would draw thee forth to perilous enterprises,
> While I at home sate full of cares and fears
> Wailing thy absence in my widowed bed.[44]

This is uxoriousness, not love, because of its close relation to sloth. Man's task is perilous enterprises, woman represents the temptation to stay in bed.

The existence of these two contrasting images of woman's sexuality makes male ambivalence plain. The sexless wife can always be seen two ways: we can speak of purity, and admire, or of frigidity, and condemn. The Victorians succeeded in dividing the two attitudes, with a neatness never before attained, between the wife and the prostitute. It is a division that has not lasted: we have reverted to Blake's demand that wives should have the lineaments of gratified desire, though we differ from him (and the Victorians) in no longer believing this is found in whores. We now pity the prostitute, as our great-grandparents pitied the wife, for having to feign sexual desire.

Next, authority. It seems obvious to twentieth-century eyes that the angel in the house is part of patriarchal ideology. We only have to remember that the most valuable of all feminine qualities was self-sacrifice. It is mentioned—and praised—by everyone, and what it means can be seen in the oblique insistence of Mrs Ellis. 'Oblique' because *The Wives of England* attacks, with apparent indignation, those who expect women to be paragons of self-sacrifice. When we look at her attack, however, we find that it is only over domestic trivia that the expectation is unreasonable:

> In my remarks upon the subject of self-sacrifice, I would of course, be understood to refer only to those trifling and familiar affairs in which the personal comfort of daily life is concerned. The higher and more sacred claims of trial and calamity with which the experience of every human being is occasionally chequered, admit neither of doubt, calculation, nor delay.[45]

There is no doubt about feminine submissiveness in Mrs Ellis. It is the privilege [*sic*] of a married woman in company 'to show, by the most delicate attentions, how much she feels her husband's superiority to herself'. There seems no need to say more: if that is not patriarchy, what is?

Yet so many Victorians (including Ruskin) saw their wifely ideal as a middle course, between self-assertion and oppression, or as a step forward in the position of woman from the bad old days of mere inferiority. Let us therefore take a look at the old days. The main source for the Victorian ideal is probably seventeenth-century Puritanism (spiced with Romanticism, and some remote recollections of chivalry), and I shall therefore take as a text for comparison the *Domestic Duties* of William Gouge (1626). A glance at this puts us in another world. Criticizing the 'fond conceit, that Husband and Wife are equal', he reminds the reader that there is no 'common equity' between them, 'for the husband may command his wife but not she him'; he concedes that wives are less inferior than children and servants,

> Yet because God hath placed authority in the husband over his wife, she is every way to testify her reverent respect of her husband.

Follow a number of suggestions on the occasions when it would be appropriate 'to declare her reverence by some obeisance'.

> This cannot but much work on the heart of a good and kind husband, and make him the more to respect his wife, when he beholdeth this evidence of her respect to him.[46]

And what should a wife call her husband? There is plenty of scriptural warrant for calling him 'Lord', though the best and most usual title is 'husband'. A title there must be: he should not be addressed by his Christian name (worse still if contracted!), nor by words implying matrimonial familiarity, 'sweet', 'sweetheart', 'love'—let alone 'duck', 'chick', 'pigmy'; and

> What may we say of those titles ... which are not fit to be given to the basest men that be, as *Grub*, *Rogue* and the like, which I am even ashamed to name.[47]

What are the limits of wifely subjection? The list of what a wife ought not to do, even if her husband commands, is short and Puritanical: to go to mass, to a stage play, to play at dice, to prostitute her body ... to go garishly or whorishly attired.[48] The list of actions for which a husband's consent is needed is far longer; and it goes without saying (though Gouge says it) that wives have no property in the common goods of the family.

After all this, who can doubt that the Victorians were right when they believed they had come a long way? If in Mrs Ellis's drawing room the wife who was showing 'by the most delicate attentions' that she appreciated her dear John's superiority had suddenly taken to calling him 'husband' (let alone 'my Lord'), and taken the opportunity to make a curtsey or other suitable form of obeisance, it would have been assumed she was play-acting. Partly, this is the change from a ceremonial to a more restrained culture: the curtseying of wives belongs with the elaborate bows that men might make to one another in the seventeenth century. But partly at least it is a change from mere subordination to a more civilized, more respectful attitude to wives.

Can we know whether the move from severity to mildness took place not only in ideology but also in behaviour? Lacking a time machine and a concealed camera, we must look to the comments of observers. Gouge's tone has a stridency that suggests he had heard wives calling their men 'chick' and even 'grub', though no doubt they were not godly or pious women; but much of the time he sounds (as Mrs Ellis does all the time) as if he is describing a (no doubt perfected) version of what women actually did.

What must surely be a reliable piece of observation comes from John Stuart Mill. In 1867 he said in Parliament:

> We talk of political revolutions, but we do not sufficiently attend to the fact that there has taken place around us a silent domestic revolution: women and men are for the first time in history, really each others companions ... they had been separate in their amusements and in their serious occupations ... the man no longer gives his spare hours to violent outdoor exercises and boisterous conviviality with male associates ... when men and women are really companions, if women are frivolous men will be frivolous ... the two sexes must rise and sink together.[49]

Mill's feminist opinions are what make this testimony reliable: the fact that he was so genuinely critical of the position of women is surely evidence that he would not testify to an improvement like this unless firmly convinced.

What seems to me a confirmation of Mill's observation, though presented in geographical not in chronological terms, comes from Mrs Frances Trollope's *Domestic Manners of the Americans*. Mrs Trollope believed women should be feminine, and that motherhood was the central event in a woman's life; at the same time, she intensely disliked the way the Americans segregated the sexes. By thus preventing women from having a civilizing influence on men, they were impeding Mill's silent domestic revolution. 'It is not thus that the women can obtain that influence in society which is allowed to them in Europe, and to which, both sages and men of the world have agreed in ascribing such salutary effects.'[50]

An empirical investigation into whether women were better treated and more listened to in the nineteenth century would have to begin from the question of class. The angel in the house was largely (though not exclusively) a middle-class ideal: it did not obtain among the more relaxed or raffish aristocrats, nor among the disreputable poor. It is not easy to say if the Victorian working-class wife was better or worse off than the middle-class angel. If we compare courtesy with abruptness, gentleness with violence, and Mill's praise of companionship with separate leisure pursuits, she was worse off; but she was far more likely to have earned her own living before marriage, and to enjoy a sexual and perhaps economic independence that would have made her mistress shudder.

It would be very naive not to remark at this point that the idealization of the wife, though it may represent a kind of emancipation, can also be a bulwark against further emancipation: the granting of something trivial in order to resist claims on what really matters. This would then be what the Bulloughs call rhetoric as compensation for underprivilege, or the rewards of the inferior position.[51] 'This,' wrote Sarah Grimke, the American feminist, quoting the sentiment 'Her influence is the source of mighty power'—'this has ever been the flattering language of man since he laid aside the whip as a means to keep woman in subjection.'[52] Such indignation is understandable, and indeed rather splendid; but we would be quite wrong to dismiss the respect with which the Victorian wife was treated as mere rhetoric. She no longer had to curtsey; and having to curtsey was not merely a sign of subjection, it was in terms of experience, part of subjection; and the Victorian wife had gained a kind of dignity that was more than a token. But she had only gained it within the home; and even in the home, she had only gained it in the field of human relations, not in terms of legal or economic status. It is worth noticing how often the ideal is set forth in the context of a discussion (indeed, a refusal) of woman's rights. This is the case with the *Edinburgh Review* article already quoted. The reason why it is so important for men to feel that consulting a wife is appealing *from* their passions and prejudices is so that the immense influence of women will 'flow in its natural channels, namely domestic ones'. If women interpose in political affairs they will lose the moral stature that is truly theirs, and even a ladies' gallery at the House of Commons is to be frowned on.[53]

The *Edinburgh Review* article was written by a man; but we are not dealing with an ideology simply imposed by men on women. It would be quite false to maintain that Victorian women did not accept the feminine ideal imposed on them, and insufferably patronizing to claim that they did not 'really' accept it. There is no better example of this than the celebrated 'Appeal against Female Suffrage' of 1899, which put forward a conception of citizenship for women based on the feminine qualities of sympathy and disinterestedness, and not involving the franchise. What is striking about this document is its intelligence and its awareness (and to a considerable degree acceptance) of social change. This is no mindless conservativism, nor are these women parrotting what their

menfolk have told them: they are making a carefully thought-out statement of their involvement in public life. The signatories are a roll-call
of the most eminent names in contemporary England—prefixed by
'Mrs'. If we compare them with the supporters of female suffrage cited
in Millicent Fawcett's reply, we can say that the latter list contains far
more women of intrinsic distinction (Emily Davies, Dorothea Beale,
Florence Nightingale, Josephine Butler, Elizabeth Blackwell *et al.*), and
that the former, as Mrs Fawcett did not fail to point out, consisted both
of women who had done little to advance the recent improvements in
women's position they claimed to rejoice in, and also of the comfortable
and the prosperous. There is no doubt that Mrs Fawcett's list, like her
arguments, represents the future; but in a society in which women took
their husband's name, the anti-suffrage list of the wives of the eminent
is more representative of the present. In 1899 the ideal of Victorian
womanhood had worked, and was, by representative women, accepted.[54]

If then we say that family reverence, though real, hindered further
emancipation, we are not saying anything about the consciousness, or
even the happiness, of Victorian women, but offering our own subsequent analysis. With this proviso, the analysis is valid. One way of
demonstrating this is to look at the terms in which conservative writers
accept the role-differentiation that the ideal involves. Compare, for instance, these two passages:

> And after all, this great dignity of man, is not much of it artificial, or at
> least put on like a robe of state to answer an especial end? Yes; and a pitiful
> and heart-rending spectacle it is, to see the weakness of man's heart disrobed
> of all its mantling pride—the utter nakedness, I might almost say, for
> woman has even something left to conceal her destitution.[55]

> Ask James's mother and three sisters what it cost to save James the trouble
> of doing anything but be strong and clever and happy. Ask me what it costs
> to be James's mother and three sisters and wife and mother to his children
> all in one. Ask Prossy and Maria how troublesome the house is even when
> we have no visitors to help us to slice the onions. Ask the tradesmen who
> want to worry James and spoil his beautiful sermons who it is that puts them
> off. When there is money to give, he gives it: when there is money to refuse,
> I refuse it. I build a castle of comfort and indulgence and love for him, and
> stand sentinel always to keep little vulgar cares out. I make him master here,
> though he does not know it.[56]

They are both saying What Every Woman Knows: that the strength
and dignity of the husband rests, though he does not know it, on the
unobtrusive support of the wife. The difference is that Mrs Ellis, author
of the first, believes unquestioningly in male authority and female
submissiveness, while Bernard Shaw, author of the second, writes as a
feminist (though less of one, and less of a realist, than he perhaps thought).

The orthodox account is so open about the basis of the masculine role, that when it is being rejected all the critic has to do is state the same doctrine in a different tone.

So much then for male authority; I turn now to the religious aspect of the ideal. The angel in the house: it could after all be a figure for Incarnation. If we put it next to modern marriage, in which everything is so completely secularized (the ceremony, in a registry office; the meals, without grace; Sunday, without church-going; the health visitor and the psychiatrist, for the curate and the priest) we cannot fail to see the religious elements. Yet, once again, if we go back to the seventeenth century, the contrast changes.

There cannot be any doubt about the explicitly Christian nature of Protestant marriage. Gouge's treatise on man and wife is based closely and unquestioningly on scripture: a domestic duty is demonstrated by finding a text for it. As for married life, mutual piety is at the centre. Husband and wife will pray together, will be concerned for each other's salvation, will help each other to control sin. The obedience owed to a husband is explicitly compared to, and derived from, the obedience due to Christ. In all this Gouge is of course thoroughly representative; and compared with such explicitness, what are we to make of the Victorian ideal?

> This is the true nature of home—it is the place of Peace; the shelter, not only from all injury, but from all terror, doubt and division. . . . It is a sacred place, a vestal temple, a temple of the hearth watched over by Household Gods before whose faces none may come but those whom they can receive with love . . .[57]

The biblical rhythms are still there, but not the biblical references. The ideal is shot through with religious sentiment and embodied in religious imagery, but there are no longer injunctions to particular religious observances, and pagan references are as prominent—and as reverently handled—as Christian:

The ability of married love, because of its religious aura, to fill the gap left by the retreating Sea of Faith can be seen in a passage from one of Leslie Stephen's letters to his future wife Julia in 1877 which has become famous.

> You must let me tell you that I do and always shall feel for you something which I can only call reverence as well as love. *Think* me silly if you please. Don't say anything against yourself for I won't stand it. You see, I have not got any saints and you must not be angry if I put you in the place where my saints ought to be.[58]

Or there is *Dover Beach*. No one thinks of this as a love poem. The figure of the woman is so shadowy, the presence of the sea (first literal then made symbolic) and the build-up of melancholy and self-examination so deeply moving, that we think of it, rightly, as one of our great introspective poems, one of the great Victorian statements about honest doubt and the human condition. Yet the woman is crucial: introduced casually in the matter-of-fact opening section, she is standing there for him to turn to at the climax. 'Ah love, let us be true to one another': how trite, and yet, in context, how enormously moving, for the whole weight of the poem's sad reflexion comes bearing down upon it. It is a rash thing, poetically, to lay such a heavy weight on such an ordinary line, and it succeeds by a miracle (Arnold thought miracles do not happen). And corresponding to that poetic rashness is a human rashness in the situation: it is an enormous burden to lay on a frail human relationship. Why should their love have to bear—somehow to atone for—the fact that the world

> Hath really neither joy, nor love, nor light,
> Nor certitude, nor peace, nor help for pain.

One can see modern divorce looming, the divorce that follows too much trust, too high an expectation.

Two of the great agnostics, then, provide us with examples of the intensity of Victorian love, even its fragile intensity; and of the displacement of religious feeling into sexual love. Whether we say that the ideal of the angel in the house is a religious one is really a matter of definition. In an important sense, it has been secularized, for the religion is no longer explicit and no longer asserted; it has been diverted, almost (one wants by analogy to say) sublimated, or rather desublimated. Suppose we ask who believed more firmly in God, the men of 1650 or those of 1850? In one sense the question is unanswerable, for in both ages the belief of the majority was unquestioning, but one feels there are ways in which the palm goes to the seventeenth century: in 1850 there were a handful of sceptics, the urban working classes largely did not go to church, economic and professional life was more secularized. Now suppose we ask which age believed more firmly in angels. In the seventeenth century— in Protestant England, at any rate—men did not pray to saints, did not believe in Purgatory, did not preach often about the hierarchies of God's angels: in this post-Reformation world, the dead, the unborn, the spiritual guardians, the innumerable ranks of supernatural creatures that interposed between God and the devil, had all been removed. This is a commonplace among historians of the age. In the nineteenth century they had in one respect come back—not as objects of belief, in any clear intellectual sense, but as symbols of the emotional life, above all of grief. The death of children is one of the searing emotional experiences of the Victorian family, presumably because the expectation that every child might live was for the first time faintly aroused: and the way this emotion was expressed was in seeing the child as an angel. The wife might die too, though (once again) it was now less likely; and she too, while on earth, was an angel, if not always a purely Christian one. We can argue endlessly over the term 'believe'. The Victorians believed in angels as no one had ever done before in the sense that they invested more emotion in them, and associated living (or dead) individuals with them. It may even be that this is a sign of the incipient decay of other, more clear-cut kinds of belief.

The Angel in Literature

And the poets and novelists: what did they make of this ideal? There is no shortage of minor novels about what a good wife should be like—books like *Agatha's Husband* (1851) by Mrs Craik, in which an ingenious plot shows why a wife should trust her husband rather than demand explanations.

'We women', she continued softly, 'the very best and wisest of us, cannot enter thoroughly into the nature of the man we love. We can only love him. That is, when we once believe him worthy of affection. Firmly knowing that, we must bear with all the rest; and where we do not quite understand, we must, as I said, have faith in him.' (II.63)

When the young wife hears her husband talking in company she has a practical lesson in the Mrs Ellis system: his clear views, his wit, his keen far-seeing intellect, are a revelation to her:

She sat attentive, beginning to learn what strange to say was no pain—her own ignorance, and her husband's superior wisdom. She had never before, felt at once so proud and humble. (I.275)

Here the ideal is pushed almost back to the seventeenth century, so clear is wifely submission and male superiority—almost but not quite, for the submission still does not show itself in curtseying but in appreciation, as Agatha has just learned from her friend Emma: ' "How well my husband talks—doesn't he?" whispered Emma, with sparkling eyes.'

If we go slumming among the forgotten novelists it will be easy to find further examples, pressing the angel ideal to the edge of mere submission, and pressing the literary expression over the edge of mere cliché. And on one level, this is true of Dickens and Thackeray as well: both of them were obsessed by the angel-wife, and both put her into their books.

The most famous example in Dickens is certainly Agnes Wickfield.

She is devoted to her father (the ideal bride is primarily a daughter); she is sexless (David is not allowed to think of her body, but the villainous Uriah is, with a grotesque and disgusting lust); she has long loved David, but with a love free from jealousy (she acts the devoted sister to Dora); and she is a paragon of self-sacrifice. And she is quite untouched by Dickens's genius: if most Victorian heroines are dead from the waist down, Agnes is dead from the waist up as well. The complex faultiness of Esther and Bella and Dora, a mingling of artistic success and failure in a way that is psychologically fascinating, gives place in Agnes and Ada and Florence Gay to mere sugarstick.

With one quaint and revealing exception. The one truly devoted wife in Dickens who is also entertaining appears in the same novel. Artistically, there is nothing in common between Agnes and Mrs Micawber, yet what is her constant reiteration that she never will desert Mr Micawber (she even addresses him with Gouge-like deference) but the same wifely devotion that Mrs Craik commended? Mrs Micawber is forgiving, but she remembers—and reminds others—that forgiveness is necessary:

> Mr Micawber may have concealed his difficulties from me in the first instance.... The pearl necklace and bracelets which I inherited from mama, have been disposed of for less than half their value.... But I never will desert Mr Micawber.   (Ch. 12)

A comic figure can state the full situation when the true angel has to suffer in silence. The relation between serious and comic in Dickens's art is, here as ever, complex and teasing: as if mocking at the ideal he accepts enables him, for once, to enjoy it.

Thackeray's ambivalence is more far-reaching, and his angels come to life according as he is willing to be critical of them. Laura, the most unquestioningly praised, is the least interesting; Rosey (in *The Newcomes*) more so, and Amelia most of all. What are we meant to think of Amelia, the devoted wife who refuses to see what a blackguard her husband is, who worships his memory, and from single-minded wifely adoration turns to single-minded maternal love? 'She was a dear little creature', Thackeray tells us in the first chapter:

> I am afraid that her nose was rather short than otherwise and her cheeks a great deal too round and red for a heroine; but her face blushed with rosy health, and her lips with the freshest of smiles, and she had a pair of eyes which sparkled with the brightest and honestest good-humour, except indeed when they filled with tears, and that was a great deal too often; for the silly thing would cry over a dead canary-bird:
>
> (*Vanity Fair*, Ch. 1)

This rather elementary irony is of course meant to work in favour of Amelia; it hints that what is folly to the hard-headed world may be the wisdom of the heart. Yet if one discusses *Vanity Fair* with students today, one can't fail to notice how they detest the saintly Amelia. What offends them? Partly no doubt it is that Thackeray protests too much. 'What do men know about women's martyrdoms? We should go mad had we to endure the hundredth part of those daily pains which are meekly borne by many women.' To the twentieth-century reader such authorial slobber is highly unacceptable; and even contemporaries were critical of it—and of her.[59] Indeed, a good deal of the hostility to Amelia comes from Thackeray himself. First, she is such a fool. In the case of her husband she is love's fool, but there are other, more incidental, touches that stick like little arrows in the tender flesh of the dear creature. When Napoleon escapes from Elba, the English continue to flock to the continent on holiday; the newspapers are convinced that the Corsican wretch cannot withstand 'the armies of Europe and the genius of the immortal Wellington. Amelia held him in utter contempt; for it needs not to be said that this soft and gentle creature took her opinions from those people who surrounded her, such fidelity being much too humble-minded to think for itself' (Ch. 26). But even this doesn't take us to the bottom of things. For the accusation most violently made at Amelia is not just that she is a fool but that she is selfish. Thackeray himself once called her selfish, in a letter to his mother;[60] though that was said when he had only written a quarter of the book, and it seems to be announcing an intended change of heart in her that we are never given. The remark is clearly made to agree with something his mother had already said ('you are quite right about *Vanity Fair* and Amelia being selfish'). What is significant is that she said it: this pious lady was anticipating the modern sophisticated reader.

And is Amelia selfish? For nine-tenths of the story (perhaps more) Thackeray keeps emphasizing her unselfishness, but it is in the remaining tenth that he is at his most brilliant—in the scene, for instance, in which Amelia shouts at her mother in blind maternal rage for giving Daffy's Elixir to little Georgy. This is not exactly selfishness: it is the harshness that flows out of a too single-minded unselfishness. Living only for her son, she is capable of insensitivity to those who seem to her to act against his interests. A parallel with *Philip* can show us the great superiority of *Vanity Fair*. Amelia's jealousy of her mother is very like Charlotte's jealousy of Caroline, Philip's 'adoptive' mother. In both cases it is prompted by maternal possessiveness. But whereas it is sentimentalized in *Philip* by subsequent and rather fulsome remorse ('friend Charlotte leans her head against her husband's shoulder, and owns humbly how good, how brave, how generous a friend heaven sent them in that humble defender'), Amelia's relationship with her mother never recovers from the lingering bitterness of a memory they can ignore but not obliterate. Even while it happens the conflict is sentimentalized in *Philip*: Caroline's unremitting goodness leads her to accept Charlotte's cool suggestion that she leave the nursery, and Thackeray immediately adds: 'Poor Little Sister! She humbled herself and grovelled before Charlotte.'[61] This is utterly different from the flaring up of Amelia when she finds her mother giving Daffy's Elixir to George:

> Amelia flung the bottle crashing into the fireplace. 'I will *not* have baby poisoned, Mamma!' cried Emmy, rocking the infant about violently with both her arms round him, and turning with flashing eyes at her mother.
> 'Poisoned, Amelia!' said the old lady, 'this language to me?'   (Ch. 38)

Nowhere else does Amelia come to life like this: her sudden anger rejuvenates even such a cliché as 'flashing eyes', and the petulant indignation of her self-pitying mother ('you think I'm a murderess then') somehow gives Amelia, by contrast, something near to dignity.

It is not quite the case that Amelia lives only for her son; she lives for her husband's memory too. Is that unselfishness? Amelia is not an egoist, in that she wants nothing from the outside world for herself, and is more used to giving than to claiming; but in a less moral, more psychological, sense her love for George's memory is egoistic, for what she worships exists and had always existed only in her. And this devotion is now used against Dobbin. Amelia accepts Dobbin's worship without ever dreaming of returning it, and her devotion to her husband is psychologically very useful to her: it enables her to trample on Dobbin (the word is Thackeray's) while accepting his love. 'She didn't wish to marry him, but she wished to keep him.'

Vanity Fair has a conventional happy ending, but the happiness is muted in two ways. First, because Dobbin had to wait so long, it is a romantic marriage transposed on to the sober plane of middle-age; and second, there lies on their happiness the taint not only of time but also of selfishness. When *Vanity Fair* was appearing as a serial, and Thackeray was urged to let Dobbin marry Amelia, he replied, 'Well he shall, and when he has got her, he will not find her worth having.'[62] It is a more savage, perhaps a more powerful remark, than anything in the novel, and it makes one speculate on whether such remarks, beyond the fringe of the text, are in a sense part of the book's artistic impact: they draw their power from the fact that they were not made in the book. There is an exact parallel to this in the famous remark to his mother, in the letter already quoted, that he was going to kill George off 'well dead with a ball in his odious bowels'. How much stronger this is than the text, which with less courage planted the ball in George's heart! If we turn to the ending of the novel and ask if Thackeray carried out his promise that Dobbin would 'not find her worth having', we find another interesting shift. Dobbin does tell Amelia that she is not worthy of the love he has devoted to her: it is by far the most impressive thing he says in the book, but he says it *before* he marries her, not after; and indeed it is this speech which (after a delay) causes her to marry him. This is less cynical than what Thackeray promised his reader, but more moving.

Thackeray's contemporary reputation was for cynicism and sneering; yet he was also the most sentimental of the great Victorians. To move, as he does, from tears of warm indulgence to comments of cool contempt can produce some exhilarating moments of truth in—and even more round the edges of—his novels, but it does not produce the higher achievement of a George Eliot or a Tolstoi, the integration of the contrasting extremes into a complex attitude. Only in the final glimpse of Dobbin and Amelia married do we get a hint of such a synthesis. Is there a shadow on their happiness? We hear no word of complaint from Dobbin, but there is a sad remark from Amelia. Col. Dobbin picks up his little Janey

> of whom he is fonder than of anything in the world—fonder even than of his 'History of the Punjaub'. Fonder than he is of me, Emmy thinks, with a sigh. But he never said a word to Amelia that was not kind and gentle, or thought of a want of hers that he did not try to gratify.

(Ch. 67)

That innocent paragraph is a true revelation of Thackeray's genius as a novelist. Dobbin's disillusion is not even, perhaps, present in his consciousness, but Amelia (she has really learned something after all) has seen it, and has had to scale down her ideal of marriage accordingly. And with perfect tact Thackeray, telling us of her secret disappointment, uses the marital endearment Emmy, and reassuring us that Dobbin behaved impeccably steps back and uses the more formal Amelia.

The lovely glorious nothing that is an angel is too insubstantial for the complex prose of the great Victorian novelists: either they are critical of it, or their writing becomes as thin as air. The realism with which Dorothea Casaubon is treated has nothing to do with angelology. Perhaps prose is too gross a medium to contain an angel; to find its voice and shapeless flame, would we not do better to look to the poets—to Patmore, for instance, from whom comes the title of this discussion. Nothing in Patmore's text is nearly as famous as his title: this often admirable poet has his immortality buried in a phrase. *The Angel in the House* (1854–62) describes how Vaughan decides to write a poem taking his wife Honoria as subject. Since the poem narrates their courtship, it is natural to locate it in the tradition of love poetry. Honoria is praised through comparisons with nature

— No idle thought her instinct shrouds,
But fancy chequers settled sense,
Like alteration of the clouds
On noonday's azure permanence.— (I.iv.)

and through religious analogies ('Her disposition is devout, Her countenance angelical'). The lover dreams of his beloved:

And phantasms as absurd and sweet
Merged each in each in endless chase,
And everywhere I seemed to meet
The haunting fairness of her face. (I.iii.)

The fact that the courted mistress accepts him in the end is not enough (as we saw in the case of Spenser) to turn traditional love poetry into poetry of wedded love. Yet Patmore has definitely made that transition. Partly this is by means of a matter-of-fact element in the poems that would be quite out of place in Petrarch or Drayton—the details of Honoria's family, the initial attraction to her sister, the fact that the rival (conventionally, a vaguely generalized figure) is quite precisely identified as her cousin Frederick, a naval officer, on his way to Portsmouth to join his ship 'for two years cruise in the Levant'. And partly it is by means of the flashback technique, the fact that the couple are already married, so that the courtship is a memory played against their present happiness. The happiness is of the best Ruskinian kind. The woman is patient with her husband's moods and has learnt to sacrifice herself:

She loves with love that cannot tire;
And when, ah woe, she loves alone,
Through passionate duty love springs higher,
As grass grows taller round a stone.

The role division that excludes her from masculine occupations, even masculine interests, is no disadvantage: 'She wants but what to have were loss.' This is submission: but the love it yields is a mutual benefit. From the first lines the stress is on mutuality ('his thoughts were rife How for her sake to win a name'), even to the extent of verbal patterning:

She laughed. How pleased she always was
To feel how proud he was of her.

This love poem, then, incorporates the idealization of literary convention with the new ideal of married love. It is the central Victorian poem of married love; but it is not easy to find another. Perhaps the best candidate is Tennyson's *Idylls of the King*, that public act of social affirmation that cost its author so much time and trouble. Certainly the theme of the Idylls is that the adultery of Lancelot and Guinevere destroyed the society of the Round Table. To the modern reader, social disintegration should have social causes, but to Tennyson the cause of the collapse is not social but personal, the wickedness of Modred, 'sharpened by strong hate for Lancelot', and underlying everything the sin of the Queen,

> whose disloyal life
> Hath wrought confusion in the Table Round.

This makes the *Idylls*, and particularly the penultimate one, *Guinevere*, into a kind of negative argument for wifely virtue, and Arthur comes to see that condoning adultery is unpardonable:

> I hold that man the worst of public foes
> Who either for his own or children's sake,
> To save his blood from scandal, lets the wife
> Whom he knows false, abide and rule the house. (509)

Guinevere is deeply impressed by this, and by the lofty assurance of forgiveness with which he leaves her, and her repentance leads to a kind of conversion, and so to a positive assertion of married love and chastity. It is difficult to believe that the exalted moralizing of the king ('Lo! I forgive thee as Eternal God Forgives: do thou for thine own soul the rest') was much more acceptable to the Victorians than to us, or the Queen's conversion much more convincing. In the very act of announcing it she explains that she fell because she 'could not breathe in that fine air' and 'yearned for warmth and colour', which she found in Lancelot. Arthur still lives in fine air, in 'pure severity of perfect light', and his description of how the unfaithful wife spreads moral disease around her could come from Ibsen's Torvald at his most pompous. It is still Lancelot who represents warmth and colour, and though in the zeal of her repentance she may now say 'We needs must love the highest when we see it', there is no reason to believe that her new humility represents a possible basis for married happiness. The moral assertion has left Tennyson's imagination unconvinced.

There is another reason too why it is difficult to take the *Idylls* seriously as an expression of Victorian marriage ideals, and that is the simple fact of the medieval setting. The very point that makes the whole social vision implausible to us, the personal nature of the causes, rings true if we see it as an historical poem, for that is a highly medieval way of thinking. And the same objection arises when we look round in the *Idylls* for a positive statement of wifely virtue. The intended example of this is certainly Enid, in the two Geraint poems, *The Marriage of Geraint* and (especially) *Geraint and Enid*. Geraint after marriage loses his ambition in uxoriousness: then a misunderstanding leads him to suspect that Enid has been unfaithful to him. He then tyrannizes her, forcing her to ride ahead of him and not speak to him; she disobeys only to warn him of danger, which angers him more than ever. After he is wounded—as it seems, fatally—she is captured by the fierce Earl Doorm, who pesters her to leave her apparently dead mate for him; her cry of distress wakes Geraint, who kills the Earl and is reconciled to her in a moment, without explanation given or received. Enid is misty-eyed for joy, and from then on they live together in wedded bliss.

This is clearly a Griselda-story: uncomplaining meekness in the wife leads the tyrannous husband to see the error of his ways. It hovers on the edge of miracle, and the wife hovers on the edge of martyrdom, until all comes right. This makes it a thoroughly medieval tale (in essentials it follows Chrétien), and these trials of virtue, this patriarchal bullying, and above all the feeling that in their reconciliation they are somehow above explanations, are quite unsuitable to the earnest exhortations of Mrs Ellis, the view that the wife is a guide and a friend, and the reality of the Victorian drawing room. It is a commonplace that Tennyson fell between two stools in the *Idylls*, the medieval and the contemporary. It is often held that the poems are too Victorian for their artistic health (hence the malicious nickname, *Morte d'Albert*), but they are also too medieval to put their moral message across.

Obviously it is from the Brownings more than anyone else that we would expect to find the poems of married love. Certainly they wrote the finest Victorian love poems; but the biographical fact that they were married does not, as we have seen, necessarily make these into poems of married love. The best candidate for this in Robert Browning's work is *By the Fireside* in which the speaker looks forward to 'life's November' in which he'll sit reading Greek and daydreaming about the moment by the little Italian chapel when all barriers dropped between them and they met in the 'moment one and infinite'. By itself this episode belongs in the tradition of love's uniqueness: they are not meeting for the first time, so it is not love at first sight, but it is experience concentrated into a single unique moment, a transcending of the everyday, and it ends the poem as a wedding ends a romantic love comedy: 'They had mingled us so, for once and good.' 'For once and good' is as much out of time as the happily ever after of romantic comedy; but what gives *By the Fireside* its special quality is the temporal framework. Three points in the speaker's life are dealt with—the perfect moment by the chapel, the old age from which he'll be looking back at it, and the moment in between when the poem takes place. By joining them together, the poem reintroduces them into time. The speaker boasts that the path to the chapel has led

> To an age so blest that, by its side,
> Youth seems the waste instead

'Waste' is the image we expect for the stretch of time that contrasts with the moment of love: here it refers to time that has actually passed, and so gives a more authentic because more matter-of-fact existence to the moment of recollection, and makes it a poem about marriage, not about courtship or falling in love.

> When if I think but deep enough
> You are wont to answer, prompt as rhyme.

The word that would be impossible in a Petrarchan poem is 'wont': only in married love can habit be praised. The simile makes the point neatly: rhyme is not an isolated pleasure but part of a pattern. The intimacy of the married is like a rhyme-scheme.

Elizabeth Browning's love poems are even more interesting in the context of this discussion, because of their relation to literary tradition. She not only wrote a sonnet-sequence, she used in it most of the conventions of Petrarchanism. Religious imagery is prominent; the Beloved is God's gift, and their love is a sanctuary on earth, a shadow of Heaven; love and death are almost indistinguishable; the love the poet feels is a privilege, and the fact that it is returned almost a miracle; the face of all the world is changed now the Beloved has appeared; the Beloved looks down on the poet from a lofty height. All this places the sonnets so clearly in the main tradition that the fact that they were written after marriage and addressed to the poet's spouse becomes, as with Spenser, a purely biographical and external point, which has left no trace on the poems themselves. The meaning of the poems is only affected by it if we lift them out of the context of poetic tradition and place them in that of the personal situation. There is however one other factor not present with Spenser, an element of context that can radically affect our reading—the fact that these poems are by a woman:

> Unlike are we, unlike, O princely Heart!
> Unlike our uses and our destinies.
> Our ministering two angels look surprise
> On one another, as they strike athwart
> Their wings in passing. Thou, bethink thee, art
> A guest for queens to social pageantries,
> With gages from a hundred brighter eyes
> Than tears even can make mine, to play thy part
> Of chief musician. What hast thou to do
> With looking from the lattice-lights at me,
> A poor, tired, wandering singer, singing through
> The dark, and leaning up a cypress tree?
> The chrism is on thine head,—on mine, the dew,—
> And Death must dig the level where these agree.

It is a stock situation: the lover serenading out of the darkness, leaning up a cypress tree, looking up literally (the beloved is at an upstairs window, or on a balcony) and emotionally (he regards her with awe) perhaps even socially (the minstrel sings to a lady of high degree). But the conventional lover is not really looking up, all the same: for he is a man, and the whole thing takes place in patriarchal society, the only society we know. Worship is offered that power may be denied. Surely then it makes an enormous difference to realize that this speaker really is in an inferior position, really is looking up.

> What can I give thee back, O liberal
> And princely giver, who has brought the gold
> And purple of thine heart, unstained, untold,
> And laid them on the outside of the wall
> For such as I to take or leave withal,
> In unexpected largesse?

The outside of what wall? In normal love poetry it is the wall of the castle where the princess lives, the fortress of her chastity or her pride, but now it is the wall of masculine power, and the beloved is doing a real favour, from a position of real strength. Love here is not a game, it is a concession won by women from men; when we say this we realize how much of a game love poetry had previously been. This contrast is so strong that I want to claim there are two poems, each with the same words, but with quite different meanings depending on the context we place them in. By her title, the author invites us to read one of these poems: they are translations, we are told, from what is presumably some traditional love poet in a little-read language—or, if we see through the pretence, they are meant to sound as if they were translations. But why have that pretence? Because they would otherwise seem too personal: which must mean that they *are* personal, which must invite us to relate them (or at any rate to know that they are related) to the situation of the poet, whose Christian name Elizabeth, stands there on the title page of the 1850 edition to tell us that they are by a woman, i.e. that they are the other poem. And this brings us, by a roundabout path, back to the question of marriage: for the surname stands on the title page too, and could—just—be an invitation to read them as written to her husband, so that the title page, like the presence of *Epithalamion* following after the *Amoretti*, is like an announcement of the marriage. The *Sonnets*, then, are not poems of married love: they are something whose unusualness we should not overlook, poems of romantic love, by a married woman.

Victorian literature has not done well by the Angel in the House. Only the lesser writers, and the great writers in eccentric moments or in qualified ways, treat it as an ideal to be expressed with the force of their genius. This returns us forcibly to the question adumbrated in the Preface, of hos literature relates to ideology. I have insisted that Victorian women as well as men accepted the domestic ideal and defined themselves in relation to their role: not to believe this is not to be interested in evidence. But if imaginative literature is in some sense the test of ideology, then it is a test which this ideal does not pass.

I cannot solve this puzzle. Either the great writers did not represent the society or they had not developed the techniques to express what they believed; or else there is some sense in which the Victorians were, at the deepest level, sceptical of their ideal. Or—this seems to me nearest the truth—their literature is of a kind that does not accept ideals but submits them to the inspection of its own complex greatness.

The Brangwens

There are plenty of studies of marriage in twentieth-century literature, and many of them by the great writers—Thomas Mann (*Buddenbrooks*) Arnold Bennett (*These Twain*) Marcel Proust (Swann and Odette) and many more. I wish to choose a single example, and that surely must come from Lawrence, first because he broke so much new ground, and second because he held, and expounded, an explicit ideology of marriage, so that the ideal and the literary expression can come from the same writer. This time it will be more convenient to look at the literary expression first.

If there ever was a novel about love and marriage, it is surely *The Rainbow*, perhaps the most truly exploratory novel we have, the most profound and powerful attempt to express levels of experience literature had hitherto passed over.

It is the story of three generations of Brangwens. In the first we are told how Tom Brangwen married a Polish lady and brought her to live at the Marsh Farm. In the best romantic tradition, he fell in love with her at first sight: but did love at first sight ever have the utter matter-of-fact authenticity of Tom walking down the road from Cossethay beside his horse, with a load of seed from Nottingham, seeing a woman approach while he was busy with his horse, then noticing her 'curious, absorbed, flitting motion, as if she were passing unseen by everybody', then seeing her face 'clearly, as if by a light in the air', and then: ' "That's her," he said involuntarily.' This is followed by an account of the emotion which the encounter stirs up in Tom:

The feeling that they had exchanged recognition possessed him like a madness, like a torment. How could he be sure, what confirmation had he? The

doubt was like a sense of infinite space, a nothingness, annihilating. He kept
within his breast the will to surety. They had exchanged recognition.

(Ch. I.)

We have already looked at what is surely the classic expression of love
at first sight in English, Romeo's reaction to Juliet:

> O, she doth teach the torches to burn bright!
> It seems she hangs upon the cheek of night
> As a rich jewel in an Ethiop's ear—
> Beauty too rich for use, for earth too dear!
> So shows a snowy dove trooping with crows
> As yonder lady o'er her fellows shows.
> The measure done, I'll watch her place of stand
> And, touching hers, make blessed my rude hand.
> Did my heart love till now? Forswear it, sight!
> For I ne'er saw true beauty till this night.   (I.v.46)

There is so little in common between these, that one wonders how meaningful it is to say that Lawrence is using the convention of love at first
sight. Brangwen does not praise Lydia, or think of her beauty; he does
not use the word 'love'; and Lawrence has none of the stylistic resources
of Shakespeare—instead of the images of the jewel, of the dove among
crows, he is left groping among abstractions. 'The doubt was like a sense
of infinite space, a nothingness, annihilating': this reads like a painful
confession of inarticulateness, a confession of stylistic bankruptcy. And
if we ask what the feeling is that Lawrence's powerful groping introduces
into the experience, the answer is in a way surprising. This sense of a dimly
perceived realm of being that annihilates the normal is, surely, a religious
sense; and the prose of the whole chapter, as everyone notices, is soaked
in Biblical rhythms and images (not much in this paragraph, though even
here 'exchanging recognition' can recall the sexual and mystical meanings of the Biblical 'know'). The answer is surprising because there is
so much religious imagery in Romeo's poetry: in these lines we have
'for earth too dear' and 'make blessed'. But it is a poetry of religious
concepts, not of the direct presence of Biblical rhythms and bewildered
mystical urgency.

To express Tom's experience of love, Lawrence needs to find a prose
that will show us how it transcends and contrasts with everyday experience, creates in him 'another centre of consciousness'. At the same time,
there is a tremendous sense of the everyday in the story. The Marsh Farm
is a real farm, it sells real butter, Tilly is a real servant. The interaction
of the transcendent and the ordinary informs the great scenes between
Tom and Lydia, such as that at the end of chapter 3, after Tom has paid
a visit to his brother's mistress. That has opened up to him a world of

culture he realizes he has never entered, and the discovery that his own brother has the freedom of it, that this dignified widow should say 'we read Browning sometimes', and remark 'he is quite an unusual man' is strangely disturbing—though once again Lawrence captures the surface perfectly when he makes Brangwen reply, 'I didn't know our Alfred was this way inclined.' Tom goes home despising himself, and discontented with his own way of life; then he tells himself that he does not want Browning and Herbert Spencer and a fine widow; and the second evening he sits watching his wife. He feels shut in, wants 'to smash the walls down, and let the night in, so that his wife should not be so secure and quiet, sitting there', and gets up, saying he's going into the village. Lydia is aware that his casual remark reveals a deep rejection, and insists on talking of it: imperceptibly, her calm account of his discontent turns into a rebuke of his self-centredness, their failure to make of their love a true human communion:

> Why aren't you satisfied with me?—I'm not satisfied with you. Paul used to come to me and take me like a man does. You only leave me alone or take me like your cattle, quickly, to forget me again—so that you can forget me again. (Ch. 3)

It is interesting to find Lydia delivering to her husband the reproach that has so often and so cheaply been directed at Lawrence, of being interested only in sex for its own sake. What she is asking for is of course Lawrence's conception of true marriage—a sexual union in which each recognizes the individuality of the other. (Though it is worth mentioning that Lawrence is here taking Paul like a mere emblem, to forget him again: when we learn more of Lydia's first marriage, in Chapter 9, we learn that Paul had treated her merely as his attribute).

It is necessary for Lydia to speak with this degree of frankness, though its effect is to make Tom say 'You make me feel as if I was nothing.' Only then can she offer herself to him, hesitantly at first, in a way that will bring them truly together. Her approach is unmistakably sexual ('her hands on him seemed to reveal to him the mould of his own nakedness'), but after what has passed it is the beginning of a new relationship that leads to a true marriage. We are told virtually nothing about this new coming together, which 'after two years of married life, was much more wonderful to them than it had been before', for a page later the chapter ends, with the image of Anna playing beneath the rainbow arch: simply that 'their feet trod strange ground of knowledge, their footsteps were lit up with discovery'.

The second marriage is that of Anna and Will. This time Lawrence has much more that is conventional to draw on: the lovers are 18 and 20, their discovery of each other is their virginal discovery of love, and the descriptions contain references to awakening, to wonder and birth-pain. The scene in the fowl-loft is particularly moving because of the presence of Tom Brangwen. He has followed them out into the darkness, seen them through the loft door, 'blurred by the rain, but lit up', and heard Anna saying 'I love you, Will, I love you.' It is an unbearable moment for him. 'Was he then an old man, that he should be giving her away in marriage?' The experience is common, but that is no comfort, any more than it was to Hamlet. Lawrence never evades the unkind surface, the petty hostility, of his bitterness; but beneath this we are shown the unbearable experience of having to take stock of his whole life.

> He was silent, with his hand on her shoulder. His heart was bleak.... He sat in his coldness of age and isolation. He had his own wife. And he blamed himself, he sneered at himself, for this clinging to the young, wanting the young to belong to him.   (Ch. 4.)

It is the situation of Ebenezer Holman in *Cousin Phillis*. There is one detail that Elizabeth Gaskell would not have included: her father might have blamed himself but he would not have sneered, as Tom does, here at himself and earlier at Anna: there we have the rawness of feeling that Lawrence can never quite lose and she can never quite include. All the same the passage is closer to the Victorian novel than is usual in *The Rainbow*: less about the inchoate darkness, the centres of consciousness somewhere in Brangwen's body, more about the situation, more a statement of the universal grief here impinging on him. Less Lawrentian, in fact. And more moving because more direct, many readers will feel though not the passionate Lawrentian readers. For those, the inchoate somethings and somewheres are the truest writing he did.

The marriage of Will and Anna contains the first real honeymoon in English fiction, describing the physical intimacy, the blissful irresponsibility, the sense of being cut off from the world:

> But it was so sweet and satisfying lying there talking desultorily with her. It was sweeter than sunshine, and not so evanescent. It was even irritating the way the church-clock kept on chiming: there seemed no space between the hours, just a moment, golden and still, whilst she traced his features with her finger-tips, utterly careless and happy, and he loved her to do it.
> (Ch. 6)

Where else can we find such directness—taking us into the lover's room, into the bed, showing us their irritation with the outside world?

> Busy old fool, unruly Sun,
> Why dost thou thus
> Through windows and through curtains call on us?
> Must to thy motions lovers' seasons run?[63]

In the next paragraph but one, Lawrence writes: 'Inside the room was a great steadiness, a core of living eternity'—a true metaphysical conceit, though without Donne's perfect poise and eloquence. Prose can hardly hope to capture the breath-taking paradoxes of Donne's poetry, but the comparison is not wholly to Lawrence's disadvantage; for Donne can hardly hope to capture that sense of complete authenticity, vivid enough here, and even more vivid in the scene when Will fetches a tray of food:

> 'How good!' she cried, sniffing the cold air. 'I'm glad you did a lot.' And she stretched out her hands eagerly for her plate—'Come back to bed, quick—it's cold.' She rubbed her hands together sharply. (Ch. 6)

Anna is more totally absorbed in the intimacy, Will is the one who feels guilty at staying in bed at all; and perhaps for that reason she is sooner ready to come back to the world. So she gives a tea party, while he still wants their isolation, and that leads to their first quarrel, whose fierceness is a consequence of the intensity of their intimacy: they are not living on a level of reasonableness and arrangements, but in response to the ebb and flow of their emotional needs, for each other and for the world, and nothing can be done when the rhythms don't fit.

> He came into the house. The sound of his footsteps in his heavy boots filled her with horror: a hard cruel malignant sound. She was afraid he would come upstairs. But he did not. (Ch. 6)

It does not matter, at a moment like this, what the other says or does, for quarrels like this have no cause, they arise from the discord of souls that makes his very boots malignant. The way to make up such a quarrel is simply to wait: after a while the need for reconciliation will assert itself, and draw them back to intimacy.

Lawrence's famous letter to Edward Garnett saying 'You mustn't look in my novel for the old stable *ego* of the character,' tells us that he is after another, deeper *ego* that no novelist has yet explored, where the individual is unrecognizable.

> Like as diamond and coal are the same pure single element of carbon. The ordinary novel would trace the history of the diamond—but I say, 'Diamond, What! This is carbon.' And my diamond might be coal or soot, and my theme is carbon.[64]

The history of the diamond would describe who came to Anna's tea-party, and explain the quarrel by means of what Will said or did wrong. But the profoundest quarrels are not 'about' anything: they are carbon. It is Lawrence's greatness to be able to show us that hate is an allotropic state of love, when the couple offend each other by their very being.

But there is also a sense in which the quarrelling of Will and Anna is very much about something. It is not an accident that Anna is the one who first feels the need to return from their intimacy to the world. Will is the mystic, the one who turns away from the intellect, whose religion is 'a dark nameless emotion', who loves Lincoln cathedral because it 'leaps on into the infinite in a great mass' and his book on Bamberg all the better for its unintelligible German text; Anna is the one who clings to human knowledge, who is hard, sceptical, ironical, matter-of-fact. Their quarrels are not simply an allotropic state of love, they also express this fundamental contrast. This is a kind of explanation, but it is still not the diamonds of the 'ordinary novelist': it accounts for the quarrels in terms of the personalities of Will and Anna, but not in terms of anything particular they say or do—it is, shall we say, coal rather than diamonds.

What makes *The Rainbow* a great novel about marriage? There are two ways of answering this question, and the main purpose of my discussion is to show the connexion between them. In the first place, there is Lawrence's relationship to realism. The two modes that his writing moves between can be called the exploratory and the realistic. The exploratory is the attempt to show the carbon, to express the mysterious forces that the characters themselves are not fully aware of. Its methods are abstract nouns and groping ('He was aware of some limit to himself, of something unformed in his very being')—the most inescapable but the least successful method—and appeals to archetypal human situations, above all to the images and rhythms of the Bible ('They felt the rush of the sap in spring. . . . They knew the intercourse between heaven and earth') but also to such pagan symbols as the moon ('which seemed glowingly to uncover her bosom every time she faced it'), and to the stuff of ecstatic nature description as it might be found in Hardy (Will and Anna with the sheaves; Tess and Angel at the early morning milking) or even in Wordsworth (the maturing of Paul Morel, or of Ursula, reminding us of *The Prelude*). The realistic is what Lawrence has in common with contemporaries like Wells, Galsworthy and above all Arnold Bennett: an awareness of social change and an eye for significant detail, a mastery of dialogue, in which no novelist in English surpasses Lawrence. There is a tendency among readers of Lawrence to prefer one or other of these modes. Those for whom Lawrence is above all a modernist choose the first: for them, the exploration of these deeper layers of consciousness is what gives him his special rank among novelists, and to emphasize the modernism we can call this mode of writing 'symbolist'. The readers who prefer the realistic Lawrence are probably more numerous, if on the whole less sophisticated. The difference is often seen as chronological and sometimes the dividing line is seen as running through *The Rainbow* itself, with symbolism becoming dominant when Ursula is made the centre of consciousness; but this is an oversimplification, for there is as much symbolism in Lawrence's first novel, *The White Peacock*, as in any of the others, and the vivid realism of the tales continues all through his career. What is far more important to say, is how great a beneficial effect each of these modes has on the other. By itself, Lawrence's symbolism easily becomes turgid, and the best restraint is that exercised by the realism: the groping and the rhetoric are often controlled by the need to put down what the character actually said or did, which is often far more resonant as a result of the exploration that has gone before. Lawrence at his best may look very like Bennett, but has a profundity that Bennett's accurate dialogue never suggests. Anna calling 'I want my mother' when Lydia's labour pains begin, then being taken into the barn by her stepfather to feed the animals, must be one of the most moving episodes Lawrence—or anyone—ever wrote: its surface is utterly genuine, its dialogue and detail brilliant, yet it constantly moves into a reminder of the mysterious depths below.

As for the division in *The Rainbow*, it is not true that symbolism is absent from the first half of the book: it dominates the first page, after all. It is true however that realism is largely absent from the Ursula–Skrebensky episode. As several critics have pointed out, the writing deals so much with the inchoate state of her feelings, that it is not clear at what point she and Skrebensky first have intercourse. What a Victorian novelist would have left unclear by conventional imagery or simple omission, Lawrence leaves unclear by such phrasing as 'it was bliss, it was the nucleolating of the fecund darkness'. That is the reason (even more than the fact that it is not, strictly, a marriage) that I have not included a discussion of this third affair.

The interpenetration of realism and symbolism can take place with any subject; but it has a very close connexion with the theme of love, as we can see if we turn to the other way of stating why *The Rainbow* is a great novel of marriage. For it joins together, as no novel before it had ever done, the mode appropriate to marriage with that appropriate to love. It shows love as a transfiguring experience, one that cannot be measured or understood by the standards of the everyday: Will and Anna in the cornfield recall the *Song of Songs*, Will and Anna in bed recall (as we have seen) Donne's poetry of transfiguration. At the same time, Will and Anna squabble with her parents over whether they are ready for marriage, their relationship develops with all the particularities of individual interaction. This is where the true originality of *The Rainbow* lies—not that it puts sex into marriage, but that it puts love in. The notorious suppression of the book, along with Lawrence's general reputation, has misled both readers and critics on this point. There is little or no outspoken description of sex in the two marriages of the novel: it only enters the account of Will's marriage after his attempt to seduce a young girl in Nottingham, and the conscious shift in his relationship with Anna towards a more deliberate seeking of sexual pleasure. To the late twentieth-century reader, what is striking about their honeymoon is the restraint, even modesty, of the writing. The scene which led to the book's suppression is shocking enough (or was then), but it is not an account of sexual intercourse: it is the description of the pregnant Anna dancing naked (and, for most of the time, alone) in her bedroom.

I believe *The Rainbow*, for all its faults, is a crucial work in the long history we are concerned with. It really does what Spenser's *Amoretti* is thought to do: it joins the poetry of love to the prose of marriage, it shows the interpenetration of transfiguring and ordinary experience. That is what marriage was, for the Victorians; if any lived to read *The Rainbow* it is a pity to think that the furore and the newness probably prevented them from realizing that their ideal had at last been expressed.

Phallic Marriage

Turning now to look for a statement of the ideal of marriage expressed in *The Rainbow*, we cannot do better than take it from Lawrence's essay *Apropos of Lady Chatterley's Lover*. To many readers that essay is a more memorable work than the novel it defends; its unforgettable eloquence is vibrant with a truer, a less sneering humanism, than anything said by Connie or Mellors. Its true literary expression is not *Lady Chatterley's Lover* but *The Rainbow*.

'I want men and women', wrote Lawrence, 'to be able to think sex, fully, completely, honestly and cleanly.' The view of sex he advances comes between the puritan ('likely to fall into sexual indecency in advanced age') and the frivolous (scoffing at sex and taking it 'like a cocktail'). Both these extremes treat the body without reverence, and Lawrence is deeply reverent towards the body:

> And this is the meaning of the sexual act: this Communion, this touching on one another of the two rivers, Euphrates and Tigris,—to use old jargon— and the enclosing of the land of Mesopotamia, where Paradise was, or the Park of Eden, where man had his beginning. This is marriage, this circuit of the two rivers, this communion of the two blood-streams, this, and nothing else: as all the religions know.[65]

Through phallic worship, through such reverence for the body we keep in contact with the rhythms of earth:

> Marriage is the clue to human life, but there is no marriage apart from the wheeling sun and the nodding earth, from the straying of the planets and the magnificence of the fixed stars.[66]

And we keep in contact with one another: it is one of Lawrence's great imaginative insights, expressed in some of his finest writing, that intimacy between man and woman is not a state but a rhythmic pattern, of coming and going, of consummation and withdrawal. To recognize this is to make possible the 'true phallic marriage' that will regenerate our society.

'As all the religions know': the doctrine of phallic marriage is deeply religious, but it is a religion of this world, ritualistic, accepting, pagan. Those who like to associate Lawrence with the Puritan and Nonconformist tradition need to ignore this essay, with its attack on Protestantism, which 'came and gave a great blow to the religious and ritualistic rhythm of the year, in human life', and on Nonconformity, which almost finished the deed. Against these Lawrence places the 'Old Church', with its pagan acceptance of life:

> The Old Church knew that life is here our portion, to be lived, to be lived in fulfilment. The stern rule of Benedict, the wild delights of Francis of Assisi, these were coruscations in the steady heaven of the Church. The rhythm of life itself was preserved by the Church hour by hour, day by day, season by season, year by year, epoch by epoch, down among the people, and the wild coruscations were accommodated to this permanent rhythm.[67]

What then of the apparently Puritanical rules of the Roman Catholic Church, that women shall cover their naked flesh in church? These rules drew the scorn of Bernard Shaw, who says 'clothes arouse sex and lack of clothes tend to kill sex', and scoffs at the Pope for wanting to cover women up, 'saying that the last person in the world to know anything about sex is the Chief Priest of Europe: and that the one person to ask about it would be the Chief Prostitute of Europe, if there were such a person'. These remarks rouse Lawrence to fury. It is Shaw who is the puritan, whose vulgar idea of sexual attraction needs tricks of dressing up or half undressing; 'when the Pope insists that women shall cover their naked flesh in church, it is not sex he is opposing, but the sexless tricks of female immodesty'. It is the Church which shows true reverence for sex, of a kind Shaw is incapable of.

This doctrine of phallic marriage has now become the orthodoxy of our age. Lawrence's enormous influence is based upon the fact that like him we believe in sex, and believe its truest fulfilment is within marriage. A thousand marriage manuals and their million readers tell us that we are all Lawrentians today—or were until recently and perhaps, for the most part, still are. We seek happiness, not the fulfilment of our role and duty, we accept sex and expect it to be mutually rewarding; we combine monogamy and idealization (and the result is unstable). Birkin and Ursula are the representative couple of the age.

Since *Apropos* is greatly concerned with the contrast between past and present, a look at its historical perspective will bring this chapter full circle. I have in the exposition so far passed over the element of *laus temporis acti* that is so prominent in the essay. Lawrence believed that modern man had lost touch with his deeper emotions, that 'love is a counterfeit feeling today', that 'the spirit of the day' was one that turned real emotions to ridicule. He even erected a theory of how class-hate and class-consciousness develop when 'the old blood-warmth has collapsed'. The question of tradition is so important to Lawrence's essay that we cannot ignore it if we are to take the argument seriously. Let us look at the most prominent and (if eloquence is to be our guide) the most powerful part of its concern with tradition, its view of the Church. When we put together the nostalgia for old times with the praise of the old Church, we clearly have a view of Roman Catholic tradition, and what it has represented, that could be true or false. Lawrence's way of showing it is true is to look at the present, and then trust his intuitive sense of what sort of past must lie behind it. That is not the only way: we can also look at the evidence from the past itself.

No dictum on marriage from the early Church is as famous as that of Jerome, that he who loves his wife too passionately commits adultery. Here is Jerome's view stated slightly more fully:

> In the case of wife of another, truly all love is shameful; in the case of one's own, excessive love. The wise man should love his wife with judgement, not with passion. Let him control the excesses of voluptuousness, and not allow himself to be carried away precipitately during intercourse. Nothing is more infamous than to love one's wife like a mistress.[68]

There were four motives for marriage in orthodox scholastic doctrine, procreation, 'yielding the debt to one's partner' (i.e. satisfying his or her sexual desires), preventing incontinence, and pleasure. It is not easy to be sure what the difference is between the last two: the third may refer to satisfying the sexual urge and the fourth to stirring it up, for instance by aphrodisiacs, or simply to indulging it more often than nature compels. There was general agreement that the first two were sinless (though the act itself could be considered sinful); there was controversy whether the third was sinless or a venial sin, and whether the fourth was a venial or a mortal sin.[69] In all the controversies that make it impossible for us to attribute a clear-cut position to 'the Church', a few things stand out. One is the constant stress on preventing incontinence, which means that no intrinsic value is given to the sexual act: the famous text here is Paul's 'It is better to marry than burn.'[70] A second is the strange but widespread doctrine that 'paying the debt' is more laudable than satisfying one's own desires. It is a neat way of making sexual pleasure legitimate after all, to make that of the other person more acceptable than one's own; it is even touching in its appeal to unselfishness, but it excludes completely any idea of mutual love in the sexual act. The idea of a debtor and a creditor is so prominent in the medieval vocabulary of sex that there seems no place for the concept of mutuality. Indeed, the vocabulary has, to us, an even more startling gap, there seems no conception of sexual love, as opposed to sexual pleasure. It was widely held in the medieval church that any man found any woman sexually attractive, and vice versa.[71]

Is this Lawrence's old Church? 'It was not until the eighteenth century,' writes Stone, 'that Catholic theologians finally identified the purpose of intercourse with the spiritual purpose of marriage itself as a union of two human beings for mutual comfort and support.'[72] Lawrence's old Church was much older than the eighteenth century, surely: in the powerful rhythms of his prose it seems timeless. St Benedict and St Francis are coruscations in its steady heaven; Augustine's view is cited, that God created the universe new everyday, but if Lawrence is claiming (as he surely is) that the act of sex is a type of that divine creation, then he is simply wrong. Augustine maintained that sexual intercourse for pleasure could be excused as long as it was not too excessive and did not interfere with the times that should be given over to prayer.[73]

But long before the eighteenth century, as we have seen, the Protestants whom Lawrence so despised had formulated a doctrine of married love that included sex and freed it from the Pauline taint. Lawrence has made the mistake of assuming that the Puritans were puritanical about sex: this is not even etymologically correct.[74] It is the old Church which was puritanical, and which deserves little of the praise Lawrence lavished on it.

It might be interesting, in conclusion, to try and observe the transition. A seventeenth-century Protestant who was still in active contact with the medieval tradition was Jeremy Taylor, and in his *Holy Living* we can find a view of marriage that looks intermediate between Jerome's austerity and the new Protestant enthusiasm; and that makes a good comparison with Lawrence's own. It is still a medieval view in that virginity is preferred to marriage, though in a qualified way: not natural virginity but that which is chosen voluntarily for religious reasons, and even that only because of its potential for spiritual use. The married state is praised, but with insistence on sexual moderation—or, as he calls it, married chastity. The order of nature and the ends of God must be observed; and sexual gratification must always be controlled by the following desires: to have children, to avoid fornication, to lighten and ease the cares and sadnesses of household affairs, or to endear each other. The last two items are more liberal than the usual medieval doctrine, and the fourth seems very close to a conception of sexual love. Taylor's next two principles are strict but also rather Lawrentian: there must be no high and violent lusts with arts and misbecoming devices, and we should be restrained and temperate in the use of lawful pleasures. The Shavian view of sex, or that of the young people who take it like a cocktail, could be described as full of misbecoming devices; and the last injunction could be seen as resembling Lawrence's belief in the natural rhythms of abstinence. But the central element of Taylor's view is not rhythm but moderation: he is against waste of time, violent transporting desires, or too sensual applications. Both Taylor and Lawrence use nature as a criterion, but they are not the same nature, and Birkin and Mellors would be unnatural lovers to Taylor—but not Will and Anna, for it is only when the heart has gone out of their marriage that they enter the phase of sensual obsession with each other's bodies.[75]

The distinction between lust and a conjugal love which is sexual is so familiar to us that it is not easy to adjust to an idea of marriage which does not know it. The Middle Ages often did not, and when the seventeenth century began to draw it they had to use symbolic language, describing true conjugal love as 'visiting thy habitation without sin' or as 'drinking of the floods of milk and butter and honey', and lust as a form of idolatry. Here we are on the edge, once the religious cocoon has burst, of a modern conception of marriage—phallic, based on love, and secularized, the culminating point of a long development.

Developments do not stand still when they reach their peak; and the ideal of marriage that I described as widely accepted in the twentieth century has already come under attack. The most important of these attacks will concern us in the next chapter.

5

Feminism and Love

There have been two feminisms. That of the nineteenth and early twentieth centuries, which was mainly Anglo-American, was concerned with the hard, measurable aspects of woman's position: its goals were education, ownership of property, career opportunities and the vote. That of the last dozen years or so, American in origin, now prominent in England, Germany and (increasingly) all over the world, is at least as much concerned with intangibles: mopping up the pockets of legal, political and (more than a pocket, this one) economic male privilege is, for it, only a preliminary goal. Centrally, its aim is to change the way women see themselves and the way men see them: to reconstruct their personal emotional life, their sexual, social and (to use the jargon) familial and interpersonal relationships. Aims that are altogether vaster, vaguer and more difficult to realize.[1]

The literary mind may well feel ambivalent about this change. On the one hand, emotions are the true stuff of literature as of human life: has not the new feminism left the superficial and the trivial and turned to what really matters? On the other hand, emotions are the stuff of literature not of politics, of intimate living not of organized movements: setting out to change them by laws, pressure groups or reform programmes is surely to make a category mistake, and, indeed, to trivialize the emotional life.

I cannot resolve this ambivalence. It may well be that the women's movement is attempting the impossible, that its subsidiary goal of capturing the last bastions of privilege will turn out to be its one lasting achievement, that its larger, nobler aim will merely make it ridiculous. Even if this is true, it may be a mistake that has to be made; and when the men have finished laughing at the absurd postures and impossible demands of the liberationists, their laughter may look like the common sense of the smug and the unimaginative. Sometimes, it's not even clear who's laughing at whom:

> When in the course of the progressive dialectic of history it becomes necessary for people oppressed by caste to off the nuclear family which stabilizes the capitalist, imperialist, military complex economy which of necessity and by its very nature causes the writing of male oriented reformist revisionist

opportunist adventurist papers, a decent respect for the opinions of our sisters in struggle, compel us to assume the responsibility of the vanguard.[2]

If I had just made that up in order to parody the clichés of radical rhetoric, I would rightly be accused of crassness. It is in fact the opening of a statement by the women's caucus within the Youth International Party, and it ends with the single word 'SCREWEE! (Society for Condemning the Rape and Exploitation of Women, etc. etc.)'. Is it a joke? Is 'off' being used as a verb, or has a word dropped out? Is the solecism of the plural verb ('compel') deliberate? Can *anyone* pile up fashionably denunciatory adjectives like that and mean it? Perhaps those familiar with the rhetoric would instantly know; or perhaps the authors do not know themselves. With Valerie Solanis we seem to be on surer ground.

> Life in this society, being, at best, an utter bore and no aspect of society being at all relevant to women, there remains to civic-minded, responsible, thrill-seeking females only to overthrow the government, eliminate the money system, institute complete automation, and destroy the male sex.[3]

This time the writer is clearly in control. The list of adjectives is mischievously incompatible, the list of aims is a cool blend of impossible but genuine wishes. And not only in control: she is (surely) enjoying herself, as is Jayne West suggesting as an Essay Subject 'Discuss the variations in tone possible when asking a male druggist "Have you Tampax Super?"'[4] Extreme rhetoric, simply because of its element of gusto, needs only a spice of intelligence to hover on the edge of self-criticism: it can be a saner attitude than the milder, more earnest rhetoric of the insistently obstinate. Instead of mere hostility, it can become satire.

I have not quoted these passages because I believe them representative of responsible feminism today, but because it may be as well to begin with the extremes, to remind ourselves that it is in the nature of Women's Liberation to raise high passions, not only because of the radicalism of its demands, but because they invade our most intimate lives. Feminism always raises passions: how much more a feminism that seeks to affect our personality as well as our rights. And how much more necessary, in that case, to turn to imaginative literature to see what change is possible, and with what kind of pain, in terms of human experience.

When we compare the views of the two feminisms on love and marriage, the contrast is revealing and, in many ways, expected. Both have had a good deal to say on marriage, an institution with identifiable rules. The first feminism wanted to reform and not destroy it—was, indeed, urgent in its wish to retain it, its insistence on total respectability, on total harmlessness where the sanctity of the home was concerned. Today's feminism is not so sure: its criticisms are more fundamental, its preference uncertain. The first feminists had less to say on love, which, it saw, was clearly not the stuff of politics; yet if we look at their responses to novels and their personal attitudes, with the eye of literary curiosity or modern feminist insistence, we can see that these earnest women are implying something about the politics of love. Today's feminism has been far more ready to rush in and condemn (or reform) the passion, but once again there is a complication of voices when we listen.

Clearly we need a fourfold discussion: two feminisms, two subjects. And so I begin with the first feminism on marriage.

An Anti-Marriage League?

Nineteenth-century feminism was not only respectable, it was strict. Some of the opposition to it came from men who were afraid that women would use their power to 'impose impossibly strict standards of morality, and endeavour to enforce them by penalities for non-obser-vance'.[5] A look across the Atlantic, where the feminist movement had close connexions with temperance, might seem to justify this, as did the famous slogan of Christabel Pankhurst, 'Votes for Women and Chastity for Men.' No doubt it was tactically important for the feminists to be respectable. The public controversy over the Marriage and Divorce Act of 1857 pointed up their dilemma. On the one hand, the Act was of only doubtful benefit to women, since it incorporated an imbalance of rights, recognizing adultery in the wife but not in the husband as adequate grounds for divorce; and on the other hand it prevented serious consideration of the measure which the feminists did care about, the Married Woman's Property Act, which did not take even its first step into reality for another 13 years.[6] Any association with divorce or attacks on the family could be damaging to feminism. This is clearly seen in the agitation surrounding Josephine Butler's campaign against the Con-tagious Diseases Acts. These Acts allowed for compulsory inspection of prostitutes in garrison towns, in order to check the spread of venereal disease among soldiers. Only the prostitutes and not their clients were inspected, and Mrs Butler regarded this as an unwarrantable interference with the liberty of women. Her campaign was long-drawn-out, courageously fought, and (in the end) successful; and what is above all striking is its iron respectability. Mrs Butler considered any form of state regulation of prostitution to be unacceptable, because it set an official approval on the activity and tended in practice to its increase. In all her work with prostitutes, which was devoted and humane, she started from the belief that prostitution itself was the evil.[7] Her approach was so re-spectable that she is open to the charge of evasiveness: this realistic and heroic woman was indifferent to the element of genuine concern that underlay the Acts, the concern to check the spread of venereal disease.

It is no accident that there were connexions between the Repeal Movement, the reforming zeal of W. T. Stead (author of 'The Maiden Tribute of Modern Babylon') and the fierce puritanism of the National Vigilance Association.[8]

Yet the campaign was not respectable enough for the suffrage movement; and there were constant attempts to keep them separate, to the point of a split in the London Society for Women's Suffrage, for even those who supported both felt that the connexion with the campaign was damaging.[9] In part this was tactics; but the concern to stay respectable included a perfectly genuine belief in marriage. Even John Stuart Mill, for all his attacks on marriage as a 'school of despotism', behaved scrupulously towards Harriet Taylor. There was clearly no sexual irregularity when she was not yet free; yet if that (and the discreet delay after her husband's death) is the sign of a low sexual drive on his part, it is striking that they did marry—and if it is not, the concern for respectability is equally striking. It could even be argued that the ponderously rational praise he bestows on her never quite conceals an almost chivalrous devotion.[10]

The respectability of the feminists can be seen in their attitude to Mary Wollstonecraft. Since she has a better claim than anyone to being considered the first explicit feminist they could not fail to revere her; but they found her irregular union and illegitimate child an embarrassment.[11]

We can make a rough division of radical movements into two kinds, according as their ideology is specific or general. The specific want to change one thing only, either because they are only interested in that, or because they are conservative on other matters; the general want to change society, and though they may start with a single issue, they believe that to liberate one group is to set in motion a wider process of liberation. The first feminism stands at the extreme of the specific, and many of its supporters were perfectly satisfied with the social order to which they wished to admit women; there is nothing in their vocabulary corresponding to the modern term of condemnation, 'the system'.

If they did not attack marriage, would it not have been even harder to attack love? What would that mean: to be for hate? To be attacked, love must be clearly identified as romantic love, a particular doctrine with a very specific ideology: then perhaps there will be some who want to draw the curtain on the long history that began with the troubadours. Even so, it will not be easy to attack it as an institution like marriage can be attacked: political movements cannot choose sentiments as their target. Or if they can, the feminists didn't.

They did recognize love as the basis of literature; and so if they had a criticism to make, it could take the form of literary comment. Beatrice Webb, for instance, asserted curtly in her diary that novels are bad for

An Anti-Marriage League? 169

young girls because 'the whole of their thought is wasted on making up love scenes, or building castles in the air, where she is always the charming heroine without fault'.[12]

How can the feminists have failed to realize, as they read the novels, that love could be a conservative sentiment? If they read them with the rather Philistine eye of the single-minded reformer, they would be more struck by the social implications of the passion than by its aesthetic function—hence the hostile reception they gave The Princess.

Tennyson certainly intended The Princess as a satire on female education: the resemblance between the woman's college and the men's academy in Love's Labours Lost is not an accident, and the project collapses not only through external pressures but because femininity proves too much for intellect: though the Princess never quite climbs down explicitly, she behaves at the climax as a woman should—first by (unaccountably) accepting her brother's offer to settle the dispute by fighting, then by nursing the wounded Prince, finally and by now inevitably by falling in love with him. In this clash between femininity and intellect it is the former which, for Tennyson at least, is the source of poetry; and he caused the Princess to realize this: for after she has listened to 'Tears idle tears' she comments 'with some disdain':

If indeed there haunt
About the mouldered lodges of the Past
So sweet a voice and vague, fatal to men,
Well needs it we should cram our ears with wool.

Fixing one's thoughts on reform means turning away from poetry that 'moans about the retrospect', 'toward that great year of equal mights and rights' that she looks forward to. Since there is no doubt that Tennyson's genius (as he knew) was for poems that moaned about the retrospect, this enabled the Athenaeum reviewer, praising the beauty of the songs, to claim that they 'delicately indicate that bias of Woman's heart towards the affections which neither the example nor the discipline of the Princess had been able effectively to counteract'.[13]

For all his satiric intent, Tennyson cannot fail to convey the actual running of the woman's college with some sympathy: his eloquent account of the Lady Psyche's lecture on Woman's Studies offers a blend of modern science and feminist history that is quite astonishing for 1847. Any reader who read this with enthusiasm would inevitably feel betrayed when the Princess is made to find her true mission as angel in the house, and one can understand feminist anger at the poem.[14]

How could the feminists attack what Tennyson had done without attacking his poetry? Tennyson had seen that what the Princess stood for was inimical to his poetic sensibility, and responded by betraying her venture; now we see that his most cunning, most treacherous act of all (though the cunning was purely unconscious) was to force the feminist critic into Philistinism. Not merely the romances denounced by Beatrice Webb but love poetry itself, and Tennyson's marvellous lyric gift, can be seen as 'fancies hatched in silken-folded idleness'.

Marriage and Liberation

Did any women in the nineteenth century attack marriage? The New Women of the 1890s—distinguishably different from the organized feminists—were certainly associated with a rejection of marriage, but it is not easy to discover the reality of these bloomered bicycling cigar-smoking creatures, the Sue Brideheads and Herminia Bartons. Were they all of them the figments of male novelists' imaginations? One who certainly existed was Olive Schreiner, who refused to dress any differently than usual on her wedding-day, and was sufficiently unfeminine (if also unsocialist) to wish 'I could have my food cooked for me and my clothes made, like a man.'[15] It is here surely, rather than from Millicent Fawcett, Josephine Butler or the Pankhursts, that we hear the anticipations of Women's Liberation, and the rejections of marriage that are now so familiar. 'If women are to effect a significant amelioration in their condition,' says Germaine Greer, 'it seems obvious that they must refuse to marry.'[16] Roxanne Dunbar, a radical Marxist (destroy one and you destroy them all) sees the female liberation movement as revolutionary because it aims to destroy the family unit.[17] Juliet Mitchell contrasts love and marriage in a way that forms an unexpected extension of the first chapter of this book:

> There is a formal contradiction between the voluntary contractual character of 'marriage' and the spontaneous uncontrollable character of 'love'—the passion that is celebrated precisely for its involuntary force. The notion that it occurs only once in every life and can therefore be integrated into a voluntary contract, becomes decreasingly plausible in the light of everyday experience—once sexual repression as a psycho-ideological system becomes at all relaxed.[18]

The literary tradition, in other words, was wiser than the social norms: the passion of romantic love should be preferred to the responsibilities of matrimony. The 'notion' of the second sentence is the attempt to deny the contrast, to base married love on romantic love. The conservative Denis de Rougemont[19] and the radical Juliet Mitchell come together in their scorn for marrying Iseult, the one because romance is no basis for marriage, the other because marriage is no basis for romance. Simone de Beauvoir makes the same point, linking it explicitly with the literary tradition: 'Since the rise of chivalric love it is a commonplace that marriage kills love.'[20] Neither of these women is quite at ease with the term 'love', and perhaps it is their cultural backgrounds that determine their way of avoiding it: the Frenchwoman replaces it by 'eroticism' while the Englishwoman retains it in inverted commas.

The immediate origin of the modern attack on marriage can be seen in Betty Friedan's description of the problem that has no name. The great retreat from feminism in the 1940s and 50s, according to her, returning women to their domestic roles, created a problem of identity—'a stunting or evasion of growth that is perpetuated by the feminine mystique'. Looking at all the 'fine, intelligent American women, to be envied for their homes, husbands, children, and for their personal gifts of mind and spirit', she asks why they felt driven, why so many had breakdowns and so many more hated their situation.[21] That those who are best off, on most rational criteria, should be more miserable and more unstable than the underfed and overworked is perhaps one of the most puzzling things in our society. To a follower of Durkheim this may not be puzzling at all. The Friedan goals of self-actualization, growth and purpose outside the self can be seen as an aspiration so high that few will ever attain them in this imperfect world: they amount to an impossible aspiration, and will therefore produce *anomie*, the condition that everywhere accompanies the 'morbid desire for the infinite'.[22] The contrast between this and the feminist analysis shows clearly the conservative nature of Durkheim's thought, for it is the difference between accepting the ills that flesh is heir to and identifying their causes, even when (as here) they seem causeless. A list of causes is spelt out explicitly by Elizabeth Janeway. First, women are made to feel that bringing up children is their most important function, yet it lasts, nowadays, for not much more than a decade; second, they fit their children for a questionable society, one in which 'the most admired goals are pretty well closed to these women themselves'; third, the process of child raising now consists only of an emotional relationship, no longer, as in the past, of 'economic activities and social processes that relate to the larger world'; finally, children are expected to grow out of the relationship in which the mothers have invested so much. 'In view of these expectations, it does not seem odd that the mothers of Orchard Town are rated as having "relatively high emotional instability".'[23] Those items in this list which are most general seem most vulnerable to a Durkheimian analysis: thus the complaint that our society has questionable aims sounds like a demand for perfection that could be made of any society, and thus like a recipe for *anomie*; whereas the second half of that same point, the contrast between what they are preparing their children for and what is available to them, is a specific criticism that could be met by specific measures. The next point, that a compound activity with practical elements has been simplified to an emotional relationship, is one where the Durkheimian would

172 Feminism and Love

agree with the feminist, for it seems to empty the process of running a home of its most clearly attainable elements.

I have set the feminist analysis of marriage against a postulated Durkheimian one because each exposes the limitations of the other: the choice between them is partly ideological, and each reader will make it for himself. I have no doubt that the social change resulting from progressive goals does increase *anomie*, but it is still of course open to the radical to maintain that this is a price worth paying for the improvement.

Here then is the modern feminist indictment of marriage. There are two main comments to offer on it. The first is that it needs to be made comparative. To say that society is imperfect, and some people unhappy, risks being merely obvious; whereas if we can see what has changed, which social imperfections have grown worse or better, or just different, and even (perhaps) whether unhappiness has increased, we shall be able to criticize with more precision. Yet to compare the situation of today's wives with that of their great-great-grandmothers must give us pause. Did not Elizabeth Janeway's points apply equally to the Victorian wife? True, she might have splent longer bringing up her children—say three decades rather than one and a half. But she too was preparing her sons for positions that were closed to her; she too if wealthy enough to have servants was reduced (or elevated) to offering her family mainly an emotional relationship; and yet she did not say 'I am desperate', she did not wake up one morning with nothing to look forward to; she did not take tranquillizers like cough drops or try to commit suicide[24]— did she? If the unhappiness of wives seems to have increased so sharply, we must come to one of three conclusions: that modern feminists are making a fuss about nothing; that Victorian women bottled it all up; or that there has been a change which cannot be explained in terms of the roles expected of the wife.

There is some objective evidence that the first hypothesis is wrong: Woman's Liberation, in its attack on marriage, is not making up the problem. This is documented in Jessie Bernard's excellent study *The Future of Marriage* which shows that in our society marriage tends to benefit men at the expense of women. Distinguishing between two marriages, the husband's and the wife's, it claims that the former, in terms of mental health, survival and happiness, is better than being single, whereas for wives the reverse obtains. The popular view of the carefree bachelor and the frustrated spinster is the opposite of the truth.[25]

And the second hypothesis? Though in the nature of things we cannot interview Victorian wives about menstrual pains or the servant problems, I do not think it possible to doubt that the angel in the house was contented with her lot, and often proud of it. The only clear evidence to the contrary which I know is Florence Nightingale's astonishing essay

'Cassandra' written in 1852 and privately printed in 1859, which presents a Friedan–Janeway critique of the Victorian family. From the heart of respectable society it delivers a savage and shrewd attack on the domestic ideal: 'The family? It is too narrow a field for the development of an immortal spirit, be that spirit male or female.' It mentions the temptation of suicide, from which some are only deterred for religious reasons 'and because it is "no use".' It compares the wife to the prostitute. It makes the point that children grow away from their family of upbringing, and leave home as early as possible. It mocks at the rites of the family, in which 'dinner is the great sacred ceremony of the day'.[26] If writing this essay was not as far-reaching as reorganizing the nursing profession and the administration of India, it was surely at least as subversive.

If we removed the stylistic traces of its origin, could 'Cassandra' be mistaken for a document of the 1960s? The answer is very nearly yes, so astonishingly does it attack what it is supposed to revere. The only difference, perhaps (and that is slight) is that there is a more specific purpose running through it than is the case with analyses of the problem that has no name. For Florence Nightingale it had a name, which was idleness. Her plea is that women be allowed to work, and work systematically and responsibly: 'So many hours spent every day in passively doing what conventional life tells us, when we would so gladly be at work.' Yet in the course of making this point it offers an indictment so generalized, it so deliberately overturns the idols of the culture, that it could well be entitled an attack on the Feminine Mystique, or an account of Man's World, Woman's Place.

But it is unique. When we read the chorus of acceptance that the angel ideal elicited from woman as well as men, and that the previous chapter tried to record, we have to recognize that woman's consciousness, true or false, was a consciousness of the domestic mission. That leaves our third hypothesis, which is obviously the correct one: that a change has taken place not only in woman's role but in her readiness to accept that role. Revolution is the result of social change as much as its cause.

My second comment on the indictment of marriage is to point out that to indict is not necessarily to reject. There are two directions to which the feminist complaint can lead, rejection or reform, and the latter has quite as strong a tradition behind it. Marriage can be seen either as an institution in which men dominate women, or as one in which men are tied to women. Because women necessarily bear the children, and have always in our society, as in most societies, had responsibility for their early care, the alternative to marriage could be an even greater burden on women. If it is true, as folklore has it, that men are naturally less committed to monogamy than women, marriage can be seen as a way of preventing them from leaving her holding the baby. This view can be found in feminist writings:

> When my father had got both his daughters off his hands he thought, I'm going to get out of it. But my sister and I said, no you're not, not now. You can't leave Mother alone at this time of life. Maybe we shouldn't have done it, but we couldn't see our mother and the kind of person she was ever making a life of her own at that age.[27]

Here marriage is clearly seen as protection for the woman. True, one party will say that it was an imperfect society which rendered the wife so feeble in the first place; but if marriage is being defended not as a sacrament but on pragmatic grounds of usefulness to women, it is women as they are who must be the starting point. By far the clearest statement of this view that I know is the following:

> I should coax him to take me before the parson straight off, and have done with it, if I were in your place ... then, you see, if you have rows, and he turns you out of doors, you can get the law to protect you, which you can't otherwise, unless he half runs you through with a knife, or cracks your noddle with a poker. And if he bolts away from you—I say it friendly, as woman to woman, for there's never any knowing what a man med do— you'll have the sticks o' furniture, and won't be looked upon as a thief.[28]

It is no answer to this to say that the law has given (even gives now?) a less adequate protection to the wife than it might; for since pragmatic judgements are comparative, the relevant comparison is with how much protection is enjoyed by the unmarried woman—as Arabella sees. At the time of this writing, there are signs that the law is changing, extending to cohabiting women the same property rights as wives enjoy: if that happens, it may be a verbal quibble whether we say that marriage is now less necessary for the protection of women, or that the idea of what counts as marriage has been extended.

Denouncing marriage and the evils it produces is easy rhetoric; if denunciation is to lead to reasoned rejection then rhetoric must give way to proposing alternative arrangements for the three main functions of marriage, economic, sexual and the rearing of children. The economic function may be in process of solving itself, as the rights of spouses are disentangled and marriage moves towards separate holdings or a set of rules for dividing joint holdings when necessary. Sex will concern us in a moment, when we turn to the alternative views of emancipated female sexuality. Child-rearing is not an easy problem for feminism to find a consistent position on, for there are two very different tendencies that beckon. On the one hand, there is the view that children are entirely a woman's concern: abortion is a woman's right to choose, which men have denied them; family allowances should be paid to women only (as the Post Office does but not the Inland Revenue); custody of children on separation should normally go to the woman (which it does); child-birth is a female affair, better left to wise women than handed over to medicine men; and so on.[29] On the other hand there is the view that men must take their share of responsibility, change nappies, get up in the night, and treat children as belonging to both parties; even that each partner might take a half-time job in order to achieve complete role-sharing. There need be no formal opposition between these two sets of demands, and they can be tailored so that they do not actually contradict each other: to that extent, it is possible for the same person to support both. But I do not see how it can be denied that the tendency of the first set is to weaken marriage, and the second set to strengthen it; and on a perhaps deeper level than the logical it might be difficult to belong to both camps. As for feminism, it may incline to the former position because it is easier to turn into specific political demands: but this will not apply to a Woman's Movement that has deliberately extended its scope beyond the strictly political. If the leaders of Women's Liberation do in practice belong to an Anti-marriage League,[30] there is no logical compulsion for their followers to do likewise.

Love and Liberation

Contraception has enabled women to separate consummated love from marriage, and to avoid the plight of being left holding the baby by not conceiving one. This has produced a doctrine of emancipated sexual fulfilment that we associate especially with our own time; yet it was stated—by a fictitious woman—in 1724. Defoe's Roxana is finan-cially independent, indeed comfortably off, when she is courted by a Dutch merchant, a widower, who has obliged her in the past. She likes him but does not wish to marry for she has found that 'a wife is looked upon as but an upper servant, a mistress is a sovereign'. She maintains

> That the very Nature of the Marriage-Contract was in short, nothing but giving up Liberty, Estate, Authority, and every-thing, to the Man, and the Woman was indeed, a meer Woman ever after, that is to say, a Slave.[31]

Here are all the modern feminist objections to marriage, which is seen as an institution based on male authority and property; and what makes this genuinely modern is the conviction that to forego marriage need not mean to forego sex. For the merchant persuades her to sleep with him (she does not need much persuading) in the belief that it will be the best way to get her to marry him, and then is astonished when she still refuses. She has nothing against him, and would be happy to con-tinue as his mistress, but objects to 'divesting myself of my estate, and putting my Money out of my hand'. The merchant, whose moral notions are orthodox, urges that what she is doing is unnatural and against custom, that 'he had reason to expect I should be content with that which all the world was contented with', and even that marriage was decreed by Heaven. But Roxana is a true moral radical: she realizes that it would be the sensible course to follow the world's doctrine, but 'I could not reconcile my judgement to marriage.' When she reveals—rather reluctantly—that she is pregnant he is of course able to add the argument that she is being unkind to the child that is yet unborn, who 'must be branded from its cradle with a mark of infamy': but she has made her plans, and they are realistic, for coping as a one-parent family.

Liberated women will perhaps be disappointed to learn of Roxana's repentance and change of mind. Her narration of the episode is accompanied by expressions of disapproval of her own conduct ('these were my wicked arguments for whoring'), and when she meets the merchant ten years later she does marry him. This certainly makes Defoe less of a feminist, but it does not deprive *Roxana* of its place in the story of emancipated sexuality, for this is the way radical sentiments normally appear in fiction—in contest with orthodoxy and often, in terms of plot, defeated by it. What matters is not simply which side the author comes down on, but his ability to express for us the full human meaning of a new point of view.

The idea of sexual emancipation has now become a commonplace among the liberated; 'the chief instrument in the deflection and perversion of female energy', writes Germaine Greer, 'is the denial of female sexuality'.[32] It is a widespread view, by now; the problem, as so often with the reform of manners, is to be sure just what sexual emancipation means. There seem to be four main possibilities: a more equal physical and emotional relationship within the existing institutions, the replacement of marriage by free unions, promiscuity, and 'sex without men'. Each has its supporters.

The demand for greater sexual equality in marriage could concern frequency of sexual intercourse, and who initiates it; concern for the woman's pleasure (or ceasing to fuss over it); greater privacy (a room of one's own); abolition of the double standard (fidelity by both, or freedom for both). There is plenty of ambiguity here. One strand of this can be seen as a demand that husbands carry out the programme they have always professed, for the nineteenth-century ideal of marriage combined, as we saw, legal subordination with an ideal of personal equality. A new conception of woman's sexuality could be fitted into the ideal, leading to the claim that the consideration given to women's intellectual potential ought to be extended to their bodies. Fidelity by men and orgasms by women is not only easily derived from Victorian doctrine, it almost certainly represents what Kingsley (and perhaps Patmore) believed. This demand then is either an appeal from men's practice to existing ideals, in which case, like most attacks on hypocrisy, it need have no radical implications; or else (if it means sexual freedom for both parties for instance) it points to one of the other demands, those that lead away from marriage.

The replacement of marriage by free unions is also ambiguous, as the case of Sue Bridehead showed. Insofar as it specifically concerns sex, it is either an attack on fidelity, or an attack on contracts. To attack fidelity is to support promiscuity (which is of course a matter of degree), and that can be described cynically as the claim that women are entitled to take their pleasures as freely as men have always done. The attack on contracts, if it is linked specifically with sex, amounts to the view that any form of public commitment or declaration of responsibility is sexually inhibiting, perhaps to the degree of producing impotence or aversion, certainly to the degree of removing the sense of freedom essential to sexual enjoyment. This view can be considered one of the quainter forms of modern individualism (only the totally unconstrained act is satisfying) and its view of sex can without distortion be labelled anarchist.

Sex outside marriage was not a problem for nineteenth-century feminists; and sex within marriage was not one they discussed. Now that we discuss everything, especially sex, it is possible to look at the sexual opinions of Women's Liberation, and I suggest that we can find in it both an anti-erotic and a pro-erotic tendency. Systematic discussion of this is not only difficult, it could be seen as unfair.

> To have the right to sleep alone is essential.... A woman needs time alone—after a day of being a public servant to the rest of the family.... To then have to touch, caress, console yet another person is too much.... Oh God, he wants his rights again.[33]

Solemnly to classify a cry of pain like this as an example of the anti-erotic view might goad the author to understandable fury: asking for bread, she is given the stones of logic. But logic is not the enemy of pain, in the long run.

The anti-erotic derives from nineteenth-century feminism. From the reasonable assertions of Beatrice Webb that women with strong natures should remain celibate so that motherly feeling should be forced into public work to the hysterical fantasies of worlds ruled by women and virgin births,[34] a strong dislike of sex has been handed down to the Movement, and it is startlingly alive today: 'This obsession with frigidity and orgasms. Frankly I get bored with the subject.'[35] This has led to perhaps the most celebrated of all the Movement's slogans, the refusal to be treated as a sexual object. I may have split enough hairs to drive the feminists bald, but I have to ask what that means too. For if it is an attack on commercialization, on the exploiting of sex to sell cigarettes or motor-cars, it joins hands with one of the most conservative positions of all, hostility to the vulgarity of modern life. And if it is a demand to be treated by your man as a person, not as a mere sexual convenience, then it does not differ from another very old idea, the difference between love and lust. In either case, it can be seen as an essentially conservative demand. If however it is not either of these, how does it differ from a simple hostility to sex itself?

This is how it is seen by Midge Decter, in the most perceptive criticism of Women's Liberation that I know.

> What the new sexual freedom of women has indisputably brought them, however, is ... new sexual freedom: the freedom of each and every individual woman to have a large hand in the determination of her own sexual conduct and destiny, the freedom to decide very largely, for herself, what to do and that other freedom, which is its inevitable concomitant, to pay very dearly—if for some reason the payment should be exacted—for her decision.
>
> This condition of freedom Women's Liberation has called enslavement; this state of controlling one's choices Women's Liberation has called being a sexual object.[36]

Midge Decter sees some of the more frenetic demands of the liberationists not as a demand for freedom but as a retreat from it. Freedom—including sexual freedom—is not a comfortable state, and its demands, in terms of decision and responsibility, may be more than all but the strongest can bear. But in an age where the rhetoric of freedom is so universal, it will not be easy to admit that one wants less of it; just as the rhetoric of sex makes it difficult to admit that one wants less of that. But if one peers beneath the rhetoric that, according to Midge Decter, is what one finds. For her, the anti-erotic is dominant in the movement, and its drive is 'for the right of women to step back, retire, from a disagreeable involvement in, and responsibility for, the terms of sexual equality with men'. If the drive is willing to express itself as conservatism, we get a return to the hearth: there is Ruskin waiting, an eager ally in attacks on the commercial exploitation of sex. If it has to be radical at all costs we can be led to Lesbianism and masturbation, propounded with ideological fervour by some. Some demonstrators are said to have carried posters reading 'Don't Fuck—Masturbate.' This is the anti-eroticism of the emancipated.

As for the pro-erotic element in Women's Liberation, here there is a similar dilemma. It may be a defence of sexual love, in which case it is not really radical; or it may be a defence of a new ideal of female sexuality—in which case?

> We and our sisters are a lot less hung-up about sleeping with different people

and we recognize that our need to fuck is a sexual need and we aren't concerned about the love bullshit routine.[37]

That seems about as extreme as you can ask for. If it is offensive, we
should ask whether it is language or content that offends. How far does
it, for instance, differ from this?

> I send a brief, fervent wish toward the future, more honest and clean than
> most of my wishes, that by the time my little girls are old enough for sex,
> convention will allow them to enjoy it for its own sake and not to feel
> morally bound to confuse it with loving.[38]

There is an aggressive promiscuity about the high-school girls that
matches the aggression in their language; but the sensitive wife in Gillian
Tindall's novel has also taken the step that would have shocked all our
grandmothers (or perhaps, by now, great-great-grandmothers), the dissociation of sex from love.

It is rash, in a time of social change, to claim that there is nothing
new under the sun. But it does look as if the programme of sexual emancipation contains some old and familiar elements. If the anti-erotic see
woman as Mary after all, do the pro-erotic not see her as Dalilah? One
good reason for maintaining this is the resurgence of the claims about
woman's insatiable sexual appetite—but this time, made by the women.
The claim is connected with the controversy about vaginal and clitoral
orgasms, the doctrine of vaginal orgasm being seen as patriarchal
because of the way it makes women dependent on men for sexual satisfaction, and the clitoral orgasm representing sex in dissociation from reproduction, and giving a woman full control of her own responses—
though there is no clear correlation between feminism and this belief.
There are some very bold statements about the 'universal and physically
normal condition of women's inability ever to reach complete sexual
satiation'. Mary Jane Sherfey supports this assertion with some evidence
from Masters and Johnson on the cure of frigidity by 'frequent pro-
longed coitus'. If there is evidence we must doubtless accept it, even
though it sounds like the male pornographer's dream; but one hopes
it is better than the evidence that leads her to assert that from 12,000
to 8000 BC 'woman enjoyed full sexual freedom and was often totally
incapable of controlling her sexual drive'.[39] Mary Jane Sherfey's view
that the ungovernable sexual drive of women needs to be brought under
control before civilization can develop sounds almost like a boast, but
it is sufficiently alarming for her editor (Robin Morgan) to disown it
in an anxious footnote. It is one of the quainter ironies of the whole
long story that the bitterest enemies of women, the long line of saints,
preachers and satirists who denounced them as composed of mere appetite, should posthumously be told by the most advanced women that
they were right.

Love is a matter not only of sexual activity but of emotional involvement: what is the relation of emancipation to the traditional emotional patterns? 'In the domain of men–women relationships, the wish to be free emerges as romantic love,'[40] writes Edward Shorter, succinctly stating a view that is set forth more fully by Talcott Parsons,[41] and implied by the main tradition of our literature, glorifying romantic love by inviting us to identify with the young couple resisting their parents. We have caught glimpses of why this view can be rejected: for what sort of freedom is it that enslaves you to an irrational force?

Several explanations are possible of why love needs to be irrational. It may represent the power of sex, the impossibility of totally containing so violent a drive. It may represent the necessary basis of any defiance of social norms: the strength to withstand parental power and prudential pressures can only come from believing that you are part of something vaster than yourself. Or it may represent an implicit condemnation, an awareness that unconstrained freedom is disastrous, that choosing a life partner without guidance is too mad for reason.[42] Love can be glorified for its irrationality, or the taint of irrationality could be a propaganda weapon by society's institutions.

Sooner or later, those who wanted freedom were bound to reject its association with irrationality. There is no reason, in strict logic, why it should be women rather than men who do this,[43] unless there is something in the very idea of romantic love that implies male dominance. Support for this view comes from the most improbable quarter conceivable, from that great anti-feminist, Nietzsche:

> Our joy in ourselves seeks to preserve itself by again and again transforming some new thing into *ourselves*—that is what possessing means.... Sexual love betrays itself most clearly as impulse towards property; the lover wants unconditional power over her soul as over her body, he wants her to love him alone and to dwell and rule in her soul as what is highest and most desired.[44]

So far from being the opposite of egoism, love for Nietzsche is its most unconstrained expression. Here is a splendid basis for those attacks on love from the modern feminists Nietzsche would have so loathed.

> Love, tailored to marriage or an affair, only keeps women isolated, dependent and inferior in personality. As there is no possible equality in any presently conceived relationship of woman to man, or in any functioning relation of the people to the controlling class, love must exist as some greater or less perversion of human awareness. The bitter flavour of this observation is not the result of my knowing you or any other individual, but is a summation of my total perception of men, beginning with my father, his God and his Reality....[45]

There may be a good deal of pain behind such a statement. Nothing

can invalidate suffering, but suffering does not in itself validate conclusions, and the very generality of the conclusion ('in any presently conceived relationship') seems to make the writer incapable of drawing distinctions. We are on the path here to the extremists we have already
glanced at—Beverly Jones, for instance: 'women have got to reject the
blind and faulty categories of thought foisted on them by a male order
for its own benefit'. These include romance, 'the love which overcomes
or substitutes for everything else'. Romance is the rabbit at the dog track
'which for the benefit and amusement of our masters keeps us running
and thinking in safe circles'.[46]

How it is possible, holding such a view, to respond to the world's
love poetry? No doubt Othello felt marvellous when saying 'O my
soul's joy', as we do when we listen: but—*amused*? And no doubt Juliet
was in fact running and thinking in circles when she called Romeo back
and then confessed 'I have forgot why I did call thee back:' but—*safe*
circles? Romeo thought he was following the same rabbit; Desdemona
thought Othello was *her* soul's joy. The literary implications of the rejection of love are enormous. Even if we dismiss Beverly Jones as an extremist, she (and others) have taught her moderate sisters to see with new
eyes.

We should not underestimate the revolutionary nature of today's
feminism. It seeks to query what not only our society but most, perhaps
all, societies have taken for granted. Margaret Mead claims to know of
no culture 'that has said, articulately, that there is no difference between
men and women except in ... generation; ... in which it has been
thought that all identifiable traits ... are merely human traits'.[47] The
attempt to abolish role differentiation is an attempt to do what has hardly
ever been done before. This does not necessarily make it absurd, for we
do not have to allow anthropology to force us into conservative
postures: we may now be in a position to do something for the first
time. But it does mean that the programme is revolutionary—even more
so than the more obviously militant wing of Woman's Liberation, that
sees women consolidating their own roles with renewed strength. But
this need surprise no one who is not slave to the superficial view that
revolution depends on violence. And of the many possible consequences
of such a revolution, its effect on how we read imaginative literature
is the one that must concern us. For this effect, the rejection of love is
more important than the rejection of marriage, simply because love is
a sentiment, marriage an institution.

If literature tells us that role division corresponds to something deep-
seated in women, then it can never be an ally of feminism; if it tells
us that love, as traditionally conceived, is the highest experience available
to us, comparable to religious ecstasy, then it can never be an ally of

the wing of feminism that regards romance as the rabbit at the dog track. The only choice for such feminism would then be Philistinism, or creating a new literature, or a new way of reading old literature. If all feminists were Philistines, their interest for this discussion would cease forthwith. We need therefore to consider the other two possibilities, first by looking at the work of some living woman novelists, then by looking at work which antedates feminism. The former will enable us to compare the feminist critique with how their sisters' imagination has actually seen things; the latter will open the possibility of seeing in earlier literature what contemporaries passed over or rejected and even the author may have been uneasy with.

Sisterly Imaginations

We could begin from a rough division of women novelists into the sensitives and the feminists—those who are and are not willing to begin from the traditional 'feminine' virtues, and draw on these for their talent. As examples of each, I suggest Elizabeth Jane Howard and Doris Lessing.

The sensitive, elaborate stories of Elizabeth Jane Howard, told with great professional competence, explore the intricate emotional relationships between men and women, in and outside marriage. The characters are usually rich, and express their feelings freely in the way they spend money: but like Virginia Woolf, she is able to set against the rich in the main plot a subplot (in *Odd Girl Out*, for instance) that shows, bluntly, the cruel effect of being poor. The sense in which her novels are and are not conventional is important, for she sometimes drops into literary convention at the point at which she departs from conventional morality. To explain this it will be necessary to tell one of her elaborate plots: I have chosen *After Julius*.

When Esmé, wife of Julius, was in her mid-thirties, she had an affair with Felix, 14 years younger than she. Twenty years later he gets in touch with her again, and the novel begins. We now learn that the foolishly heroic death of Julius at Dunkerque was partly because he'd found out about them. Cressy, the elder daughter, had married soon after her father's death; now she is a widow of 37, who has affairs, is unhappy, and longs for love. She is fiercely resentful at Felix's reappearance; now we learn that she had found out about the affair and told her father, so that she was really responsible for his death, though she blamed it on Esmé and Felix. Felix and Cressy fall in love—embarrassingly, since Esmé, a well-preserved 58, indicates she is still available just as Felix is on the point of saying, I've fallen in love with your daughter; but they extricate themselves, not without comedy.

Here we have an involved and touching family drama (this summary has greatly simplified the elaborate plot). Cressy had hated Felix because he spoilt her parents' marriage; she had kept her resentful picture of him as a layabout who went round wrecking marriages, and that resentment precipitated their quarrel, which precipitated their new feeling for each other. The interactions of sexual, parental and filial feeling, between Felix, Cressy, her mother and her dead father (there is a sister too) are studied sensitively and with a due sense of their complexity—until the final revelation is made. The first love-making of Felix and Cressy is very awkward, and in explaining her unexpected dread, she tells him, You were the first man I loved. It turns out that at the age of 17 she has fallen in love with Felix and that was why the discovery of his affair with her mother had hurt so.

This transforms the novel. Up till then, Cressy had apparently hated Felix because he spoilt her parents' marriage. She had been deeply attached to her father—hence her hasty marriage on his death, hence (perhaps) her telling him about the affair. Now we find that her main motive was sexual jealousy; a study of how a basically affectionate woman grows up insecure and even bitchy because of her shattered trust in her parents' marriage turns out to be the drama of a woman scorned. As a piece of respectable morality, this is less conventional, but as a plot much more so.

The Long View is also built on a move back into the past, as it tells the story of the Fleming marriage backwards, from their break-up at the beginning to their first meeting on the last page: a way of getting (ironically) some of the artistic effect of a happy ending. This novel is cynical about marriage: 'this act of folly ... did not seem to be graced by a spark of romantic selection, desire or bravado,—seemed nothing more ... than the next thing these two were to do in their lives'. This is as bitter as Penelope Mortimer, for whom marriage is chiefly an opportunity to be wounded. The frightening intensity of her urbane, desperate pessimism tells us that 'pain and evil are there for the asking, nobody's going to protect you from them'. Yet for both these novelists there is, for women, no escaping the need for a man. The crises in Mrs Fleming's life are linked to being noticed by a man, even a man casually met at a party, as if unhappiness makes her, in a way, available. More serious is woman's need of monogamy. The reason that these middle-aged wives are so vulnerable is because of their emotional need of the husband who bullies or abandons them. The narrator of *The Pumpkin Eater* is destroyed because she could not grow indifferent to her husband:

> You learn nothing by hurting others; you only learn by being hurt. Where I had been viable, ignorant, rash and loving I was now an accomplished bitch, creating an emptiness in which my own emptiness might survive.

In *The Home*, Penelope Mortimer goes further. All round the heroine, Eleanor, sexual partnerships form and rearrange, in varying degrees of happiness, but for her there is only the ache caused by her emotional need of the husband she has lost, that need on which 'enlightened' separations so often founder. Marriage, the book tells us, is not needed by the happy, only by the unhappy. Eleanor, like Mrs Fleming, finds that she needs monogamy when she can no longer have it.

Conrad Fleming had been in love, in his way, when he married the wife he learns to treat with such dignified indifference. During their honeymoon he set out to mould her, with the calm patience of a sculptor. Not surprisingly, the bewildered young bride complained that he did not take her seriously, and his reply to that reveals his conception of marriage.

> 'I married you', he said slowly and clearly, 'because you are going to be extremely beautiful, which means for me that you will be a pleasure to see, a delight to be with, and because, possessing you, I shall be envied by others.... You see why I cannot help laughing when you say that I don't take you seriously.'

It is important to the novel that we find Mr Fleming mysterious and impressive, that realizing his tremendous egoism, we also realize his fascination and his wife's attraction to him. The novel was published in 1956; and the two decades that have passed may have made it very difficult for the feminist reader to do this. In the present climate of opinion, his egoism looks too like certain stereotypes of male possessiveness to emerge as an individual variant. The detail that gives most away in this passage is his use of the future tense: at the beginning of his marriage he cannot yet recognize that his wife already has a character.

Two things are meant to prevent us from impatiently dismissing Mr Fleming as a bully. One is his wife's emotional need of him, especially as a middle-aged woman when the marriage breaks; the other is a sense of his enormous talent and mysterious charm, but here the author seems to underestimate our resistance. When Mrs Fleming is given a picture by her father-in-law, her husband says, in the vividly written quarrel that ensues: 'I have put that picture away. I do not want it hung in my house. I have told you, I detest it.' Put in context, that declaration is meant to sound less crude, less bullying, than it does; but it is exactly the sort of statement that to the feminist ear now has a crudity that no charm or talent can modify.

Frustration versus need: the unsatisfactory functioning of the institution, the emotional dependence that makes its break-up so painful. That would be the pessimist's version of the wife's dilemma: the optimists would set the delights of freedom against the reassurances of love and commitment. Two first novels enable us to see something of this contrast in action. *The L-Shaped Room* by Lynn Reid Banks can be seen as a rejection of marriage, insofar as the heroine finds it necessary to maintain her emotional independence in a situation in which she needs a husband because of external pressure (pregnant, unmarried and insecure) and because she is in love. It is a novel highly conscious of conventional opinion, and of the boldness of flouting it, to a degree that could make the radical reader impatient of its timidity, though this is a clear advantage in terms of plot tensions. It is also a novel in which we are intended to like almost all—perhaps all—the characters, and the dilemma is not simply one between forms of pain. Frances Jessup's *The Fifth Child's Conception in the Runaway Wife*, funnier and nastier, contrasts marriage and freedom the other way round, starting from marriage; and it expresses the contrast by changing its mode of narrative. Beginning with a witty realistic account of Josephine's day as housewife and mum (pestering children, salestalk from milkman and vicar) it tells the story of how she runs off to live for a few days with an improbably eloquent dustman. It is a fantasy of escape—living in dirt not tidiness, her birth pills thrown away, meeting her husband at a party when she is dressed only in a sheet—and is followed by an equally fantastic account of the husband's disintegration and her return (a successful supermarket manager, he gets the sack for ordering a thousand extra frozen chickens). The housewife's escape wish is directly fulfilled and turns to hysterical farce, accompanied with constant reminders of how it could all, in matter-of-fact terms, be seen as disaster. The implications of this light-surfaced book could be as pessimistic as Penelope Mortimer, and the writer of the Penguin blurb clearly incorporates some of the feminist critique of marriage when he sees the reunion with the husband not as a happy ending but as showing her 'humiliating need for dependence'.

For every one of these novelists marriage, however varied their view of it, is a present reality; and love will be conscious of having to come to terms either with marriage or its lack. We need now to look at a novelist whose characters take their independence more for granted. Doris Lessing is such a novelist, and the novel within her novel is actually called 'Free Women'. The contrast with Elizabeth Jane Howard is revealing on several counts: she is experimental and modernist where the other is conventional, actively concerned with politics where the other writes only of the private life, outspoken where the other is discreet, and far more directly concerned with the subject matter of feminism.

The Golden Notebook is an elaborate set of stories about what it is like to live without some of the traditional moral norms. The unmarried women in these stories learn from their sexual experiences that men are vain, bullying and self-centred, using sex to bolster their own egos, and turning, when they fail, on the woman. The man who insists on sleeping with Julia, turns out to be impotent, and then accuses her of being a castrating woman, is not much worse than the rest. The Victorian way of handling the selfishness of men was the self-sacrifice of women, who by their moral superiority absorbed it and perhaps shamed the men out of it. Though it was not given this cynical justification, the ideal of the Angel in the House is quite compatible with Doris Lessing's picture of what men are like in sexual situations. Her women, however, are 'free', without permanent ties though sexually emancipated, and it is clear that free women see the worst side—perhaps the truest side—of men. To realize this is to be on the edge of bitching, that vocal enjoyment of your superiority to and exploitation by the others: the Victorian angel was never allowed to bitch. Doris Lessing's characters are aware of this danger, and watch themselves carefully in the attempt to avoid it.

These free women are not happy; and it seems natural to ask what positives such a portrayal implies. One implication could be the case for monogamy, but the social group she is depicting have given that up, and the novel is not a treatise. If we ask whether, in the end, it suggests that marriage is in women's interests, it is not easy to answer: the question is interesting simply because the novel is not a treatise. There is plenty in it to suggest that marriage can be constricting and tyrannical, but there is even more to suggest that the absence of it leads to frustration and the constant threat of humiliation.

Though Doris Lessing is a far more down-to-earth realist than Elizabeth Jane Howard, displaying an explicit and lengthy concern with politics, she is also, in the end, more experimental. The painful dilemmas of being a Communist in the 1950s are circumstantially and vividly conveyed, from a standpoint apparently so committed as to seem unaware how completely the anti-Communist reader will be confirmed in his initial opinions (or prejudices); but on the other hand the elaborate stories-within-stories, and the interplay between Anna's story and her four notebooks, enclose the urgency of the issues in a self-contained aesthetic structure—less so than this device usually does, because of the realism of the actual telling, until the concluding device of the golden notebook seems to suggest that human and political issues can be resolved aesthetically.

Perhaps the most striking paradox of the comparison is the way the committed realist shows herself finally to be more of a formalist than the sensitive explorer of personal intimacies. If the feminist reader grows impatient with Elizabeth Jane Howard's lack of impatience over marriage, the same reader might see Doris Lessing as a sister who has given up the cause for art. But such a reader would be an activist so simple-minded that literature could offer her little; and in an issue so complex as the politics of love this would not make her much of an activist either.[48]

Ideology can teach us to see with new eyes, and so to reinterpret literature; though it may also teach the impatient to throw down novels that reveal the openness of the imagination. That is why literature can never merely illustrate an ideological position: it will also to some degree test it. But we can also reverse the formula: the literary imagination may teach us to see with new eyes, for it can perceive social relationships in a way that ideology has not yet formulated. To test this we need to go well back into the past, before the first feminism, and read with our modern eyes.

Protofeminism: Charlotte Brontë

Two things were central to Charlotte Brontë, the need for love and an awareness of the difficulties of woman's lot. Perhaps we would not know about the first if she had never written novels: her advice to Ellen Nussey ('no young lady should fall in love, till the offer has been made, accepted—the marriage ceremony performed and the first half year of wedded life has passed away')[49] sounds like the controlled staidness of a young ladies' manual, though we know, as no doubt Miss Nussey did too, that she is writing against her own temperament (and the remark surely owes some of its poise to this). Her burning views on the treatment of women do however emerge from her correspondence: she wrote to her publisher in 1849, 'Something like a hope and a motive sustains me still. I wish all your daughters—I wish every woman in England had also a hope and a motive. Alas! there are many old maids who have neither.'[50] She felt with peculiar bitterness that society imposed an impossible situation on old maids, preparing them for nothing except a marriage they were quite likely not to make, and then expecting them gladly to embrace a life that brought only loneliness and contempt. There is an interesting chapter in *Shirley* in which the heroine reflects bitterly on the situation of old maids who 'have no earthly employment but household work and sewing, no earthly pleasure but an unprofitable visiting, and no hope, in all their life to come, of anything better.' This is clearly not only the heroine but also the author talking, and both the bitterness and the sarcasm belong to Charlotte herself:

> What do fathers expect them to do at home? If you ask, they would answer, sew and cook. They expect them to do this, and this only, contentedly, regularly, uncomplainingly all their lives long, as if they had no germs of faculties for anything else—doctrine as reasonable to hold as it would be that the fathers have no faculties but for eating what their daughters cook, or wearing what they sew.[51]

The artistic consequences of these two central concerns in Charlotte's nature are so different, so near to being opposites, that we can be led to seeing the concerns themselves as opposites. The need for love fits without difficulty into well established literary conventions: it will lead to the kind of love story that invites the reader to identify with the hero— or in this case heroine—and find vicarious emotional satisfaction in her fulfilment. This is one of the oldest of fictional patterns and though it was clear to contemporaries that Charlotte treated it in a new and more realistic way ('The democratic principle has ordered romance to descend from thrones and evacuate the palace,' wrote one reviewer of *Villette*),[52] it could be argued that this democratic principle—the ordinariness of Jane Eyre and Lucy Snowe—simply reveals more clearly than ever the basic pattern of reader-identification. Charlotte's indignant views on the role of women, however, lead in her fiction to a realism that defies convention, to a direct presentation of what woman's situation is like that ignores, or directly flouts, the expectations of the ordinary novel reader; and that, like most realism, extends the traditional subject matter of fiction. If in some ways Charlotte is a deeply traditional storyteller, in others she is concerned to offer us the truth as she shows it, whether or not that is what her readers expect.

It would be an oversimplification, however, to say that as a writer of love stories she is conservative, giving her readers what they expect; and that as a writer about woman's role she is subversive. For respectable contemporaries were, if anything, more shocked by the former: *Jane Eyre* aroused more enthusiasm, but also more indignation, than *Villette*. Since *Jane Eyre* is above all a love story, and since *Villette* deals more or less explicitly with the tensions between love and work, the best way to arrange the discussion of Charlotte Brontë will be to look first at *Jane Eyre* and her treatment of love; and then at *Villette* and her treatment of woman's work and independence.

'Every page burns with moral Jacobinism,' said the *Christian Remembrancer* of *Jane Eyre*.[53] The *Quarterly Review* did not 'hesitate to say that the tone of the mind and thought which has overthrown authority and violated every code human and divine abroad, and fostered Chartism and rebellion at home, is the same which has also written *Jane Eyre*'.[54] Conservative indignation often makes future generations rub their eyes with astonishment. What is there in this Cinderella-like story to make these worthies so cross? Is this the voice of Mrs Reed and Mr Brocklehurst, heard from outside the pages of the book?

Jane does not behave as a well brought up girl ought to: her character, with which generations of readers have identified so fiercely, is weak on Christian humility and feminine submissiveness. This is most exhilaratingly apparent in the childhood scenes.

Me, she had dispensed from joining the group, saying 'She regretted to be under the necessity of keeping me at a distance; but that until she heard from Bessie, and could discover by her own observation that I was endeavouring in good earnest to acquire a more sociable and childlike disposition, a more attractive and sprightly manner—something lighter, franker, more natural, as it were—she really must exclude me from privileges intended only for contented, happy little children.'
'What does Bessie say I have done?', I asked. (Ch. 1)

That bluntness is a new voice in English fiction. There had been ill-disciplined, rebellious children before, like the Middletons in *Sense and Sensibility*; there had been idealizations of childhood innocence and sensitivity, in Wordsworth, in Blake and (in more complex form) in Rousseau; now we are being invited to identify with the child who answers back, who goes straight to the factual basis (or lack of it) underlying the moralized nonsense. Here on the very first page is the defiance that shook the *Christian Remembrancer* as it shook Mrs Reed:

'I am not deceitful: if I were, I should say I loved *you*; but I declare I do not love you: I dislike you the worst of anybody in the world except John Reed: and this book about the Liar, you may give to your girl, Georgiana, for it is she who tells lies, and not I.'

Suddenly the bullied child turns, spurning humility, and insists on truth and justice. And—the little Jacobin— she feels marvellous for it. 'Ere I had finished this reply, my soul began to expand, to exult, with the strangest sense of freedom, of triumph, I ever felt.' This ability to stand up for herself never leaves Jane: 31 chapters later, she speaks out to Rivers with similar bluntness, and he is surprised—'He had not imagined a woman would dare to speak so to a man.'

Jane's character is established not only directly but by means of foils. The most obvious is Helen Burns, her schoolgirl friend, who is a model of Christian submissiveness, who believes 'it is far better to endure patiently a smart which nobody feels but yourself, than to commit a hasty action whose evil consequences will extend to all connected with you', acts on that belief, and when she listens to Jane's tale of her own woes is able to say with startling shrewdness. 'She has been unkind to you, no doubt ... but how minutely you remember all she has done and said to you.' In the course of arguing with Helen, Jane formulates (as perhaps Charlotte may have done in arguing with her sister Maria) her moral Jacobinism ('When we are struck at without a reason, we should strike back again very hard') and her rejection of self-sufficiency ('I cannot bear to be solitary and hated'). There is a connexion, we see, between her need for love and her unchristian defiance.

Less obvious, but equally interesting, is the use of her cousins, the Reed sisters, as foils. Eliza Reed is a monster of discipline and organization, planning every hour of the day, beholden to no one, and contemptuous of her 'fat, weak, puffy, useless' sister: 'Instead of living for, in and with yourself, as a reasonable being ought, you seek only to fasten your feebleness on some other person's strength.' Each of these unattractive girls is an exaggeration, even a parody, of one half of Jane's nature: Georgiana of her need for love, which is not simply fastening her feebleness, Eliza of her independence, which is not hard or mean.

But to the modern reader Jane will not, at first, seem independent. This demure and submissive governess, who calls Rochester 'Sir' when they are engaged—is *that* a free spirit? The tension between defiance and surrender in Jane's love is the most subtle and powerful thing in the novel. It is central to the plot, of course, when she is struggling with the temptation to stay with Rochester instead of leaving him once the secret of his wife is out. This struggle, between love and duty, is conventional enough: though written with the eloquence that won Currer Bell so many readers, it has little of the Brontë genius. But the tension within the love itself is altogether more interesting. Rochester is aware of it: she pleases and masters him even while he is 'turning the soft silken skein round my finger'. Her defiance issues in a refusal to be treated in Turkish fashion: she resists presents, objects to feminine luxury, and actually repulses Rochester physically when she feels he is treating her as a sultan treats a slave. It is after he has taken her to a silk warehouse and a jeweller's shop that she has one of her most modern thoughts, the wish to be financially independent. In terms of literary convention, too, this proud independence involves a rejection. Rochester uses the images of the *Minnegrotte* when talking to the little girl, Adèle:

> I am to take mademoiselle to the moon, and there I shall seek a cave in one of the white valleys among the volcano-tops, and mademoiselle shall live with me there, and only me. (Ch. 24)

He talks like this to Adèle because he is not allowed to do so to Jane: these images of love's self-sufficiency do not answer to her insistence on being treated as what she is. She will not respond to such poetry, and nor does Adèle, whose childish matter-of-factness remarks 'she would get tired of living with only you in the moon'.

Most subtle of all is the way Jane uses the formulas of deference to stand up for herself. She keeps Rochester at bay by formality, refusing to dine with him because

> 'I never have dined with you, Sir; and I see no reason
> why I should now: till—'
> 'Till what? you delight in half-phrases.'
> 'Till I can't help it.' (Ch. 24.)

We need to divest ourselves of our egalitarian passion for informality to see how necessary it is for Jane to continue calling him 'Sir'. It protects her individuality, enabling her to keep her identity as an employee who has chosen to marry her employer, rather than a doll or a Danaë for whom only one kind of relationship is now possible. Jane herself is quite conscious of this tension. On the one hand, she insists on showing herself to Rochester, when they are engaged, as 'naturally hard—very flinty'; and her reason is that 'he should know fully what sort of a bargain he had made, while there was yet time to rescind it'—once again, employee's language, that will enable her to feel that both parties are marrying of their own free will. But on the other hand, she is not at all free emotionally: 'My future husband was becoming to me my whole world.... He stood between me and every thought of religion, as an eclipse intervenes between man and the broad sun.' The more helplessly in love she is, the more she feels she must keep her distance.

Because this tension is so central to her love, it is always possible for the oversimplifying critic to see one half of it only: to regard Jane as bold and unfeminine, or as the submissive Victorian woman. To see how central the element of paradox is, we can look at her most famous speech:

> 'I tell you I must go!' I retorted, roused to something like passion. 'Do you think I can stay to become nothing to you? Do you think I am an automaton?—a machine without feelings? ... Do you think, because I am poor, obscure, plain, and little, I am soulless and heartless? ... I am not talking to you now through the medium of custom, conventionalities, nor even of mortal flesh: it is my spirit that addresses your spirit; just as if both had passed through the grave, and we stood at God's feet, equal—as we are!'
>
> (Ch. 23)

That is not how a penniless governess is supposed to talk to her employer. If he were trying to seduce her she is allowed (in novels, anyway) to defend her virtue in such fiery language; but to defend her right to love with such an assumption of equality savours of immodesty. But what is she saying? The demand she is making with such 'hunger, rebellion and rage' (the virtuous phrase is Matthew Arnold's) is not a demand to be free of him but to be tied to him. 'Equal as we are': is Jane demanding anything more than what is traditional, the admission that beyond the discrepancies of wealth and rank there is an emotional equality in love? Is she not simply being immodest in asking, instead of waiting for the man to offer it?

In the end, what we think of this today depends on what we think of love. Is sexual love a situation of mutual dependence, a rescue from the emptiness of self-sufficiency that benefits both parties? Or is there, in our society at least, a built-in imbalance, so that in the inevitable give and take it is mostly the woman who gives, mostly the man who takes? If the latter, feminist questioning of the ideal of love is understandable;

if the former, it is mere encouragement to emotional selfishness. It is a modern question, not one over which Charlotte Brontë would have hesitated: so though it is inappropriate to a historical understanding of what her books originally said, it can be a necessary problem for us.

At that point we could leave the issue, if it were not for the two episodes with which the book concludes—meeting the Rivers family, and the fire. Once again, the least interesting thing about them is the plot: that the cottage where Jane Eyre knocks when she is faint with cold and hunger turns out to contain her long-lost cousins, and to bring her a legacy, is the sort of contrivance for which we must now indulgently forgive the nineteenth-century novelist. The question of marrying St John Rivers, however, has nothing to do with his being her cousin, and does contribute a great deal to understanding her emotional life. Here again there is a tension, but this time it is not one that Charlotte Brontë intended. She saw marriage to Rivers as repressive and old-fashioned, and to make the point quite clear, he had to love someone else (it would be too much to expect a Victorian novelist—and Charlotte Brontë above all—to depict a loveless proposal without syphoning off the love onto a beautiful rival). Though he is a good man, he 'forgets, pitilessly, the feelings and claims of little people'. His insistence that it is Jane's duty to marry him and accept the call to work as a missionary is a kind of bullying; her true call is to marry the man she loves, and it comes to her, quite literally as a call. Yet what the author does not say, and does not see, is that in some respect marriage to Rivers represents something new. 'I scorn your idea of love,' Jane says to him proudly. Why? Because he has just admitted there are obstacles in the way, and said they must be hewn down. 'Undoubtedly enough of love would follow upon marriage to render the union right even in your eyes.' Rivers offers a marriage in which love will grow with habit: to use the terminology of our last chapter, married love and not romantic love—or, we can say, at the risk of being impertinent, the kind of marriage Charlotte Brontë actually made. It is true that Rivers is a bully; but it is also true that his view is closer to modern companionate marriage than anything Rochester has to offer. Rivers despises 'domestic endearments and household joys', and prefers the bond that comes from working together. If we can disentangle his conception of marriage from the pious hectoring of his religious dogmatism, we can see that it is rational and level-headed. Any woman who really wanted to reject the eternal feminine might choose Rivers rather than Rochester.

Finally, reader, as all readers know, she married Rochester. The happy ending might have seemed inevitable to that contemporary reader waiting eagerly for the consummation, though Charlotte Brontë was later to show how very moderate her enthusiasm for happy endings was. And even in this novel, marriage has to be preceded by a savage alteration in their relationship. The fire in Thornfield kills off the obstacle of Mrs Rochester, but once again that plot function seems comparatively uninteresting. It also leaves Rochester blind and crippled, thus giving Jane a totally different kind of marriage. Why? There is the inevitable psychoanalytic proposal that the blinding is a symbolic castration, that the marriage has to be desexualized before it can take place. We shall turn to Charlotte Brontë's handling of sex in the next chapter: here I will just say that if psychoanalytic interpretations ever allow themselves to be refuted, this one is easily refuted. Jane sits on Rochester's knee, he is jealous, and their physical contact is closer than ever, after he is blinded, and the intensity of their domestic intimacy suggests nothing is missing from the marriage. The reason Charlotte Brontë offers for the maiming is in fact a good feminist point: that Jane is happier in a situation where she is needed than 'in your state of proud independence, when you disdained every part but that of the giver and protector'. Yet this is surely not the whole story. In becoming a nurse, Jane has taken on the true feminine role: like Tennyson's Princess, she finally expresses her love by looking after a helpless man. Though in one respect she is now on terms of truer equality, in another she has declined into the Angel in the House. There will be no more taunting, no more resisting, and the *Christian Remembrancer* could have felt at ease. Angels are never Jacobins.

Jane Eyre and Lucy Snowe have a good deal in common. Both are plain; both are sturdily independent; both have demure and conventional surface, and fires underneath. Jane's character is described explicitly by Rochester in his disguise as a gipsy: 'Reason sits firm and holds the reins.... The passions may rage furiously, like true heathens, as they are.' Exactly the same contrast applies to Lucy, and its importance is stressed by her name. We know that it was deliberately chosen to indicate her cold exterior (at one time she was to be called Frost), and the difficulty of knowing what lies beneath that exterior is repeatedly emphasized. Lucy takes some satisfaction in the thought that everyone she knows has a different version of her character; and is sardonically amused when M. Paul, in contrast to everyone else, diagnoses the volatile and the versatile under the melancholy sobersides. She may not paint Jungian pictures like Jane, but she responds to nature with the same intensity:

> I could not go in: too resistless was the delight of staying with the wild hour, black and full of thunder, pealing out such an ode as language never delivered to man. (Ch. 12)

They are also alike in their situation: both are orphans (in Lucy's case this is left deliberately vague, but she has, effectually, no family), both have to make their own way. Here there is a striking contrast. Jane passes quite consciously into the stage of needing to assert her independence ('I tired of the routine of eight years in one afternoon'), advertises for a situation, and sees herself as representing rebellion against one's lot in a passage of virtually explicit feminism ('Women are supposed to be very calm generally: but women feel just as men feel'). Lucy however takes her decisions by accident, almost in a state of trance. She has no explicit reason for going to London, and even less for taking ship to Labassecour, nothing but 'a strong, vague persuasion, that it was better to go forward than backward, and that I *could* go forward'. On the boat she meets Ginevra Fanshawe, who asks her where she is going:

> 'Where Fate may lead me. My business is to earn a living where I can find it.'
> 'To earn!' (in consternation). 'Are you poor, then?' (Ch. 6)

Ginevra's snobbery and superficial sympathy must be established, but even she would surely have been struck first by the absurdity of a young girl setting out for a foreign country with no plans, no contacts and no knowledge of French. The series of accidents that leads Lucy to Madame Beck's academy (at which Ginevra is a pupil) is quite as far-fetched as that which leads Jane to knock at her cousin's cottage, but its function is quite different. Coincidences towards the end of the story, that wrap it up with long-lost relatives and a legacy from an uncle, serve a providential function; coincidences like Lucy's that set the story going, are not needed in the same way: Lucy could have arrived at Madame Beck's in a more rational manner, and these arbitrary events seem to express the trance-like state in which she finds herself led to begin her story.

The point is important, and mysterious. For *Villette* is far more concerned with the heroine's career than is *Jane Eyre*. We are told very little about the teaching of little Adèle: Jane's job is a way of getting her into the family, so that she and Rochester can fall in love. But we are told a great deal about Lucy's work: *Villette* is a novel about a woman making her way in life. It could be argued that Jane's long reflection on women needing a field for their efforts ought really to be given to Lucy, that it ought to be Lucy who advertises and decides rationally what to do. Yet in a way that perhaps eludes understanding the sense of being swept along by a force that eludes *her* understanding seems a fitting start to her career.

The career in question is always the same: what else could she do but teach? There were 24,770 governesses in England in 1851, and their significance was out of proportion to their numbers. They represented the one opportunity of employment for the respectable unmarried woman, even though the majority of them were paid a wretched salary for their often wretched talents. To raise the level of the profession was an urgent task in the 1850s; but the thousands of women who flocked into the office of the *Englishwoman's Journal* desperate for work—any work—showed that however badly paid and treated a governess was, it seemed to many a better fate than uselessness.[55] And fiction, realistically in touch with social reality for once, saw that the situation of the governess enacted some of the most urgent social issues in the form of individual experience. Badly paid and usually undervalued, she belonged to the same class as her employer; if the employer was unkind or snobbish, this placed her in a highly embarrassing, even unfair position. Plenty of fictional employers *were* unkind, as for instance the Harringtons in E. M. Sewell's novel *Amy Herbert* (1844). An elaborately improbable accident results in the illness and eventual death of their daughter Rose; the parents assume it is the fault of the governess, Emily Morton, who is in fact innocent, and dismiss her unheard. It is a thoroughly simplified situation of victim and unjust employer. Miss Morton is a paragon, who had in fact been visiting a worthy old retainer on an errand of charity; she has come down in the world after her genteel education, her parents being dead. As we might expect, all is cleared up at the end, and she gets a better employer, but if we leave out the ending we can see that the governess is simply too good for a society that wrongs her. Harriet Martineau's *Deerbrook* (1839) is a more intelligent novel, but its governess, Maria Young, is almost identical in character and situation. The governesses of fiction, it seems, were all Jane Fairfaxes, but without her ability to protest. We have, of course, a comparison much nearer home for Charlotte Brontë, *Agnes Gray*, the short novel about a governess by her sister Anne. It is the simplest imaginable version of a tension betwen work and love. Agnes is forced to go governessing because her father's death has left them poor: her mother is warmly supportive, and Agnes is heartbroken at leaving home. Mr Weston the curate, the flattest and worthiest of virtuous heroes, eventually rescues her; and between these two domestic havens, as daughter and as wife, Agnes undergoes her ordeal (no milder word will do) first in the Bloomfield, then in the Murray family, where she has to endure the spite and aggression of unruly children, and the unfairness of parents who will neither exercise discipline nor give the governess any real authority:

> If I were quiet at the moment I was conniving at their disorderly conduct; if (as was frequently the case) I happened to be exalting my voice to enforce order, I was using undue violence, and setting the girls a bad example by such ungentleness of tone and language. (Ch. 4)

It is educationally reactionary, since it attributes to children no wish to learn, and believes above all in the need for discipline; and it is reactionary on the woman question, since there is no hint that career, as well as marriage, might be fulfilling. Work is for those women who lack a secure domestic place of their own.

Charlotte does not go so far (how could she, in 1850?) as to make her heroine prefer teaching to being looked after; but she does present the experience of teaching in subtly different terms. For one thing, Lucy is in a school. Teaching in a school can be more fulfilling, and also more of an assertion of independence, than going as a governess. In a school the teacher is part of an institution into which the pupil has to fit, instead of having to fit into the family of which the pupil is part. This gives her role more of an existence in its own right, and makes the whole activity more professional, more like a career. Not that Charlotte necessarily thought this in real life: when she was teaching at Roe Head, she wrote an account in her journal of how she had sat all day in a dream that 'showed almost in a vivid light of reality the ongoings of the infernal world', while at the same time she had to toil 'for nearly an hour with Miss Lister, Miss Marriott and Ellen Cook striving to teach them the distinction between an article and a substantive'.[56] That is pure romanticism, in which work appears as everyday dullness, not as opportunity for self-fulfilment. When it comes to *Villette*, however, teaching is something to be taken seriously: it is not simply an ordeal, as it is for Agnes Gray, it is a challenge. True, Lucy is bullied and spied on by Mme Beck in ways that are comparable to how Agnes is treated by the Bloomfields; but it makes a great difference that Mme Beck is a teacher too—i.e. that Lucy's struggles are within the profession. The accounts of learning how to assert authority, how to master and deliver material, make this one of the earliest novels that is genuinely about professional work. The scene in chapter 8 in which she is thrust in front of a class for the first time has no parallel before the twentieth century. Sent in at a moment's notice, not yet able to speak the language properly, warned savagely by her employer that she is likely to fail and need expect no help, it reads like an impossible test devised in the fantasy of a frightened novice. But though it may on a matter-of-fact level be quite unrealistic, it is a superb rendering of the subjective experience:

> As I mounted the estrade.... I beheld opposite to me a row of eyes and brows that threatened stormy weather—eyes full of an insolent light, and brows hard and unblushing as marble.

There is not much in common between Charlotte Brontë and D. H. Lawrence, but this scene is startlingly like the marvellous thirteenth chapter of *The Rainbow*, Ursula's experiences as a primary teacher in a slum school, Both are about learning to control a hostile class; and in both cases, the battle of wills has to begin as a physical battle, with

the public defeat of the most unruly pupil. It is not a accident that
both teachers are women, and Lawrence's chapter is called 'A Man's
World', making explicit what is also prominent in *Villette*, that we are
concerned with a woman's struggle to prove her ability to join a profession. The differences, too, are striking. One very instructive difference
concerns social class, and indicates how the social function of education
had changed in half a century: in Madame Beck's academy the pupils
are socially superior to their teacher, and despise her for being a 'bonne
d'enfants', whereas in Brinsley Street School the poor children are
resentful of the respectability that the 1870 Education Act is trying to
impose on them. In both cases the teacher is afraid, but fear of one's
betters whom one also despises has a different flavour from fear of the
'pale quivering class, whose childish faces were shut in blank resentment'.
The other main difference concerns teaching itself. Lawrence does not
really believe in the value of the whole activity: he sees it as a situation
of conflict rather than an opportunity to learn, and the effect on the
teachers is, in the end, degrading. But for Charlotte Brontë learning
how to teach is a real achievement; the first lesson ends with quiet
triumph (C'est bien,' said Madame Beck, when I came out of class,
hot and a little exhausted, 'Ça ira.') and from then on Lucy has a skill
she is pleased and proud to exercise. When later she is offered the chance
to live with Paulina and her father for thrice her salary, she refuses
because it is not her vocation: 'I could teach; I could give lessons: but
to be either a private governess or a companion was unnatural to me.'
Ursula, when she marries Birkin, does not hesitate to accept his proposal
that they both give up their posts. It is not misleading to connect
this difference with Charlotte's feminism and Lawrence's rejection of
society's institutions. Feminism means wanting women to succeed, and
is therefore incompatible with cynicism about the success.

If *Villette* is about independence and a career, it is certainly a feminist
novel; and the temptation of the feminist who admires Charlotte Brontë
is to see it is as simply about that. Hence Kate Millett's reading, by which
Lucy makes use of Paul Emmanuel to climb out of her position of economic slavery and is then neatly rescued from having to pay the usual
price:

> As there is no remedy to sexual politics in marriage, Lucy very logically
> doesn't marry. But it is also impossible for a Victorian novel to recommend
> a woman not to marry. So Paul suffers a quiet sea burial.[57]

Patricia Beer will have none of this. *Villette* is a love story, and the hint
of disappointment at the end is not an oblique assertion of emancipation
but a note of tragedy: 'She does not rise above the lures of marriage....
She is an unhappy and deprived woman for the rest of her life.'[58] It

is a contrast between the critic who trusts the author and the critic who is palpably cleverer than the author. In an obvious sense, Patricia Beer is right; as we can see if we ask what a contemporary feminist made of the book. Harriet Martineau was looking for the same thing as Kate Millett, but she was sure that she hadn't found it:

> all the female characters, in all their thoughts and lives, are full of one thing, are regarded by the reader in the light of that one thought—love.... It is not thus in real life. There are substantial, heartfelt interests for women of all ages, and under ordinary circumstances quite apart from love.[59]

The tone is very different but the content is comparable to that of the sisterly exhortations to reject romance, 'the illusive, fake, and never-attained reward which for the benefit and amusement of our masters keeps us running and thinking in safe circles'. Harriet Martineau saw that Charlotte was not on the side of liberation; her firm rebuke is, really, a rebuke to literature. She is unjust: substantial, heartfelt interest in teaching does find its way into the novel. Yet in the end she sees rightly where Charlotte's heart lay, and she is against her.

Is Kate Millett nonetheless, in an obscure way, in touch with something in the deeper dynamic of the novel? She senses, for instance, a feverish quality in the fourteenth chapter ('The Fête') which it is not easy to account for. Why should Lucy, bullied into acting by M. Paul, locked up in the attic to learn her part, suddenly enter into it with such frenetic animation, even to the extent of misrepresenting the character and wooing Ginevra with more enthusiasm than she was meant to? It is ingenious to suggest a Lesbian attraction and 'the desire such beauty [as Ginevra's] arouses in her. Kate Millett sees the amateur theatricals as 'one of the most indecorous scenes one may come upon in the entire Victorian novel', and Lucy as having to express, and then conquer, 'a masculine lust for Fanshawe'. But we can account for the frenzy in a more plausible if more complicated way. There is a good deal of sexual feeling present: from Dr John to Ginevra, from Lucy to Dr John, and (incipiently) between Lucy and M. Paul—so far from hiding this, the narrative makes it very prominent in the account of how Mme Beck invites young men to the dance and then chaperones savagely; there is the intense, inbred excitement of a school function, in which it matters enormously who does and doesn't act well; and there is Lucy's frightening discovery that she can act—a discovery she makes even before the play begins by the skill with which she half-dresses as a man. It is frightening because 'it would not do for a mere looker-on at life': social inferiority and proud egoism mingle in that self-castigation. It is not implausible, surely, that in her sudden frenzied desire to excel she should throw herself into wooing Ginevra as if it was real. It is not sexual attraction but self-assertion that so dangerously looms; and the suggestion of Lesbianism oversimplifies a strange and powerful episode.

It is important to see that *Villette* is a love story; for when Charlotte's two concerns encounter each other, there is no doubt that the romantic scores an easy victory over the feminist. It is only on behalf of single women that she grows indignant at the lack of outlets: the real fulfilment, for any woman, is love, and Charlotte's fiery feminism takes second place to her need for a man. This was realized from the beginning, with cruel insight, by Thackeray:

> The poor little woman of genius! The fiery little eager brave tremulous homely-faced creature! I can read a great deal of her life as I fancy in her book, and see that rather than have fame, rather than any other earthly good or mayhap heavenly one she wants some Tomkins or another to love and be in love with. But you see she is a little bit of a creature without a penny worth of good looks, thirty years old I should think, buried in the country, and eating up her own heart there, and no Tomkins will come.[60]

I could understand any woman's fury at this condescending masculinity (though, interestingly, Thackeray's correspondent here is female); but how shrewd he is—how clearly he has anticipated Freudian views that trace intense writing back to the intensity of deprivation, and how right he is that patriarchal society had, in the end, nothing to fear from this fiery creature.

Villette is a love story: yet so strange and original a love story that the love-interest is as disturbing, in its way, as the feminism. In the first place, Lucy's need to love is even stronger than Jane's. This might seem impossible to the reader fresh from Jane's passion for Rochester: to pass beyond such emotional intensity would be to pass beyond the normal, and that is what happens in *Villette*. It is the study of a neurotic, a woman in whom 'secret but ceaseless consciousness of anxiety lies in wait on enjoyment, like a tiger crouched in a jungle'; and who undergoes perhaps the most frightening nervous breakdown in the Victorian novel, in the haunting chapter called 'The Long Vacation'. Though its plot is more messy, its style more contorted, it is a profounder and more disturbing novel than *Jane Eyre*.

What sort of men do the Brontë heroines love? Rochester is not like anyone Charlotte can ever have met: ugly, moody, a man with a past, he derives from the Byronic hero and (as we can see from the Zamorna of the *Angria* stories) from an emotional pattern that goes right back to her own childhood. By sheer imagination, she has found the words for what it would be like to love such a man: 'the sarcasm that had repelled, the harshness that had startled me once, were only like keen condiments in a choice dish'.[61] This is strong stuff, from the parson's daughter; but in *Villette* she went further in the direction of frustrating the expectations of the conventional reader. For Lucy does begin what looks like an ordinary love story, pining for the sort of handsome masculine Englishman every eager brave tremulous female is supposed to long for in life and be rewarded with in fiction. This is Dr John, the 'born victor' for whom everything in life has been a little too easy, as both author and heroine realize before the story is over. Lucy never quite ceases to love him, even after she has fallen in love with Paul Emanuel; Thackeray (the pig!) noticed and was amused by 'the author's naive confession of being in love with two men at the same time; and her readiness to fall in love at any time'. The other lover is 'a dark little man, ... pungent and austere', as different as can be from the conventional hero: 'a harsh apparition, with his close-shorn, black head, his broad, sallow brow, his thin cheek, his wide and quivering nostril, his thorough glance, and hurried bearing'. To see him as a bullying male chauvinist is to ignore the grotesque comedy with which he is treated, and the importance of there being two heroes instead of one. The subdued suggestion at the end that Lucy will not after all marry Paul Emanuel has obsessed readers of *Villette*: it is important, of course, as a sign of impatience with a literary convention, a wish to upset the reader almost for the sake of doing so. But it has distracted attention from what is in another way more important, the fact that she doesn't marry Dr John. That is the real departure from convention and it is arguable that it is emancipatory: to move from a handsome 'born victor', the answer to every maiden's prayer, to a vain, bullying, bigoted (Papist and anti-feminist) and yet vulnerable 'apparition' is to move from the stereotypes of romance to the individuality of a particular creation, and Lucy would lose less individuality as Mme Emanuel than as Mrs Bretton.

So is Charlotte Brontë a proto-feminist? Not in the easy ways: to see her as preferring career to love may be a tempting misreading, but it is certainly a misreading, and the tension and equality she depicts in the love relationship is superimposed on a total surrender of the self to the beloved. But we do not in the end value great literature for which side it is on. We value it for the way it increases awareness, and there are few problems of the mid-nineteenth-century woman of which these two novels do not make us more fully aware. She was not a virago of talent but something finer, a poor little woman of genius.

Since there was so little feminism in the 1840s, and Charlotte Brontë had so little contact with what there was, we have moved almost to a pre-feminist age in discussing her; but now I want to move even further back, to a time when the modern feminist consciousness indubitably did not exist. If we find it anticipated even then, this can only be by pure literary insight.

Protofeminism: Samuel Richardson

Samuel Richardson believed in parental authority. 'I have a better opinion of your good sense,' he wrote to Frances Grainger, 'than to think that you have a low Idea of the Parental Authority.'[62] He believed that wisdom grows with experience, and that mothers must be expected to have more sense than their daughters; even when this was not the case, 'let the child's good Sense, Superior Sense, be shewn in concealing her Parent's faults'.[63] The child ought therefore to try and accept a husband proposed by the parents; but if she could not, it was then wrong for the parents to force her. In a matter so important as marriage, real aversion was ground enough for a veto by the child. In writing *Clarissa*, he set out to illustrate this doctrine, and also to attack 'that pernicious Notion, that a Reformed Rake ... makes the best Husband'.[64] And so he chose as his situation a dutiful and beloved daughter, normally more than willing to submit to her parents, who is forced to accept a loathsome suitor by a tyrannical family, while being courted by an aristocratic rake whom (for various reasons, some good, some unjust) her family hate. Parental tyranny drives Clarissa into putting herself under the protection of the rake (though if left alone she would have rejected him, and was in any case willing to obey her parents on the negative point of refusing Lovelace, though not on the positive point of accepting the detestable Solmes). Lovelace takes advantage of this, and after a long-drawn-out cat and mouse game, Clarissa is ruined. Moral to parents: don't force your child to accept someone she has a real aversion to. Moral to daughters: however strong the provocation, however attractive he is, don't trust a rake. Various subsidiary morals all reinforce the same position of moderate conservatism.

That was the book Richardson set out to write; quite clearly, it is not the book he wrote. If there ever was a case where we should trust the tale and not the artist, it is *Clarissa*: generations of readers have responded with passion to what they saw as an indictment of parental tyranny and a spirited rejection of bourgeois respectability. Lovelace the villain has all the gusto: though Richardson knew hardly anything about the aristocratic circles in which such young gallants flourish, he somehow found in himself the material to create one of the superb characters of English literature. Such 'misreading' of the book took place from the beginning. 'Would you not wonder,' he wrote to the Misses Hill in (simulated?) astonishment, 'were you to hear that there are such as prefer Miss Howe to Clarissa?'[65] 'Little did I think at the time,' he complained to Lady Bradshaigh, 'that those Qualities ... would have given Women of Virtue and Honour such a liking to Lovelace, as I have found to be the case with many.'[66] Deep down in Richardson, there must have been

an identification with Miss Howe and with Lovelace, the kind of identification on which such a dramatic genius necessarily draws; but it is not
necessary, in accounting for the unplanned (even unwanted) power of
the book, to rush into Richardson's unconscious, for much of it is simply
due to his craftsmanship. He did not wish to make Lovelace a monster;
in depicting Miss Howe he deliberately 'threw in a few Shades, a few
Failings consequent to so lively a Character'.[67] Though Mr Richardson
was pained at how much his reader warmed to these failings, at how
eager they were to defend Lovelace, he did not respond with the hysterical over-reaction of someone shown the repressed contents of his own
mind; but rather with the stern disapproval of the moralist. He tried
to put things right by inserting the notorious footnotes that call the
reader's attention to Lovelace's machinations and defend the conduct of
Clarissa. Her failure to get herself married as soon as she went off with
Lovelace, for instance, was seen by readers as over-niceness, and she is
told by Miss Howe that she has 'modestied-away' her opportunities; the
footnotes insist that it was not niceness but delicacy, and point out that
Lovelace took care to make his proposals in a way that made it difficult
for her to accept.[68] This is true (and Lovelace even boasts of it); but
it is also true that with shrewdness Clarissa could have managed things
better. Some of the eager and romantic readers certainly oversimplified;
but the footnotes eversimplify in the other direction, and fail to do justice
to the complexity of Richardson's own creation. I find it a touching
sign of his artistic integrity that he confined them to footnotes rather
than changing the text, rebuking his readers for agreeing that she
modestied-away her chances without removing that brilliant phrase.

It will be the argument of this discussion that *Clarissa* does contain
a good deal of proto-feminism, though not in any clear-cut form and
though Mr Richardson, the teller, would not have accepted what I find
in his tale. Lovelace will only be peripheral to the argument, which will
concentrate more on Anna Howe, and I therefore cannot offer it as a
complete and central reading of the novel. But I do believe that no complete interpretation can omit these points, just as I believe Richardson
is a key figure in the depicting of woman in fiction.

We must begin by remarking that although there is so much propaganda against the arranged (or at any rate the imposed) match in the
novel, there is no corresponding exaltation of romantic love. Indeed,
there is virtually no romantic love in *Clarissa*, as there was none in
Pamela. The happy marriages at the end (Belford and Lady Charlotte,
Anna and Hickman) have no touch of it; the only character who could
be said to feel it is Clarissa herself, in whom we can find something like
a romantic feeling for Lovelace. She is more drawn to him than she will
admit, even to herself; and she feels jealousy (most notably over the

Rosebud episode). But it is made quite plain that if left alone she would have conquered this inclination and refused Lovelace, for romantic love has a weaker hold on her than virtue. No one else in the novel even feels it, with the possible exception of Sally and Polly, two of the girls whom Lovelace earlier ruined; and the romantic credo, that reason and love keep little company together, is given to Lovelace in one of his fierce denunciations of Clarissa: 'Love, that deserves the name, never was under the dominion of *prudence*, or of any *reasoning* power' (III.175). From this, we are clearly justified in concluding that love in Clarissa *is* under the dominion of prudence and reason, and that the true contrast to parental tyranny—the golden mean, in fact, between parental tyranny and romantic folly—is reasonable love.

Golden mean: prudence: reasonable love. Nothing subversive about these respectable concepts, redolent of moderation. Yet as we have already seen, reasonable love is a radical doctrine if romantic love is conservative, and the feminist rejection of romance can make its appeal to reason. Is there any case for reading *Clarissa* in this way? Only if reason is used to probe and question established institutions; only if the issue of the position of women is explicitly brought into question. And this is just what happens.

The character through whom the issue first arises is Clarissa's mother. She is, we are repeatedly assured, the best and tenderest of mothers; yet she joins the rest of the family in trying to force Clarissa to marry Solmes, not because she is convinced but for the sake of domestic peace, and because it is her duty to submit to her husband. Anna Howe has no hesitation in condemning her for this:

> *You* pity her mother—so do not *I*! I pity no mother, that puts it out of her power to show maternal love, and humanity, in order to patch up for herself a precarious and sorry quiet. (II.287)

That is to Mrs Norton, Clarissa's nurse; and she had already said the same thing more than once to Clarissa herself, in terms which betray little respect for wifely submissiveness. That might be part of Anna's pertness; but Clarissa herself, paragon of obedience though she is, utters the same sentiment. Even before the story has got under way, she delivers the opinion 'that had she been of a temper that would have borne less, she would have had ten times less to bear than she has had'; and in one of her last letters she observes, speaking this time of her aunt and her mother

> Shall we wonder that kings and princes meet with so little control in their passions, be they ever so violent, when in a private family an aunt, nay, even a mother in that family, shall choose to give up a once favoured child against their own inclinations, rather than oppose an aspiring young man,

who had armed himself with the authority of a father, who, when once
determined, never would be expostulated with?   (IV.194)

Questioning of male authority here involves questioning a good deal
of other authority too. The parallel between the government of the
father and that of the king was a commonplace in the seventeenth century, and Richardson, showing himself a good son of the Glorious
Revolution of 1689, is also questioning male authority in the family.
Constitutional monarchy can imply constitutional patriarchy. We do
not need to rely on the comments of Anna or even of Clarissa to see
that the submissiveness of the Harlowe women is unworthy of them;
if we attend too exclusively to Clarissa's praises, we may not notice what
her mother sinks to. Early on in the story, she appears agitated because
(I presume we are meant to take Clarissa's interpretation as correct) she
has been 'expressing herslf with warmth' against Clarissa, in order to
'clear herself' (*sic*—and to her other daughter!). Much later, when
Clarissa is dying, she is capable of saying that her daughter's grief and
present misery 'must be short of what I hourly bear for her'.

There is then what we may call objective evidence that submission
to male authority is not always right; and the constant reiteration of
this view comes from Miss Howe, who after Lovelace is the liveliest
and most brilliant of Richardson's creations. We shall need to look at
her character and her opinions in some detail.

'Pert Anna Howe' represents, above all, standing up for yourself. She
does not like to be told what to do; she sees conflict everywhere, and
has decided that one must join in—hence her brilliant fable of the chicks.
Enraged at 'a game chicken that was continually pecking at another (a
poor humble one, as I thought him)' she had its neck wrung—whereupon the other grew insolent and began pecking at one or two under
him. 'Peck and be hanged, said I.' Here we have the very opposite to
Clarissa's meekness, as both of them very well see, and the consequences
of this difference are stated unequivocally by Anna. Clarissa is better
suited for the next world; Anna is better suited for this. Clarissa is no
Griselda, but all the same what she lacks, and what Anna has, is survival-
value. Anna owns when she has been too warm; but 'the treatment you
meet with is very little encouragement to me to endeavour to imitate
you in your dutiful meekness'. Anna is not aggressive; but in a world
of 'peck and be hanged' you need to cultivate at least the aggressions
of self-defence.

So Anna is pert: but to say this simply as a point about her personality
would be to remove the social dimension of the novel. For what is she
pert about: that is, against what does she feel it necessary to stand up
for herself? Almost invariably, against the two forms of established auth-

ority, that of parents and that of men (and since her mother's main endeavour is to get her to marry Hickman, the two acts of defiance often coincide). Anna delivers herself of a steady critique against marriage, which (like a good feminist) she sees as an institution for keeping women down.

> When I look round upon all the married people of my acquaintance, and see how *they* live, and what *they* bear who live *best*, I am confirmed in my dislike to the state. (IV.477)

You have to keep your eyes open to see how the obsequious lover, once he is accepted, gives place to the imperative husband:

> in short, how he *ascends* and how I *descend*, in the matrimonial wheel, never to take my turn again, but by fits and starts, like the feeble struggles of a sinking State for its dying liberty. (I.340)

Clarissa, in contrast, accepts the institution of marriage, and indeed it is her high sense of its duties that leads her to refuse a man she knows she can never respect; yet she too is capable of a shrewdness fraught with potential cynicism, as when she remarks that 'the men were the framers of the matrimonial office, and made *obedience* a part of the woman's vow'. Anna could easily say that; but when she does say it, we recognize a verbal violence—and brilliance—utterly beyond the range of the estimable Clarissa. Be careful, she warns, lest you be brought at last,

> so *prettily* and so *audibly*, to pronounce the little reptile word OBEY, that it will do one's heart good to hear you. (I.342)

It is mainly in her remarks on marriage that Anna shows her streaks of feminism; but sometimes she can show it direct, in tones that sound even more like the twentieth century:

> But I, who think our sex inferior in nothing to the other but in want of opportunities, of which the narrow-minded mortals industriously seek to deprive us, lest we should surpass them as much in what they chiefly value themselves upon, as we do in all the graces of a fine imagination....
> (IV.497)

All this by way of forthright but theoretical criticism. Anna, however, is no theoretical critic: she is intensely involved emotionally, and her attack on marriage is fuelled by a fierce dislike of men with which she can on occasion touch a nerve. Never more intensely, perhaps, than when suggesting that Clarissa runs off with her instead of Lovelace:

> A woman going away with a *woman* is not so discreditable a thing, surely! and with no view but to *avoid the fellows*! (I.449)

The last three words come from a genius of empathy in which no one has equalled Richardson: from below all the elaborations and arrangements comes the utter directness of sheer sexual dislike. And she knows that any woman will understand her; for at that very moment Clarissa is writing (in milder tones, of course) that she would be glad of a breach with Lovelace if it could be combined with escaping Solmes, and so 'make way for the single life to take place, which I so much prefer: and then I would defy the sex'. Only the stylistic genius of Richardson could have seen so unerringly that defying (especially if combined with the abstraction of 'the sex' rather than those vividly imagined 'fellows') is so much milder than avoiding.

There are other examples of Anna's hostility to men ('O my dear! How pleasantly can these devils, as I must call them, pass their time, while our gentle bosoms heave with pity for their supposed sufferings for us!'—I.351); and not surprisingly it joins with her criticism of marriage to produce an attack of rare power and conviction, the *cri de coeur* of one who has learnt her feminism the hard way:

> If I lose you, my more than sister, and lose my mother, I shall distrust my own conduct, and will not marry. And why should I? Creeping, cringing in courtship! O my dear, these men are a vile race of *reptiles in our day*, and mere *bears* in *their own*. . . . Is it to be expected that I, who could hardly bear control from a mother, should take it from a husband?   (IV.265)

But there is a further complication. This Diana-like figure likes the 'blushing fellows' much more than Clarissa does. She is capable of suggesting that she and Clarissa have the wrong men, and that she is the right woman for Lovelace—a view that Lovelace himself shares, though we can attribute to his own vanity the opinion that Anna Howe is in love with him. Anna had herself (before the story begins) fancied a rake, Sir George Colmar, but had been talked out of him. She has more in common with Lovelace than the saintly Clarissa ever could have, and her violent hostility to him must contain a kind of attraction. Anna the man-hater has stronger sexual feelings than her friend, and this issues in an ambivalence that can be seen above all in her reactions to Hickman.

Hickman's courtship of Anna is one of the great comic sequences of the English novel; and like the finest comedy, it runs deeper than its uproarious surface. It is essential to realize that the disdain with which she treats his earnest addresses is ambivalent. She despises him because he is not one of the blustering fellows, because his deference and his formality show that he is willing to be trodden on; at the same time, she resents him because he is a man, and so is capable (or will be capable) of exercising authority over her. She is at the same time tyranness and victim; and since marriage turns the tyranness into the victim, the more willing she is to marry Hickman, the more necessary it is for her to bully him now. Here on the one hand is her contempt:

> I am so much accustomed, for my own part, to Hickman's whining, creeping, submissive courtship that I now expect nothing but whine and cringe from him: and am so little moved with his nonsense that I am frequently forced to go to my harpsichord to keep me awake and to silence his humdrum. (II.104)

If Lovelace—or Sir George Colmar—was courting her, she would at any rate not be bored. (If she *is* bored? she may simply be relieved that Hickman is mild enough to enable her to pretend it.) And here on the other hand is the opposite reason for treating him badly:

> Mr Hickman, like the rest of his sex, would grow upon indulgence. One distinction from me would make him pay two to himself. Insolent creepers, or encroachers, all of you! To show any of you a *favour* today, you would expect it as a *right* tomorrow. (IV.475)

Or, as she put it more succinctly earlier, 'if I do not make Hickman quake now and then, he will endeavour to make me fear'. This ambivalence makes Anna a much less unambiguous spokeswoman for proto-feminism than she might be, but we need not be surprised to find that the very greatness of a work obscures its ideological implications. In a passage like the following Richardson is at his most complex and most ambiguous:

> The man has certainly a good mind. Nor can we expect in one man every good quality. But he is really a silly fellow, my dear, to trouble his head about me, when he sees how much I despise his whole sex; and must of course make a common man look like a fool, were he not to make *himself* look like one, by wishing to pitch his tent so oddly. (II.116)

Affection, contempt and a kind of admiration for Hickman; her own superiority and her own inferiority; all jostle, all buckle here, and the passage asserts that woman is the glory jest and riddle of the world.

I believe Anna Howe is the richest study of a rebellious woman until we come to George Eliot and Henry James;[69] I know of only one character to compare with her, and that too is by Richardson. There was a time when *Sir Charles Grandison* was read by everyone interested in literature; now it is read by virtually no one. To offer a rather unorthodox reading of it is therefore to tilt at windmills, but I still find it worth expressing surprise that nobody, to my knowledge, has remarked how interesting—and how subversive—is the figure of Charlotte Grandison.

I begin with the orthodox. *Sir Charles Grandison* takes up a moderate position on marriage. On the one hand, parents should not force their children to marry against their inclination; one the other hand, young girls whose heads are filled with romantic nonsense are liable to make fools of themselves, and ought to listen to the wisdom of their parents. Richardson holds explicitly the carefully balanced view that Thackeray held implicitly, and against the horrifying account of parental tyranny in *Clarissa* we can set some entertaining accounts of the folly of romantic love in *Grandison*. A responsible account of Richardson's fiction—one he would himself have assented to—would have fitted very appropriately into the chapter on choosing a mate.

But because Richardson so often wrote at his best when departing from his own purpose, I once more prefer to offer an irresponsible account of the book: that is, to place at the centre not the estimable characters who speak for the author, but the irrepressible Charlotte Grandison, the pert sister of the flawless hero. She is Richardson's La Rochefoucauld: 'We can be very generous for others, Harriet, when we apprehend that one day we may want the same pity ourselves. Our best passions, my dear, have their mixtures of self-love.' (IV: letter 8). The shrewdest and most cynical character in the book, she sees the self-love in the motivations of others and (especially) of men;[70] and her willingness to dismiss the code of honour is because she sees it as coming entirely from 'these Lords of the creation'. She is easily the wittiest character in an (admittedly) stodgy book, and some of her most effective sallies consist of undermining in passing the vocabulary of marrying:

O, Sir, what a memory you have! I hope that the man who is to call me *his* (thats the dialect, i'n't it?) will not have half your memory....
(III letter 17)

Charlotte's wit is not, of course, disinterested: it arises mostly out of her own situation, and in particular out of her marriage to Lord G. This is by Richardsonian standards an admirable match. Lord G. is approved of by her family: that is, since she has no parents, by her elder sister and the virtuous brother who is wiser and more insupportably virtuous than any father. At the same time he loves her passionately, and longs to call her his (that's the dialect). Both propriety and love support the marriage, and there is no one Charlotte likes better, but she rebels—not enough to refuse him, for that might suggest that she was waiting for a more suitable man; but she mutters all the way to church ('I don't like this affair at all Harriet') and up to the altar ('You don't know what you are about, man. I expect to have all my way'), and once married she leads her husband a dance, picking quarrels, resenting his behaviour at every opportunity.

What is the content of Charlotte's rebellion—or rather of the perversity and wit she has recourse to as a way of not, in the end, actually rebelling? Part of the answer may be that it is her resistance to sex, the maiden's resentment of the interference with her privacy that sexual surrender will entail. In so discreet a writer as Richardson it is hard to offer direct evidence for this, but I have little doubt that it is true both of Charlotte and of Clarissa. Charlotte's resentment is for instance stirred up when

> last night, the week from the wedding-day not completed, Lord G. thought fit to break into my retirement without any leave....
> What boldness is this, said I!—Pray, Sir, begone—Why leave you your company below?
> I come, my dearest life, to make a request to you.
> The man began with civility enough, had he had a little less of his odious rapture; for he flung his arms about me, Jenny in presence. A husband's fondness is enough to ruin these girls. Don't you think, Harriet, that there is an immorality in it, before them? I refuse your request, be it what it will. How dare you invade me in my retirement? (IV letter 27)

'The week from the wedding day not completed': The wedding day was the abandonment of her right to be left alone, and if she must lose this she feels at least entitled to the courtesy—the pretence, even—that permission is needed before he comes in, at any rate till she is more used to it. And why was the embrace so much worse in Jenny's presence? Not, clearly, for the reason she gives, that it is bad for the girl's morals: what is immoral about married love? Surely it is because Jenny's presence emphasizes the lack of privacy. That a sexual advance should be seen by someone who is still a virgin makes it more of an outrage—and even if Jenny is not a virgin, she is supposed to be, and knows very well that her mistress was until a week ago: Charlotte has lost face as a young woman in the first case (she has lost what Jenny still has), as a member of her class in the second (she has sunk to Jenny's level).

Not that we are to imagine Charlotte frigid. The intensity of her sexual reluctance (as with that of Anna Howe, as with that of any normal woman) is connected with the loss of independence: marriage is a reminder of woman's oppression, since this so desirable condition simply exchanges one underprivileged state for another. There is in fact a good deal of more or less explicit feminism in Charlotte's petulance. She is angry with her husband because he takes a house without consulting her; she mocks her sister for handing over the thousand pounds Lord W. gave her to her husband, 'to take part of it back from him, by four or five paltry guineas at a time, at his pleasure' (IV.17); she is hoity-toity because 'my Lord may go where he pleases, without my leave—very fit he should. He is a *man*' (IV.10). I am not at all sure that

Richardson agreed with Charlotte on any of these points, but all the same she speaks for the future, and we trust the tale.

If any reader is now getting enthusiastic enough to think of reading *Sir Charles Grandison*, I must warn him that Charlotte sees the error of her ways, takes it all back, and declines into a wife. She even hands over her thousand pounds, insistently, though Lord G. urges her to take it back; and like so many pert characters she is, in the end, defeated by her author. The contrast with Anna Howe is interesting, since there is no corresponding sense of anticlimax in Anna's case. True, we do not see her married to Hickman, but I see no reason why Richardson could not have shown her as a pert wife, as he after all does with Charlotte, whose recantation does not come with her marriage (indeed, and interestingly, she grows if anything more rebellious as a wife). The difference is that the ambivalence of Anna's feelings towards Hickman, and towards her own situation, is split into two in the case of Charlotte, so that instead of the tension between submission and rebellion that makes Anna so profound a study, we have rebellion followed by submission. There is only one moment, after her recantation, at which Charlotte is once more interesting. Her brother has returned from Italy, and she is describing the pleasure of everyone in the family, including her husband:

> My bustling nimble Lord enjoyed over again his joy, at that of every other person; and he was ready, good-naturedly, to sing and dance—That's *his* way, poor man, to shew his joy; but he is honest, for all that. Don't despise him, Harriet! He was brought up as an only son, and to know that he was a Lord, or else he would have made a better figure in *your eyes*. The man wants not sense, I assure you. You may think me partial; but I believe the most foolish thing he ever did in his life, was at church, and that at St George's Hanover-Square.   (V.43)

Here is Anna Howe once more, expressing the full complexity of the feminine state, and here is the only point in the novel at which Charlotte reformed is as interesting as Charlotte in rebellion.

The three most successful characters in Richardson's fiction are Lovelace, Anna Howe, and Charlotte, and none of them speaks for the sober bourgeois morality of the author, with its admiration for duty, routine, good works, careful bookkeeping and a moderate acceptance of the status quo. Lovelace represents something older, the carefree irresponsible gaiety of the natural aristocrat who has never known the curb of real authority; and the two pert women, though Mr Richardson would have been distressed to learn it, represent the future: for they rebel against their situation as women, and rebel with the unreasonableness that so often seems to belong with premature allegiance to future morality.[71] And in both cases, their rebellion takes the form of impatience with both the current criteria for marriage choice. They do not want to submit tamely to the choice made by their family; but they do not want a romantic love match either. For romantic love is unreasonable, and a proper respect for the individuality of a woman would allow her the exercise of reason. Unreason easily becomes conservative, for in depriving us of the insight that could criticize existing institutions, it thereby supports them. Here we have the seed of the modern feminist attack on love. Incipient in Anna and Charlotte are Kate Millett and Shulamith Firestone. I am delighted to point this out, since the alliance will benefit both parties.

6

Sex

Perhaps this chapter should have come first. What is love, after all, but the epiphenomenon of sexual appetite, what is marriage but an institution for the regulation of sexual behaviour? Whether or not we take this reductive view (whether or not we consider it reductive) there is an obvious sense which sex is the basis of love and marriage. We have constantly stumbled, in earlier chapters, against the underlying fact of sex, and it is now time to confront this directly, to offer an account of the basis after building the superstructure.

Since we know so little about sexual behaviour, and so much about sexual ideology, one of the stories that can be told is that of what could and could not be publicly mentioned. Conventions of reticence are clearly of great interest for literature, which is so centrally concerned with what can be said, and what must be conveyed without being said; and so this chapter will look at the shift from reticence to outspokenness over the last hundred years or so, and at its literary consequences.

If this shift is a pendulum swing, then the arc has increased enormously. From one of the furthest extremes of prudery our society has known, we have shifted to what must be the furthest extreme of openness, and there is no sign of a reversal. If it was once improper to use the words 'breeches' and 'shift' (even, we are told, 'legs'),[1] we are now fast losing the very idea of impropriety in language (of this more later). The causes of Victorian reticence lie in the Evangelical movement of the late eighteenth and early nineteenth centuries.[2] The casual disreputability of the eighteenth-century Church, when a man could advertise for 'a curacy in a good sporting country where the duty is light and the neighbourhood convivial'[3] gave place to a Church under pressure first from Dissent, then from Catholicism, then from unbelief, and so generating those three diverse forms of nineteenth-century earnestness, the Evangelical, the High Church and the Broad Church movements. At the same time the sexual casualness of the propertied classes of the eighteenth century gave place to the concern with purity, so that Lord Chesterfield would have been as much out of place in 1840 as Thomas Arnold in 1740. The sexual nature of woman ceased to be a permissible subject; the threshold of obscenity dropped sharply; and the bedroom door became impenetrable to words. If we want a representative figure for this change it will surely be Thomas Bowdler.

Bowdler's *Family Shakespeare* appeared in 1818. Its aim was to render the plays of the immortal bard 'unsullied by any scene, by any speech, or if possible by any word that can give pain to the most chaste, or offence to the most religious of his readers'. The blasphemy, Bowdler explains, has been comparatively easy to remove; the indecency was more of a problem. (It is difficult to know if this is an objective judgement, or if he had higher standards for indecency.) Nonetheless, he claims to have rendered the text fit for family reading without there being any danger of encountering 'words and expressions which are of such a nature as to raise a blush on the cheek of modesty'.[4]

Forms of Reticence

What Bowdler shows us is a change in the conventions of social behaviour; and this of course has literary consequences, not only for reading, but for writing also. Its effect on the novelists was varied. They could accept it without fuss; they could complain bitterly; they could conform eagerly. George Eliot is an example of the first, Thackeray of the second, Dickens of the third. There is no suggestion in George Eliot's fiction that she found the conventions irksome: she included the scenes it was customary to include on the evident assumption that this enabled her to say all she needed to say about her characters. By the same token, there is no suggestion that if convention had required her to say more she would have had any difficulty. When she describes Grandcourt's pleasure in kissing Gwendolen while she is furious with him

—The rage was silent and therefore not disagreeable to him. It followed that he turned her chin and kissed her, while she still kept her eyelids down—[5]

it is not difficult to extrapolate to what happened in the bedroom.

Dickens and Trollope, on the other hand, show exaggerated care not to bring a blush to the cheek of modesty. There are three kinds of young woman in Dickens's fiction: the virtuous (Florence, Agnes, Esther, Amy, Lizzie), devoted daughters and totally sexless; the pretty and delicious (Dolly Varden, Dora, Bella Wilfer); and the passionate (Rosa Dartle, Alice Marwood, Fanny Dorritt, and—in former years—Lady Dedlock). The last group are tormented by their twisted sexuality, marvellously symbolized in Rosa by the scar on her face, given her by the man she loves, that under the stress of strong emotion seems to move independently of the face it is on. The second group provide clear examples of evasiveness: because their curls, their rosy cheeks and their demure manner are sexually attractive, and because the author seems determined not to admit this (for the heroes who love them do not seem to love their bodies), we can accuse him (which means, also, them) of being coy.

The most interesting example is perhaps Dora Copperfield, and we can begin with her death. How many contemporary readers realized— how many modern readers would realize if their teachers had not got into the habit of pointing it out—what Dora Copperfield died of? She dies off-stage, while David sits grief-stricken and watches her little dog die in sympathy. He knows she is going to die, for 'they' (Betsy Trotwood and Agnes) have told him 'that my child-wife will soon leave me'. Our glimpses of the dying Dora consist simply of her being made trim by his aunt, and her pretty hair persisting in curling upon the pillow. We can be forgiven for wondering if she dies of anything but the need to bow out so that he can marry Agnes, unless we spot the clue 70 pages earlier:

> But, as that year wore on, Dora was not strong. I hoped that lighter hands than mine would help to mould character, and that a baby-smile upon her breast might change my child-wife to a woman. It was not to be. The spirit fluttered for a moment on the threshold of its little prison, and, unconscious of captivity, took wing.   (Ch. 48)

From then on Dora is never well. It is not clear how much longer she lives but we can presume that she died of this very discreet miscarriage.

And was that foetus who died so surreptitiously, just as surreptitiously conceived? There is a strong streak of youthful sexual attraction in Dora, and the point of her story is that this is not enough for marriage. She needs, and could never learn, to accept the responsibilities of being a wife. If we said that seeing yourself as a sexual object is not enough we could make Dickens (even Dickens!) sound like a proto-feminist; and if there is anything in Dickens for which this case could be made, it is surely the treatment of Dora, who was treated like a child and so learnt to treat herself as one. But this would be a misleading interpretation, for the maturity that Dora should have had was not that of equality but of submissive acceptance of the expected role.

And is it even correct to say that Dora's immaturity consists in only seeing herself sexually? How are we meant to read the descriptions of Dora sitting on David's knee when they are married, Dora coaxing him not to scold, Dora acting the helpless innocent over the housekeeping, and responding to his frowns with this:

> 'Oh, what ugly wrinkles in my bad boy's forehead!' said Dora, and still being on my knee, she traced them with her pencil; putting it to her rosy lips to make it mark blacker, and working at my forehead with a quaint little mockery of being industrious, that quite delighted me in spite of myself.   (Ch. 44)

This sort of writing is familiar to all readers of Dickens: what it describes is a sexual invitation, accompanied by the presentation of the girl as innocent. Dora was like that from the beginning, delightful in her curls, caressing her dog, not noticing (or pretending not to notice) the effect she has on the enamoured David. But by this stage in the story much has changed: she has now advanced to sitting on David's knee; and she and David are married. Dickens may still pretend that what she is doing with her pencil is not immodest, and Dora may be trying to pretend it too; but we know perfectly well that the couple will, before long, end up in bed. The fact of marriage makes the naivety impossible, as Dora must by now have learnt. True, we could postulate an innocent maiden as the reader, one so innocent (there must have been some such who read *David Copperfield*) that she did not know what Dora was doing (and so did not know how unscrupulously she was using her charms to distract from her failings). Can Dickens really have believed he was writing only for such readers? If coyness is the non-admission of the sexual element, can it have extended to married flirting? It is as if this scene can be read on two levels: the truer and less evasive also gives us a nastier Dora.[6]

The case of Thackeray is as interesting. Adopting the man-of-the-world posture he was so fond of, Thackeray complained that it was impossible to depict a MAN in English fiction. 'We must drape him, and give him a certain conventional simper.' Yet although he claimed to show that young men had passions to feel, he is capable of being as coy as Dickens. Perhaps the most brilliant episode in all Thackeray— Becky's intrigue with Lord Steyne—shows this. It is full of marvellous observation (Lord Steyne ordering his wife to invite the Crawleys to dinner) and marvellous ironies—Becky sitting down to the piano after everyone has cut her to sing 'religious songs of Mozart which had been early favourites of Lady Steyne, and with such sweetness and tenderness that the lady . . . listened until the tears rolled down her eyes'. If we compare Lord Steyne bowing over Becky's hand to kiss it after she has sung, with Edith Dombey's fit of shrill Victorian virtue in a French hotel after she has run off with Carker, we can see the difference between omission and evasiveness. And then, after the climax and Rawdon's discovery of the truth he had perhaps always half-known, Thackeray spoils it. 'Was Rebecca guilty or not?' he asks, more than once, and suggests that the answer may have been, no. Why does he make this utterly implausible suggestion? It is after all a touch of the same squeamishness that can only allow Edith Dombey to run off with Carker if she repents in time to refrain from getting into bed with him and repents with all the fury of the indignant *paterfamilias* reading—and it is all the more cowardly on Thackeray's part because of his bold attacks on squeamishness in this very novel.

Several modern critics have offered defences of this passage. Barbara Hardy suggests that by refusing to answer the question of Becky's adultery, Thackeray is showing 'a larger and more profound sense of value' than those critics who have complained of his evasion. Becky has betrayed Rawdon in so wide and deep a way that the question of sexual guilt becomes trivial: 'Thackeray is interested in truth and lies rather than in chastity, fidelity and adultery.' This point is understood by Rawdon, when he says 'If she's not guilty, she's as bad as guilty', and part of the effect of the scene should lie in our discovery of the 'superior moral intelligence' of Rawdon.[7]

The point is shrewd and, in a way, right: Becky has betrayed Rawdon in ways that go deeper than adultery. But it is not based on what Thackeray has actually done. For the way to show us that the adultery does not matter would be either to say nothing about it, or else to mention in passing that it had taken place, treating it as a mere detail. But we are given a prurient harping on the point which is too like an imitation of the gloating curiosity of servants and neighbours, exactly the curiosity that lacks superior moral intelligence.

There is an exactly parallel case in *Pendennis*. Pen's affair with Fanny Bolton, the young working-class girl who nurses him devotedly through his fever, is ended by the indignant arrival of his virtuous mother and his virtuous Laura. This glimpse of the cruelty of virtue is also a glimpse of Victorian squeamishness: young men have mistresses before they settle down, but 'the most squeamish if not the most moral of societies is determined to ignore it!' For a moment Pen stands up against the hypocrisy, even to the extent of being beastly to his mother; but again, Thackeray spoils it. He cannot admit that his hero had a mistress. The situation is saved by Pen declaring himself innocent and all is forgiveness between him and his mother and Laura. Instead of giving Pen the really interesting anger at being confronted with the hypocrisy of a class-structure he himself profits from, he gives him the much safer anger of protesting against an unjust accusation.[8]

What could the novelist do who was dissatisfied with reticence? Elizabeth Gaskell set out to write a novel on the forbidden subject of the fallen women, and drew down showers of abuse when she published it. *Ruth* appeared in 1853, and was denounced because it treated 'an unfit subject for fiction'. One London library withdrew it as 'unfit for family reading', and two members of her husband's congregation burnt the first volume ('they sit next to us in Chapel and you can't think how "improper" I feel under their eyes').[9]

This 'improper' book is the story of an unmarried mother who almost succeeds in redeeming herself. Taken into the house of a kindly Congregationalist clergyman who passes her off as a distant connexion and a widow, she gradually becomes accepted as a member of the local Dissenting and money-making community; the discovery of the truth produces the plot-complications of the climax and Ruth's saintly death. What is most striking to the modern reader is the lengths which the author has gone to in order to make Ruth's fall excusable. She is apprenticed to a horrid old beast of a dressmaker, who virtually drives her into her seducer's arms; the seducer himself is a fop and a cad, and when he falls ill Ruth's reward for her devoted nursing is to be bundled out (like Pen's Fanny) when his mother turns up; the whole of her subsequent life is blameless and unselfish, and her death virtually a martydom. Ruth has to pay very high for our support. Is this simply a rhetorical device on Mrs Gaskell's part, or did she believe that fallen women needed to be saintly to deserve charity?

It is striking to look at Mrs Gaskell's own response to the book's reception. There is no doubt she was deeply hurt—'I had a terrible fit of crying all Saturday night at the unkind things people were saying'[10]—and she compared herself to St Sebastian tied to a tree to be shot at with arrows. Yet she was not surprised. She knew the subject was painful and would offend, for indeed it was *not* a fit subject for family reading, and *Ruth* was a forbidden book in her own household![11] It is clear that she shared the contemporary feeling about the delicacy of the subject, and that what she was pleading for was charity to the sinner and not any softening of attitude towards the sin. The seduction itself is narrated with the utmost discretion, without a word Dr Bowdler would have needed to remove. We are far more conscious of Victorian prudery when reading *Ruth* than with any other of the author's novels. Nothing, in short, shows the strength of convention better than a mild resistance to it.

Jude the Obscure has a far better claim to defying the sexual conventions, and was greeted with louder howls of indignation than *Ruth*. 'Jude the Obscene', one review was entitled; others were 'Hardy the Degenerate', 'A Novel of Lubricity'. It too was burnt, and this time by a bishop: William Walsham How seems to have been a progressive and dedicated social worker, but he is now remembered for his Pecksniffian letter to the *Yorkshire Post* on 'the intolerable grossness and hateful sneering' that so disgusted him in the novel 'that I threw it into the fire'.[12]

In two respects, *Jude* is a more radical novel than *Ruth*. It goes further in outspokenness, for it not only tells us exactly when Jude and Sue first went to bed together, but makes it clear that Sue's motive in yielding was sexual jealousy, and that she offered her body to keep Jude from going to help Arabella. Worse still, the fact is pointed out, with casual coarseness, by Arabella herself. Hardy even does what so few Victorians did, he takes us into the bedroom. First that of Jude and Arabella, where he discovers that she wears false hair, sees her practising her dimples, and is told that she isn't pregnant after all. Then—more daringly—that of Phillotson and Sue, where we learn of Sue's frigidity, see her jump out of the window in terror, and—nastiest of all—eventually see her grit her teeth and return to her husband's bed.

As well as being more outspoken than *Ruth*, *Jude* is more subversive. For Sue is not a victim but a rebel, is not seduced but deliberately leads an unorthodox life, until she finally repents and is beaten down by the Big Brother of conversion. On her first appearance she is buying copies of classical statues—a Venus and an Apollo—'so very large ..., so very naked', and hiding them from her pious landlady. Timid as she is, she accepts neither orthodox religion nor orthodox sexual morality, and the indignation of contemporaries was fed because they saw in her example of the New Woman. 'A highly-strung, nervous, hysterical woman,' said the *Morning Post*, 'who throws quotations from eminent economists at her husband'; and the critic does not conceal his sympathy with the husband's response, 'What do I care about J. S. Mill, I only want to lead a quiet life.'[13]

Yet is the novel really outspoken? Hardy himself did not think so. 'I think you will admit,' he wrote to Florence Henniker, 'that if the story had to be told, it could not be told with more reticence.'[14] Its account of Sue leaves us uncertain on the question whether her sexual aversion was to Phillotson in particular, or to men in general. There are indications both ways—on the one hand, the suggestions that Sue was not suited to marriage, on the other the confession that she still loves Jude 'grossly'. The difference is crucial: has Hardy made a genuine attempt at portraying frigidity? The subject is startlingly rare in fiction: the earliest (and perhaps still unsurpassed) treatment of it that I know is *Le Baiser au Lepreux* by François Mauriac (1922). In a famous letter to Edmund Gosse, Hardy explained that he could not say all he wished to about Sue's nature: 'her sexual instinct being healthy as far as it goes, but unusually weak and fastidious'. He regrets that he could not 'dwell upon' the point that 'although she has children, her intimacies with Jude have never been more than occasional'.[15] This certainly suggests that Sue is a study in frigidity, and her aversion was not simply to Phillotson; and it is not clear why Hardy felt he could not say so, since there is nothing in the letter any more outspoken than the novel. The problem is not what the novel does not but what it does say—the suggestions of Sue's genuine sexual passion for Jude, mainly at the end, and no doubt as a contrast to the aversion for Phillotson.

I believe this uncertainty about Sue's sexual nature springs from Hardy's uncertainty about where he stands. The novel offers a parallel between education and sex: Jude defies the reluctance of society to give him an education, and fails; Sue defies the sexual conventions and fails.

The parallel is a truer one than Hardy knows, for on both issues two contradictory interpretations are possible. On the one hand, there is the radical reading, by which it is the callousness of society that denies opportunity to such talented scholarship material, and the rigidity of the marriage laws that kept Jude and Sue apart, though they were so suited to each other, on the pedantic grounds of an earlier contract by each. This is how most contemporaries saw it, especially (but not only) the indignant ones; and though Hardy liked to deny this ('I hold no theory whatever on the subject [of marriage])[16] there is no doubt that much of the book shows such a commitment. The letter from the Master of Biblioll College, advising Jude to stick to his station, is clearly meant to be a slap in the face from the home of complacency; and there are frequent remarks on the folly, even wickedness, of binding oneself by the impossible promise of continuing to love indefinitely.

> There seemed to him, vaguely and dimly, something wrong in a social ritual which made necessary the cancelling of well-informed schemes ... of foregoing a man's one opportunity of showing himself superior to the lower animals ... because of a momentary surprise by a new and transitory instinct.
>
> (I.ix)

With a passage like this to quote, Mrs Oliphant can hardly be blamed for heading her review 'The anti-marriage league'.[17]

Yet Hardy also thought that Jude's drive to education, and Sue's unconventional morality, were examples of the modern vice of unrest. The 'true illumination' falls on Jude when he first enters the stonemason's yard that here 'was a centre of effort as worthy as that dignified by the name of scholarly study', but he puts it aside. There is similar ground for seeing this vice in Sue. Her effect on ordinary decent folk is one of bewilderment, even resentment. Phillotson's friend Gillingham speaks for conventional Philistine opinion when he opposes the generous act of giving Sue her freedom; but he also speaks for a sturdy common sense when he responds to her high-minded shilly-shallying by calling her a little hussy. Even Jude is driven to something near resentment at times, and when she calls herself an Ishmaelite he replies 'an urban miss is what you are'. Sue's frigidity can be seen as a sign of the essential artificiality of the New Woman, the fact that she is not in touch with the deeper organic rhythms of life: she can live with a man in defiance of convention, but she can torture him (first the student, then Jude) by refusing his advances. Sex in the head is her complaint, and she succeeds in neither having her cake nor eating it. This very conservative view is certainly present in the novel, but not consistently: it does not represent Hardy's judgement of Sue, but a part of his own contradictory position. Sue's objections to marriage may be partly sexual but they are also legal, not for coherent feminist reasons but because of her aversion to a binding promise, her dislike of a form which says '"Names and Surnames of the Parties" (they were to be parties now, not lovers, she thought)'—as if she were Lydia Languish. Sue speaks for her author at this point, for Hardy keeps shifting attention from the important question of the sexual relation between the pair to the more superficial question of her aversion to the ceremony—and shifting in a way that cannot be simply explained by his fear of censorship.

For all its power, *Jude* is a confused novel. It is not resonant with the ambivalence of a masterpiece that cannot be tied down to opinions, for it does advance opinions, but contradictory ones. It inclines at times to being a novel of social criticism, with progressive implications, at others to asserting the traditional values that modern unrest is destroying. It is this confusion which shows itself in the uncertainty with which the sexual material is handled. Sue, as the emancipated woman, ought to be Roxana. It turns out that she is Mary, not idealized for her purity, but resented for her frigidity. If she were a true woman, in touch with traditional values, would she not be more like Arabella, who is of course Dalilah, divesting Jude of his modern unrest and his ambitions as if they were hair to be cut off?

Forms of Outspokenness

What do we mean when we say that sexual reticence is over, and the novelist can now say anything? The simplest illustration would obviously be an episode in which sexual intercourse takes place in front of our eyes.

'I want to know what it really means,' I told myself in a mirror whose cracks had been pasted over with the trimmings of postage stamps. I meant of course the whole portentous scrimmage of sex itself, the act of penetration which could lead a man to despair for the sake of a creature with two breasts and *le croissant* as the picturesque Levant slang has it. . . . How far had our feelings carried us from the truth of the simple, devoid beast-like act itself? To what extent was the treacherous mind—with its interminable catalogue raisonné of the heart—responsible? I wished to answer an unanswerable question; but I was so desperate for certainty that it seemed to me that if I surprised the act in its natural state, motivated by scientific money and not love, as yet un-damaged by the idea, I might surprise the truth of my own feelings and desires. Impatient to deliver myself from the question I lifted the curtain and stepped softly into the cubicle . . .

The bed was inhabited by an indistinct mass of flesh moving in many places at once, vaguely stirring like an ant-heap. It took me some moments to define the pale and hairy limbs of an elderly man from those of his partner—the greenish-hued whiteness of convex woman with a boa-constrictor's head—

a head crowned with spokes of toiling black hair which trailed over the edges of the filthy mattress ...

They lay there like the victims of some terrible accident, clumsily engaged, as if in some incoherent experimental fashion they were the first partners in the history of the human race to think out this peculiar means of communication. ... From this sprang all those aspects of love which the wit of poets and madmen had used to elaborate their philosophy of polite distinctions. From this point the sick, the insane started growing; and from here too the disgusted and dispirited faces of the long-married, tied to each other back to back, so to speak, like dogs unable to disengage after coupling.[18]

It is now possible for the novel-reader to be taken into a brothel, and to be shown, with this blend of scientific curiosity, amusement and incipient disgust, what goes on there. The narrator's assumption here is that of naturalism, that the true basic meaning of the sexual act is what it shares with the animals: 'the simple devoid beast-like act itself'—that last word, 'itself', shows the naturalistic assumption. But the writing confirms none of this naturalism. The setting is very human, involving payment and legality, the fear of a police raid, the willingness of the woman to accommodate a new client, ('Wait one moment,' she cried, waving a white blotched hand in the direction of the curtain, 'I will not be long'). The constant comparisons with animals do not at all convey a continuity with nature, but, by their clash with what we expect of the act of love, an effect of the grotesque: the naturalist who wishes to show the continuity between human and animal sex would hardly choose a boa-constrictor. The expectation that human sex will involve thoughts beyond the naturalistic is so explicit and so prominent ('the whole protentous scrimmage') that the determined neutrality of the observer clearly does not represent what he believes about sex but a counter-attitude that he is trying to set up against his beliefs—and trying with complete lack of success, for he is never able to shake off the grotesque discrepancy between the mere bodily posture and the richness of traditional connotation. Perhaps no detail conveys this better than the ant-heap, the impossibility of being sure, at first, how many individuals the mass of flesh divides into. Indeed the very choice of narrator—the sophisticated, even world-weary man with his knowledge of (and detachment from) Levant slang—renders naturalism impossible, as we can see if we ask ourselves how the truly naturalistic novelist will handle sex.

Lise Buteau in Zola's *La Terre*, gives birth to her baby at the same time as their cow gives birth to her calf. She has been expecting this, and joking about it, for some time:

Dragging her huge belly into the cowshed, Lise would cease to think about herself as, with a worried eye, she watched the cow, whose belly had also swollen immeasurably.[19]

They go into labour together, and the reader's attention is constantly switched from one to the other. The vet is called to help with the cow, but too late, after the crude peasant methods have made sure the calf is killed; the same meanness prevents them calling the doctor for Lise. The vet's reaction to the double labour is amused, coarse and even abusive: after Lise's groans have startled him, he tells her 'Va donc faire ton affaire chez toi, et laisse-moi faire la mienne ici!' So we have Lise crouching on three chairs in one room, Coliche (the cow) moaning in the byre, and the neighbour, la Bécu, running from one to the other to bring her news. It is a richly comic episode, the main figure being Patoir, the vet; and as a climax the second (and living) calf is brought in and shown to Lise in labour, so that she is seized with giggles like all the others, and the pains of labour are confused with the aches of laughter.

How like Durrell, in one way: the parallel between the human and the animal turning into grotesque comedy. Yet how utterly different, for two reasons. First, we are on a farm; and the parallel exists not only in the narrator's thoughts, but in front of our eyes, in the form of two actual births: this is not a novelist of sophisticated sensibilities, but of realism and action. And second, because for all the contrasts and for all the humour, Zola really does believe in the parallel. We have known this from the very first chapter, in which that calf was conceived. Françoise (sister of Lise) brought Coliche to be serviced, and her unembarrassed helping of the bull to carry out his task is something Jean, as he watches, finds it impossible to be coarse about: 'C'etait la nature.' That sums up Jean's response to Françoise; and Françoise has the same response during her sister's labour. Unable to bear the sight of the vet cutting up the calf in order to save the life of the cow, she drops her candle (almost causing a fire) and run to where Lise is in agony, and where the yawning gap between her legs does not distress her, 'comme s'il se fût agi d'une chose naturelle et ordinaire, après ce qu'elle de venait voir'.

The whole of *La Terre* is a long exploration of the interaction of the human and the natural, and any one formula must oversimplify. But it is not misleading to say that the parallel is accepted: with little question in some of the choric passages, such as the account of indiscriminate sex during the grape-harvest, and modified by the moral issues raised but still, basically, accepted in the main story. A glance at Zola makes it clear that Durell is no naturalist.

We had to wait till the twentieth century for *Justine*, and that episode in the brothel would be inconceivable in a nineteenth-century novel. But *La Terre* was published in 1887. True, they order these matters differently in France, and any good English bishop would have been likely to burn Zola, especially if he read far enough to come upon the description of the body of Lise when in labour ('le trou baillant d'un tonneau défoncé, la lucarne grande ouverte du fenil, par òu l'on jetait le foin, et qu'un lierre touffu herissait de noir': even in 1978 I am glad to quote in the decent obscurity of at any rate a foreign language). But there were obscenity trials in France too,[20] and it seems fair to conclude that naturalism is less shocking than the sophisticated reflections of Durrell's narrator. It is after all easier (shall we say, more natural) to wax indignant over the thoughts of a mind you can see as corrupt than over what keeps the livestock going. Françoise's gesture as she firmly seizes the bull's pizzle to guide it safely into the cow may not be modest, but it is a farm girl's work: it is hard to see it as corrupt. Furthermore, the vision of natural processes which infuses Zola's novel is so universalized, so strongly rendered in terms of timeless rhythms, that it could (and for large areas does) dispense with the particularities of description that give offence. Naturalism is a more reductive view of man than the tortured amusement of Durrell's narrator; but it is not their view of men that makes bishops burn books, it is the presence of particular unmentionable details.

Outspokenness can mean different things; and so we need more than one modern example. It can, for instance, simply mean an enlargement of subject matter, by which the same kind of exploration of motive and morality is offered for sexual behaviour as is offered elsewhere in the novel for other behaviour. Doris Lessing's *The Golden Notebook*, as we have already seen, is concerned with what it is like to be an independent woman. This involves politics, bringing up children, earning one's living, and writing; it involves handling complex relationships with woman friends, with colleagues, and with men. It involves love-affairs, and also sex when one is not in love. Sex is very prominent, but there is no claim that it is a special area, where behaviour, and moral criteria, are fundamentally different; the author has simply declined to cut off the exploration by excluding one area of her characters' lives. This is a kind of equivalent to George Eliot's calm acceptance of the conventions of reticence. George Eliot accepts them, Doris Lessing rejects them, but for both of them the conventions themselves are unimportant.

Lawrence stands in clear contrast to this. Since he stands out among early twentieth-century novelists for his belief in the fundamental importance of sex, and since *Lady Chatterley's Lover* is the most important single landmark in the fall of reticence, a scene from that novel belongs inescapably in this discussion. The love-making between Mellors and Connie at the end of chapter 12 is at first unsatisfactory, and Connie feels inert and finds the act absurd; she 'sobs in her heart', and, when Mellors realizes how upset she is, sobs aloud. Then, as he's dressing, she begs him not to leave her. He comes again (and yet again) with tremendous joy to her. Afterwards they talk about it happily, avoiding dangerous areas.[21]

The scene contain four kinds of writing. There is dialogue, which as so often in the love scenes contrasts Connie's agonized, educated voice with the very different register of Mellors' dialect:

'Nay, nay,' he said, 'Ta'e the thick wi' th' thin. This wor' a bit o' thin for once.'
She wept bitterly, sobbing: 'But I want to love you, and I can't. It only seems horrid.'

Second, there is analysis of Connie's feelings:

Yes this was love, this ridiculous bouncing of the buttocks, and the wilting of the poor insignificant, moist penis. This was the divine love! After all, the moderns were right when they felt contempt for the performance; for it was a performance. It was quite true, as some poets said, that the God who created man must have had a sinister sense of humour, creating him a reasonable being, yet forcing him to take this ridiculous posture, and driving him with blind craving for this ridiculous performance. Even a Maupassant found it a humiliating anti-climax. Men despised the intercourse act, and yet did it.

The sentiment in this is very traditional, and only Connie's ignorance attributes it to 'the moderns'. What is new is the physical description, and we can ask what is the difference between Augustan elegance ('the position undignified, the pleasure momentary and the expense considerable') and this anatomical explicitness. Explicitness is not, after all, necessary: the point had been made often enough without it. Is it an extra detail that helps prove the point on the pulses (and elsewhere!) or is it obstructive, since sex is best discussed at one remove? That depends on what can be done by other methods.

The third method of writing is metaphoric, as in the account of the act itself in terms of 'dark waves rising and heaving', a long description of intercourse through images of the sea ('the depths parted and rolled asunder from the centre of soft plunging'). This too is traditional: both the sea as symbol and the heavy, cumulative rhythms (partly biblical, but recognizably Lawrentian) belong to the poetry of sex as it has always been written. It is clearly impossible to maintain here that symbolic writing is based on censorship, and that the symbols express what cannot be admitted to consciousness.

Finally, there are the four-letter words. Strictly this is part of the first method, the use of dialogue, but since it aroused so much controversy it is worth singling out. Mellors teaches them to Connie as part of teaching her dialect, and to convey tenderness (*Tenderness* being the original title of the novel); unless we are offended simply by the printing of the words, it is hard today to find that scene offensive:

'What is cunt?' she said.

'An' doesn't ter know? Cunt! It's thee down theer; an' what I get when I'm i'side thee, and what tha gets when I'm i'side thee; it's a' as it is, all on't.'

'All on't', she teased. 'Cunt! It's like fuck then.'

'Nay, nay! Fuck's only what you do. Animals fuck. But cunt's a lot more than that. It's thee, dost see: an' tha'rt a lot besides an animal, aren't ter? even ter fuck! Cunt! Eh, that's the beauty o' thee, lass!'

She got up and kissed him between the eyes, that looked at her so dark and soft and unspeakably warm, so unbearably beautiful. 'Is it?' she said. 'And do you care for me?'

Mellors's rejection of naturalism is vivid and true to the scene we have witnessed, but the linguistic basis he gives it is pure fiction. This is not an area where dictionaries can help us, but I know of no evidence for claiming that the one word describes what you do, and the other its human associations. Indeed, he seems plain wrong when he says 'animals fuck'; idiomatically animals mate, or copulate, and only humans fuck.

The monosyllables have now been almost completely reinstated (or instated) in public speech and writing. This has been a real linguistic revolution, and its implications are not necessarily those which its advocates (or its opponents) have claimed. Sometimes it is seen as an assertion of naturalism (sex is no more than this), sometimes as a celebration of the richness of sex, and the very fact that such varied associations can be given to the monosyllables suggests that the implications of value are imposed on the words rather than drawn out of them. If 'fuck' were to become the normal term for sexual intercourse in polite speech, the result would be not simply liberation but also impoverishment. Sensitivity to language involves an awareness of contrasting registers, that the term has customarily belonged in situations of monosexual frankness, and that it has heavy associations of abuse and aggression (and is therefore quite inappropriate to the celebratory and perhaps also the naturalistic). In Edward Albee's play *All Over* a woman is telling her lover, in languorous, deliberate prose, that it was not their affair that hastened the death of his wife, but his divorcing her.

It wasn't *us* that did her in—our ... late summer ... arrangement: there had been others. Our ... mercy to each other, by the lake, the city ... *that* didn't (...) send her spinning back into the animal brain; no, my dear; fucking—as it is called in public by everyone these days—is not what got at her; yours and mine, I mean.[22]

The whole play is written in these elaborate Jamesian cadences, used to draw delicate moral distinctions about often grossly selfish behaviour—as they are by James. But there is one word, of course, James could never have used. This is a stylistic effect only possible because of linguistic change: the clash between the circumlocutions (our ... late summer ... arrangement; our ... mercy to each other) and the vulgarism not only relates the prose to another kind of prose as James never could, it helps draw attention to the contrast between the two superficially similar circumlocutions. But before hailing this as a triumph of linguistic emancipation we must realize it is a kind of effect that cannot last, for it depends on the vulgarism not yet being at home among the cadences. Emancipated language will not only destroy James, but Albee too.

Sublimation

If outspokenness can mean several things, so can reticence. George Eliot, I have suggested, comes as close as a novelist can to simple unembarrassed omission; other Victorians used elaborate processes of apology and evasion; and, of course, like anyone else, they used symbolic representation. Symbols are as old as love poetry: 'he brought me to the banqueting house, and his banner over me was love'. A flower may open, a wave break, fire may burn or the sun rise, and the meaning be sexual.

Theodor Fontane's novel *Unwiederbringlich* (1891) is the story of Graf Holk, his marriage and his love affair with the court lady Ebba, finally culminating in adultery. Fontane is the most discreet of writers, as far as physical details are concerned, and after Holk has insisted on staying behind after the other guests have left in order to speak to her, looking at her confused and passionately, and she teases him, the chapter ends; and when the next begins, an hour later, it is soon clear what has happened. This might seem to be simple omission if it were not for the previous chapter. A skating expedition by the court has taken them to an inn on the edge of a larger, not yet frozen lake; Holk has been separated from Ebba, whose exuberant skating with her two male companions has made him jealous, and the chapter ends like this:

> There was something like jealousy in Holk's look, and when Ebba's eye seemed to be answering this with a half-mocking 'everyone is the master of his own happiness', he seized her hand violently and pointed to the West, far away, where the sun was going down. She nodded agreement, almost in bravado, and now they flew, as if the astonishment of those remaining behind was a further spur to them, to the spot where the ever receding arm of water, glittering with ice between its shores, lost itself in the broad surface of Lake Arre. They came ever nearer to the danger, and now it really looked as if both of them wanted to cross the belt of ice, now no more than a hundred steps across, and make their way onto the open lake: their looks searched for each other and seemed to ask, 'Is it to be so?' And the answer was at any rate not a denial. But at the very moment when they were about to pass the line where a row of pines marked the boundary of what was safe, Holk swerved right with a quick turn, dragging Ebba with him.

'This is the boundary, Ebba. Do we want to go beyond it?' Ebba kicked her skate into the ice and said 'He who thinks about returning wants to. And I'm content. They'll be waiting for us....'[23]

During the drive back, and the party that evening, there are frequent references to this escapade. Ebba loves to play with danger, they remark, but has the gift of coming out of it unharmed. Dr Bie, the retired ship's doctor, drinks a toast to her (she is the hostess) as an example of true Nordic courage: 'To hover on the edge of death, so that a single false step takes us into the depths for ever, is the greatest charm in life.' The guests start to make up fairy stories of what might have happened if they'd been carried onto the open water, and this leads to a dispute on whether love performs the same miracles nowadays as in old times. It is as this party breaks up that Holk stays behind, in a mixture of passion and embarrassment.

Clearly Fontane has enacted symbolically for us the coming adultery that he does not then describe. Just as in the skating escapade, Holk makes the first approach but is embarrassed, Ebba is the one who is willing to surrender herself. In both episodes we have a mixture of public and private: what actually happens is seen by no one, but it is clear to onlookers that something has taken place. The fire that breaks out in the tower throws an unwanted publicity on their affair, and brings out the contrast in their characters—Ebba more frightened of the comedy of concealment than of discovery, Holk withdrawing to protect her reputation though it almost costs them their lives—in a way their earlier conduct had adumbrated.

What does the escapade symbolize? There is a distinction between symbolizing the love affair or, more narrowly and specifically, the sexual encounter. All the details which are stressed, and the comments of the party, suggest the former, and their turning back would then correspond to Ebba's refusal to marry Holk, her judgement of him having been delivered when she said 'Wer an zurück *denkt*, der *will* zurück.' I am sure Fontane has this in mind, though in so matter-of-fact a realist there will be no close parallelism of detail; but in that case, the symbolism has nothing to do with reticence, for the interaction of personality and motive in their affair is precisely what he deals with explicitly. Is not the skating episode there to express the one thing he does not tell us about, the sexual act itself? This would account for its strange power; and though in this case the drawing of particular analogies (Holk turning back as the moment of withdrawal) would be positively ridiculous, there is a deep appropriateness in the imagery of water, open sea and passing the boundary, along with the rhythmic nature of the skating, as a form of symbolic representation.

For a very different example we can turn to Charlotte Brontë. How is sex handled in *Jane Eyre*? Is the novel, for instance, centrally concerned with Jane's sexual development, as Elaine Showalter maintains? For her, the red room into which Jane is locked as a child is a symbol of the adult female body, and the early chapters are filled with sexual (and flagellatory) fantasy; Lowood disciplines its pupils by punishing and starving their sexuality; Bertha Mason is the incarnation of female sexuality, and is recognized by Jane as embodying parts of herself.[24] This is an attentive and intelligent but (I believe) deeply mistaken reading. It is of course as difficult to argue with as Freudian interpretation always is: if for instance we object that to lock Jane in the red room as a punishment can hardly be an attempt to deny her sexual potential if the room represents the adult body, and can hardly be a menarchal ceremony that accepts her sexual potential since it is administered as a punishment by those who hate her, we can be met with the usual appeal to ambivalence, reaction-formation and over-determination. More seriously, by completely omitting any consideration of how far Charlotte Brontë was conscious of (or could accept) these meanings, it ignores the whole question of reticence as a means of discourse. We need a conception of what the novel means that draws on symbolism not in defiance of explicit statement, but in order to explore the interrelation of the two.

There is never any doubt that Jane is physically attracted to Rochester: he is clearly a man of strong sexual energy, and when she opposes his physical brusqueness with a mixture of responsiveness and resistance, she is clearly provoking him sexually:

> I assured him I was naturally hard—very flinty ... and that, moreover, I was determined to show him diverse rugged points in my character.... On the whole I could see he was excellently entertained, and that a lamb-like submission and turtle-dove sensibility ... would have ... suited his taste less.
>
> (Ch. 24)

No sexual meaning of these images is offered us: they are all intended to refer to their discovery of each other's characters, their jostling for power through words, not through caresses. Reading it today, we can say that in a situation so highly charged sexually, the images of flint and rock, of lamb and turtle dove, cannot be accidental: but it is not easy to know how far Charlotte Brontë could have admitted this. The idea of *double entendre* is alien both to her modesty and to her literary method, yet it is as if the imagery enables her to include something of the element that reticence naturally avoids. The end of chapter 15, when Jane is still falling in love with Rochester, is interesting here:

> I regained my couch, but never thought of sleep. Till morning dawned I was tossed on a buoyant but unquiet sea, where billows of trouble rolled

under surges of joy. I thought sometimes I saw beyond its wild waters a shore, sweet as the hills of Beulah; and now and then a freshening gale, wakened by hope, bore my spirit triumphantly towards the bourne: but I could not reach it, even in fancy—a counteracting breeze blew off the land, and continually drove me back.

The same image as Lawrence used, describing Connie's experience of intercourse; but this time for the girl alone in her single bed. Once again, the official tenor of the metaphor concerns emotions and decisions, but in a book so vividly aware of the bodily element in feeling, so filled with the physical presence of Rochester ('strange energy was in his voice, strong fire in his look'), how can we fail to feel that these are the experiences of Jane's body? The resemblance between Connie's billows rolling away to some shore, and Jane's billows of trouble rolling under surges of joy, ought to be confined to the vehicle, but the tenors may not be as distinct as either author would have assumed.

These three passages of symbolic writing represent the three possible relations of symbol to explicitness. In *Jane Eyre* no overt sexual activity takes place, so that explicitness, on the level of fact, is impossible. Passion exists only as emotion; when this is expressed symbolically, we have a language so appropriate to sexual activity that the physical nature of the feeling can be expressed without loss of modesty. In *Unwiederbringlich* no overt sexual activity is described: the facts have changed but there is still reticence in describing them, and symbolism is used, quite consciously, instead of explicitness—not only verbal symbolism but a displacement in terms of action: they actually are skating. In *Lady Chatterley's Lover* sexual intercourse takes place and is described explicitly, then is accompanied by a symbolic account. The fact that we know exactly what is happening makes the passage more outspoken than any nineteenth-century novelist is likely to offer us, though the images are traditional. After all, there are not many new images to draw on, and it is not in the vehicle of metaphors that originality consists.

We now need a single concept to explain how these symbolic accounts are related to the sexuality they do not (or do) explicitly describe; and this means that some theoretical discussion is required. The concept I propose to use is that of sublimation, which we owe mainly to psychoanalysis, though it is not easy to find a precise account of it in Freud. He uses the term as follows in the *Three Essays on Sexuality*:

> It enables excessively strong excitations arising from particular sources of sexuality to find an outlet and use in other fields, so that a not inconsiderable increase in physical efficiency results from a disposition which in itself is perilous. Here we have one of the origins of artistic activity.[25]

Freud here seems to have in mind a neurotic or at any rate unstable state of mind. But nothing is commoner in Freudian thought than for a neurotic condition to be offered as a model for ordinary psychic processes, for we are all ill. Sublimation could then be a normal process, as, elsewhere in Freud, it clearly is. Sublimation is the redirecting of libido into socially acceptable channels. 'This capacity to exchange its originally sexual aim for another one, which is no longer sexual, but which is psychically related to the first aim, is called the capacity for *sublimation*.'[26]

Sublimation can be looked at in two ways, according as our concern is individual or social. Here is a revealing statement by Freud's orthodox but lucid disciple Ernest Jones:

> The wishes, desires, etc. which had previously found unsatisfactory expression in the creation of various symptoms, are now free to be applied through the process of sublimation to non-sexual, social aims.[27]

Jones is describing how analysis can replace repression by sublimation. and he clearly believes that the neurotic symptoms were both 'unsatisfactory' to the individual, and anti-social in aim. But is the world so well ordered that more constructive aims are necessarily those that cost the individual less? The optimism which believes that the social benefit of more acceptable aims can also mean the easing of psychic stress in the individual is very different from the pessimism of *Civilization and its Discontents*, in which Freud is concerned with the high cost, in frustration and repression, that is paid by individuals for the deprivation of instinctual gratification that makes civilization possible.

I believe this pessimism is less wise than Jones's optimism, and that the deprivations exacted by civilization can enrich as well as frustrate. This is certainly the view of John Dewey, who in *Art and Experience* puts forward a theory of art that emphasizes its continuity with the rest of life: 'esthetic emotion is something distinctive and yet not cut off by a chasm from other and natural emotional experiences'. He distinguishes between experience, as an undifferentiated flux, and 'having an experience', an activity that is fulfilled and carried through, with a structure, or plot, of its own, in which the 'varied parts are linked to one another, and do not merely succed one another'. An experience can be very simple, like poking the fire, but it is the basis of art. The distinguishing element of art is expression, which is 'the clarification of turbid emotion'. Expression is contrasted with the mere naturalistic discharge of emotion by its relation to a medium (the emotion takes on its identity by its interaction with the external world), by its higher degree of coherence and consciousness, and (here is the overlap with psychological theories) by the 'existence of conditions that impede direct manifestation, and that switch it into a channel where it is coordinated with other impulsions'. The richness of expressed emotion depends on this inhibition of direct discharge: 'that which elevates the embrace of lovers above the animal plane is just the fact that when it occurs it has taken into itself, as its own meaning, the consequences of these indirect excursions that are imagination in action'.[28]

The common element between Freud and Dewey is found in Max Weber, whose concept of sublimation occurs in his treatment of religion, as part of the discussion of the tension between religion and sex. In ritual, which Weber regards as the original form of religion, the relation between the two is intimate and direct. Religion however develops into the salvation religions of which there are two versions, active and passive; and sex develops into eroticism. Between these higher forms there is a necessary hostility. 'Inner-wordly rational asceticism must reject every sophistication of the sexual into eroticism as idolatry of the worst kind.'[29]

Our concern here is with the transformation of sex into eroticism, which takes place by means of sublimation. It is a turning away from the naive naturalism of sex, hiding its natural and organic basis, and raising it to the sphere of conscious enjoyment. It is, in fact, a deflection of libido: not however into unrelated spheres, only into a more consciously accepted, more wide-reaching form of sexuality. The reason why this is now in contention with religion is that it makes fuller claims on our whole being, including our social life.

We can see Weber's sublimation as a particular version of Freud's. The deflection is less far-reaching, an inhibiting of immediate naturalistic discharge that results in its enrichment. It has much in common with what Jones calls idealization ('a sexual object can be idealized'), and distinguishes (perhaps unnecessarily) from sublimation, the former referring to the view taken of the object, the latter to the impulse behind it (so that idealization is love, and sublimation is loving).[30] All three thinkers are offering a concept based on the diversion of libido from immediate gratification, thus providing the psychic energy for a remoter goal. The Freudian concept is the most far-reaching, in that the goal need no longer have any overt connexion with sex; and it therefore presupposes, as the others do not, that the whole process must take place unconsciously. Since we are concerned with love poetry, and not with the unconscious libidinal element in all human activity, we have no need to use the wider concept, and I shall use 'sublimation' essentially in its Weberian meaning, to mean the raising of sexuality from direct naturalistic discharge (Dewey's phrase, which equals Weber's 'naturalism') to a conscious activity of the whole person, which Weber calls eroticism.

The parallel with Dewey makes it clear that the process is central to artistic expression. Can we, indeed, have art without sublimation?

On one level, the answer must obviously be no, since writing is not a naturalistic activity. Perhaps speech is not really immediate enough to count as naturalistic discharge. Shouting at an enemy could be seen as at least a momentary deflection from the most direct form of aggression, and the fifteen-year-old male whose attitude to women was expressed as 'man, I wanna fuck' was at least pausing long enough to verbalize. Clearly the deflection of impulse is a matter of degree, and if we are to find the concept of sublimation useful for drawing distinctions in language we must start from the possibility of some language being unsublimated. We must say that go-to-hell statements and what we may call I-fuck-her poems are the verbal equivalent of direct naturalistic discharge. Sublimation is a way of enriching such verbal acts.

In theory, there will be two contrasting positions that do not involve sublimation, the naturalistic and the Platonic. The naturalistic presents sex as it is, not raised to the level of eroticism; and the Platonic presents a love relationship that is non-sexual, and therefore does not draw on any deflection of sexuality. That naturalism is possible was made clear earlier in this chapter. Zola is a naturalist, Hardy has touches of it, and Whitman comes close at times to being the poet of naturalism:

> Through me forbidden voices,
> Voices of sexes and lusts, voices veil'd and I remove the veil,
> Voices indecent by me clarified and transfigur'd.

> I do not press my fingers across my mouth,
> I keep as delicate around the bowels as round the head and heart,
> Copulation is no more rank to me than death is.

> I believe in the flesh and the appetites,
> Seeing, hearing, feeling, are miracles, and each part and tag of me is a
>   miracle.[31]

Yet a passage like this makes it clear that naturalism can hardly exist except as a counter-statement. Our thought and our vocabulary are so deeply committed to the belief that human beings are not merely animals, that to assert that they are is to undo the way we think, to 'remove the veil'. It is only significant to say 'I sound my barbaric yawp over the roofs of the world' because the poet is expected to sound his civilized song; and the lines quoted start from the fact that some voices are forbidden, some smells rank.

Naturalism can function in love poetry as a counterblast to over-idealization, a moment of shocking or refreshing reductionism. Platonic love has a more respectable history, yet logically its status is even weaker. It is a doctrine based on the difference between love and lust, and though it has little to do with Plato it can take as its starting point the following passage from the *Laws*.

He that treats carnal appetite as out of the question, that puts contemplation before passion, he whose desire is veritably that of soul for soul, looks on enjoyment of flesh by flesh as wanton shame; as one that reverences, aye, and worships, chastity and manhood, greatness and wisdom, he will aspire to live with his love in constant purity on both parts.[32]

The question which this forces on us is, what happens to carnal appetite when it is suppressed. 'The task of mastering such a powerful impulse as that of the sexual instinct by any other means than satisfying it,' wrote Freud, 'is one that can call for the whole of a man's forces.'[33] There are two possible consequences of this task. Either the impulse is driven down by the brute force of the superego, raging unsatisfied and providing dynamic material that strives for outlets, direct or indirect; or else it in some sense provides the energy for the desire of soul for soul. The first is repression, the second sublimation. There is a third, and impossible, outcome, that the powerful impulse admits defeat and obligingly ceases to exist. This is Platonic love, the doctrine that love differs from lust in having no sexual element. Since it is sexual love that is in question (admittedly in Plato's case it may be homosexual, but conceived of as being as natural as heterosexual), language itself shows the contradiction in the doctrine. The poets have not hesitated to confirm this:

Love's not so pure and abstract as they use
To say, that have no mistress but their muse.[34]

Donne loves to write about Platonic love, but he always treats it as astonishing. The fact that he and the Countess of Bedford, he and Mrs Herbert, loved without being interested in difference of sex, without 'touching the seals', is constantly dwelt on, and we are invited to marvel at the miracle, to realize that there must be some explanation (difference of age, existence of a spouse, moral principle—the poems don't tell us, the biography sometimes does).[35] Nothing emerges more strongly from these poems than the opinion that Platonic love is unnatural.

Love differs from lust as eroticism differs from sexuality: it raises carnal appetite to the level of a fully conscious human activity. Naturalism, the denial that there is any difference, can be very attractive when we are tired of cant, but it is untrue because it is merely reductive. Platonic love, the denial that love has anything to do with lust, is a perverse doctrine that common sense can blow away. Theories of sublimation remind us where all the ladders start: in the foul rag-and-bone shop of the sexual impulse. These two doctrines try and pretend there is no ladder.

That then is the theory underlying the celebration of human love. To put it into practice we can turn now to love poetry itself.

Poetry and Eroticism

The poetry of eroticism will replace direct statements of sexual desire with those forms of poetic indirection that involve the fullness of a conscious human activity. In literary terms, this means wit, rhythmic power, suggestiveness, irony and (above all) the use of symbol. This corresponds to those psychological processes that render delayed gratification possible: the enjoyment of pre-coital tension (or forepleasure), and the concentration on secondary sexual characteristics. As used by Darwin this term refers to those characteristics not directly connected with the act of reproduction, for instance organs of sense or locomotion. Since courtship in the animal kingdom is done by the male, and choosing by the females, the secondary characteristics are more highly developed in the male; but since among human beings it is men who choose, 'women are everywhere conscious of the value of their own beauty; and when they have the means they take more delight in decorating themselves with all sorts of ornaments than do men'.[36] A love poem then will celebrate a woman not merely for her availability for copulation, but for her beauty, her voice, her ornament, her wit: those qualities by which the man makes his choice. This makes it an expression of the total activity, not merely of the consummation. How, for instance, do Romeo and Juliet express their love?

> It seems she hangs upon the cheek of night
> As a rich jewel in an Ethiop's ear—
> Beauty too rich for use, for earth too dear!   (I.v.45)

What turns the speech to poetry is not the statement of love's uniqueness in the last line, but the haunting image that precedes it. Can we say something about how this works? The image haunts because it is used ambiguously. Is the Ethiop too ugly to deserve the jewel, so that night is a foil that contrasts with Juliet's beauty; or is the jewel enhanced by the black skin, as love is enhanced by the opportunities of night? The ambiguity is enhanced by the last line, which is of course proleptic, and announces that Juliet is not long for this world. The Capulet party is taking place at night: is Juliet then out of place at the party as the jewel would be on the Ethiop? But the party is also taking place on earth, in this life, in a blaze of lights: if she is out of place there she belongs with night (and death) as the jewel belongs best on the black skin. Ambiguity like this is not confusion but a poised exploration of alternative ways of relating love to experience. By means of the resonance of the image, love is raised to the sphere of conscious enjoyment.

In this case we are certainly attending to secondary sexual characteristics; but the poetry also makes frequent reference to the sexual act itself, and in particular to the loss of virginity. That high-spirited naturalist, Mercutio, who so loves to remind us of where the ladders start (though he also loves to climb them—acrobatically) is lavish with reference to sexual intercourse, and hints that forepleasure is wasting time: fair comment, we are to believe, on Romeo's euphuistic passion for Rosalind, for we all know what he's really after. But Romeo and Juliet are after the same, though not in a way Mercutio must any longer be allowed to mock:

> Lovers can see to do their amorous rites
> By their own beauties; or, if love be blind,
> It best agrees with night. Come, civil night,
> Thou sober-suited matron, all in black,
> And learn me how to lose a winning match
> Played for a pair of stainless maidenhoods.   (III.ii.8)

The wit places us at a distance from the experience; but the experience is—quite unambiguously—copulation.

Open reference to sexual intercourse, combined with metaphoric enrichment, reaches its extreme in a poem like *A Rapture*, by Thomas Carew. It is in one sense a highly indecent poem, for it goes through the whole story of an act of coition, from beholding 'thy bared snow and thy unbraided gold', through caresses

> —There my enfranchised hand on every side
> Shall o'er thy naked polish'd ivory slide—

and the intertwining of limbs, to consummation:

> Yet my tall pine shall in the Cyprian strait
> Ride safe at anchor, and unlade her freight.

Yet at the same time it is highly decorous, for not only does it avoid crudity, it is written throughout in what Renaissance critics called the high style, that appropriate to 'matter stately and high', which is lifted up and advanced 'by choice of words, phrases, sentences and figures, high, lofty, eloquent and magnific in proportion'.[37] The poem is a *tour de force* in its combination of explicitness and indirection, telling us, in the language of the highest eroticism, that plain copulation is marvellous fun.[38]

This means that it will necessarily ignore any distinction between mere copulation and a higher, more fully human, form of sexual activity—between lust and love. How will this distinction be drawn in non-Platonic poetry? The best poet to turn to for an answer is Spenser, and just this distinction is very important in *The Faerie Queen*, where there is a true and a false Cupid. Of its four allegorical retreats of love, two represent the temptation of lust: the Bower of Bliss, with its lake, its imitation ivy made of gold, its naked damsels disporting, its lovely *carpe diem* song, and the fearful House of Busyrane, whose entrance is guarded by fire; the other two, the Garden of Adonis and the Temple of Venus, celebrate sexual love.[39] The Garden of Adonis, drawing heavily on neo-Platonic tradition, is a version of the Earthly Paradise in which Spenser celebrates generation by blending the two main elements of his style, the philosophic and the sensuous:

> The substance is not changed nor altered,
> But th' only form and outward fashion:
> For every substance is conditioned
> To change her hue, and sundry forms to don. . . .
> And that fair flower of beauty fades away,
> As doth the lily fresh before the sunny ray.

What is the difference between lust and love, true and false Cupid? One answer we could expect from Spenser, who set out to be one of the great poets of marriage, would clearly be that the one represents married love, the other fornication. But how can this distinction be applied to the Garden of Adonis, where there is no marrying or giving in marriage, and where the climax is a description of Venus enjoying 'Her dear Adonis' joyous company'? We need a poetical distinction, one that could be perceived by the reader of each episode, and felt as an active difference between the passages. Though he is not quite systematic in using it, I have little doubt that Spenser intended this distinction to concern fecundity. The true Cupid is constantly associated with fertile, the false with sterile love, with sex for its own sake, not as part of the cycle of generation. Thus Scudamour's description of the Temple of Venus shows us a richly populated garden,

> And therein thousand pairs of lovers walked
> Praising their god, and yielding him great thanks:

and the song in praise of Venus commends her for presiding over generative nature:

> Then doth the deadale earth throw forth to thee
> Out of her fruitful lap abundant flowers . . .

> So all the world by thee at first was made,
> And daily yet thou dost the same repair.

In contrast, the House of Busyrane, when Britomart finally penetrates inside, is strangely deserted:

> But more she marvelled that no footing's trace
> Nor wight appeared, but wasteful emptiness

And solemn silence over all that place:
Strange thing it seemed, that none was to possess
So rich purveyance, ne them keep with carefulness.

This contrast does in a way correspond to the moral point about the difference between fornication and married sexuality. Marriage is an institution for the rearing of children and for allotting to the couple a place in society: in two senses, it cannot be solitary. The isolation of the *Minnegrotte* does symbolize the difference between adulterous passion and wedlock. Now this certainly fits the celebratory nature of Spenser's best poetry, but it presents a special aesthetic problem to the modern reader. As birth-control propagandists know to their cost, the values of pre-industrial society include an acceptance of fertility. The large family, to the peasant, represents insurance for his old age, a good contribution (since mortality is high) to the survival of the community and, beneath these rational considerations, a feeling of well-being and rich human affection. Twentieth-century man has had to unlearn this: to the extent that those for whom overpopulation is an urgent danger now suggest that parents of large families should be systematically presented in the mass media as incompetent buffoons. It is doubtful if our values can change quite so quickly as this, but we have already, in urban industrial culture, learned to associate large numbers of children with poverty, dirt, Roman Catholicism and (probably) low intelligence. But our literary values are frozen in an earlier stage, and it is difficult for us to feel that sterility can provide images of poetic beauty. Does this not present us with a divided reaction to Spenser's celebratory language? How can we react unenthusiastically to a line like 'Out of her fruitful lap abundant flowers', and how can we fail to realize that what is being celebrated is not just botany? In this case, the implied association with human reproduction is contained in 'lap'; just as in the previous stanza a line that clearly unites man and the other creatures

—In generation seek to quench their inward fires—

offers sexual satisfaction and procreation as indissolubly associated.

I am not of course suggesting that we love our children less than our pre-industrial ancestors; but I am suggesting that we do not love them because they are numerous—even that we wonder whether the parents of ten can be as fond of any as we are of our one or two. Yet our aesthetic values have retained a preference that we have as citizens abandoned; so that our response to Spenser's poetry is, in an interesting sense of the term, an anachronism. But this coin has another side: the love that stands in opposition to marriage has little to do with fertility, and we may now have a new reason for valuing it.

Fertility is the most striking criterion for true love in *The Faerie Queene* but there is also another: the fact that Venus has a temple. Love is placed, as lust is not, in a queer–religious setting. Ritual is missing from the Bower of Bliss, which has one important thing in common with *A Rapture*, that it does not enter into competition with religion. Carew's poem might be suppressed for indecency, but it does not threaten the religious ethic of brotherhood by setting up rival claims. That is done by those forms of eroticism that see love as a sacrament, that 'offer the unsurpassable peak of the fulfilment of the request for love in the direct fusion of the souls of one to the other'[40]—Weber's language sounds like a description of Donne's love poetry. Again this throws new light on the love–religion parallel explored in chapter 2: it is not simply a parallel, we see, but a rivalry. Rivalry on the ideological level can of course appear in poetry as the tension generated by the imagery, can indeed be the source of poetic power.

The effect of celebrating love as a sacrament will depend on the religion: the sacraments of an other-worldly religion have a different meaning from those of a religion of this world, and we ought therefore to look at two examples, one Christian and one pagan. Sixteenth-century erotic narratives, most of them heavily indebted to Ovid, are deeply pagan, and also rich in celebrations of sexuality. The extraordinary fruitfulness of Ovid's central device in the *Metamorphosis*, of emphasizing, as the common element in all myths, the miraculous change undergone at the climax, must depend on a mysterious connexion with sexuality: Nature emerges as unpredictably obsessed with changes of state, and so as the Nature of procreation, pupation, gestation and birth.[41] In itself this might bring a poetry simply of sexuality not of eroticism, until a religious dimension is added by the myth. Sometimes this may be merely cursory:

> Adonis' lips with her own lips kindly she kissed,
> Rolling tongue, moyst mouth with her own mouth all
>   to be sucking,
> Mouth and tongue and lips, with Jove's drink nectar
>   abounding.[42]

So strong is the stress here on the purely physical, that to speak of the saliva as 'Jove's drink, nectar' is to change little, like the eager man who can barely pause in his pawing to pay a verbal compliment. In Marlowe's *Hero and Leander*, however, paganism is taken very seriously. Hardly any natural function is without its god, and the world of natural processes is one rich with stories and similes:

> His body was as straight as Circe's want;
> Jove might have sipt out nectar from his hand....[43]

A description of Leander's body is an opportunity to bring in the myths, for what they are, essentially, is a celebration of bodily delights.

Perhaps the most brilliant detail in Marlowe's poem was making Hero into Venus's nun. She has charge of Venus's temple, which is richly jewelled and devoted to the celebration of love. The mosaics are high spirited and uninhibited:

> There might you see the gods, in sundry shapes,
> Committing heady riots, incests, rapes.... (I.143)

It is so uninhibited as to be a huge joke; yet there is no suggestion that actual orgies take place in the temple. Everything is symbolized, not enacted; and 'chaste Hero' has dedicated herself with virgin modesty to performing sacrifices and due rites. This paradox associates renunciation and gratification in a way that denies sex in order to celebrate it more fully: exactly the process that turns naturalistic sex into eroticism.

If Weber is right about the rivalry between eroticism and religion, it should not surprise us that a poem which presents love as a Christian sacrament is actually by a pagan. Keats's *Eve of St Agnes* tells a simple story based on folk-belief: a young girl performs the rites that, on St Agnes Eve, are supposed to cause her to dream of her lover. She wakes to find the lover there in person, and they elope into the night. The rites are presented as if they were a formula for sublimation:

> If ceremonies due they did aright;
> As, supperless to bed they must retire,
> And couch supine their beauties, lily white;
> Nor look behind, nor sideways, but require
> Of Heaven with upward eyes for all that they desire. (Stanza 6)

The preparation for dreaming of love is a series of renunciations; the exact opposite of this would be a preparation for the act of love by means of a series of stimuli, and this is what the watching Porphyro has:

> Stol'n to this paradise, and so entranced,
> Porphyro gazed upon her empty dress,
> And listened to her breathing, if it chanced
> To wake into a slumberous tenderness. (Stanza 18)

A poem that enacted love's rites to the full would begin with foreplay and culminate in sexual intercourse. This is certainly the case in *Hero and Leander* and may be in *The Eve of St Agnes*. Here is Marlowe on secondary sexual characteristics:

> and as she spake,
> Forth from those two tralucent cisterns brake
> A stream of liquid pearl, which down her face
> Made milk-white paths, whereon the gods might trace
> To Jove's high court. (I.295)

Religious imagery enhances Hero's physical charms: in that way, this can be seen as the early stages of an erotic rite. The range of Marlowe's tone—frank sensual delight, celebration, mockery, awe—prevents the poem reading as consistently like a sacrament as the more uniform tone of *The Eve of St Agnes*:

> Full on this casement shone the wintry moon,
> And threw warm gules on Madeline's fair breast,
> As down she knelt for heaven's grace and boon;
> Rose-bloom fell on her hands, together prest,
> And on her silver cross soft amethyst,
> And on her hair a glory, like a saint:
> She seem'd a splendid angel, newly drest,
> Save wings, for heaven:—Porphyro grew faint:
> She knelt, so pure a thing, so free from mortal taint.   (Stanza 25)

The beauty of these lines is breathtaking, for without diminishing Madeline's sexual attractiveness at all they draw constantly on the enhancing suggestions of religious feeling. The religion involves no turning from the flesh, simply its celebration. Madeline's purity is equated with her being nubile, and Porphyro's faintness is both awe and sexual desire. To a pious reader, the lines could seem intolerable simply because of their beauty.

That foreplay leads up to intercourse is quite plain in *Hero and Leander*, in the first place because of the setting in Venus's temple, a constant reminder of where all these charms are meant to lead, and furthermore, because the story does culminate in an act of sexual intercourse. Once again there is great variety of tone, but once again the celebratory is prominent:

> Leander now, like Theban Hercules,
> Enter'd the orchard of th' Hesperides;
> Whose fruits none rightly can describe, but he
> That pulls or shakes it from the golden tree.   (II.297)

Sexual experience, like religious, can be understood only by those who have undergone it. The accident that Marlowe died after writing only two sestiads makes the sexual climax even more prominent, for it becomes the actual climax of his part of the poem.

It is not easy to say whether there is the same clear movement in *The Eve of St Agnes*, through preliminaries to climax, establishing the erotic description as foreplay; for it is not certain whether Porphyro and Madeline actually consummate their love in the poem. The crucial moment in the text is stanza 36:

> Beyond a mortal man impassion'd far
> At these voluptuous accents, he arose,

Ethereal, flush'd, and like a throbbing star
Seen mid the sapphire heaven's deep repose;
Into her dream he melted, as the rose
Blendeth its odour with the violet,—
Solution sweet.

How literally do we take these lines: do they refer to Porphyro's bodily presence as she wakes, or to sexual intercourse? And does Madeline's lament in the next stanza ('Thou forsakest a deceived thing') mean that she has lost her virtue, or simply that she does not believe he will stay, even that he is real? An interesting piece of external evidence, the correspondence between Woodhouse and Taylor, makes it clear that there were textual revisions here which we no longer fully possess. Woodhouse complained that Keats had altered the poem so that it was no longer possible for '*we* innocent ones (ladies and myself)' to read it as 'right honest chaste and sober' love, for now 'as soon as Madeline has confessed her love, Porphyro winds by degrees his arm round her, presses breast to breast, and acts all the acts of a bona fide husband ...'. The textual variants that have survived are not as explicit as this, and at least one crucial stanza must be lost. According to Keats, however, it was anyway not necessary:

> He says he does not want ladies to read his poetry: that he writes for men, and that if in the former poem there was an opening for a doubt what took place, it was his fault for not writing clearly and comprehensibly.[44]

This seems to settle matters, and to show that those modern critics who assume that sexual consummation takes place[45] must be right. But it is never wholly safe to move from poem to poet. The objections that Woodhouse made 'a full hour by the temple clock', and the 'Keats-like rhodomontade' in reply, make it clear that there was a good deal of annoyance in the air, and Keats may have been more interested in shocking Woodhouse than in being faithful to the spirit of his poem. For the 'innocent ones' (including Taylor, Keat's publisher, who was not prepared to allow any impropriety) were not stupid prudes: they expected the poem, like most love poems, to stop short of explicitness, and they did not consider that evasive. The no-nonsense attitude Keats expressed to Woodhouse could lead to a direct expression of sexuality, and undo the enriching effects that raise it to eroticism.

That an erotic poem need not describe or even include consummation should not need arguing: for in the very source of our love poetry, consummation is carefully excluded. The *fin amors* of the troubadours has an ambivalent relation to the physical: on the one hand, what the poet wishes is left in no doubt, but on the other hand he never attains it. So important is this contradictory element in their love that it leads them to announce, often quite explicitly, that possession is incompatible with love, that he who wishes to possess his lady entirely knows little of the service of women.[46] This had led to a great range of interpretations, some highly ingenious,[47] from those who cannot tolerate paradox: in particular, to the claim that their love is really religious, and *midons* (the lady) represents the Virgin Mary, despite the fact that she is described as fickle (by Cercamon) or that Bernard de Ventadour longs to kiss her and hold her white body, plump and smooth (*so cors blanc, gras e le*). There is no need to explain away the doctrine that perfect love is begotten by Despair upon Impossibility: we saw in chapter 2 that it is widespread, and now we see one kind of explanation for it. The best commentators on troubadour poetry have been driven towards psycho-analytic concepts,[48] for the poetry is built on the belief that delayed gratification enriches the experience, even if it means that gratification never comes.

The absence of consummation can spring from this paradox, but it can also simply indicate that consummation is yet to come. This fact may be obvious but in an age of reticence it may not be mentioned.

Now sleeps the crimson petal, now the white,
Nor waves the cypress in the palace walk;
Nor winks the gold fin in the porphyry font.
The fire-fly wakens; waken thou with me.

Now droops the milk-white peacock like a ghost,
And like a ghost she glimmers on to me.

Now lies the Earth all Danaë to the stars,
And all thy heart lies open unto me.

Now slides the silent meteor on, and leaves
A shining furrow, as thy thoughts in me.

Now folds the lily all her sweetness up,
And slips into the bosom of the lake.
So fold thyself, my dearest, thou, and slip
Into my bosom and be lost in me.[49]

This marvellous poem is perhaps the supreme example of how the great-ness of erotic poetry can depend on the distance it has travelled from sexuality. It is undoubtedly about love; it is drenched in a physical aware-ness of the body, and contact with the world through the senses; and there is nothing in it to which Dr Bowdler need take exception. The contrast with *Venus and Adonis* is striking. Both poems create a state of sexual tension and avoid consummation—Shakespeare explicitly and teasingly, Tennyson silently. His poem renders the heightened awareness that accompanies a state of sexual tension; and if we ask whether it admits that this is what it expresses, it is not easy to answer. The tension is generalized, contains no direct reference to coition, and even though Tennyson must have known that the hush of expectation, the intense sensitivity, the constant references to gentle movement, are the products of sexual expectation, he can write as if there is no need to say that. If we carry Marlowe's paradox to the point of absurdity, Hero would pretend (or naively believe) that Venus had nothing to do with copulation; as the naively innocent reader who enjoys the rich sensuousness of this poem without thinking about sex is not actually misreading it. It is the perfect poem for Venus's nun.

Tennyson is at the opposite extreme not only to Shakespeare but to Carew, for whereas their metaphors apply very clearly to particular sexual acts, Tennyson is interested in expressing a generalized tension. It would be quite wrong to offer specific interpretations of his images, as we can see if we think about that powerfully sexual word 'in'. When Porphyro melts 'into' Madeline's dream the sexual meaning of penetration is possible, though not (*pace* Keats himself) necessary; but in the phrase 'in me', which occurs twice in Tennyson's poem, this meaning would be simply wrong. We can be sure of this because it is the man and not the woman speaking; but I think we could be sure anyway. Juliet's appeal to night, the 'sober-suited matron', is also a kind of opposite to this poem:

> Hood my unmanned blood, bating in my cheeks,
> With thy black mantle till strange love grow bold,
> Think true love acted simple modesty.   (III.ii.14)

Who is closer to the act of coition, Juliet or Tennyson's lover? In one sense Juliet, since she talks about it, and knows that she is going to blush when it takes place; but the state of physical tension implied by Shakespeare's conceit is directly rendered by the heavy rhythms, the hypnotic trance that Tennyson creates. This speaker is actually on the brink of the climax that Juliet is still thinking about.

We can arrange the poems so far discussed on a kind of scale. At the one extreme are Juliet's speech and *A Rapture*, in which references to sexual intercourse are prominent but distanced, by wit in the one case, by mischievous use of metaphor and mythological reference on the other. Next comes *Hero and Leander*, in which we move towards sexual intercourse through a delight in secondary sexual characteristics and a lingering on the forepleasure. Next *The Eve of St Agnes*, in which there is more lingering and more ritual enrichment, and a less explicit culmination in intercourse. Finally, 'Now sleeps', in which there is no climax and no explicit reference to intercourse, but a more intense awareness of the physical tension than in any of the others.

The scale is not one of greater or lesser sublimation, for all the poems use sublimation. It is one of diminishing explicitness in its references to copulation but at the same time of increasing immersion in the absorbing state of sexual tension. In at least one important sense of the term, the scale is one of increasing eroticism.

Conclusion

The sublimation of sex into eroticism can take place outside marriage, and usually did. Weber has pointed out that religion cannot admit so powerful a rival: we may ask, can any institution? Marriage is a set of social arrangements into which sex has to be fitted: could it be that to make too high a claim for sexuality will threaten even marriage? That is a view that could follow from Weber's theory, and it would explain the contest of love and marriage. The literary tradition would, in that case, have shown a kind of inarticulate wisdom, an awareness that no social arrangement can carry the intensity of demand made by Tristan and Othello, Lancelot and Phèdre, that eroticism will threaten any attempt to contain it.

This takes us back to our first chapter, and suggests several corollaries to its argument. Before drawing them, I ought (belatedly) to deal with an objection to that argument that has not yet been explicity mentioned, but that might have been silently building up all through the book.

What sort of love is it that flies to the *Minnegrotte* because it dare not live in the world, that strangles an innocent wife in her wedding sheets, that hangs itself to bring about the death of the now hated beloved? Can it be love, if it fails to treat its object like a responsible human being? When Porphyria's lover finds that he and she have attained complete confidence in each other, he preserves this moment of perfect love in the only infallible manner:

> I found
> A thing to do, and all her hair
> In one long yellow string I wound
> Three times her little throat around
> And strangled her.

Porphyria's Lover is intended as a *reductio ad absurdum* of romantic love, as the subtitle 'Madhouse Cells' indicates;[50] but the power of the poem comes from the fact that we cannot dismiss the speaker as mad with quite the ease that Browning appears to assume. Not only the calm lucidity of his narrative, but also the deeply traditional nature of the love–death he gives her, force us to take him seriously; and to the modern reader who takes the title ironically and remarks that he clearly did not really love Porphyria, one can ask if Othello really loved Desdemona, or Tristan really loved Isolde.

We live in the middle of an anxious debate about the future of marriage. Not only feminists but various forms of social relativism assure us that monogamy based on intense intimacy is both unstable and doomed. This may be announced in moral language, as a disaster; in radical language, as a triumph; in anthropological terms, as too inevitable, in a plural world, to need worrying about.[51] We have seen that a kind of silent irony announced this possibility from the beginning, in that one of our first great defences of married love comes in a treatise defending divorce. Against this stands the conservative optimism that defends marriage and admires the humane doctrine of married love: love that grows with the relationship between two individuals over a lifetime. That doctrine has produced its own literature—a counter-tradition to the marvellous literature of romantic love. And, inevitably, it has produced a critical tradition that wonders whether Othello really *did* love Desdemona, or Phèdre Hippolite.

One of the best known examples of this criticism is F. R. Leavis's essay on *Othello*.[52] Against Bradley's interpretation, by which the noble hero is tragically destroyed by a diabolical intellect,[53] Leavis maintains that Othello's 'nobility is really egoism', that Iago is lucky and Othello destroys himself—even, in a sense, deserves what happens to him. It is true that, reading Bradley's account of Othello's last moments ('pity itself vanishes, and love and admiration alone remain'), you would never suspect he had just murdered his wife; but it is equally true that reading Leavis you would wonder what makes a tragic hero, and how, if our view of the hero is so steadily critical, we can feel any emotional involvement with Othello. A balanced view of the play needs to admit Othello's responsibility, without ceasing to feel his splendour, to see him not as pompous, not as self-approving, but as magnificent and dangerous. Since it is Iago who does the damage, we need to say that Othello is particularly vulnerable to Iago, that something in Othello gives purchase to Iago's scheming, without feeling that by saying this we are denigrating him. There are various ways of making such a point, and I find Maud Bodkin's particularly valuable:

> Those aspects of social experience that a man's thought ignores leave their secret impress on his mind.... Iago seems to Othello so honest, so wise beyond himself in human dealings, possessed of a terrible power of seeing and speaking truth, because into what he speaks are projected the half-truths that Othello's romantic vision ignored, but of which his mind held secret knowledge.[54]

The obverse of Othello and Desdemona are Beatrice and Benedick. Their obsessive teasing of each other is a kind of talking-out cure as preparation for marriage. Beatrice's ambivalence about sex ('I could not endure a husband with a beard on his face; I had rather lie in the woollen'), and Benedick's reluctance to lose his liberty, make them 'too wise to woo peaceably': a deep unconscious wisdom, that begins with the hostility that love represses, brings it to the surface and so renders it harmless. Once their love is declared, Benedick will not call Beatrice a rotten orange in public, or feel his confidence threatened by the hints of an honest Iago.

But would it be reasonable to expect this kind of self-therapy from *Othello*? Only if we are also willing to foregoe the high poetry. An Othello who could enjoy the teasing of a Beatrice would not be a romantic lover; he would have learned not to rely so much on his own consciousness of worth, but he would have ceased to be capable of saying:

> My soul hath her content so absolute
> That not another comfort like to this
> Succeeds in unknown fate.

It is necessary first, to maintain that Leavis's view of Othello is deeply mistaken; but it is an important, indeed valuable, mistake. For it concerns the relation between our interpretation of literature and our values as social beings. There is a deep paradox here. Any reader whose response to literature is purely passive, whose concern is to understand every work on its own terms, suspend disbelief and receive the experience without then going on to do anything with it, is displaying a form of scholarship that is somehow subhuman: why should we care about literature unless it is of some use in living our lives? But the reader who sets out to *use* literature, who takes from it what he needs as a human being of this time, of that place, with these problems, will soon find that he is cheapening it. Literature, that supremely useful institution, will not submit to being used, will not allow itself to be judged by our values, even our deepest values.

It could be a humane and responsible view of love that finds Othello to be a self-deceiving egoist, Porphyria's lover a madman, Phèdre a vicious bitch, Guinevere an irresponsible adultress. Such ignorant and imperceptive criticism is in a way admirable: it is prepared to rebuke, and dismiss, the world's great lovers in the interests of another and ultimately more worthwhile conception of love. The long line of morally concerned critics, from Plato onwards, who have wanted literature to be right-minded have sometimes operated from outside and sometimes from within: the first group denounce, the second misread. They have to be refuted but they should also be envied, for they treat literature as if it mattered. It does matter—enormously—but we also have to treat it humbly, and not remould it nearer to our heart's desire.

Notes

Chapter 1

1. Quotations are from the Penguin version, in prose, by A. T. Hatto (1960).
2. *Ibid.*, p. 195.
3. *Ibid.*, p. 58.
4. For revelant discussions see Hatto's Introduction; W. T. H. Jackson, *The Anatomy of Love: The Tristan of Gottfried von Strassbourg* (1971); Bossert, *La légende chevaleresque de T. et I.* (1902); R. G. Kunzer, *The Tristan of Gottfried von Strassbourg: an Ironic Perspective* (1973).
5. A free and—O wê—inadequate rendering of the second stanza. For text, translation and comment see Peter Dronke, *The Medieval Lyric* (1968), p. 180; and all of ch. 5, which deals with the *Alba*.
6. Chrétien de Troyes, *Cligés* (late twelfth century): I use the prose translation of W. W. Comfort, in his Everyman *Arthurian Romances* (1914).
7. *Op. cit.*, l. 3145: Comfort, p. 132.
8. *Op. cit.*, l. 5309: Comfort, p. 160.
9. *Op. cit.*, l. 4471: Comfort, p. 149.
10. See Gaston Paris, 'Cligés', in *Mélanges de littérature française du moyen âge* (1912); Denis de Rougemont, *L'amour and l'occident* (1938): transl. as *Passion and Society*; W. T. H. Jackson, 'Faith Unfaithful—The German Reaction to Courtly Love', in *The Meaning of Courtly Love*, ed. F. X. Newman (1968).
11. Comfort, *op. cit.*, p. 270ff.
12. The long prose romance, *Lancelot* (French, thirteenth century), and especially the final section, *La Mort le Roi Artu*: closely imitated by Malory, especially in his last two books, *The Book of Sir Lancelot and Queen Guinevere* and *The Most Piteous Tale of the Morte Arthur Saunz Gwerdon* (c. 1470).
13. Malory, *Morte d'Arthur*, Vinaver's edition (1947), Vol. III, p. 1253; Caxton, Bk 21.
14. Andreas Capellanus, De Arte Honeste Amandi: translated by J. S. Parry as *The Art of Courtly Love* (1941).
15. Gaston Paris, 'Le Conte de la Charrette,' *Romania*, Vol. XII (1884).
16. Lewis' *Allegory of Love* (1936) has been described by one medievalist as 'a charming and seductive book that has led many a fair young man astray'. Two of its severest critics are Peter Dronke, *Medieval Latin and the Rise of the European Love-Lyric* (1965–6) and D. W. Robertson, 'The Concept of Courtly Love as an impediment to the Understanding of Medieval Texts', in *The Meaning of Courtly Love*, ed. F. X. Newman (1967); and *A Preface to Chaucer* (1962), p. 391ff.
17. H. A. Kelly, *Love and Marriage in the Age of Chaucer* (1975).
18. B. Malinowski, *Sex and Repression in Savage Society* quoted in *The Anatomy of Love*, ed. A. M. Kitch (1960), p. 19.

19. See H. A. Kelly, *op. cit.*, part III; also J. L. Fiandrin, *Familles* (1976), p. 128ff; Ernest Schanzer, 'The Marriage Contracts in *Measure for Measure*, *Shakespeare Survey 13* (1960), p. 81ff.
20. E. T. Donaldson, 'The Myth of Courtly Love', in *Speaking of Chaucer* (1970).
21. First pointed out (I believe) by Robert Bridges in *The Influence of the Audience: Considerations Preliminary to the Psychological Analysis of Shakespeare's Characters* (1926), and excellently discussed by Granville-Barker, in his Preface to *Othello* (1930), §3, 'The Ambiguity in Time'.
22. Saint-Beuve, 'Sur la reprise de *Bérénice*', *Portraits Littéraires* (1843); nouvelle edition, p. 113.
23. Gower, *Confessio Amantis* (1390), Bk III, 1431.
24. Lyly, *Campaspe* (1584), III.v.
25. Elizabeth Gaskell, *Cousin Phillis* (1863–4): *Works*, ed. Ward (1906), Vol. 7, pp. 68, 94.
26. Donne, *The Canonization* (*c.* 1603), 1. 5.
27. See R. W. Chapman, *Jane Austen: Facts and Problems* (1948), ch. 5.
28. See D. W. Harding, Regulated Hatred, *Scrutiny*, VIII (1940), and widely reprinted; and Marvin Mudrick, *Jane Austen: Irony as Defence and Discovery* (1952). For a delicately sceptical conservative reception of Mudrick see the *TLS* review, 19 Sept. 1952.
29. Charlotte Brontë, *Jane Eyre* (1948), ch. 24. For discussion, see below chs 5 and 6.
30. G. H. Lewes, 'Criticism in Relation to Novels', *Fortnightly Review*, Vol. 3 (1865), p. 354. See also 'The Novels of Jane Austen', *Blackwood's Magazine*, Vol. 86 (1859), p. 99ff; 'Dickens in Relation to Criticism', *Cornhill Review*, Vol. II (NS) (1872), p. 141ff; and *The Literary Criticism of G. H. L.*, ed. Kaminsky (1964).
31. Roman Jakobson, 'Über den Realismus in der Kunst'. *Texte der russischen Formalisten*, ed. Striedter and Kosny (1969), I, 373ff.
32. E. R. Curtius, *Europäische Literatur und Lateinisches Mittelalter* (1948): transl. as *European Literature and the Latin Middle Ages* (1953), p. 386, fn. 17.

Chapter 2

1. Francis Hutcheson, *An Essay on the Nature and Conduct of the Passions and Affections* (1728), p. 96.
2. *Evalina* (1778): quoted in OED s.v. 'romantic', meaning A-4.
3. The OED (surprisingly) does not even recognize the modern meaning. The editors have kindly supplied me with material from their files, but none of their quotations is as early as the Hutcheson (which I owe to my colleague David Morse).
4. Flandrin, *Les Amours Paysannes* (1975), p. 89. Other proverbs are: 'Amour ne set raison garder' (love cannot preserve reason); 'Qui t'aime te fera pleurer' (the one who loves you will make you weep); etc.
5. Marlowe, *Hero and Leander* (1593), I, 167ff.
6. Thomas Lodge, *Rosalynde: Euphues Golden Legacy* (1590): *Narrative and Dramatic Sources of S.*, ed. Bullough (1958), II.223.
7. Wagner, *Tristan and Isolde* (1865), I.v.

8. D. de Rougemont, *L' Amour and l'occident* (1938) : *Passion and Society* (1956 ed.), p. 132ff.
9. Shakespeare, *The Phoenix and the Turtle* (1601), 125ff.
10. E. B. Greenwood, 'Marvell's Impossible Love', *Essays in Criticism* (1977), XXVII, pp. 100–9.
11 .F. W. Bateson, Comment on the above, *ibid.*, pp. 109–11.
12. Texts from *Poesie lyrique au Moyen-Age*, Vol. I, ed. Picot.
13. Text in Picot, *op. cit.* The legend dates from the thirteenth century.
14. 'In weiz niht wol wiez dar umbe si ...': from 'Sumer unde winter beide sint' (L. 99, 20). See H. Kolb, *Der Begriff der Minne (und das Entstehen der höfischen Lyrik)* (1958).
15. *Ibid.*, p. 110ff.
16. 'Ai! fin 'amors, fons de bontat': Marcabru, XL, 36ff. See Kolb, *op. cit.*, p. 17.
17. 'Pax odio, fraudique fides, spes juncta timori
Est amor, et mistus cum ratione furor ...'
Alanus de Insulis, *Liber de planctu Naturae*; text from Kolb, *op. cit.*, p. 102.
18. The most famous medieval allegorizing was the 86 (fortunately brief) sermons of Bernard of Clairvaux (*c.* 1136) : see the *Works* of Bernard Vol. II (Shannon 1971). For a modern example, see André Feuillet, *Le Cantique des Cantiques*, 1953.
19. Guinizelli, *Amore e Cor Gentile* (thirteenth century), translated by D. G. Rossetti.
20. Carlyle, *Past and Present* (1843), Bk I, ch. 4.
21. C. S. Lewis, *The Allegory of Love* (1936), ch. I; Peter Dronke, *Medieval Latin and the Rise of the European Love-Lyric* (1965–6), esp. Excursus II: On Courtly Love.
22. Dronke, *The Medieval Lyric* (1968), p. 175.
23. Nor does Max Weber. See the further discussion in ch. 6, below.
24. Aucassin and Nicolette (thirteenth century), transl. Pauline Matarasso, §6.
25. Thomas Carew, 'Song: To my Inconstant Mistress', from *Poems* (1640).
26. Andreas Capellanus, *De Art Honesti Amandi* (early thirteenth century): *The Art of Courtly Love*, transl. J. J. Parry (1941); see A. J. Denomy, *The Heresy of Courtly Love* (1947); and W. T. H. Jackson, 'The De Amore of AC', *Romantic Review* (1958), Vol. 49, p. 243ff.
27. Chaucer, *Troilus and Criseyde* (*c.* 1480), V, 1835ff.
28. Malory, *The Most Piteous Tale of the Morte D'Arthur Sanz Guerdon* (*c.* 1470), Caxton, Bks 21 and 22.
29. E.g. Denomy, *op. cit.*; and see ch. 1 above, fn. 16 and 20.
30. Dante, *La Vita Nuova* (*c.* 1293) §2: translated by D. G. Rossetti.
31. Charles Singleton, *An Essay on the Vita Nuova* (1949), ch. 4.
32. *VN*, §13.
33. Thomas Mann, *Der Zauberberg* (1924) : *The Magic Mountain*, Penguin ed., p. 322ff ('The Walpurgis-Night').
34. E.g. L. F. Mott, *The System of Courtly Love as Introduction to the VN* (1896).
35. See also Colin Hardie, 'Dante and the Tradition of Courtly Love', in *Patterns of Love and Courtesy*, ed. Lawlor (1966).
36. See Singleton, *op. cit.*, p. 4ff.
37. See Zuckermann, *A Hundred Years of Tristan*, 1964.
38. 'Sind es Wellen/sanfter Lüfte ...', *T and I*, III.iii. I have translated freely.

39. See Leo Spitzer, 'Drei Gedichte der Ekstase', in *Eine Methode, Literatur zu Interpretieren* (1966).
40. Gottfried von Strassbourg, *Tristan* (*c.* 1210), transl. Hatto §17.
41. *Much Ado*, V.ii.102 and *King Lear*, IV.vi.197.
42. *R. & J.*, II.vi.10.
43. The OED does not recognize the sexual meaning at all. This is clearly an oversight, and the editors have kindly supplied me with a number of quotations from their files—all of which, however, are examples of literary word-play.

Chapter 3

1. Le Play's views, stated in *Les ouvrières européens* (1855) and *La reforme sociale* (1864), are summarized by Peter Laslett in his Introduction to *Household and Family in Past Time* (1972).
2. For a systematic account of anthropological terminology, see G. P. Murdock, *Social Structure* (1949). For useful proposals on the systematic use of every day terms (household, family, dwelling, inmates) see Peter Laslett, *op. cit.*
3. Murdock, *op. cit.*, p. 2.
4. For convenience I shall use this term loosely, to cover all forms larger than the nuclear or conjugal family, thus subsuming under it both the multiple and the extended family in the narrower sense (i.e. with or without more than one married couple). Both the patriarchal family and the *famille souche* of Le Play are multiple.
5. Laslett, *HFPT*, p. 40.
6. See M. Anderson, 'Household Structure and the Industrial Revolution—mid-19th-Century Preston in comparative perspective' in Laslett (ed.), *The Comparative History of Family and Household* (1971); and Harold Perkin, *The Origins of Modern English Society 1780–1880* (1969), ch. 5.
7. See C. Bell, 'The Social Significance of Kinship'; M. B. Sussman and L. G. Burchinal, 'The Kin Family Network in Urban–Industrial America'; both in M. Anderson (ed.), *Sociology of the Family* (1971).
8. Wm J. Goode, *The Family* (1964) and *World Revolution and Family Patterns*, 1963 (paperback ed., p. 75). See also Laslett, *The World We Have Lost*, 1965 (paperback ed., pp. 95, 206), and *HFPT*, p. 72; and the comments of J. L. Flandrin in *Familles*, 1976, ch. 2.
9. See Flandrin, *Familles*, p. 75ff.
10. Lawrence Stone, 'Marriage among the English Nobility in the 16th and 17th Centuries', *Comparative Studies in Society and History*, Vol. III (1960-1); and *The Crisis of the Aristocracy 1558–1641* (1965), pp. 589–671.
11. Emile Durkheim, 'La Famille conjugale', *Revue Philosophique*, Vol. XCI (1921).
12. Sussman and Birchinall (cf. note 7); and Talcott Parsons, 'The Family in Urban–Industrial America' (also in Anderson's Penguin).
13. See Laslett, *HFPT*, p. 18.
14. *Ibid.*, ch. 4.
15. *Ibid.*, p. 38, and chs 14–19.
16. Flandrin, *Familles*, p. 75.
17. Sir Rowland St John in 1639, quoted in Stone, *CA*, p. 634.
18. Laslett, *WWHL*, p. 249.

19. See Alan MacFarlane, *The Family Life of Ralph Josselin* (1970), chs. 5, 6, 7.
20. Flandrin, *Familles*, p. 50.
21. Stone, 'The Rise of the Nuclear Family in Modern England', in *The Family in History*, ed. Charles E. Rosenberg, 1975, p. 20; and *The Family Sex and Marriage*, 1500–1800 (1977), p. 131.
22. Retif de la Bretonne, *M. Nicholas*, Vol. I (1794): cited by Flandrin, *Familles*, p. 45.
23. *Ibid.*, p. 26.
24. See the opening paragraph of ch. 2, above.
25. Linton C. Freeman, 'Marriage without Love: Mate-Selection in non-Western Societies', in *Selected Studies in Marriage and the Family*, ed. Winch and Goodman, 1953. For the recipe for disaster, see Margaret Mead, *Male and Female*, 1950, ch. 17.
26. Flandrin, *Familles*, p. 44.
27. *Amours paysannes (Collection Archives)* 1975, p. 74.
28. *Ibid.*, p. 58.
29. David Hunt, *Parents and Children in History: the Psychology of Family Life in Early Modern France* (1970), p. 58.
30. *Mémoires*, 1694, ch. VIII: cited by Flandrin, *AP*, pp. 48–9.
31. Sir William James (ed.), *The Order of Release: the story of John Ruskin, Effie Gray and John Everett Millais told ... in their Unpublished Letters*, 1947, pp. 32–3.
32. *CA*, p. 670.
33. Stone's conclusions, as he makes clear, are drawn from his work on the aristocracy. That class differences can be almost as important as chronological differences, where marriage customs are concerned, is recognized by almost all the historians who have treated the question. See Flandrin, *Familles*, ch. 2 and *AP*, passim; Laslett, *WWHL*, esp. pp. 67, 181; Shorter, *The Making of the Modern Family*, 1975, ch. 2. Although Stone elaborates his view at much greater length and complexity in *FSM*, he still seems to me to cling to chronological patterns that the evidence does not support.
34. MacFarlane, *op. cit.*, ch. 6.
35. Michael Walzer, *The Revolution of the Saints* (1965) (Atheneum paperback ed., p. 193–4.)
36. Flandrin, *Familles*, p. 129–30.
37. H. A. Kelly, *Love and Marriage in the Age of Chaucer* (1975), pp. 164–8.
38. See Hunt, *op. cit.*, p. 64.
39. *FSM*, p. 151ff.
40. Walzer, *op. cit.*, p. 185.
41. Quoted by Flandrin, *Familles*, p. 128. See Stone, *RNF*, p. 34ff; also Christopher Hill, 'The Spiritualization of the Household', in *Society and Puritanism in Pre-Revolutionary England*, 1964.
42. Goode, *WRFP*, p. 19.
43. *FSM*, p. 192.
44. Text from Flandrin, *Familles*, p. 168.
45. Bernard Farber, *Guardians of Virtue: Salem Families in 1800* (1972), p. 32.
46. Flandrin, *AP*, p. 40.
47. 'Ten Precepts by Lord Burghley to his second son Robert Cecil', printed in *Desiderata Curiosa*, ed. Francis Peck—Bk I, p. 47.

48. Pasquier, *Lettres* (Lyons 1607), III, letter 1. I take the text from Mandrou, *Introduction to Modern France*, trans. Hallmark, 1975, p. 85.
49. *The Ladies Calling*, 1673, II.i. The context is a discussion of marrying without parental consent. Cited in Roger Thompson, *Women in Stuart England and America*, p. 153.
50. *Ibid.*, p. 119.
51. Edmund S. Morgan, *The Puritan Family* (1944), Harper Torchbook ed., p. 53.
52. *Thraliana*, ed. K. C. Balderston (1942–51), 4 Nov. 1782 (I, p. 549).
53. *Ibid.*, 20 Sept. 1782 (p. 544).
54. *Ibid.*, 19 Nov. 1782 (p. 550).
55. *Ibid.* 20 Sept. 1782 (p. 544).
56. *Aucassin and Nicolette* (13th century), §2, translated Pauline Matarasso.
57. Dickens, *Nicholas Nickleby* (1838–9), chs 47, 51, 53–4.
58. See fn. 26.
59. George Eliot, *Daniel Deronda* (1876), ch. 22.
60. Thackeray, *Mr Deuceace at Paris* (*Yellowplush Papers*), 1847–8; *Pendennis*, 1848–50; *Barry Lyndon*, 1844; *The Book of Snobs*, 1847; *Vanity Fair*, 1847–8; *Henry Esmond*, 1852; *The Newcomes*, 1853–5.
61. *The Spectator*, 24 Sept. 1853: see *Dickens: Bleak House, a Casebook*, ed. A. E. Dyson (1969), p. 57.
62. *Bentley's Monthly Review*, Oct. 1853: *ibid.*, p. 67.
63. See Lukacs, 'Der Alte Fontane', in *Deutsche Realisten des 19en Jahrhunderts* (1952).
64. *The Autobiography of Anne Lady Halklett*, ed. John Gough Nichols (1875). See also Stone, *FSM*, p. 304ff.
65. S.C., *The Life of the Lady Halklett* (1701).
66. *John Constable's Correspondence*, ed. R. B. Beckett (1964), Vol. II.
67. Trollope, *The Last Chronicle of Barset* (1867), ch. 76.
68. Thackeray, *The Virginians* (1857–9), ch. 92.
69. Constable to Maria, 13 Dec. 1812. *Op. cit.*, p. 100.
70. Maria to C., 4 Nov. 1811. *Ibid.*, p. 53.

Chapter 4

1. Lawrence Stone, *The Family Sex and Marriage 1500–1800* (1977), p. 136; W. Haller, *The Rise of Puritanism* (1938), and 'Hail Wedded Love', *ELH*, Vol. XIII (1946), p. 79ff; W. & M. Haller, 'The Puritan Art of Love', *Huntingdon Library Quarterly*, Vol. V (1942), p. 235ff; R. M. Frye, 'The Teachings of Classical Puritanism on Conjugal Love', *Studies in the Renaissance*, Vol. II (1955), p. 148ff.
2. Stone, *op. cit.*, p. 14.
3. Wm Perkins, *Christian Oeconomie* (1609), quoted in Haller, *PAL*, p. 245.
4. Thomas Becon, Preface to *The Christian State of Matrimony* (1543): cited in Haller, *PAL*, p. 244.
5. Thomas Gataker, *A Good Wife God's Gift* (1624), p. 244.
6. Gataker, *A Wife in Deed*, p. 27.
7. *Ibid.*, p. 40.
8. Milton, *The Doctrine and Discipline of Divorce* (1643), Bk. I, preface.
9. *Ibid.*, Bk. I, ch. 9.
10. Milton, *Tetrachordon* (1645), § on Gen. II.18.

11. Milton, *DDD*, I, ch. 4.
12. The point was raised by Dr Johnson in his *Life of Milton* (1779). See also William Empson, 'Milton and Bentley' in *Some Versions of Pastoral* (1935); E. M. W. Tillyard, *Milton* (1946); David Daiches, *Milton* (1957); John Peter, *A Critique of PL* (1960), ch. 5.
13. I have discussed this in *The Uses of Nostalgia* (1972), ch. 10.
14. Damaris Marsham, *Reflections upon Marriage*: quoted in Maurice Ashley, *The Stuarts in Love* (1963), p. 19.
15. William Gouge, *Domestical Duties* (1626): *Works*, Vol. I., p. 132.
16. *Ibid.*, p. 132.
17. Gataker, *GWGG*, p. 11.
18. Henry Smith, *A Preparative to Marriage* (1591): cited in Haller, *PAL*, p. 258.
19. See Roger Thompson, *Women in Stuart England and America* (1974), p. 116.
20. William Cobbett, *Advice to Young Men* (1829), §99.
21. *Ibid.*, § 121.
22. See Roger Thompson, *op. cit.*, p. 117.
23. Denis de Rougemont, 'The Crisis of the Modern Couple': first published 1949: I have taken it from *The Anatomy of Love*, ed. A. M. Krich (Laurel edition 1960), p. 107.
24. de Rougemont, *L'Amour et l'occident* (1938): translated as *Passion and Society* (enlarged ed., 1956).
25. Margaret Mead, *Coming of Age in Samoa* (1928), Penguin ed., pp. 88, 127.
26. Wm J. Goode, 'The Theoretical Importance of Love', *American Sociological Review* (1950), Vol. 24, p. 38ff.
27. E. Legouis, *Spenser* (1926), p. 77.
28. A. B. Grosart (ed.), *Complete Works of Spenser* (1882), I, 527–8. See also W. L. Renwick, *Edmund Spenser* (1925), pp. 192–4; J. C. Smith, 'The Problem of Spenser's Sonnets', *MLR*, V (1910), pp. 273–281.
29. Shakespeare's *Sonnets*, published 1609, no. 57.
30. John Ruskin, *Lilies: of Queens' Gardens* (1865), §91.
31. [T. H. Lister] 'Rights and Conditions of Women', *Edinburgh Review* (1841), LXXIII, 205.
32. Eliza Lynn Linton, *The Girl of the Period* (1883).
33. Anna Jameson, *Winter Studies and Summer Rambles in Canada*, III, 307: see John Killham, *Tennyson and the Princess* (1958), p. 110ff.
34. Anna Jameson, *The Romance of Biography* (1837), Vol. II, p. 44.
35. W. R. Greg, 'The False Morality of Lady Novelists', *Literary and Social Judgements* (1869).
36. Layard, *Mrs Lynn Linton* (1901), p. 104.
37. David Newsome, *Godliness and Good Learning* (1961), p. 76.
38. John Morley, *Critical Miscellanies* (1866), III, 213ff.
39. *Ibid.*, p. 219.
40. William Acton, *The Functions and Disorders of the Reproductive Organs* (1857): text from Steven Marcus, *The Other Victorians* (1964), p. 31.
41. Cobbett, *op. cit.*, §200.
42. *Ibid.*, §221.
43. Bernard of Cluny, *De Contemptu Mindi*: quoted in John Peter, *Satire and Complaint in Early English Literature* (1956), p. 31. See also G. G. Coulton, *From St Francis to Dante* (2nd ed. 1907), and *Five Centuries of Religion*

(1923), Vol. I, ch. 11; Keith Thomas, *Religion and the Decline of Magic* (1971), ch. 18; Vern L. Bullough, *The Subordinate Sex* (1973), ch. 8.

44. Milton, *Samson Agonistes* (1671), 803–6. See William Empson, *Milton's God* (1961), ch. 6.

45. Mrs Ellis, *The Wives of England* (1843), p. 104.

46. Gouge, *op. cit.*, p. 164.

47. *Ibid.*, p. 166.

48. *Ibid.*, p. 191.

49. Cited in Roger Fulford, *Votes for Women* (1957).

50. Mrs Frances Trollope, *Domestic Manners of the Americans* (1832), ch. 26.

51. Bonnie Bullough, 'Some Questions', in Vern L. Bullough, *op. cit.*, p. 339ff.

52. Sarah Grimke, *Letters on the Equality of the Sexes* (1838): text from Rossi, *The Feminist Papers* (1973), p. 308.

53. *Op. cit.*, p. 205.

54. 'An Appeal against Female Suffrage', *The Nineteenth Century*, June 1889, p. 781ff; replies by Millicent Fawcett and M. M. Dilke, July 1889, p. 86ff.

55. Mrs Ellis, *op. cit.*, p. 89

56. G. B. Shaw, *Candida* (1895), Act. III.

57. Ruskin, *Lilies*, §68; See Alexander Welsh, *The City of Dickens* (1971), Part III.

58. Cited in Noel Annan, *Leslie Stephen* (1951), p. 75.

59. E.g. John Forster, *The Examiner*, 22 July 1848: text in *Thackeray: The Critical Heritage*, ed. Tillotson (1968).

60. 2 July 1847. *Letters and Private Papers of WMT*, ed. by Gordon N. Ray (1945), II, p. 309.

61. Thackeray, *Philip* (1861–2), ch. 36.

62. *Letters*, ed. Ray, II, 642.

63. Donne, 'The Sun Rising' (*c.* 1603), lines 1–4.

64. Letter to Edward Garnett, 5 June 1914.

65. Lawrence, *Apropos of LCL* (1930): *Phoenix II*, p. 506.

66. *Ibid.*, p. 504.

67. *Ibid.*, p. 503.

68. St Jerome, *Against Jovinien*, I, 49. Quoted in Flandrin, *Familles*, p. 157.

69. See Kelly, *Love and Marriage in the Age of Chaucer* (1975), p. 245ff.

70. 1 Corinthians, VII, 1–9.

71. See Flandrin, *Familles*, p. 158; *Amours paysannes*, p. 84ff.

72. Stone, *FSM*, p. 624.

73. Kelly, *op. cit.*, p. 284.

74. The nickname derives (mid-sixteenth century) from the attempt to purify the doctrines and ceremonies of the church; the earliest usage I can find in the OED where the meaning is primarily sexual is dated 1607 (*s.v.* 'puritanical').

75. Jeremy Taylor, *Holy Living* (1650), II, iii.

Chapter 5

1. Of the many explicit statements of this contrast, see esp. Kate Millett, *Sexual Politics* (1971), Abacus ed., p. 85; Miriam Kramnick's Introduction to the Penguin edition of Mary Wollstonecroft's *Vindication*, pp. 64–5; and Sheila Rowbotham, *Woman's Consciousness, Man's World* (1973), p. 12.

2. Taken from *Sisterhood is Powerful*, ed. by Robin Morgan (1970), p. 532.
3. Valerie Solanis, SCUM Manifesto: *ibid.*, p. 514.
4. *Ibid.*, back cover.
5. F. W. Pethick-Lawrence, *Fate Has been Kind* (1943), p. 68. See Constance Rover, *Love, Morals and the Feminists* (1970), ch. 1.
6. See Ray Strachey, *The Cause* (1928), p. 72ff.
7. See A. S. G. Butler, *Portrait of Josephine Butler* (1954), esp. ch. 7.
8. Eric Trudgill, *Madonnas and Magdalens: the Origins and Development of Victorian Sexual Attitudes* (1876), p. 237.
9. Strachey, *op. cit.*, p. 267ff.
10. J. S. Mill, *Autobiography* (1873), ch. 6 (opening pp.), and ch. 7 ('Marriage'); and see M. St J. Packe, *The Life of J. S. M.* (1954).
11. See Constance Rover, *op. cit.*, p. 53.
12. Beatrice Webb, Diary typescript p. 1 (?1869), Passfield Papers, LSE. I owe the reference to my friend Norman MacKenzie.
13. J. W. Marston, *Athenaeum*, 1 Jan. 1848: text from Tennyson, *The Critical Heritage*, ed. John D. Jump (1967), p. 169.
14. I have discussed this more fully in *The Context of English Literature: the Victorians*, ed. Lerner (1978), ch. 11.
15. Vera Buchanan-Gould, *Not Without Honour (The Life and Writings of Olive Schreiner)* (1948), p. 147.
16. Germaine Greer, *The Female Eunuch* (1971), Paladin edition, p. 319.
17. Roxanne Dunbar, 'Female Liberation as the Basis for Social Revolution', in *Sisterhood is Powerful*, ed. Morgan (1970), p. 477ff.
18. Juliet Mitchell, *Woman's Estate* (1971), ch. 5 (Penguin ed., p. 114).
19. See discussion in ch. IV above, and ch. IV, fn. 23, 24.
20. Simone de Beauvoir, *Le Deuxième Sexe* (1949): *The Second Sex* (Penguin ed.), III, i, p. 219.
21. Betty Friedan, *The Feminine Mystique* (1963), esp. chs 10, 12.
22. Durkheim, *Le Suicide* (1897): *Suicide* (1952), Bk. II, ch. 5.
23. Elizabeth Janeway, *Man's World, Woman's Place* (1971), ch. 12.
24. See Betty Friedan, *op. cit.*, ch. 1.
25. See Jessie Bernard, *The Future of Marriage* (1972).
26. Text from Ray Strachey, *The Cause*, p. 395ff.
27. *The Body Politic*, ed. Michelene Wander (1972), p. 54.
28. Hardy, *Jude the Obscure* (1896), V.ii. I am breaking my methodological rule (see *Preface*) by quoting from a novel in this part of the discussion, but the point here made by Arabella is so self-contained it can be lifted from context without loss.
29. See Ann Oakley, 'Wise Women and Medicine Men: Changes in the Management of Childbirth', in *The Rights and Wrongs of Women*, ed. Mitchell and Oakley (1976).
30. I take the phrase from Mrs Oliphant's review of *Jude* in *Blackwood's Magazine*, Jan. 1896.
31. Defoe, *Roxana* (1724), Oxford English Novels ed., p. 148.
32. Greer, *op. cit.*, p. 67.
33. *The Body Politic*, p. 33.
34. See Elaine Showalter, *A Literature of their Own* (1977), p. 187ff.
35. 'Women Rap about Sex' in *Avatar* magazine: text from Edward Grossman, *In Pursuit of the American Woman*, Harper's magazine, Feb. 1970.
36. Midge Decter, *The New Chastity* (1972), (Wildwood ed., p. 94).

37. Women's Collective of the New York High School Student Union, in *Sisterhood is Powerful*, p. 372.
38. Gillian Tindall, *Fly Away Home* (1971), p. 72. See fn. 28.
39. Mary Jane Sherfey, 'A Theory on Female Sexuality' in *Sisterhood is Powerful*, p. 220ff.
40. Edward Shorter, *The Making of the Modern Family* (1975), p. 259.
41. Talcott Parsons, 'The Kinship System of the Contemporary United States', *Essays in Sociological Theory* (revised 1954), p. 177ff.
42. See Max Gluckmann, *Custom and Conflict in Africa* (1955), ch. 3.
43. See ch. 3 above, § 'The Arranged Match'.
44. Nietzsche, *Die Fröhliche Wissenschaft* (1882–7): *The Gay Science*, §14.
45. Hilary Langhorst, 'A Final Word', *Journal of Female Liberation* 3 (Nov. 1969), 114–16. See Jessie Bernard, *The Future of Marriage*, p. 215.
46. Beverly Jones, 'The Dynamics of Marriage and Motherhood', in *Sisterhood is Powerful*, p. 46ff.
47. Margaret Mead, *Male and Female* (1950), p. 8.
48. Elizabeth Jane Howard, *The Long View* (1956), *After Julius* (1965), *Odd Girl Out* (1972); Penelope Mortimer, *The Pumpkin Eater* (1963), *The Home* (1971); Lynn Reid Banks, *The L-Shaped Room* (1960); Frances Jessup, *The Fifth Child's Conception in the Runaway Wife* (1970): all in Penguin. Doris Lessing, *The Golden Notebook* (1962).
49. 20 November 1840: Winifred Gerin, *Charlotte Brontë* (1967), paperback ed., p. 167.
50. To W. S. Williams, 3 July 1849: *ibid.*, p. 394.
51. Charlotte Brontë, *Shirley* (1849), ch. 22.
52. *Putnam's Monthly Magazine*, May 1853: text from *Jane Eyre and Villette: a Casebook*, ed. Miriam Allott (1973), p. 95.
53. *Christian Rembrancer*, April 1848: *ibid.*, p. 58.
54. Elizabeth Rigby, *Quarterly Review*, Dec. 1848: *ibid.* p. 72.
55. See Hester Burton, *Barbara Bodichon* (1949).
56. Journal, 11 August 1836: Gerin, *op. cit.*, p. 103.
57. Kate Millett, *op. cit.*, p. 142.
58. Patricia Beer, *Reader I Married Him* (1974), p. 93.
59. Harriet Martineau, *Daily News*, 3 Feb. 1853: Miriam Allott, *op. cit.*, p. 76.
60. To Lucy Baxter, 11 March 1853: *The Letters and Private Papers of WMT*, ed. Ray (1946), III, 233.
61. To Frances Grainger, 21 Dec. 1749: *Selected Letter of S.R.*, ed. John Carroll, p. 138.
62. To the same, 22 Jan. 1750: *ibid.*, p. 146.
63. To Aaron Hill, 29 Oct. 1746: *ibid.*, p. 73.
64. 17 Dec. 1748: *ibid.*, p. 102.
65. 15 Dec. 1748: *ibid.*, p. 113.
66. To Sarah Chapone 25 March 1751: *ibid.*, p. 181.
67. E.g. Vol. I, p. 501 or Vol. II, p. 33. Quotations from *Clarissa* are taken from the Everyman edition, the only one readily available, and are identified by volume and page.
68. For an appreciative but rather different view of Anna, see Mark Kinkead-Weekes, *Samuel Richardson, Dramatic Novelist* (1973), p. 205ff.
69. See e.g. VII letter 43: the silly young girl and Sir Arthur Poinings.
70. Caution compels me, Richardson-like, to add a disclaiming footnote. The

morality of the future, imported into the present, usually looks unreasonable. This does not mean that unreasonableness or rebellion necessarily represent the future.

Chapter 6

1. See G. R. Taylor, *The Angel-Makers* (1958), pp. 34–6, 102.
2. See Maurice Quinlan, *Victorian Prelude* (1941); Muriel Jaeger, *Before Victoria* (1956); Walter E. Houghton, *The Victorian Frame of Mind* (1957).
3. Jaeger, *op. cit.*, Introduction.
4. Preface to the first edition of Bowdler's *Family Shakespeare* (1818).
5. *Daniel Deronda* (1876), ch. 48.
6. For a different but (I believe) compatible view of Dora, see Jenni Calder, *Women and Marriage in Victorian Fiction* (1976), ch. 7.
7. Barbara Hardy, *The Exposure of Luxury: Radical Themes in Thackeray* (1972), pp. 24–33. See also G. Armour Craig, 'On the Style of VF' in *Twentieth Century Interpretations of VF*, ed. by M. G. Sundall (1969).
8. *Pendennis* (1848–50), chs 47–56.
9. To Eliza Fox, February 1853: *The Letters of Mrs Gaskell*, ed. Chapple and Pollard (1966), p. 223.
10. To Anne Robson, January 1853. *Ibid.*, p. 221.
11. *Ibid.*
12. *Yorkshire Post*, 8 June 1896. Text reprinted in *Thomas Hardy and his Readers*, ed. by Lerner and Holmstrom (1968), p. 158.
13. *Morning Post*, 7 Nov. 1895: *ibid.*, p. 109.
14. 10 Nov. 1895: *One Rare Fair Woman—TH's Letters to Florence Henniker*, ed. Hardy and Pinion (1972), p. 47.
15. 20 Nov. 1895: text in F. E. Hardy's *Life of Thomas Hardy* (1928–30), 1962 edition, p. 272.
16. To Florence Henniker, 1 June 1896: *op. cit.*, p. 52.
17. *Blackwood's Magazine*, Jan. 1896: Lerner and Holmstrom, *op. cit.*, p. 126.
18. Lawrence Durrell, *Justine* (1957), Part III (Dutton, New York, p. 185).
19. Zola, *La Terre* (1887). All the passages quoted are from Bk III, ch. 5.
20. *Les Fleurs du Mal* was tried for obscenity, and six poems suppressed, and *Madame Bovary* tried and acquitted: both in 1857.
21. *Lady Chatterley's Lover* (1928; unexpurgated 1960), ch. 12.
22. Edward Albee, *All Over* (1972), p. 32.
23. Theodor Fontane, *Unwiederbringlich* (1891), ch. 25. My translation.
24. Elaine Showalter, *A Literature of their Own: British Women Novelists from Brontë to Lessing* (1972), ch. IV.
25. Freud, *Three Essays in Sexuality* (1905), Standard Edition, VII, 238.
26. Freud, 'Civilized Sexual Morality and Modern Nervous Illness' (1908). Standard Edition IX, 187. See also *Five Lectures on Psycho-Analysis* (1910), SE IX, lecture 5.
27. Ernest Jones, *Papers on Psycho-Analysis* (1912), 4th ed., p. 18.
28. John Dewey, *Art as Experience* (1934), esp. chs 3 and 4.
29. Max Weber, *Religious Rejections of the World and their Directions* (1915), §7: 'The Erotic Sphere'. Text in *From Max Weber*, ed. Gerth and Mills, paperback ed., p. 349.
30. Jones, *op. cit.*, p. 45.
31. Walt Whitman, *Song of Myself* (1855), §24.

32. Plato, *Laws* (transl. A. E. Taylor), Bk. VIII, §837. See M. C. Darcy, *The Mind and Heart of Love* (1945), ch. 8.
33. Freud, 'Civilized Sexual Morality ...', SE IX 193.
34. Donne, 'Love's Growth' (159?) lines, 11–12.
35. Poems to these two ladies include: 'The Undertaking', 'The Will', 'The Funeral', 'The Blossom', 'The Primrose', 'The Relic', 'The Damp', and 'Twickenham Garden'.
36. Darwin, *The Descent of Man* (1871). See esp. pp. 911, 939.
37. Puttenham, *The Art of English Poetry* (1589). Text from *Elizabethan Critical Essays*, ed. Gregory Smith, II, 157.
38. Thomas Carew, *A Rapture* from *Poems* (1640). The lines quoted are 29–30, 85–6.
39. Spenser, *The Faerie Queene* (1590–6), II.xii. 42–87; III.xi.21–55 & xii; III.vi. 29–54; IV.x. 5–58.
40. Weber, *op. cit.*, p. 347.
41. See William Keach, *Elizabethan Erotic Narratives* (1977), esp. ch. 1.
42. Abraham Fraunce, *Amintas Dale* (1592): quoted by Keach, p. 54.
43. Christopher Marlowe, *Hero and Leander* (1593), I, 61–2.
44. Richard Woodhouse to John Taylor, 20 Sept. 1819: *The Keats Circle*, ed. H. E. Rollins (1948), I, 92.
45. E.g. Jack Stillinger, 'The Hoodwinking of Madeline'. *Studies in Philology* (1961), Vol. 58. Stillinger's argument, that Porphyro is up to no good and Madeline is hoodwinked by superstition, places him in the critical tradition I discuss in my conclusion.
46. See Denomy, *The Heresy of Courtly Love*, p. 24.
47. E.g. Flandrin, *Familles*, p. 25 (courtly love as coitus interruptus), or de Rougemont, *Passion and Society*, Bk. II, ch. 10 (courtly love as Tantrism).
48. Leo Spitzer, 'L'amour lointain de Jaufré Rudel', *Univ. of N. Carolina Studies in Romance Language and Literature*, no. 5 (1944); H. Kolb, *Der Begriff der Minne* (1963), p. 127 fn.; and above all René Nelli, *L'Erotique des Troubadours* (1963, ch. IV, 3. 10/18 Edition, I, p. 373. See also pp. 277, 280, 296.
49. Song from Tennyson's *Princess* (1847), V, 161.
50. Browning, *Porphyria's Lover*: first published 1836, reprinted in *Bells and Pomegranates* (1842), along with its companion piece, *Johannes Agricola in Meditation*, under the common heading 'Madhouse Cells', which was dropped in 1863.
51. For the last, see Edmund Leach's Reith Lectures for 1967, *A Runaway World*, no. 3.
52. F. R. Leavis, 'Diabolic Intellect and the Noble Hero': or 'The Sentimentalists' Othello', *The Common Pursuit* (1952).
53. A. C. Bradley, *Shakespearean Tragedy* (1904), lectures 5 and 6.
54. Maud Bodkin, *Archetypal Patterns in Poetry* (1934), V.i.

Index

Index

Acton, William 134
Alanus de Insulis 42
Albee, Edward 225–6
Allestree, Nicholas 72
Andreas Capellanus 13, 45
Appeal against Female Suffrage 139
Arnaldi, Jean 57–9
Arnold, Matthew 141–2, 191
Astell, Mary 123
Aucassin & Nicolette 44, 76
Augustine 163
Austen, Jane xiii, 25–9

Banks, Lynne Reid 184–5
Bateson, F. W. 39–41
Beaumont & Fletcher 22
Beauvan, Jean de 67
Beauvoir, Simone de 170
Becon, Thomas 111
Beer, Patricia 197
Benedicti, Jean de 67
Bernard of Cluny 135
Bernard, Jessie 172
Blake, William 136
Bodkin, Maud 245
Bowdler, Thomas 213
Brontë, Anne 195
Brontë, Charlotte 31, 187–200, 228–9
Brooke, Arthur xv
Browning, Elizabeth 151–2
Browning, Robert 150–1, 244
Brussels Catechism 71

Bullough, Vern & Bonny 139
Burghley, Lord 72
Butler, Josephine 167

Carew, Thomas 45, 235, 238, 243
Cercamon 242
Chaucer, Geoffrey 45
Chrétien de Troyes 11–12
Cobbett, William 123, 135
Coleman, Benjamin 122
Conrad, Joseph 28
Constable, John 105–10
Contagious Diseases Act, 167
Craik, Dinah 143
Curtius, E. R. 33

Dalilah 135–6
Dante 46–50
Darwin, Charles 234
Decter, Midge 178
Defoe, Daniel 175–6
Dewey, John 230–1
Dickens, Charles 80, 84–5, 94–7, 143–4, 213–5
die, pun on 54–5
Donaldson, E. T. 13
Donne, John 26, 156–7, 233
Dronke, Peter 44
Dunbar, Roxanne 170
Durkheim, Emile 62, 171
Durrell, Lawrence 220–1

Edinburgh Review 131, 139
Eliot, George 29–32, 34–5, 87, 213
Ellis, Mrs 136–7, 140

Fawcett, Millicent 139
Flandrin, J-L. 66–7
Fraunce, Abraham 238
Freeman, Linton C. 66
Freud, Sigmund 229–31, 233
Friedan, Betty 170
Fontane, Theodor 97–101, 226–7, 229

Gaskell, Elizabeth 8–10, 24–5, 216–17
Gataker, Thomas 112, 120
Goode, William J. 125
Gottfried von Strassbourg 1–4, 11, 54
Gouge, William 121, 137–8, 141
Gower, John 20
Gray, Effie 67–8
Greene, Graham 50–2
Greenwood, E. B. 39–40
Greer, Germaine 170, 176
Greg, W. R. 132–4
Grimke, Sarah 139
Guinizelli 43

Halklett, Lady Anne 102–5
Hardy, Thomas 174, 217–220
Hill, Christopher 69
Howard, Elizabeth Jane 182–4

Jakobson, Roman 33
James, Henry 225–6
Jameson, Anna 131–2
Janeway, Elizabeth 171
Jerome, 162

Jessup, Frances 185
Jolivet, Thomas le 67
Jones, Beverly 181
Jones, Ernest 230

Keats, John 239–41, 243
Kelly, H. A. 13
Kolb, H. 42

Lancelot story 12
Laslett, Peter 63
Lawrence, D. H. 153–64, 196–7, 223–5, 229
Le Play 60, 62
Leavis, F. R. 245
Lessing, Doris 185–6
Lewes, G. H. 32–4
Lewis, C. S. 13, 44
Liebestod 53–9
Linton, Eliza Lynn 131–3
Lodge, Thomas 37
Lydia Languish 76, 79
Lyly, John 22–3

Malinowski, B. 13
Malory, Thomas 12, 45
Mann, Thomas 48–9
Marcabru 42
Marlowe, Christopher 37, 238–40, 243
Marriage & Divorce Act 167
Married Women's Property Act 167
Marsham, Damaris 120
Martineau, Harriet 195, 198
Marvell, Andrew 38–40
Mary (Virgin) 134–5
Massachusetts Statute 73
Mather, Increase 71
Mead, Margaret 181
Meredith, George 101

Mill, John Stuart 138, 168
Millett, Kate 197–8
Milton, John 112–20
Mitchell, Juliet 170
Mort le Roi Artu 12
Mortimer, Penelope 183–4

Naturalism 116–7, 221–6, 232
Nietzsche, Friedrich 180
Nightingale, Florence 172

Pankhurst, Christabel 167
Paris, Gaston 13
Parsons, Talcott 179
Pasquier, Etienne 72
Patmore, Coventry 147–8
Perkins, William 111
Plato 232–3
Poe, Edgar Allan 51

Racine, Jean 17–19
Retif de la Bretonne 64
Richardson, Samuel 201–11
Roman Catholic Church (on marriage) 161–3
romantic love (the term) 36
Rudel, Jaufré 40–1
Ruskin, John 67–8, 130–2, 141, 148, 178

Sabina, Karla 86
Saint-Simon 67
Schreiner, Olive 170
SCREWEE 165
Sewell, E. M. 195
Shakespeare, William
 Antony & Cleopatra 15–16, 32,
 As You Like It 20–22, 37
 Love's Labour's Lost 23

A Midsummer Night's Dream 19–20
Much Ado about Nothing 245–6
Othello 14–17, 245–6
The Phoenix & the Turtle 38
Romeo & Juliet xv, 5–8, 23–4, 55, 76–9, 154, 234–5
The Sonnets 128–30
The Tempest 24
Venus & Adonis 245–6
Shaw, G. B. 140
Sherfey, Mary Jane 179
Sheridan, R. B. 76
Shorter, Edward 179
Showalter, Elaine 228
Smith, Henry 122
Solanis, Valerie 166
Song of Songs 42
Spenser, Edmund 123–30, 235–8
Stephen, Leslie 141
Stone, Lawrence xii, 62, 68–72, 104, 111, 163
Suffragist movement 167

Tait, Catherine 133–4
Taylor, Jeremy 163–4
Tennyson, Alfred
 Aylmer's Field 80–86
 Idylls of the King 148–50
 'Now sleeps the crimson petal' 242–3
 The Princess 168–9
Thackeray, W. M. 88–94, 106–8, 144–6, 199–200, 215–6
Thrale, Mrs Hester 74–5
Tindall, Gillian 179
Tristan & Isolde 1–4, 11–13, 37–8,
Trollope, Anthony 107–8
Trollope, Mrs Frances 138

Ventadour, Bernard de 242

Wagner, Richard   53–4, 57
Walter von der Vogelweide   41–2
Webb, Beatrice   168, 177
Weber, Max   231, 238, 244
West, Jayne   166
Whitman, Walt   232

Wigglesworth, M.   73
Wollstonecraft, Mary   168

Zola, Emile   221–2